87

The
AMERICAN HERITAGE
History of the
1920s & 1930s

The
AMERICAN HERITAGE
History of the
1920s & 1930s

By the Editors of **AMERICAN HERITAGE**

Editor in Charge
Ralph K. Andrist

Narrative
Edmund Stillman

With Two Chapters by
Marshall Davidson

Pictorial Commentary
Nancy Kelly

AMERICAN HERITAGE/BONANZA BOOKS
New York

EDITOR
Ralph K. Andrist

MANAGING EDITOR
Nancy Kelly

ART DIRECTORS
Lester Glassner
Thomas Morley

COPY EDITOR
Joan Rehe Wilkinson
Assistant: Lynn A. Ramsey

PICTURE EDITOR
Nancy French Oakes
Assistant: Linda Silvestri Sykes

ASSISTANT EDITORS
Rosemary Klein
Susan H. Baker
Jaleh Bakhshayesh

Copyright © MCMLXX by American Heritage
Publishing Co., Inc., a division of Forbes, Inc.
All rights reserved.

This 1987 edition is published by Bonanza Books,
distributed by Crown Publishers, Inc., 225 Park
Avenue South, New York, New York 10003, by
arrangement with American Heritage, a division
of Forbes, Inc.

Printed and Bound in Hong Kong

Library of Congress Cataloging-in-Publication
Data

The American heritage history of the 1920s &
1930s.

 Reprint. Originally published: The
American heritage history of the 20's & 30's.
New York : American Heritage Pub. Co., 1970.
 Includes index.
 1. United States—History—1919-1933.
2. United States—History—1933-1945.
I. Andrist, Ralph K.   II. Stillman, Edmund O.
III. American heritage.
E784.A67   1987   973.91   87-14611

ISBN 0-517-63169-5

h g f e d c b

Picture Credit, Pages 4–5: Brown Brothers

REGINALD MARSH, PRINTS DIVISION, NEW YORK PUBLIC LIBRARY

Contents

Introduction

It is not easy to write an unromanticized history of the 1920's and 1930's. With the passing years, myth has become entangled with fact, and the two decades are already half lost in a haze of legend. Readers have come to expect that the Twenties will be depicted as a glittering, lighthearted era of flappers, the Charleston, and speakeasies; they have been led to believe that the bitter Depression years were almost the good old days, when the sharing of adversity brought people closer to one another.

But there were millions who never drank bootleg liquor during the Twenties, never bought a share of stock during the most frantic days of the Great Bull Market on Wall Street, never wore a coonskin coat. And in the Thirties there were many who went through the Depression very comfortably, suffering no distress or privations.

The purpose of this history is to tell the whole story of these two singular decades and not the romanticized version that has become popular. It also aims to explain the place of the Twenties and Thirties in the long sweep of American history. Why, for instance, did so many Americans cast aside long-standing moral and ethical restraints in the Twenties? Why did the seeming prosperity of the Jazz Age collapse into the most bitter hard times in our history? The chronicles of the two decades pose a hundred questions. It is our hope that some of the answers will be found between these covers.

The Editors

In the mural above, last in a series of panels called Contemporary America, *painted in 1930, Thomas Hart Benton recalls the 20's in places and faces of the times. "They are real people," he says, "in real situations." Among them: Benton's wife, Rita, and son Thomas (foreground) and the artist himself (far right) toasting completion of the murals with Dr. Alvin Johnson, founder of New York's New School for Social Research.*

In his canvas of the signing of the peace treaty at Versailles, William Orpen depicts the historical moment in the Hall of Mirrors. Wilson sits slightly left of center holding a copy of the treaty; Clemenceau with his walrus mustache, to the right of Wilson, is unmistakable among the notables present at the signing. The German delegates are in front nearest the artist.

Retreat from Versailles

At four twenty in the morning of December 13, 1918, long before dawn lit the waters of the eastern Atlantic, the watch aboard the presidential liner *George Washington* spied the lights of American warships steaming along the horizon. The flotilla of warships—nine battleships and twelve destroyers in all—turned westward to meet the presidential convoy, nine days out from the United States; by a little after seven each of the battleships had delivered a twenty-one-gun salute.

By midmorning the entire flotilla and the presidential liner lay off the French port of Brest, and at one o'clock the shore batteries began to thunder out their greeting. For the first time in history an American President during his term of office had entered the territory of a European state. This was Woodrow Wilson, twenty-eighth President of the United States, former schoolmaster, college professor, president of Princeton University, governor of New Jersey, framer of the New Freedom, and now, at the moment of victory in Europe, the passionately acclaimed leader of the coalition of "Allied and Associated Powers," which had humbled the mightiest and most ruthless military machine in history.

Woodrow Wilson, the scholar in politics, the evangelistic visionary of a world order based on world law, had come from the New World to redress the imbalance of the Old.

The luncheon party on the ship was correct enough: French officers of imposing rank, political leaders, the President's daughter Margaret, who had been escorted aboard (she had been singing for the troops in Europe) by General John J. Pershing, commander of the American Expeditionary Force. But if the transatlantic trip had been relaxing, if the novelty of reaching Europe while cloaked with the immense powers and prestige of the American Presidency was exhilarating, nothing for Woodrow Wilson would thereafter be quiet—or good—again.

Ashore the scene that met the American party was total hysteria: the military bands, the marine guards, the banners whipping in the December wind, above all the press of the crowds wildly cheering the President in a volume that became an inconceivable animal roar. "Welcome to the Founder of the Society of Nations," the banners pro-

11

claimed. "Hail the Champion of the Rights of Man." "Honor to the Apostle of International Justice."

But the welcome in Brest was nothing compared to that of the next day as the presidential party entered Paris. There thirty-six thousand crack French troops stood guard along the route of entry, the city shuddered under the booming of ceremonial cannon, and hundreds of thousands crowded the line of march from the Madeleine to the Bois de Boulogne. According to the British journalist William Bolitho, who reported the event: "No one ever had such cheers. I, who heard them in the streets of Paris, can never forget them in my life. I saw Foch pass, Clemenceau pass, Lloyd George, generals, returning troops, banners, but Wilson heard from his carriage something different, inhuman—or superhuman."

No man could have escaped the effect of the frenzy, for it was repeated again and again in the days and weeks that followed. Hysteria in London, hysteria in Milan, hysteria in Rome.

In America Wilson had left a strangely sullen and divided country. The wartime exaltation, the spirit of self-sacrifice—and the anti-German vengefulness fed by propagandist George Creel's millions of hate pamphlets—had been succeeded in November by anticlimax. The victorious Allied armies had not marched to Berlin; the German people did not groan under the occupation lash; the Kaiser did not hang from the limb of a linden tree.

A vast war economy had been disbanded without forethought. American industry, which had made few airplanes before the war, had by 1919 manufactured sixteen thousand military planes and thirty-two thousand Liberty aircraft engines. It had produced thirty-four million more tons of steel in 1918 than in 1914. At the same time the farm lands sent abroad in 1918–19 three times as many tons of wheat and flour and almost as greatly increased an amount of meats and fats as they had exported annually during the prewar period. Most of this intensified effort was abandoned soon after the end of the war.

In America there was also a kind of spiritual exhaustion directly attributable not to the sacrifices of the American people (which by European standards were slight) but to the false exaltation, stimulated by wartime propaganda, of the preceding two years. With this emotional flattening came the painful threat of unemployment to the only recently affluent labor force.

Added to all this, there was a sullen Congress. Indeed Wilson's Democratic party had lost its majority in both the Senate and the House of Representatives in the November, 1918, elections.

Yet, for Wilson, Europe made up for everything. A caviling press at home sneered at his messianic pretensions, pretensions coupled, they said, with a low taste for party politics. (Had Wilson not appealed to the country to elect only Democratic candidates even though Republicans had loyally helped prosecute the war against the Kaiser?) But in Europe the cheers echoed everywhere, and for Wilson the fatal error was that in hearing the hysterical throngs and seeing about him the faces suffused with unreasonable hope, he did not realize that it was not Wilson the Man, nor even Wilson the Political Architect, that they acclaimed. It was Wilson as incarnation of all the lost hopes of four agonizing wartime years. For when Europe cheered him, it was cheering, in effect, its own lost innocence, its own lost capacity for hope blasted on the bloody fields of Passchendaele, the Marne, and the Somme.

hough the Central Powers had been defeated—Austria-Hungary, successor to the ancient Holy Roman Empire, had been ruined utterly and the Hohenzollerns, makers of modern Germany, had been driven into exile—the cost had been immense. In Russia, far to the east, the Romanovs had been brutally murdered and a vast civil war was raging between Reds and Whites, with the French, British, American, Czech, and Japanese forces still in Russia in futile combat to halt the Communists. The Red menace seemed to be spreading westward. The Italian monarchy and the French republican authority had been undermined. Great Britain, so long the arbiter of world politics, was slipping into social conflict and economic stagnation.

Europe had bled. Almost three-quarters of France's eight-and-a-half-million-man army had died or been wounded in the Great War. A million men from Great Britain and its overseas Empire and Commonwealth—truly a "lost generation"—had died. Six hundred and fifty thousand Italians had been slain in futile battles in the barren limestone frontier region between Austria and Italy's northeast provinces. Eastward the toll of war had been even higher and can perhaps never be known. It is certain that at least one million seven hundred thousand Russians were killed between 1914 and 1917, the year when the tsarist war effort collapsed. One-third of a million Rumanian fighting men died, nearly half of that nation's entire armed forces.

On the side of the Central Powers the toll likewise had been heavy. At least one and three-quarter million German soldiers had died, and in the ramshackle empire of the Hapsburgs one million two hundred thousand had lost their lives. None of these figures include the huge civilian losses by violence, hunger, and disease.

But it was not merely the killing—it was the way the men had died. For the men who had fought it, the war had been a moral as well as a physical catastrophe. It was a war mindlessly waged by the generals according to the *attaque à outrance*, the "attack to the death," which as often as not in practice meant a brutal pitting of strength against strength to obtain ultimate victory by demonstrating a superior ability to bleed. The French novelist (and later to turn Fascist apologist) Fernand-Louis Céline was to write of the war:

Lost in the midst of two million madmen, all of them heroes, at large and armed to the teeth! . . . sniping, plotting, flying, kneeling, digging, taking cover, wheeling, detonating, shut in on earth as in an asylum cell; intending to wreck everything in it, Germany, France, the whole world, every breathing thing; destroying, more ferocious than a pack of mad dogs and adoring their own madness (which no dog does), a hundred, a thousand times fiercer than a thousand dogs and so infinitely more vicious! . . . Clearly it seemed to me that I had embarked on a crusade that was nothing short of an apocalypse.

Verdun in 1916 cost the French 315,000 men and the Germans 281,000; the net result was that the Germans made a penetration of five miles in four and a half months. The Battle of the Somme cost the British and the Germans together more than a million men; the gain to the British was five miles—into nowhere but a limitless inferno of high-explosive shell fire, barbed wire, mud, and death.

The British historian Alistair Horne quoted a German who was at Verdun. It would not end, it seemed to the German, "until the last German and the last French hobbled out of the trenches on crutches to exterminate each other with pocket knives or teeth and fingernails."

This was the war that Europe had endured; it was not America's war. If the American Expeditionary Force had won the admiration and astonishment of the Allies —and the Germans—in battle, it was not so much for any superior manliness that they brought to the combat of 1918. Rather, fighting alongside comrades and against enemies long since devoid of hope, they brought to the battlefield the same dash and innocence that had made German schoolboys at Ypres in 1914 charge again and again against the coolly aimed rifle fire of the British regulars, who shot them down on the slopes in windrows so that the incident has gone down in German history as *"Das Kindermord von Ypern,"* "the Massacre of the Innocents at Ypres." The American troops, fresh and still believing in their cause, sustained casualties as high as 40 per cent in many units in clearing Belleau Wood and contributed in large part to Marshal Ferdinand Foch's stemming of the German last-gasp offensive during the summer of 1918. But at home the war brought, in material terms, only a new prosperity and the trifling inconveniences of voluntary meatless Tuesdays and wheatless Mondays and Wednesdays.

Thus Woodrow Wilson's hysterical reception in Europe was a confrontation between American innocence and European experience and exhaustion. The encounter left plenty of opportunity for misunderstanding and mistrust on both sides as soon as the cheering had ended and the cold business of bargaining began.

Perhaps nothing could have prevented mutual disillusionment and disaster. For their ordeal the Europeans wanted compensation; for their part the Americans sought to build a new political order in the world. Wilson had justified American entry into the war in 1917 as a crusade to end war. The war was—in the phrase that has, decades later, become a black joke— "to make the world safe for democracy." Each of the parties was moved by an overriding concern—the Europeans to seek territory and revenge, Wilson in turn to seek to thwart them in the interest of a higher vision of the peace. And in the end both parties failed.

Even after half a century, Woodrow Wilson is a difficult figure to evaluate dispassionately. His sincere piety and commitment to idealism in politics cannot be doubted even though his piety had about it something of the Pharisee who thanks God that he is not a sinner as other men are. He was, on his visit in the winter of 1919 to the little English church where his grandfather had preached and his mother, as a little girl, had worshiped, apparently moved almost beyond expression. He was also a man who, in the French Premier Georges Clemenceau's characterization, spoke like Jesus Christ but acted like David Lloyd George, the clever, shallow Prime Minister of England who completed the trinity at the Versailles negotiations of the Big Three.

That he was vain is certain, but there seems to have been about him too a genuine humanity, which did not mean, however, a liking for association with people. This humanity lay behind his proclamation in 1912 of the New Freedom, a forerunner of this century's later New Deal, New Frontier, and Great Society, but did not prevent his bowing to racist pressures at home and firmly rejecting the demand of his cobelligerent Japan that a clause on racial equality be inserted into the draft of the League of Nations Covenant.

Certainly Wilson was damaged by the worship of the crowds, coming so sweetly in the wake of his defeat—some of the American press called it a "repudiation"—in the congressional elections of 1918 at home. But everything else aside, it may be that Woodrow Wilson failed in his great quest because he was a good American—a special breed of political animal, something new under the sun. The American typically sees his nation as unique in history, a society different from any other in the world. He persists in projecting his nation as a prototype for all mankind, and as a result, a powerful current of political evangelism suffuses American life at all levels. America was founded in the deliberate effort to create a better ordering of affairs— a New Jerusalem in the wilderness. There has been, from the beginning, a sense of America as mankind's ark—the mechanism for the social and moral redemption of mankind.

The conceit of perfection entered early into the American national consciousness—a social and moral perfection achieved, in the American belief, primarily through laws. As the early visitor (and convert) Michel Guillaume Jean de Crèvecœur put it in his *Letters from an American Farmer:*

Here are no aristocratical families, no courts, no kings, no bishops, no ecclesiastical dominion, no invisible power giving to a few a very visible one. . . . The rich and the poor are not so far removed from each other as they are in Europe. . . . We have no princes, for whom we toil, starve, and bleed: we are the most perfect society now existing in the world. Here man is free as he ought to be; nor is this pleasing equality so transitory as many others are.

Woodrow Wilson, and America, distrusted Europe, for Europe, at the very least, was the place from which Americans had come—or fled. In asserting the moral superiority of the New World over the Old, Wilson was true to the national myth of American identity. Americans, isolationist or interventionist, had always proclaimed their sense of larger purpose.

Thus Wilson was faithful to the American tradition when he seized on the notion of a League of Nations as the cornerstone of a lasting peace. When America had fought, it had been to bring about the new and to expunge the old.

Wilson himself understood this, for at the lunch with President Raymond Poincaré of France after his tumultuous arrival in Paris, he rose to deliver a toast and, with humble mien, confessed:

All that I have said or tried to do has been said and done only in the attempt to faithfully express the thoughts of the American people. From the very beginning of this war the thoughts of the people of America turned toward something higher than the mere spoils of war. Their thought was directed toward the establishment of the eternal principles of right and justice.

The sentiments were noble and no doubt sincere. But a cynic might have remarked that they were sentiments appropriate to a nation that sat secure behind its ocean frontiers, had apparently been endowed to the point of superabundance by a benign Diety who did not similarly favor his European children, and had not, since the end of the Civil War, tasted the bitterness of ruin and hate.

In any event, the leaders of the other Allied nations were not quite ready to accept Wilson's vision of what the postwar world should be, nor to agree with his proposals on how to bring that world into being. The President had made a speech in Manchester, England, in which he proclaimed that the doctrine of the balance of power had been responsible for most of Europe's troubles in the past and that it must therefore be banished from the new order that was to be forged in Paris. Clemenceau, after reading the speech, growled, "We are going to have difficulties with this Presbyterian." To the French Premier the balance of power was an eternal verity, a cornerstone of his nation's security, and he told the Chamber of Deputies that "this system of alliances, which I do not renounce, shall be my guiding thought at the Conference . . . so that there can be no separation in peace of the four powers that have fought side by side." Thus, from the outset there were irreconcilable differences at the conference table.

Once the peace conference got under way and the ceremonial obeisances to the giant power of the West had ended, the hard bargaining began. For it was all very well for Wilson to chant the slogan "the establishment of the eternal principles of right and justice," but what were they?

 urope was an old continent, drenched not merely with the blood of 1914–18 but with that of centuries of crime and countercrime. Where were the frontiers to be drawn? The Fourteen Points proclaimed by Wilson in January, 1918, as the basis of American policy were explicit on one thing: in clause after clause the principle of self-determination was reiterated. In Article Nine, for example, it was asserted that "a readjustment of the frontiers of Italy should be effected along clearly recognizable lines of nationality," and Article Ten assured the subject "peoples of Austria-Hungary, whose place among the nations we wish to see safeguarded and assured," that they would "be accorded the freest opportunity of autonomous development."

This was heady stuff as well as potent wartime propaganda subversive of the morale of the subject populations conscripted into the armed forces of the Central Powers. But it was unspecific to a degree. Where were the frontiers of Italy to be drawn? The Italians claimed the former Austro-Hungarian areas of the Trentino-Alto Adige, but tens of thousands of Austrians (or better, German-speaking Tyrolese) dwelt in the mountain valleys that Italy not only coveted but, so the Italians argued, had a right to because they had bought those valleys with ample Italian blood.

On the eastern march of Italy, adjacent to the new South Slav state of Yugoslavia, lay the city of Fiume. That the inhabitants of the city were principally Italian was not to be denied, but the backlands on which the city—the best port on the Adriatic coast south of Trieste—depended were Slavic-speaking. Without an Adriatic outlet, the Yugoslavs argued, Yugoslav commerce would die.

As for Article Ten, to apply it in practice meant, in effect, to play with that quality of the Nightmare Absurd that even then the surrealist Franz Kafka, a representative of one of the ethnic minorities of the former Austro-Hungarian Empire, was adumbrating in his short stories.

There were no just frontiers in Central Europe—there was only a hopeless tangle and geographical interpenetration of Germans, South Slavs, Magyars, Rumanians, Ukrainians, Poles, Lithuanians, and Jews, all living cheek by jowl and hating every minute of it.

What was to be done?

Before setting out for Versailles, Wilson, not altogether unaware of the complexities awaiting him in the vicious and complicated stews of Europe, had commissioned an extensive survey. This early American foray into the would-be science of politics had produced The Inquiry, a vast research by American academics on nationality and other sociopolitical problems of the peace.

Wilson's confidant Colonel Edward House organized the survey, which he placed under the direction of his wife's brother-in-law Sidney Mezes, then president of City College in New York. One major effort focused on international law, another on international business, still another on the problems of "suppressed, oppressed, and backward peoples," a category that included, among others, Poles, Bohemians, and Yugoslavs.

Wilson, though, did not much care for facts. His imagination was elsewhere, seized by a vision that, after half a century, would still seem to be the American nation's dream. Certainly it was not foreign to the American people at that time, for it is an irony of history that the notion of a League of Nations had been espoused early in the war by the stately patrician Henry Cabot Lodge, the senior senator from Massachusetts, one of the men who, as events transpired, was to do much to destroy the dream.

All during January and February, 1919, a steady stream of petitioners flocked to the American President's door. Among them were the Committee of Mutilated and Wounded Soldiers of Milan, the National Union of Railwaymen in England, the delegation to the peace conference of the Carpatho-Russians, the President of the Albanian provisional government, representatives of the Celtic Circle of Paris, and the archbishop of Trebizond.

All these men and delegations wanted something—just what was not always certain. To deal with them while at the same time carrying on the principal business of his visit to Europe, which was, after all, to negotiate a peace treaty with Prime Minister Lloyd George of England and Premiers Georges Clemenceau of France and Vittorio Orlando of Italy, the American President worked late, very late. For working with the

15

European statesmen was far from easy. They did not really like the stiff, vainglorious American, and even if they had, they had their own peoples to answer to.

The Italian demands were relatively simple: large areas of the former Austro-Hungarian domains in the Alps and on the eastern shore of the Adriatic. But clearly these demands clashed with the doctrine of self-determination. Eventually, unsatisfied by the American President, Orlando was to stalk out of the peace conference while in the United States tens of thousands of Italian-Americans grew sullen.

The withdrawal of Orlando and the Italian delegation was not the only untoward incident during the conference, where conflicting interests, national pride and prestige, and mutual distrust led to situations in which compromise or accommodation became unthinkable. The Japanese threatened to walk out over the issue of the Shantung Peninsula, which they thought they should retain, as a reward for taking it from the Germans, rather than return to China. President Wilson at one point directed that the presidential liner *George Washington* be made ready to take him home. And there was a touchy moment during an acrimonious exchange between Lloyd George and Clemenceau when the French Premier was on the verge of assaulting the British leader.

On the question of dividing the spoils—Germany's former colonies—Wilson clashed principally with the British and the Japanese, who had concluded a treaty in 1917 to divide the German Pacific possessions at the Equator. The result was a compromise: the former German colonies in the Pacific and in Africa were to be administered as "mandates" under the ultimate authority of the League of Nations, which thus became central to the peace as Wilson had wished.

But with France compromise was not so easy. The French had been overrun by Germany in 1871 and nearly so in 1914. They were obsessed with a desire for security and filled with a wish for revenge. What they wanted was in effect a partition of Germany and an ironclad treaty with the United States.

All through January and February the lights at the Hôtel de Mûrat, which was the President's residence in Paris, burned until two or three in the morning. Woodrow Wilson had not been an entirely well man when he left the United States in December; the left side of his face had developed a nervous twitch and, unaccountably, in the midst of conversation his eye would screw up. He ignored the advice of physicians, and to the lasting credit of the man, it must be said that his idealism can have been no mere sham. He asked of himself no less than he had asked of the one hundred and sixteen thousand Americans who had died to make a durable peace.

But not only the Europeans troubled him. His home front was crumbling. The Italian-Americans were unhappy; the Irish-Americans had expected that Wilson would force Lloyd George to disgorge Ireland; the German-Americans, who by and large had faithfully executed their duty during the war, now resented that the Fourteen Points had not been literally applied and that, for another thing, the blockade on Germany remained in force pending a conclusion of the peace.

The newly elected Republican majorities in both the Senate and the House of Representatives rejected his domestic policies of the New Freedom, and had no wish to see a Democratic President, whom they suspected of harboring ambitions for a third term, score a personal triumph.

 ate in February Wilson returned to Washington and asked the Senate and House Foreign Affairs committees to meet with him at a dinner at the White House. He asked that all public discussion of the League be held off until that time, but his enemies did not wait. Senator William Edgar Borah of Idaho denounced the League as "the greatest triumph for English diplomacy in three centuries," and others were hardly more temperate. The day after the dinner a Republican senator from Connecticut remarked: "I feel as if I had been wandering with Alice in Wonderland and had tea with the Mad Hatter."

Almost a week after the dinner, on March 2, Henry Cabot Lodge circulated the Republican Round Robin, a document that expressed the gravest reservations about the League of Nations Covenant in its present form and proposed, moreover, that any consideration of the League be deferred until after the peace. This was directly counter to Wilson's strategy of bargaining; in dealing with the Europeans he had refused to make concessions to them unless the concept of the League was made a central part of the peace treaty. If the League were to be deferred until afterward, then the American President, facing the vengeful and venal Europeans, would have no leverage at all.

Thirty-nine senators signed Lodge's Round Robin, but the President on March 4 struck back. In a public address in New York he declared to a throng, whose responsiveness evidently heartened him, that there would be a peace and there would be a League integral to it. "When that treaty comes back, gentlemen on this side will find the covenant not only in it, but so many threads of the treaty tied to the covenant, that you cannot dissect the covenant from the treaty without destroying the whole vital structure."

Thus there was to be no compromise. Woodrow Wilson would get all or nothing. And in the end it was to be nothing.

The President returned to Paris in a curious mood—both defiant and despondent. On April 3 his health broke and he was forced for the first time to take to his bed. But a few days later he resumed his killing schedule and bullied the Europeans by threatening to break off negotiations. This the Europeans, financially dependent on the Americans, could not face and so they capitulated. But they grumbled, and as Clemenceau put it, secretly resented the arrogance of a leader who was like the cook who threatens eternally by keeping her trunk packed in the hall.

Wilson grew irritable with his associates too, and from this period dates his estrangement from his long-time confidant and adviser Colonel House, as well as his alienation from Secretary of State Robert Lansing.

He deteriorated physically; the twitch grew more alarming. But there was more—signs of what can only be taken as a kind of incipient arteriosclerotic-paranoid syndrome. He was convinced that the French servants about him were all government spies. He began to itemize the contents of his Paris house—to which he had moved from his hotel on returning to France—convinced that article after article was being stolen. He checked on the use of the delegation's automobiles to make sure that they were being used only for official purposes. On one occasion he spent a half hour with his personal physician rearranging the furnishings of a room, moving couches and tables about to suit himself. His faithful servant "Ike" Hoover, head usher at the White House, recorded: "Coming from the President, these were very funny things, and we could but surmise that something queer was happening in his mind."

But he worked, and by early May the peace treaty was ready. The Germans had been summoned to Versailles, and in a carefully arranged ceremony designed by the French to humiliate their ancient enemies, they were handed the terms.

The actual treaty bore little resemblance to the Fourteen Points—on the basis of which the Germans could argue, not without justice, that they had put down their arms. But as Clemenceau bitingly addressed the fallen, it was "neither the time nor the place for superfluous words."

Wilson had done what he could to soften the terms of the peace. But it was neither a peace of justice nor a Carthaginian peace that the Big Three had hammered out in Paris, neither one that would reconcile the Germans nor that would, in the years to come, adequately secure France against a resurgent and embittered Germany. Sullenly the Germans signed on June 28, 1919, in the Hall of Mirrors at Versailles. But it was not peace that was made there, for both the old diplomacy and the new diplomacy had failed at Paris.

That failure was soon apparent. Wilson, physically exhausted, a fallen hero, returned to America, the fountain of his strength, to find not merely a Congress but a nation that had long since grown bored with his idealism; more foreign wars for principles that had ceased to be meaningful were no longer acceptable. And apart from this mood of national apathy, there were the personal and political vendettas: Wilson had taken no prominent Republicans to Paris to assist him. The concept of bipartisanship was foreign to his stiff and unforgiving character. He would accept no changes in his draft. Had he done so, the revised treaty would almost certainly have passed in the spring of 1919. He refused. Thus he reaped the whirlwind.

Defiant—and gallant—still, in September, 1919, he took his case to the country, barnstorming through the Middle West and the West. But he was almost sixty-three years of age, harrowed by the physical and mental ordeal of the Presidency, the responsibility of the war, and the endless wrangling in Paris. In the Far West, his old source of political strength, the response was encouraging, and with these successes behind him he planned to swing eastward to invade the territory of his chief rival, Senator Henry Cabot Lodge.

But at last his strength failed. Late in September he returned to Washington, where a few days later he suffered a massive stroke. For four months he lay helpless, attended by his wife and his personal physician—a woman and a man who in effect constituted a regency for the fallen leader. While Wilson was helpless, Lodge-Borah forces, who opposed the draft treaty, gathered strength. By an almost solid Republican vote, the Senate appended to the treaty fourteen reservations, most of them trivial—including a reaffirmation of the Monroe Doctrine—and already guaranteed by the treaty or the Constitution of the United States.

But when Wilson began to reassume leadership, he still would have no compromise. Unwisely he ordered the Democratic forces in the Senate to boycott the reservations, thereby dooming the treaty once and for all. When on November 19, 1919, the matter came to a test, the treaty with its fourteen reservations was defeated by 55 votes to 39; stripped of the reservations, it was voted down 53 to 38. Loyal Democrats joined with the die-hard antitreaty Republicans—the "battalion of death"—to defeat it.

And yet the tragedy is that even as it voted down the treaty, four-fifths of the Senate supported it in some form. But for Wilson and his foes there was to be no meeting of the minds. Four months later, in the spring of 1920, the treaty came up for a vote once again—to a replay of what had gone before. The President demanded of the Democrats that they support him against the revisions, and loyally they did.

Had he been willing to bend his stiff neck a trifle, the President even at this late date could have had his League of Nations. Colonel House later related that on his own initiative he had gone to Senator Lodge and had asked what changes would be necessary to make the treaty palatable to the opposition. The Republican senator wrote out his minimum requirements in the margin of a printed copy of the treaty. None of the changes were serious; none would have impaired the effectiveness of the treaty. Colonel House sent the annotated copy of the treaty to the White House, but it was never acknowl-

edged by the President. And so the treaty went to a vote in the Senate without the modifications that, in House's opinion, would have assured its passage.

This time the treaty won a majority—49 in favor—but fell short of the required two-thirds majority as 35 voted against it. Of the 35 nays 23 were Democrats. Thus did Wilson undo his own work and cause the League of Nations to fail.

But by the opening of the new decade America did not truly care. The war was a faded memory. A new era of normalcy lay before America, an era of new fun and new anxieties. America retreated from the world. Its failure to join the League was not the inevitable result of the existing popular sentiment in the country, but at the same time the failure was not badly out of harmony with what Americans wanted to do.

But as Americans would learn, the retreat into the old isolationism was illusory. The nineteenth-century isolationism had rested on the real interests of an infant nation guarded by a British fleet that offered free security. It had rested on the existence of a stable European power balance and a common set of political values that those nations and America agreed should form the basis of a minimally decent international order. Until the First World War all powers, even the Kaiser's Germany, respected the status quo and merely sought readjustments within the system.

But the war upset all that. In Russia the Bolsheviks came to power, proclaiming a doctrine of revolution and change. A Europe that had policed the world for three centuries was bankrupt and riven by dark forces that the world did not yet understand.

For two centuries the United States had lived in a happy isolation from international problems. Once again it retreated from the world in the Twenties. But the world would not let it escape.

® REGISTERED TRADEMARK PARAMOUNT PICTURES CORPORATION

THE EYES AND EARS OF THE WORLD
1.

World War I left Europe exhausted and in chaos, many of its cities scarred or in ruins, its peoples sick and hungry, its money inflated, its governments in turmoil. An influenza epidemic killed millions in 1918, and many more suffered severely from cold and famine. In Germany women and children combed slack heaps for bits of coal, and Austrians were forced to chop down their cherished Vienna Woods for fuel to survive the winter. With such conditions widespread, the specter of Communism loomed large. "Bolshevism . . . feeds on empty stomachs," warned General Tasker H. Bliss, an American delegate to the peace conference at Paris. Russia was already under Bolshevik control, and Communist revolutions were raging through Hungary and Germany. Nor was Communism the only threat to peace. In dividing up the spoils of war, the Allies fought among themselves: Greeks with Italians, Poles with Ukrainians, Russians with one another. Europe was shell-shocked; her recovery would be slow and painful.

The war devastated Europe. Fighting in northern France reduced places like Arras, below, to rubble.

DEPARTMENT OF NATIONAL DEFENSE, CANADA

RADIO TIMES HULTON PICTURE LIBRARY

Famine plagued Russia, and the American Relief Administration sent food to hungry peasants (above).

A starving Serbian peasant, right, begs in the streets of Belgrade in December, 1918.

Refugees in Shumitza, Serbia, right, huddle together atop boxcars, 1918.

A shattered store front in Berlin, above, after an outbreak of food riots.

Germans hurry aboard a train after raiding the fields for potatoes in 1923.

A captured British tank is used by Germans to crush a pro-Communist revolt in Berlin in January of 1919.

Right, Communists round up disguised officials of the old regime after the Bolshevik revolution in Russia.

L'ILLUSTRATION

R. CARBONE, COURTESY L'ILLUSTRATION

Benito Mussolini (in center, sporting a diagonal shoulder sash) parades with his black-shirted Fascists shortly after they occupied Rome in 1922.

New countries emerged and the old struggled for stability. Thomas Masaryk (opposite, center page) enters Prague after his election as President of newly formed Czechoslovakia. In Germany inflation drove the value of the mark downward, and by 1922 a baker (far right) picked up his wages in a cigar box. Right, a German firm collects payroll in a handcart.

In Hungary a short-lived Communist regime was established under Bela Kun. At right, new Red Army recruits.

UPI

Before the advent of the radio, the motion picture, and the Ford car, small-town America was essentially rural and unhurried. By the mid-1920's, however, the average Main Street was a bustling center of movie houses, motor vehicles, and paved streets. In the water color above, the artist, Charles Burchfield, portrays the decline of the old bucolic ways in his street scene of a decaying little village in Ohio, bypassed in the rush of "progress" of the Twenties.

Small-Town America

The First World War is a great watershed of modern history. Prior to that war the stars, as it were, had marched in their courses. The universe was knowable and benign — or thought to be so.

For the almost two million doughboys returning from the Western Front during the precipitate demobilization of 1919 that faith had been shaken. Some had seen the hell of modern war firsthand and would never again believe in flags and parades. Even many who had seen no more of war than the boredom and mindless regimentation of training camps were disillusioned and made cynical by their experiences.

For the home front, the war's end was nearly as unsettling. There has probably never been a war in history so passionately embraced in a flush of naïve patriotic ecstasy as America's war against the Kaiser. Thus, the reaction when it came was a massive retreat into cynicism and apathy.

The doughboys returning from France were met by the hysterical acclaim of vast cheering crowds. But in a matter of months roars of applause turned to callous indifference. What had been the War to End War and the War to Make the World Safe for Democracy became for all too many in the days of 1919–20 the Big Parade, a sham and a delusion.

Americans by and large had experienced a very peculiar war indeed, a vast churning up through propaganda and patriotic emotion to a sudden letdown. They were denied the satisfaction of seeing Germany invaded. No postwar millennium had dawned. Indeed, the market had slumped, jobs for veterans were scarce, farm prices slid. The economic recession of 1921 left almost five million unemployed.

There was another very important characteristic of the America that entered the postwar world. Not only were the emotions of its people stimulated and unsatisfied, but America was still fundamentally a provincial society. For all its industrial power, innovative technology, and commercial drive, America essentially still preserved a nineteenth-century rural outlook.

The industrial expansion before and during World War I had been impressive enough, as a few statistics will indicate. In 1889 electricity generated only 2 per cent of the power in American industry; by 1919 the figure had risen to 31 per cent. In 1910 there were only four thousand tractors produced; by 1920 the number had increased fiftyfold, to a conservatively estimated two hundred thousand a year. There were eight million automobiles on the roads in 1920, an increase of more than 300 per cent from 1915, and that period included the wartime years of presumed austerity.

But in 1919, as a new decade neared, almost half of America's population still lived on the land. In vast areas of the country—in the Middle West, the South, and the Southwest—the old rural folkways lived on. This was Small-town America, and it conceived of itself as being America. Novelists like Sherwood Anderson and Sinclair Lewis might chronicle the intellectual and spiritual aridity of that America, and self-conscious debunkers like the journalist H. L. Mencken might sneer at the Bible Belt and The Great American Desert, but the backlands were unmoved. In fact, they were not always aware of what the writers and the pundits in the big cities were saying about them. Said Preacher Joe Leffew to one reporter while the state of Tennessee assailed the abomination of Darwin's theory of evolution in the county seat of Dayton: "I ain't got no learnin' and never had none, glory be to the Lamb! Some folks work their hands off'n up'n to the elbows to give their young-uns education, and all they do is send their young-uns to hell." In this world of farming communities and sleepy country towns still isolated from the world, the city represented the new, and the new was sinful.

The conservatism of these predominantly rural areas would give way only gradually before the onslaught of automobiles, paved highways, radios, and motion pictures, and the process would be painful. Small-town America would strike back again and again.

The great agent of the transformation of rural society was the internal combustion engine. Invented in Europe and developed into a practical mechanism in Germany toward the end of the century, it was not a new device, and Americans were some ten years behind Europeans in adapting it to the purpose of propelling vehicles.

The automobile in the United States was for a long time largely a toy, disliked because it smelled, frightened horses, and was pretty much limited to the prosperous. Woodrow Wilson, as president of Princeton in 1907, warned students against the "snobbery" of automobil-

ing. "Nothing," he said, "has spread socialistic feelings in this country more" than this "picture of the arrogance of wealth."

What was really wrong with the horseless carriage was that it was a hybrid contrivance, neither as reliable as the horse nor as cheap. It was merely faster—faster, that is, when the roads were good and the engine worked and the tires did not blow out and the sky did not open and deluge the luckless automobilists in a torrent of rain. What was needed to transform a rich man's plaything into a popular necessity was a triad of improvements, each of which reinforced the others: first, a cheap and reliable car; second, a network of good all-weather roads; and third, readily accessible gasoline and repairs.

Of the three, the fundamental necessity, of course, was the cheap automobile. And the man responsible for its production was Henry Ford. For it was Ford who first made large-scale use of the mass production line, modernizing the old American technique of manufacture through interchangeable parts, which dated back to Eli Whitney, to the Connecticut clockmakers, and to those other canny Yankees who in pre- and post-Revolutionary days had invented the system.

The Ford technique was simple. All component parts were standardized and produced in volume. The components were assembled into larger units—engine, chassis, and transmission. The subassemblies flowed together inexorably on a moving belt in a never-ending stream. Each man, like an automaton, performed only a few limited operations, and very often only a single operation.

The work was efficient and dehumanizing. But Ford was willing to pay well—very well indeed. In 1914 he astonished the world by announcing a minimum wage of five dollars a day for his workers at a time when other manufacturers were paying scarcely half of that. And his system worked: ruthless efficiency of production, a well-trained and docile labor force, a single-model automobile. Ford brought out the Model T in 1908. In an industry unable to produce a reliable runabout for less than $1,500, Ford that year introduced a car (always a somber black, but sturdy) that sold for a reasonable $825.

For Ford had sensed the principle that lies behind America's economic success: volume pays, not high markup. His prices fell steadily as the volume of sales rose. In twelve months during 1920–21 he sold 1,250,000 automobiles. By 1924 his price was down from the 1909 high of $950 to a mere $290.

Auto sales began to boom. The flivver was useful as transport and also as a light-duty truck. By jacking up and fitting with a belt pulley one of its rear wheels, the farmer could use his Model T to perform a dozen mechanical chores. City men drove to the country on Sunday afternoons. There were two and a half million cars in 1915, eight million in 1920, and by 1925 the number had shot up to a cool seventeen million. The contributors to this success were many, among them Charles F. Kettering, who perfected the self-starter and sold it to Cadillac in 1912. Until then the automobile had been not merely uncomfortable and unreliable but dangerous even before it began to move. Few women were able to start an automobile; cranking one was a chancy job, and many men who tried it ended up with broken arms.

Building comfort into cars was a less obvious breakthrough. In 1916 98 per cent of all American automobiles were open to the weather. A thunderstorm could turn a dirt road into a quagmire and drench the car's occupants before they could get the top up and side curtains on. But by 1926 only 28 per cent of America's motorcars were open to the elements, and of those many were open because the buyers preferred them that way: convertibles.

nother important aspect of the automobile was the revolution it stimulated in buying habits and credit practices. America had always exalted the Puritan virtues, and saving was sovereign among them. Yet more than three-quarters of American cars bought in 1925 were purchased on time. That year the husband-and-wife team of American sociologists Robert and Helen Lynd, in their monumental study of middle-class America, *Middletown*, could record more than one acquisitive housewife who declared that she would rather drive than eat. "I'll go without food before I'll see us give up the car," one asserted to the startled investigators. Another opined, when it was observed that she had an auto but no bathroom: "You can't go to town in a bathtub." Mourned one small-town banker, writing for the *Atlantic Monthly* in 1925:

During a period of about four weeks I saw the following sales made: (a) a $1500 touring car to a small tailor, who had no place to keep it, had nothing to pay down on it—except an old Ford in exchange—and who could not in the course of two years pay a note of seventy-five dollars at his bank; (b) a similar car to the policeman on the post, who went in debt for half his monthly salary for a year in order to pay for it; (c) a sedan selling for about $2000 to a restaurant keeper who had just gone into business for himself. . . . After the first season, with a hard winter before him, this man deliberately—or through the efforts of a good salesman—plunged into debt for $1200. The result is that all he earns must be applied to his debts, and he now has no margin of safety at all. Before, he was sure of his ground and free from anxiety. Now, he must not only work, but he must also worry.

The transformation of the social scene worked by the automobile was profound. World War I had exposed American boys to a wider world, bringing a new awareness, expressed in the words of the old song "How You Gonna Keep 'Em Down on the Farm (After They've Seen Paree)?" But the automobile opened all of rural America to the outer world.

As the web of roads grew more extensive, it became increasingly easy to drive from outlying farms to some large town, where that other innovation of the first quarter of the century, the nickelodeon, brought awareness of an external world of adventure and glamour and where the chain store, its shelves and counters loaded with comforts in variety undreamed of in the old general store, brought the delights and temptations of material luxury to immediate hand.

The very face of the land changed. Roads were built, not just from town to town but from state to state, and increasingly they were hard-surfaced roads, even highways. Burbled a reporter for *The Outlook* in the mid-1920's, surveying the contemporary automobile migration to Florida:

The movement promises to bring momentous changes in its train. Southern states, long negligent of their roads, have been stimulated into transforming rough or sandy rural thoroughfares into straight and stately hard-surfaced boulevards, with a consequent fillip to internal intercourse. Old-fashioned Southern villages have been awakened out of their sleep, with an ensuing desire to paint up and brush up. And for the first time in history the common ordinary "fo'kes" of the North and South are meeting one another on a really large scale, mostly by means of the National chariot—the Ford car.

There were other changes brought by the motorcar. Farm boys and girls had had access to barns and haystacks, but the morality of small-town America had rested in good measure on the unavailability of bedroom space to the young (certainly the young and respectable female). Now the automobile provided a mobile bedroom, or at the very least a mobile parlor, where the young might grapple free of the surveillance of their elders. The revolution in sexual morality, to be sure, dated back to the beginnings of World War I at least, but the automobile vastly accelerated the trend.

It also accelerated the rise of suburbia. The affluent, or near affluent, now that the automobile had given them easy mobility, moved out of the cities into the suburban villages that had previously been the homes of rural Americans. They brought city mores with them. Schools were built, taxes rose. The natives adapted and usually prospered as tradesmen serving the invaders. The villages became little more than adjuncts to the city.

The new mobility had a darker side, and that was not merely the passing of the harness industry. There was the wasting away of the individual's ties to the community, the weakening of family cohesion, the breaking up of an integrated system of rural values, which while often ingrown and narrow-minded, nevertheless provided the American with roots in time and place.

In this erosion of the old rural way of life the radio was a powerful ally of the automobile. The first commercial radio station went on the air in the autumn of 1920, and within months a new craze swept the nation. An army of tinkerers retired to cellars, attics, or barns to construct the oh-so-simple crystal sets, which in the evening, when reception was best, could bring in Philadelphia or New York or Pittsburgh.

But crystal sets did not satisfy for long. In 1922 Americans purchased more than $60,000,000 worth of radio equipment. The figure soared to $136,000,000 in 1923, and in 1925 Americans were spending $430,000,000. Radio programming grew apace. More significantly, radio altered the pattern of American politics by making it possible for a candidate to reach voters he never could have appealed to in person.

Radio brought to the backlands not only a greater exposure to politics but also a new kind of music, a slightly more sophisticated brand of humor, and a better standard of speech. But even the tremendous outside influences brought by the radio, the automobile, and the motion picture would not change small-town America overnight.

There are four main themes in the story of the last-ditch stand of the rural state of mind: the moralism of Prohibition, the antiforeign politics of the Big Red Scare, the racism and exaggerated moralism of the revived Ku Klux Klan, and finally the attack on the new science by the forces of Christian Fundamentalism, which came to a head in the celebrated Monkey Trial of 1925 in Dayton, Tennessee.

As the decade opened, America as a whole was still a puritanical civilization. Its vision of the gateway to hell was the swinging door of the big-city saloon. The colors were lurid. Warned an antisaloon monthly of the time, popular in the small-town evangelical churches: "'Come in and take a drop.' The first drop led to other drops. He dropped his position, he dropped his respectability, he dropped his fortune, he dropped his friends, he dropped finally all his prospects in this life, and his hopes for eternity; and then came the last drop on the gallows. BEWARE OF THE FIRST DROP."

Dry "scholars" concurred. Dr. and Mrs. Wilbur Crafts, coauthors of *Intoxicating Drinks and Drugs in All Lands and Times*, could only conclude sadly that America was indeed far gone in decay: "In this age of cities . . . temptations about our youth . . . increase, such as foul pictures, corrupt literature, leprous shows, gambling slot machines, saloons, and Sabbath breaking. *. . . We are trying to raise saints in hell.*"

The dry crusade drew vast support from the country districts. But it was more than just a rural movement; it stemmed also from the reformist tradition in American politics, that phenomenon of periodic idealism that punctuates periods of public sloth and corruption with demands for moral regeneration and reform. Support of prohibition by such urban-oriented politicians as Theodore Roosevelt and William Howard Taft indicates that dry sentiment flourished in city as well as country.

As Finley Peter Dunne's Mr. Dooley was ruefully to observe: "Th' imprissyon [the politician] thries to give is that th' sight iv a bock beer sign makes him faint with horror, an' that he's stopped atin' bread because there's a certain amount iv alcohol concealed in it. . . . Ivry statesman in this broad land is in danger iv gettin' wather-logged because whiniver he sees a possible vote in sight he yells f'r a pitcher iv ice wather. . . ."

As a citizen of Charlotte, North Carolina, said to a

New Republic reporter investigating bootlegging in the state in 1920, "When the women, the churches, and business are united in any fight, as they are in this one, nothing can stand against them." But the reporter discovered that though the drys were triumphant in public, moonshine from the back-country stills continued in good supply.

Wartime patriotism had helped make prohibition the law of the land. Liquor in the United States is "the Kaiser's mightiest ally," the Anti-Saloon League had thundered. Beer was German, pretzels were German. The league, on the other hand, was for God, America, and a sober, steady-handed doughboy going over the top. To oppose the league was tantamount to treason.

In a flush of idealism during the war Congress "temporarily" restricted the manufacture of intoxicating beverages to conserve grain, and provided that no alcoholic beverages should be sold after June 30, 1919, until the end of the war. Thus, actually from July 1, 1919, America was dry. When the Eighteenth Amendment went into effect six months later, it was only a formal recognition of a fact already accomplished.

But the actual effects of prohibition were foreshadowed by the melancholy fact that in the three months before the Eighteenth Amendment became operative more than five hundred thousand dollars' worth of liquor was stolen from guarded government warehouses. The morality of the American people was going to be extremely hard to legislate.

For all its naïveté and arrogance, the dry crusade may be judged in retrospect with a certain amused tolerance. Not amusing in any way, however, was the Big Red Scare, the witch hunt against radicals in 1919–20.

One might suppose that since the scare was cynically exploited by Woodrow Wilson's Attorney General A. Mitchell Palmer, a careerist with ill-concealed presidential ambitions, he had deliberately fomented it to serve his own purposes. Not so. Palmer did not in fact introduce the hysteria; he augmented it and took advantage of it, as would Senator Joe McCarthy a third of a century later.

In 1919, as the President lay isolated in the White House and great armies demobilized, Americans stirred uneasily to reports of Red revolts sweeping across Europe. Concern grew as tens of thousands of coal miners and steelworkers, toiling more than sixty hours a week for a pittance—and all infected, so rumor had it, by Bolshevism and anarchism—went out on strike by the end of the year. As crises and rumors mounted, the nation was on the verge of panic.

It had been in a state of alarm for three years. The wartime assistant to the Attorney General in espionage cases related some of the fantastic stories current during the war: "A phantom ship sailed into our harbors with gold from the Bolsheviki with which to corrupt the country; another phantom ship was found carrying ammunition from one of our harbors to Germany; submarine captains landed on our coasts, went to the theater and spread influenza germs; a new species of pigeon, thought to be German, was shot in Michigan...."

The armistice did nothing at first to calm the country. Instead, the heightened tension resulted in an ugly rash of race riots: in Washington, D. C., where federal troops were called out and six persons died; in Chicago, where thirty-eight persons died in a week-long riot; and in New York, in Omaha, and in a number of parts of the rural South.

Fifteen states in 1919 declared it a criminal offense to teach in any language but English, not merely in public schools but private as well. On November 11, 1919, the first anniversary of the armistice, a disorderly crowd in Centralia, Washington, celebrated victory and saved America by seizing an organizer for the Wobblies, the radical Industrial Workers of the World, dragging him out of jail, tying a rope around his neck, and flinging him from a bridge. That year, too, fourteen states passed antistrike legislation.

Hysteria fed on rumor and on isolated outrages seized upon as evidence of a vast conspiracy. In April, 1919, a clerk discovered a bomb "big enough to blow out the entire side of the County-City Building" in Mayor Ole Hanson's mail in Seattle. The next day a luckless Negro maid in Senator Thomas Hardwick's home in Atlanta opened a package and was maimed by the explosion. And the following day a postal clerk in New York discovered sixteen brown paper parcels, similarly lethal, addressed to such worthies as Palmer himself, Postmaster General Albert S. Burleson, Supreme Court Justice Oliver Wendell Holmes, Secretary of Labor William B. Wilson, J. P. Morgan, and John D. Rockefeller.

To some, the deep fabric of America seemed threatened when steelworkers and coalworkers struck. Worst of all, that autumn the very forces of the law, the Boston police, struck too and hoodlums looted the city while citizen volunteers tried to restore order.

"It has always been plain to me," said Palmer, "the Fighting Quaker," "that when American citizens unite upon any national issue, they are generally right, but it is sometimes difficult to make the issue clear to them."

Palmer did his best, inflaming bigotry and ignorance. In September of 1919, as Wilson lay stricken, Palmer seized his opportunity. "Unaided," as he was later to put it, "by any virile legislation," he made do with the means at hand, securing a federal injunction against the nationwide coal strike by invoking the wartime food and fuel control act, though the administration, at the time it had introduced the bill to Congress, insisted it was not intended to limit the rights of workers. Moreover, the nation was still in a state of war due only to the technicality that the Senate had rejected the Versailles Treaty because of its League of Nations provision.

In late fall of 1919 Palmer's agents rounded up a number of alien Bolshevik sympathizers, and on December 21 he deported 249 of them to Russia on the steamship *Buford*, nicknamed the *Red Ark*. Public applause was loud, and Palmer, his presidential ambitions glowing, increased his efforts. On January 2, 1920, his agents arrested five thousand suspects; all were jailed without judicial proof, all were denied right of counsel. In Detroit more than a hundred suspects were locked up on unspecified charges and held in isolation for seven days. For one period of twenty-four hours they were penned up together in a nearly airless room without toilet facilities, conditions that more than one victim was to liken to the Black Hole of Calcutta. Yet among the five thousand suspects—and the two thousand more picked up in subsequent days—only three pistols were found, and no evidence at all of further little brown parcels intended for the mails was uncovered.

The witch hunt went on. Five Socialist members of the New York State legislature were expelled on the grounds that they represented a "disloyal organization composed exclusively of perpetual traitors." When Theodore Roosevelt's son denounced the action, the Speaker rebuked him harshly, comparing his patriotism unfavorably with that of his father.

Palmer fanned the flames. "By stealing, murder and lies, Bolshevism has looted Russia not only of its material strength, but of its moral force," he warned the country. The same fate threatened America. Information "showed that communism in this country was an organization of thousands of aliens," "direct allies of Trotzky," "aliens of the same misshapen caste of mind and indecencies of character." There were, he asserted, sixty thousand Communists at large—enough, if unchecked, to bring the republic down. They planned to launch an attack on May Day, 1920.

The police mobilized, the National Guard stood ready. Yet May Day came and went without incident. Though Palmer could claim that it was his stringent precautions that had saved the nation, there was something faintly comic in the spectacle of a choleric and windy defender of the nation defiantly poised to meet an assault that never came.

What a decent regard for evidence and the guarantees of constitutional liberty could not accomplish, boredom and a sense of the ridiculous did. The mood of the country began to lift. Palmer was through, and when in the fall what appears to have been a genuine anarchist bomb plot did materialize—a huge explosion at the junction of Broad and Wall streets a few minutes before noon, damaging the House of Morgan Building, killing thirty and wounding hundreds more—the country absorbed the news with surprising aplomb.

But it would be many years before the fever entirely ran its course. In 1921 America turned its back on the long-standing rule of opening the doors to the wretched of the earth and instituted legislation designed to preserve the Anglo-Saxon nature of the American population. Argued the homespun Maine novelist Kenneth Roberts in *Why Europe Leaves Home:* ". . . any promiscuous crossing of breeds invariably produces mongrels, whether the crossing occurs in dogs or in humans. . . . if a few more million members of the Alpine, Mediterranean and Semitic races are poured among us, the result must inevitably be a hybrid race of people as worthless and futile as the good-for-nothing mongrels of Central America and Southeastern Europe."

The nation accepted the argument. The Emergency Quota Act of 1921 duly protected the racial purity of America. The yearly quota of immigrants from any country was limited to 3 per cent of the total number of people from that country who were dwelling in the United States in 1910. Three years later the National Origins Act reduced the quota to 2 per cent and used the census of 1890 as its base, thus discriminating blatantly against the late-arriving Slavic, Balkan, Near Eastern, and Mediterranean immigrants in favor of Scandinavians, Britons, and other "Nordic" stocks. And the law banned all Asians, a deadly insult to the Japanese following on the heels of Woodrow Wilson's refusal to include an article denouncing racial discrimination in the League of Nations Charter.

he Red Scare was a general American reaction to a suspected outside danger; the Ku Klux Klan revival of the 1920's was a rebellion by small-town America against imagined corruption from both the big city and outside the country. The Klan, of course, had roots reaching back to the early days of Reconstruction in the South. It had been founded in Pulaski, Tennessee, in 1865 as a social club by a band of ex-soldiers, who took their name from the Greek word *kuklos,* or "circle." They soon discovered that the regalia they wore as a lark was taken seriously by the Negroes, who were terrified by the sheeted figures, and the social Klan quickly became an organization for intimidating and controlling the newly freed black man. When it began to be used as an instrument of private vengeance by some of its members, it was disbanded by Nathan Bedford Forrest, the former Confederate general who was its commander.

The new Klan, revived in the mind of a dreamy and none-too-successful Southern minister, one "Colonel" William J. Simmons of Atlanta, also placed a heavy emphasis on keeping the Negro in check, but it went further than that. Simmons founded his new Klan in Georgia in 1915, setting up shop with himself as "Emperor." His statement of principles was nicely calculated to appeal to the bigoted. Those principles—anti-foreign, anti-Catholic, anti-Semitic, anti-Negro, anti-urban—were set forth in the Kloran, or book of rules and rituals, which demanded of the initiate: "Are you a native born, white, gentile American?" "Do you believe in the tenets of the Christian religion?" "Do you believe in and will you faithfully strive for the eternal maintenance of white supremacy?"

The mumbo jumbo of the old Ku-Klux Klan ritual was expanded to the point of lunacy. The Klan members sang klodes and held klonvocations under the rule of an Exalted Cyclops and his assistant, the Klaliff. To gain entry, the Klansman would give the secret word "Kotop" and receive the equally nonsensical counterword "Potok." By the end of World War I, as frustration and anxiety swept America, the rural areas were ripe for KKK expansion. All that was missing were talents of promotion and organization, talents that Colonel Sim-

mons, for all his prophetic vision of a legion of defenders of racial purity and rural virtues, conspicuously lacked. But in 1920 he found a provincial publicity man named Edward Y. Clarke and Clarke's mistress, Mrs. Elizabeth Tyler. Thereafter they never looked back.

Clarke was a fund raiser by profession and anything but a mystical fool. He had labored successfully for the Anti-Saloon League, for the Theodore Roosevelt Memorial Fund, for Near East Relief. All this had been comparatively smalltime.

Now, applying the methods of American business to Klan organization, he systematized recruitment and ritual, dividing the United States into eight domains, each a kind of franchise in the charge of a Grand Goblin. To join the Klan cost $10, of which the recruiter (Kleagle) retained $4. Of the remainder, $1.50 stayed with the local organization and $4.50 passed on to the central coffers in Atlanta. There were profitable side lines in robes and inspirational texts.

The movement grew, and local atrocities with it. According to an investigation made by the New York *World,* by 1921 the Klan had perpetrated four murders, one castration, forty-one floggings, and five kidnappings, to say nothing of a host of mere tar and featherings and warnings to leave town.

Prompted by the *World's* exposé, Congress began an investigation in the autumn of 1921, to which Simmons piously replied that the awful doings cited by the *World* had nothing whatsoever to do with the Klan. The atrocities, if atrocities they were, were the work of impostors who sought to discredit the Klan.

More damaging to Simmons was the *World's* turning up the information that Clarke, the King Kleagle, had been arrested with Mrs. Tyler in an Atlanta brothel two years before. The brothel had been run by Mrs. Tyler herself. For the moralizers of the back country this was hard to take, and a group of Young Turks within the Klan unseated Simmons. Leadership passed to the grandest Imperial Wizard of all, Dr. Hiram W. Evans, a former dentist from rural Texas.

By 1923 the Ku Klux Klan under Evans' leadership numbered a conservatively estimated five million members and was growing by an average of well over thirty-five hundred members a day. Dealing impartially with the Democratic machines of the South and the Republicans of the Middle West, the Klan came to dominate the government of at least seven states. Setting itself up as moral censor, the Klan added a new element of fear to the ordinary public pressures that kept the small-town merchant or banker from deviant behavior. "TWK," "Trade with Klansmen," became a valuable device to display in a merchant's window. Catholic and Jewish merchants were hard pressed to stay in business. Reminisced one victim of the Klan's bigotry:

The appeal of the Klan lay in the deadly tedium of small-town life, where any change was a relief; the nature of current Protestant theology, rooted in Fundamentalism and hot with bigotry; and, not least, a native American moralistic blood lust that is half historical determinism, and half Freud. . . . Puritanism defies human nature, and human nature, repressed, emerges in disguise. . . . The Klan, which sanctified chastity and "clean living" and brought violent punishment to sinners, was a perfect outlet for these repressions. It is significant that the favored Klan method of dealing with sexual transgressors was to strip them naked and whip them, an act of sadism.

As with A. Mitchell Palmer's witch hunt, what killed the Klan was not so much reason as boredom and a new taste for frivolity, which by the mid-1920's was increasingly pronounced, even in middle America. But most of all the Klan died of scandal, this time of a nature impossible to ignore. For in Indiana, where by the mid-1920's the center of gravity of the Klan had begun to shift from Atlanta, the Grand Dragon, David C. Stephenson, high liver, big spender, and womanizer, was caught in a case of rape and death.

Why it happened is not easy to fathom. Stephenson, whose income in one eighteen-month period was estimated at between two and five million dollars, ran the Indiana statehouse from behind the scenes. Clearly he ought to have had access to more willing and certainly better looking women than Madge Oberholtzer, an obscure civil servant. Yet it was she who did him in. She was twenty-eight, a buxom 145 pounds, and rather plain, but Stephenson, for whatever dark reasons, conceived a yen for her. For weeks he squired her around Indianapolis, and then on the night of March 15, 1925, dragged her to Chicago aboard the night train.

"After the train started," she testified before dying, "Stephenson got in [the berth] with me and attacked me. He held me so I could not move. I . . . do not remember all that happened. . . . He . . . mutilated me." The next morning the luckless girl found poison and swallowed six tablets of bichloride of mercury. The panicky Stephenson smuggled her back to Indianapolis, held her in his garage, and finally breaking before her stubborn refusal to forgive or marry him, took her to her home and left her there to die.

The case was too sordid to cover up. Stephenson was arrested, tried on charges of second-degree murder, and despite his great political influence, found guilty. He was sentenced to life imprisonment. And that meant the end of the Klan as a force of any consequence.

To be sure, it did not die completely. The taint of scandal notwithstanding, the Klan recovered briefly when the Democrats nominated a Catholic, Al Smith, in 1928. And it led a half life during the Depression years of the 1930's, when demagogues like Huey Long flourished.

But the days of provincialism were passing as the decade lengthened. After the upsurge of hate, the essential kindliness of the small-town character, which along with moralism and distrust of outsiders was also a fundamental characteristic, began to reassert itself. The wave of hysteria and black hatred subsided, leaving the nation to ask how it could have given itself so unthinkingly to excess.

Finally, there was the emotional stand of Fundamentalist religion in the country, the celebrated Monkey Trial of 1925 in Dayton, Tennessee.

The war between Fundamentalism and science was not peculiar to the 1920's. Darwin's great work *On the Origin of Species* had appeared in England in 1859 and had quickly raised a storm of controversy over its central notion, that man himself was subject to evolution, which opposed the traditional view that he was a special creation only "a little lower than the angels."

Among intellectual Americans of the 1920's, Darwin was decidedly old hat. Along the Eastern seaboard, city intellectuals had long since moved on to Freud and Havelock Ellis.

Yet Fundamentalism did not quite go begging for champions in those years. It had many, among them the tub-thumping evangelist Billy Sunday and the more appealing figure of Aimee Semple McPherson, she of the sunlit soul, who made religion pay at her Angelus Temple in Los Angeles. Even clergymen like the imposing John Straton of New York's posh Calvary Baptist Church, who ought to have known better, were willing to assert the total validity of the Bible, of every jot and tittle, every trivial begat.

But the high champion of Fundamentalism, then in his fading years, was "the Great Commoner," William Jennings Bryan, thrice Democratic candidate for the Presidency and thrice defeated. Wrote a bitterly hostile

H. L. Mencken, who understood Bryan but could not forgive the idol of the backlands:

Wherever the flambeaux of Chautauqua smoked and guttered, and . . . men gathered who were weary and heavy laden, and their wives who were full of Peruna and as fecund as the shad (*Alosa sapidissima*), there the indefatigable Jennings set up his traps. . . . He liked people who sweated freely, and were not debauched by the refinements of the toilet. . . . He liked getting up early in the morning, to the tune of cocks crowing on the dunghill. He liked the heavy, greasy victuals of the farmhouse kitchen. He liked country lawyers, country pastors, all country people. He liked country sounds and country smells.

The hinterlands reciprocated the love, all the more desperately because, like Bryan himself, they could suspect that their best days were past, that as the urban centers gained the majority, the forces of modernism and skepticism and godlessness would slowly begin to prevail.

If the backlands had never been able to elect Bryan, who was their very incarnation, if the forces of skepticism grew bold, yet Fundamentalists were prepared to strike back. Bills to make the teaching of evolution illegal had been introduced into at least six state legislatures in the South by 1925; two had been defeated and three were still pending. And in Tennessee an anti-evolution bill had become law because the lower house had counted on the upper one to kill it, because the upper house had thought the governor would veto it, and because the governor, signing the bill, had depended on the good sense of the school districts not to observe it.

All were wrong. "Nobody believes that it is going to be an active statute," the governor of Tennessee, Austin Peay, was quoted as saying. But he did not reckon with the fanaticism of the countryfolk. And once a test case had been made, the era's frenzied climate of ballyhoo ensured that it would receive maximum and sensational treatment by the press.

Perhaps there would have been no need for a test at all if the forces of modern science, represented by the American Civil Liberties Union, had been content to let the fanaticism of the hinterlands work itself out in futile legislation and rhetoric. But with a singular humorlessness, the A.C.L.U. took up the challenge, announcing in the spring of 1925 that it would finance the defense if anyone brought the act into court in a test

case. The next day George Rappleyea, a superintendent of mines in the Dayton area, a local lawyer named Sue K. Hicks, and the superintendent of schools concocted a plan at Robinson's Drug Store in Dayton: John Thomas Scopes, a twenty-four-year-old schoolteacher, unmarried, unburdened by responsibility, would offer himself as sacrificial lamb to put Dayton forever on the map.

Scopes, who had been teaching evolution unhindered until then, was duly indicted for his crime. Seeing a chance to settle the score with modernism once and for all, the Fundamentalists asked the aging William Jennings Bryan to take charge of the prosecution. Bryan, forgotten in semiretirement and not averse to a little publicity, agreed to take the case.

And just as surely the modernists would promote their cause. To join an already impressive legal team they called in the formidable Clarence Darrow, fresh from his triumph in defending the young murderers Nathan Leopold and Richard Loeb against the death sentence.

ayton that hot July became a promoters' dream. Great cavalcades of mule-drawn wagons and decrepit Model T flivvers bore the pious of the hinterlands to town. Revival camps proliferated on the outskirts, offering nightly calls to salvation. The telephone and wireless facilities were overloaded as more than a hundred newsmen descended on Dayton. A Coney Island freak show offered its "Zip the Apeman" to the defense as the long-sought "missing link." Hatchet-faced country preachers demanded of passers-by whether they were saved and whether they were washed in the Blood of the Lamb. Peddlers hawked hot dogs, popcorn, Bibles, and copies of *On the Origin of Species.*

The tension rose; the heat over Dayton was palpable, the temperature soaring above 100 degrees. As the court assembled, the faithful crowded the courthouse square, singing hymns, praising God amidst the hot-dog vendors.

The prosecution was swift. Had Scopes expounded the theory of evolution, the doctrine that man was descended from the lesser animals? they asked Howard Morgan, aged fourteen.

Yes, young Morgan replied, and added that he did not think it had hurt him at all.

Darrow tried to call expert witnesses: geologists, paleontologists, other scientists. Their testimony was ruled irrelevant by Judge John T. Raulston, a mountain justice who said that the only question to be decided was whether Scopes had taught evolution. Yet the courtroom rocked as the defense read, with the jury absent, a statement saying that rather than having been created in 4004 B.C., life on the earth was fully six hundred million years old. A gasp of incredulity stirred the rows of countryfolk spectators.

The testimony of the experts having been ruled inadmissible, Darrow then attempted a final stroke: he called Bryan to the stand as expert witness—for the defense. That day, July 20, the court was meeting outdoors on the courthouse lawn in blazing heat because the judge had feared the courthouse floor might collapse under the weight of the crowd. Bryan, his face running with sweat, sat fanning himself continuously with a palm leaf fan. Darrow stood before him in shirt sleeves. It was matador and bull.

Did Bryan believe every word of the Bible? Darrow asked.

Indeed he did.

Was Mr. Bryan aware of the size of a whale's gullet? How then could Jonah have been swallowed by a whale?

He had been swallowed, said Bryan, by a "giant fish."

Had Joshua made the sun stand still?

He had.

Where had Cain found his wife?

He would let the agnostics search for her, Bryan replied airily.

So the duel continued, with Bryan insisting on the literal truth of the Bible until Darrow asked if it was true that the earth had been created in only six days.

For the first time Bryan hedged. The word "day," he said, might possibly have been used to denote some period of time longer than twenty-four hours. And now the great Fundamentalist began to appear unsure of himself, and admitted that he did not know the answer to questions on subjects about which he had earlier spoken with Olympian assurance. Finally Darrow asked how the serpent had moved about before the Lord cursed it and condemned it to crawl on its belly. Had it perhaps walked about on its tail?

The crowd broke into loud laughter. Bryan lost his temper, Darrow responded in kind, and the spectators were on the verge of rioting when Judge Raulston adjourned the court. When court was convened again the next morning, Raulston ordered Bryan's testimony stricken from the record, leaving virtually nothing of the defense case. Scopes was found guilty and fined one hundred dollars.

Bryan died five days after the trial ended. His death, though somewhat imaginatively attributed to his humiliation at Darrow's hands, was more likely due to a combination of heat, exhaustion, and too much food (he had diabetes but disregarded his diet and ate voraciously).

The plans of the defense to appeal were frustrated when the Tennessee supreme court sent the case back to the lower court on the technical point that the fine had not been properly levied, thus avoiding a clear-cut ruling on the antievolution act. At the same time the supreme court advised the district attorney not to bring to court again what it called a bizarre case.

So, although Scopes went unfined, the antievolution law remained in effect. Fundamentalists everywhere cheered a great victory and during 1926 and 1927 introduced so-called monkey bills in twelve states. The Mississippi legislature enacted one into law; when the lawmakers in Arkansas rejected a similar bill, an organization of Fundamentalist zealots was able to bring it to a state-wide referendum, in which the voters approved it.

But those were the only two victories. The Scopes trial had been the beginning of the end for the backcountry Bible thumpers. Legislators grew skillful in avoiding committing themselves to a vote on monkey bills offered by Fundamentalist colleagues—or by colleagues with large Fundamentalist constituencies. In Delaware one such bill was referred to the Committee on Fish, Game and Oysters and was heard of no more.

It would be wrong to say that the event in Dayton made many instant converts to evolution in the Bible Belt. But it did start many people wondering. Perhaps—blasphemous thought—it was not possible, or even necessary, to believe in every word in the Bible. Perhaps, the questing minds in the rural areas told themselves, these were matters that would bear some thought. And once they started thinking and questioning, the narrow old-time religion was doomed.

Into the 20's

Though some Americans had fought and bled, most, especially on the home front, had found the war rather exhilarating. They sang "Over There" and "The Long, Long Trail" (it was the last war in which they would sing with enthusiasm); they hated the Kaiser with satisfying ferocity; they knit socks and made sacrifices and sometimes expressed patriotic ardor in more unusual ways, as did the lady who made the patchwork quilt shown in part above. Then the war ended. The returned soldier put away his souvenir German helmet, the lady packed away her quilt, and the nation tried to take up where it had left off in 1917, as one might resume reading a book that had been laid aside. But there was no going back; the war had altered America and the rest of the world too much for that. Instead of returning to familiar ways, the nation found disillusion and change; instead of retracing old patterns, it passed through the Twenties and one of the wildest decades in its entire history.

Return to Peace

"ARMISTICE SIGNED, END OF THE WAR!" headlined *The New York Times*. America, awakening to news of peace that November 11, 1918, exploded in a coast-to-coast frenzy of celebration. Shops, offices, and factories closed, whistles blew, brass bands blared, and people danced, sang, and paraded in confetti-strewn streets in every town and city in the nation. Four days earlier a false report of peace, flashed over the United Press wires, had unleashed a similar delirium that fizzled out when the truth became apparent. This time it was the real thing, and the sense of elation mounted at home and abroad. "We danced in the streets, embraced old women and pretty girls, swore blood brotherhood with soldiers in little bars, drank with our elbows locked in theirs, reeled through the streets with bottles of champagne," wrote one doughboy, the critic and author Malcolm Cowley. But that high euphoria was not to last. "On the next day," continued Cowley, "after we got over our hangovers, we didn't know what to do. . . ." The same could be said of a whole generation of young men and women. Amidst the harsh realities of postwar readjustment, hope would turn quickly to disillusionment, and with the letdown, nobody would seem to know just what to do.

The festiveness and jubilation of victory are vividly portrayed in Gifford Reynolds Beal's Armistice Day, 1918. *In the first exhilarating days of peace Americans celebrated in a swirl.*

There were two Americas in the first postwar years: the real one and the one people held in their hearts and believed they could return to after the tumult of wartime. *Summer Twilight* (top right), a 1920 etching by Edward Hopper, and John Sloan's *Main Street, Gloucester* (above) of 1921 capture the essence of the small-town America of the heart, while the photograph of Mormon threshers in Utah pausing for lunch

seems to sum up the best of rural life. The elderly couple in Thomas Hart Benton's *The Lord Is My Shepherd* typify old-fashioned virtues. But the truth was rather different. America was becoming industrialized and citified; by 1920 the census bureau classified more than half the population as urban, and the idyllic rural image was shattered in 1921 by a recession that kept the farmer in distress all through the 20's.

The Way It Was

The American scene at the beginning of the Twenties was far different from what it would be in a decade or two—and a world away from what it is today. Now gone are former mainstays of everyday living, such as the iceman (left), who in 1920 made his rounds unthreatened by any mechanical refrigerator. The wintry scene below is of a vanished related occupation: cutting pond ice for summer use. The milkman above made his early morning rounds with horse and wagon, and for a completely equipped 1920 kitchen (below right) a wood-burning range was an absolute necessity. Though the bathroom (above right) may appear primitive, it was not basically different from one today. Other sights and sounds then commonplace have vanished: the clop of a horse's hoofs, a trolley bell, the whistle of a steam locomotive. Electric lights now shine through farm windows once lit by the yellow gleam from kerosene lamps. And such implements of wifely drudgery as the washboard are happily all but forgotten. The changes have been many, but not all have made life better.

ALL: BROWN BROTHERS

41

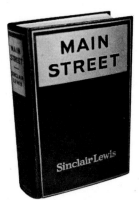

Small-town America might have had its virtues, but a disillusioned postwar generation had begun to question the long-accepted values and aesthetics of the Great American Heartland. One of the most searching and searing of those critics was Sinclair Lewis (caricatured opposite), whose Main Street, a best-selling novel published in 1920, was a devastating satire of everybody's home town, Gopher Prairie, as seen through the eyes of its city-bred heroine, Carol Kennicott. In the excerpts below he lays bare the town and the townsfolk, the drabness of the one reflecting the dullness and insularity of the other.

"the unsparing unapologetic

When Carol had walked for thirty-two minutes she had completely covered the town, east and west, north and south; and she stood at the corner of Main Street and Washington Avenue and despaired.

Main Street with its two-story brick shops, its story-and-a-half wooden residences, its muddy expanse from concrete walk to walk, its huddle of Fords and lumber-wagons, was too small to absorb her. The broad, straight, unenticing gashes of the streets let in the grasping prairie on every side. She realized the vastness and the emptiness of the land. The skeleton iron windmill on the farm a few blocks away, at the north end of Main Street, was like the ribs of a dead cow. She thought of the coming of the Northern winter, when the unprotected houses would crouch together in terror of storms galloping out of that wild waste. They were so small and weak, the little brown houses. They were shelters for sparrows, not homes for warm laughing people. . . .

It was not only the unsparing unapologetic ugliness and the rigid straightness which overwhelmed her. It was the planlessness, the flimsy temporariness of the buildings, their faded unpleasant colors. The street

was cluttered with electric-light poles, telephone poles, gasoline pumps for motor cars, boxes of goods. Each man had built with the most valiant disregard of all the others. . . .

She escaped from Main Street, fled home. . . .

That evening, at a welcoming party given in her honor, Carol Kennicott was introduced to the good citizens of Gopher Prairie.

The men and women divided, as they had been tending to do all evening. Carol was deserted by the men, left to a group of matrons who steadily pattered of children, sickness, and cooks—their own shop-talk. She was piqued. She remembered visions of herself as a smart married woman in a drawing-room, fencing with clever men. Her dejection was relieved by speculation as to what the men were discussing, in the corner between the piano and the phonograph. Did they rise from these housewifely personalities to a larger world of abstractions and affairs?

She made her best curtsy to Mrs. Dawson; she twittered, "I won't have my husband leaving me so soon! I'm going over and pull the wretch's ears." She rose with a *jeune fille* bow. She

was self-absorbed and self-approving because she had attained that quality of sentimentality. She proudly dipped across the room and, to the interest and commendation of all beholders, sat on the arm of Kennicott's chair.

He was gossiping with Sam Clark, Luke Dawson, Jackson Elder of the planing-mill, Chet Dashaway, Dave Dyer, Harry Haydock, and Ezra Stowbody, president of the Ionic bank. . . .

As Carol defied decency by sitting down with the men, Mr. Stowbody was piping to Mr. Dawson, "Say, Luke, when was't Biggins first settled in Winnebago Township? Wa'n't it in 1879?"

"Why no 'twa'n't!" Mr. Dawson was indignant. "He come out from Vermont in 1867—no, wait, in 1868, it must have been—and took a claim on the Rum River, quite a ways above Anoka."

"He did not!" roared Mr. Stowbody. "He settled first in Blue Earth County, him and his father!"

("What's the point at issue?" Carol whispered to Kennicott.

("Whether this old duck Biggins had an English setter or a Llewellyn. They've been arguing it all evening!")

Dave Dyer interrupted to give tidings, "D' tell you that Clara Biggins

42

ugliness"

was in town couple days ago? She bought a hot-water bottle—expensive one, too—two dollars and thirty cents!"

"Yaaaaaah!" snarled Mr. Stowbody. "Course. She's just like her grandad was. Never save a cent. Two dollars and twenty—thirty, was it?—two dollars and thirty cents for a hot-water bottle! Brick wrapped up in a flannel petticoat just as good, anyway!"

"How's Ella's tonsils, Mr. Stowbody?" yawned Chet Dashaway.

While Mr. Stowbody gave a somatic and psychic study of them, Carol reflected, "Are they really so terribly interested in Ella's tonsils, or even in Ella's esophagus? I wonder if I could get them away from personalities? Let's risk damnation and try."

"There hasn't been much labor trouble around here, has there, Mr. Stowbody?" she asked innocently.

"No, ma'am, thank God, we've been free from that, except maybe with hired girls and farm-hands. Trouble enough with these foreign farmers; if you don't watch these Swedes they turn socialist or populist or some fool thing on you in a minute. Of course, if they have loans you can make 'em listen to reason. I just have 'em come into the bank for a talk, and tell 'em

a few things. I don't mind their being democrats, so much, but I won't stand having socialists around. . . .

"Do you approve of union labor?" Carol inquired of Mr. Elder.

"Me? I should say not! It's like this: I don't mind dealing with my men if they think they've got any grievances—though Lord knows what's come over workmen, nowadays—don't appreciate a good job. . . . But I'm not going to have any outsider, any of these walking delegates, or whatever fancy names they call themselves now—bunch of rich grafters, living on the ignorant workmen! Not going to have any of those fellows butting in and

telling *me* how to run *my* business!" . . .

"I stand for freedom and constitutional rights. If any man don't like my shop, he can get up and git. Same way, if I don't like him, he gits. And that's all there is to it. . . . They like what I pay 'em, or they get out. . . ."

. . . The talk went on. . . . Their voices were monotonous, thick, emphatic. They were harshly pompous, like men in the smoking-compartments of Pullman cars. They did not bore Carol. They frightened her. She panted, "They will be cordial to me, because my man belongs to their tribe. God help me if I were an outsider!"

43

CLOSE THE SALOONS

U.S.A
PU
OI
RY

IF you believe that the traffic in alcohol does more harm than good —

Help stop it.

CHARLES STELZLE, *WHY PROHIBITION!*, 1918

The poster opposite appeared in Why Prohibition!, *a 1918 book dedicated "to the valiant fighters who need ammunition to batter down the bulwarks of booze." They won. Below, a final drink before the booze (right) goes down the sewer.*

At midnight on January 16, 1920, the Eighteenth Amendment went into effect and America went dry. In Chicago, it was reported, drinkers gathered to toast "the final moments of a moist United States," and in San Francisco "glorious festivals" prevailed. But for the most part, the event was undramatic—and somewhat anticlimactic. Wartime prohibition had been in effect, more or less, since July 1, 1919; Congress had passed the Eighteenth in 1917, and its later ratification really came as no surprise. It came, rather, with a conviction of

its inevitability—and its inherent rightness. "Hell will be forever for rent," cried the evangelist Billy Sunday, and the equally optimistic Anti-Saloon League of New York proclaimed, "Now for an era of clear thinking and clean living!" Most Americans sincerely believed, or at least hoped, it would be just that. Speak-easies, bootleg booze, and enterprising mobsters were all in the future. For the moment the nation could rejoice, for "an enemy has been overthrown and victory crowns the forces of righteousness," as a Long Island church leaflet put it.

Time of Strikes

Chicago steelworkers walk off the job at the beginning of a nationwide strike organized by the American Federation of Labor in September, 1919. By January the union's strike was broken.

Rising prices, static wages, and the workingman's impatience with long-endured grievances precipitated a series of violent labor disturbances at war's end. One of the bitterest clashes occurred in the fall of 1919, when some 350,000 steelworkers struck for higher wages and the shortening of a grueling twelve-hour day. Their demands were rejected and violence erupted in mill towns from Pennsylvania to West Virginia. Union organizers were harassed and one was murdered; strikers were shot down by mill guards and mounted police. That same year a nationwide bituminous coal strike crippled industry and transportation for more than a month before it was broken, and a strike by the Boston police was finally quelled with the help of the state militia. For the moment, the workingman was beaten, but labor continued to organize, and management to resist, as the battle raged on into 1920.

Big Steel used military force and private strong men against union members. Below, mounted police patrol the mining areas of Pittsburgh as the steel strike spread and gained momentum.

The Boston police strike of 1919 left citizens at the mercy of rioters and looters and made an overnight hero of Massachusetts Governor Calvin Coolidge, who would brook "no right to strike against the public safety by anybody, anywhere, any time." Above, stouthearted merchants prepare to defend their enterprise against anyone foolish enough to attempt foul play.

The Big Red Scare

WHOSE COUNTRY IS THIS, ANYHOW?

In 1919–20 Attorney General A. Mitchell Palmer (middle photograph above) led the country in a Red hunt. The Rollin Kirby cartoon (top) comments on the mass roundup of "Red" aliens, some of whom are shown above awaiting deportation from Boston.

In the wake of labor riots at home and Communist rebellions abroad, a wave of anti-Red hysteria swept postwar America. Whipped up by the fiery rhetoric of Wilson's Attorney General, A. Mitchell Palmer, who warned of "the blaze of revolution" that was "eating its way into the homes of the American workman," good patriots were ready to see an anarchist behind every alien, a Red agitator behind every union organizer,

and a Communist plot behind every labor protest. Left-wing presses were raided and destroyed, a Socialist legislator was barred from Congress, and professors were expelled for teaching "radical" (hitherto merely "liberal") theories. At the height of the madness, in 1920, over six thousand persons suspected of Communism were rounded up by Palmer's men and clapped into jail in a series of coast-to-coast Red raids unprece-dented in its disregard for civil liberties. By the end of the year the fever had subsided, and an explosion at the corner of Wall and Broad streets in September (shown in the photograph below) failed to bring on the hysteria and counterviolence against "Communist conspirators" that would have accompanied such a bombing earlier. The witch hunt was over, but it had left a bitter legacy of disillusionment and distrust.

With the resurgence of the hooded night riders of the Ku Klux Klan, bigotry, racism, and chauvinism reached a zenith in American society. The story of the Klan's rebirth in 1915 might be amusing were it not for the reign of terror that followed in the 20's. The Klan was the brain child of a Georgian named Colonel William J. Simmons, who had become intoxicated by stories of the old Reconstruction Klan told to him by his "black mammy" to "pacify us children late in the evening." His preoccupation with hooded Knights and dark rituals grew until it overwhelmed him. As he described it to a reporter for the Atlanta *Journal*, he was finally taken with a vision: "On horseback in their white robes they rode across the wall in front of me, and as the picture faded out I got down on my knees and swore I would found . . . a memorial to the Ku Klux Klan." Simmons was as good as his word, and by 1920, with the help of a good publicity agent, Klansmen were holding Konklaves, burning crosses, and initiating new recruits across the country. Their slogan was "Native, white, Protestant supremacy," and their victims included Jews, Catholics, foreigners, and Negroes as well as radicals and "intellectually mongrelized 'Liberals.'" They throve among the bigoted and ignorant ("We are demanding . . . a return of power into the hands of the everyday, not highly cultured, not overly intellectual-

ized [citizen]," declared Simmons' successor, Imperial Wizard Hiram Wesley Evans); and their most effective weapon was terrorism. Wherever they gained a foothold, their route was marked by floggings, brandings, burnings, and lynchings. "Boys, you'd better disband," warned the Houston *Chronicle* in 1921 after a bout of violence in Texas in which forty-three people were tarred and feathered and a Negro bellboy was branded with "KKK" across the forehead. "You'd better take your sheets, your banners, your masks, your regalia, and make one big bonfire." It would be four more years before the Klan would begin to disband, and not before its membership had reached an estimated five million.

The Klan

In the photograph at lower left, new members are admitted to the secret rituals of the Klan in an initiation ceremony at South Mountain near Brunswick, Maryland, in 1922. Only native-born white Americans "who believe in the tenets of the Christian religion" were accepted. Some of their white Christian fervor resulted in scenes of atrocity like the one below.

NAVY DEPARTMENT

SMITHSONIAN INSTITUTION

The United States ended the war with a fleet of surplus planes and many trained pilots, who returned to civilian life with an enthusiasm for flying and with talents now unwanted. Many, unwilling to go back to duller ways of life, bought themselves flimsy surplus planes and became barnstormers, traveling to county fairs or wherever they could draw a crowd with their stunt flying, standing on wings, or parachute jumping. The money lay in giving rides—"ten dollars for ten minutes" was a common charge. From such a precarious existence some barnstormers moved on to organize passenger airlines, set up flying schools, and become carriers of the early airmail.

The first transatlantic flight was by the Navy's NC-4, pictured (left) arriving off the coast of England after flying from Newfoundland via the Azores and Portugal. Three planes started, but only the NC-4 was able to complete the flight.

CULVER PICTURES

The U. S. Post Office began flying the first airmail service in the East in 1918; the first transcontinental airmail (above left) was delivered in New York in August, 1923. Above right, an automobile and an airplane piloted by Ruth Law Oliver, an early woman stunt flyer, race around a track in 1920. Such risky stunts helped popularize aviation. The song sheet opposite, typical of many from the early Twenties, is indicative that flying was then still considered a highly romantic adventure.

Dedicated to the Aviation Club of Chicago

Flying Around the Stars

Lieut. W.D. Phillips
U.S.A.

Eagle on Trial

Brigadier General William L. "Billy" Mitchell, brilliant World War I pilot and strategist and assistant chief of the Army Air Service from 1920 to 1925, waged a relentless war to upgrade the nation's air facilities. After the celebrated transatlantic flight of the Navy's Curtiss flying boat the NC-4 in 1919, Mitchell capitalized on the climate of public interest to dramatize the enormous potential and inadequate development of the country's aviation program. Again and again he pointed out the dangerous obsolescence of such hazardous aircraft as the Army's DH-4's, dubbed flaming coffins by the pilots, and he repeatedly urged the formation of a strong and independent air force. He believed that air power would determine supremacy in future warfare and set out to prove it in a series of aerial bombings of target warships in the summer of 1921. His most spectacular assault was against the supposedly indestructible *Ostfriesland*, Germany's onetime pride of the seas, on

July 21. With eight Martin bombers, each carrying a new 2,000-pound bomb, he sank the mighty dreadnought in twenty-five minutes flat. But even such demonstrations failed to effect a revolution in military aviation, and in 1925, after two particularly disastrous air accidents, Mitchell accused the War and Navy Departments of "incompetency, criminal negligence, and almost treasonable administration of the national defense. . . ." The charge brought him a highly publicized court-martial, in which the prosecution, conceding that he was "a good flyer, a fair rider, a good shot," accused him of being "flamboyant, self-advertising, wildly imaginative, [and] destructive." Mitchell was convicted of insubordination, but public sympathy was with him. Many would agree with the verdict of Frank Tichenor, editor of the *Aero Digest*, who said of Mitchell: "He has done more for the cause of aviation than any other man in the nation's history except the Wright brothers."

Airman Billy Mitchell, center, with Mrs. Mitchell, right, and defense attorney, Frank R. Reid, left, at Mitchell's 1925 court-martial.

A Martin twin-engine bomber, opposite, demonstrates its ability to sink a battleship in a test bombing of the U.S.S. Alabama.

The Open Road

Americans took to motoring like the proverbial ducks to water. By 1923 the automobile had become a necessity, and everybody, regardless of social or financial position, had to have one. It was a petting parlor for the young, an errand runner for the housewife, and an escape hatch for the restless. If one could afford an elegant Pierce-Arrow or a luxurious Cadillac, so much the better, but for just $290 ($5 a week on the installment plan) the country cousin could get there just as surely in his Model T runabout. And get there he did—to beaches, mountains, parks, and choice picnic spots, to city haunts and rural dives. America was on the move, and the flivver ruled the road.

The automobile was everywhere, on the open road and at crowded playgrounds. Highway conditions (above) have since improved, but parking problems, like the jam at Massachusetts' Nantasket Beach (right), have worsened.

In 1920 a twenty-four-year-old writer published his first novel and consigned the remnants of Victorian morality to oblivion. The novel, This Side of Paradise, *was an instant success, and its author, F. Scott Fitzgerald, became the spokesman for a new era of sophisticated youth. In the following excerpt he shocked and fascinated readers with his description of "petting," a new and popular pastime.*

"one vast juvenile intrigue"

On the Triangle trip Amory had come into constant contact with that great current American phenomenon, the "petting party."

None of the Victorian mothers—and most of the mothers were Victorian—had any idea how casually their daughters were accustomed to be kissed. "*Servant*-girls are that way," says Mrs. Huston-Carmelite to her popular daughter. "They are kissed first and proposed to afterward."

But the Popular Daughter becomes engaged every six months between sixteen and twenty-two, when she arranges a match with young Hambell, of Cambell & Hambell, who fatuously considers himself her first love, and between engagements the P. D. (she is selected by the cut-in system at dances, which favors the survival of the fittest) has other sentimental last kisses in the moonlight, or the firelight, or the outer darkness.

Amory saw girls doing things that even in his memory would have been impossible: eating three-o'clock, after-dance suppers in impossible cafés, talking of every side of life with an air half of earnestness, half of mockery, yet with a furtive excitement that Amory considered stood for a real moral let-down. But he never realized how wide-spread it was until he saw the cities between New York and Chicago as one vast juvenile intrigue.

Afternoon at the Plaza, with winter twilight hovering outside and faint drums down-stairs . . . they strut and fret in the lobby, taking another cocktail, scrupulously attired and waiting. Then the swinging doors revolve and three bundles of fur mince in. The theatre comes afterward; then a table at the Midnight Frolic—of course, mother will be along there, but she will serve only to make things more secretive and brilliant as she sits in solitary state at the deserted table and thinks such entertainments as this are not half so bad as they are painted, only rather wearying. But the P. D. is in love again . . . it was odd, wasn't it?—that though there was so much room left in the taxi the P. D. and the boy from Williams were somehow crowded out and had to go in a separate car. Odd! Didn't you notice how flushed the P. D. was when she arrived just seven minutes late? But the P. D. "gets away with it."

The "belle" had become the "flirt," the "flirt" had become the "baby vamp." The "belle" had five or six callers every afternoon. If the P. D., by some strange accident, has two, it is made pretty uncomfortable for the one who hasn't a date with her. The

Last summer I was at a student conference of young women comprised of about eight hundred college girls from the middle western states. The subject of petting was very much on their minds, both as to what attitude they should take toward it with the younger girls . . . and also how much renunciation of this pleasurable pastime was required of them. . . .

So far as I could judge from their discussion groups, the girls did not advise younger classmen not to pet—they merely advised them to be moderate about it, not lose their heads, not go too far—in fact the same line of conduct which is advised for moderate drinking. Learn temperance in petting, not abstinence.

Before the conference I made it my business to talk to as many college girls as possible. . . . Just what does petting consist in? What ages take it most seriously? Is it a factor in every party? Do "nice" girls do it, as well as those who are not so "nice"? Are they . . . exaggerating the prevalence of petting, or is there more of it than they admit? . . .

One fact is evident, that whether or not they pet, they hesitate to have anyone believe that they do not. It is distinctly the *mores* of the time to be considered as ardently sought after, and as not too priggish to respond. As one girl said—"I don't particularly care to be kissed by some of the fellows I know, but I'd let them do it any time rather than think I wouldn't dare. As a matter of fact, there are lots of fellows I don't kiss. It's the very young kids that never miss a chance." . . .

I sat with one pleasant college Amazon, a total stranger, beside a fountain in the park, while she asked if I saw any harm in her kissing a young man whom she liked, but whom she did not want to marry. "It's terribly exciting. We get such a thrill. I think it is natural to want nice men to kiss you, so why not do what is natural?" There was no embarrassment in her manner. Her eyes and her con-

"belle" was surrounded by a dozen men in the intermissions between dances. Try to find the P. D. between dances, just *try* to find her.

The same girl . . . deep in an atmosphere of jungle music and the questioning of moral codes. Amory found it rather fascinating to feel that any popular girl he met before eight he might quite possibly kiss before twelve.

"Why on earth are we here?" he asked the girl with the green combs one night as they sat in some one's limousine, outside the Country Club in Louisville.

"I don't know. I'm just full of the devil."

"Let's be frank—we'll never see each other again. I wanted to come out here with you because I thought you were the best-looking girl in sight. You really don't care whether you ever see me again, do you?"

"No—but is this your line for every girl? What have I done to deserve it?"

"And you didn't feel tired dancing or want a cigarette or any of the things you said? You just wanted to be——"

"Oh, let's go in," she interrupted, "if you want to *analyze*. Let's not *talk* about it."

ALFRED CHENEY JOHNSON

F. Scott Fitzgerald and his wife, Zelda, in the early days of their marriage.

science were equally untroubled. I felt as if a girl from the Parthenon frieze had stepped down to ask if she might not sport in the glade with a handsome faun. Why not indeed? Only an equally direct forcing of twentieth century science on primitive simplicity could bring us even to

the same level in our conversation, and at that, the stigma of impropriety seemed to fall on me, rather than on her. It was hard to tell whether her infantilism were real, or half-consciously assumed in order to have a child's license and excuse to do as she pleased. I am inclined to think that

both with her and with many others, it is assumed. One girl said, "When I have had a few nights without dates I nearly go crazy. I tell my mother she must expect me to go out on a fearful necking party." In different parts of the country, *petting* and *necking* have opposite meanings. One locality calls necking (I quote their definition) "petting only from the neck up." Petting involves anything else you please. Another section reverses the distinction, and the girl in question was from the latter area. In what manner she announces to her mother her plans to neck, and in what manner her mother accepts the announcement, I cannot be sure.

If Victorian mothers were shocked by Fitzgerald's exposé of the petting scene in 1920, they must have been horrified at the boldness with which their daughters were soon discussing the subject. In 1924 Eleanor Rowland Wembridge attended a Midwestern conference of coeds, and her observations, extracted here, entitled "Petting and the Campus," appeared in the July 1, 1925, issue of The Survey.

"Temperance, not abstinence"

The New Woman

Postwar woman demanded and was granted a new independence. Her unabashed use of cosmetics (above),
which once would have branded her a hussy, and her
shortening skirts were superficial; the important change
in the young lady of the early Twenties, opposite, was in
her growing poise and awareness of her new freedom.

ONEIDA LTD. SILVERSMITHS, COURTESY SY SEIDMAN

September 11, 1920

Price—15 Cents
Subscription Price $7.00 a year

Leslie's

Illustrate   vaper

VOTING
BOOTH NO 1

The Mystery of 1920

Women's long fight for the vote ended with ratification of the Nineteenth Amendment in August, 1920. Suffragists had predicted that women voters would lift the moral tone of politics, and *Leslie's Illustrated Weekly Newspaper* (opposite) wondered how the new voter would choose; two months later her overwhelming favorite was handsome Warren Harding. The two pictures above bespeak the rapid growth of women's new freedom: at top, girls are taken from a beach in 1922 for wearing indecent one-piece swimsuits; above, though there has hardly been time for suit styles to change, the young lady poses undisturbed by the sea.

UPI; OPPOSITE: *JUDGE*, SEPTEMBER 3, 1921, NEW YORK PUBLIC LIBRARY

*Swept into office with a promise of "law and order" and "return to normalcy," Warren G. Har-
ding is accompanied to his inauguration by outgoing President Woodrow Wilson, ill and weary
after two paralytic strokes and an enervating battle for the League of Nations. In front, bundled
against the cold, rides Joseph "Uncle Joe" Cannon, colorful and autocratic Speaker of the House.*

Shadow over Washington

Inauguration Day, March 4, 1921. The contrast could not have been more glaring when the two men, the old President and the new, rode together in the open Pierce-Arrow cabriolet under a sunny, cloudless sky to Capitol Hill. The crowds that lined the way saw on the one hand Woodrow Wilson, shrunken, white, tense hands gripping his invalid's cane, and on the other Warren Gamaliel Harding, of leonine head, plump, affable, the prophet of the return to "normalcy," the neologism he had coined during his staggeringly successful campaign, in which he appealed to the longings of an American people exhausted by the strain of three years of world war and its aftermath and impatient to try to return to the pleasant prewar life.

Wilson had been the autocrat, the dogmatic schoolmaster, forever dragooning the American people to work for a cause, whipping them down the unpleasant road of international responsibility. Harding asked nothing of them. Easygoing, kindly, totally devoid of intellectual qualities, he was the abstraction come to life of the average sensual man.

And he was that with a vengeance, had the nation only suspected. The man they had chosen over colorless Governor James M. Cox of Ohio by a landslide was a small-town sport and womanizer. If he was not truly a hick, he was as close to being the embodiment of the back-country politico, the practitioner of courthouse intrigue and of statehouse trafficking in shady contracts, as the American Presidency has ever known.

Warren Harding's origins were humble, a fact he made no effort to disguise, thereby endearing himself to the plain men of the nation. They identified with him, seeing him as the incarnation of the banal American dream that every mother's son, similarly devoid of qualities, might aspire to the most high. For Harding, the son of a small-town schoolteacher turned doctor, had only a mediocre schooling (he had acquired a Bachelor of Science degree in 1882 at Ohio Central College, a now-defunct freshwater academy of higher learning whose faculty totaled three). Harding had moved to Marion, Ohio, before the turn of the century and there, at the age of eighteen, with a friend, took charge of a bankrupt newspaper, the *Star*, in which his father had purchased a half interest. The job seemed to fit him.

But fate would single out this all-too-common man for greatness, or at least a kind of notoriety that has set him down in history as perhaps the worst President the United States has known, surpassing in fatuity even such presidential ciphers as James Buchanan and John Tyler and rivaling in indifference or insensitivity to rampant corruption the administration of Ulysses S. Grant. In the end fate would also prove unkind, for in Marion, Warren Harding, then scarcely twenty-five years old, met a girl, one Florence Kling, five years his senior, a divorcee, the unalluring daughter of one of the great powers of back-country Ohio. Her money, connections, and most importantly her driving ambition would propel the passive young man into politics, into the White House, and eventually into disaster.

Florence Harding, soon to be known as the Duchess for her imperious manner, believed in her young husband's star—quite literally, since she was a devotee of astrology and necromancy. She married him over her family's objections, and drove him to run successfully on two occasions for the state senate and to follow this with election as lieutenant governor in 1903.

At the close of his term in 1905, Harding retired from politics until 1910, when he ran for governor of Ohio and was soundly thrashed. But two years later the uncertain Harding was persuaded to make another try— this time for a vacant senatorial seat in Washington. By a quirk of fate, the man of small endowments won.

Thus far, except for minor setbacks, the story would seem to be one of unqualified successes. Harding, however, was shadowed, in his youth and to the day of his death, by the persistent story that he was tainted by Negro blood, that he was, in short, a "bad nigger" trying to pass. Florence Harding's father, Amos Kling, who apparently believed the story, threatened Harding in the street, and when his daughter defied him and married the young man, refused to speak to her for seven years.

Whether there is truth to the story of Harding's mixed ancestry is difficult to say. The genealogical tables reach back to one Richard Harding, of yeoman stock of England, who emigrated to New England in the seventeenth century. The Harding forebears drifted to Pennsylvania and eventually to lands that would become part of central Ohio. But the details of the genealogy in the subsequent years are obscure. It is entirely possible that some intermarriage with Negroes did take place, as

there were black Hardings in Ohio in the last third of the nineteenth century. But in Warren Harding's case the Negro blood, if it existed at all, must have been so diluted as to be of interest only to an implacable bigot.

Yet the unkillable rumors of Harding's ancestry did not seriously impede his rise. In Washington Harding found himself in his element in a Senate that was, for him, a congenial and convivial club. Recalling him in those years, one associate astutely remarked that Harding liked being in the Senate rather than being a senator —the camaraderie, the pomp, the status, the proximity to good fun like golf, baseball games, and all-night poker, and the ready opportunities for patronage suited Harding well. The duties were far from onerous: Harding voted only one-third of the time. Back home in Ohio his paper flourished, making him an independently wealthy man, and the not inconsiderable political power he wielded in his home state was itself vastly pleasing.

Nor did his position in public life, with its bright light of publicity, seriously inhibit Warren Harding's private life. In the years when he had been lieutenant governor he had entered into a long-term affair with the wife of a Marion department-store owner, which for all the banality of expression in his love letters (the contents of which are available as yet only by hearsay) apparently was a relationship of considerable depth. Phrases like "Gee, I love you, dearie" might have represented the limit of Harding's capacity for verbal self-expression, but they do not necessarily mean that the sentiments he haltingly avowed were shallow. But constancy was foreign to Harding's nature, and even before that affair had completely ended, there was twenty-year-old Nan Britton, who was to bear his bastard child.

 t was Florence Harding's ambition that would, in the end, bring him down. Joining with Harry Daugherty, a minor statehouse politician whose personal political ambitions had long since been blasted— Daugherty was compared by the contemporary *The New York Times* to a stumblebum who wisely decides to manage others —she pushed Harding relentlessly on. In 1912 Harding introduced the name of William Howard Taft in nomination for the Presidency at the Republican convention, and four years later he served as chairman of the convention. He began to catch the eye of the party's national leadership, and the

careful maneuvering behind the scenes by Florence and Daugherty bore fruit at the war's end.

For the Republicans victory was in the air in 1920. The country longed to repudiate the adventurous policies of the Wilsonians so that winning the Republican nomination would be tantamount to national victory. But there were obstacles standing in Harding's way. There was no shortage of able or famous Republicans to run, among them General Leonard Wood, Governor Frank Lowden of Illinois, Senator Hiram Johnson of California, Charles Evans Hughes, only narrowly defeated by Wilson in 1912, Senator William Borah of Idaho, and even that dark horse Herbert Hoover. But the leading figures were deadlocked. After four ballots it became clear that a compromise candidate would have to be found. Harding, running fifth in the balloting, was that man.

Summoned at two o'clock in the morning before a dozen or more party politicos in a "smoke-filled room," where the destiny of the nation was being hammered out, Harding was told of his probable nomination the following day. Were there any impediments to his running for the Presidency? he was asked.

Harding asked for time to ponder. Since his political career had to date been a cipher, the party politicos could only have been alluding to the persistent racial slurs and to his sexual irregularities. Young Nan Britton, whom Harding had established in New York and met regularly in third-rate hotels, was even then in Chicago with Harding's daughter of less than a year.

But after consulting his conscience for ten minutes, Harding found it good. The next day he was nominated on the tenth ballot with Governor Calvin Coolidge, famed for his handling of the Boston police strike, as his running mate. In November the nation went on to elect Harding by a plurality of seven million votes over Cox.

"We're in the Big League now," a gleeful Harding told his associates on being elected to the Presidency, but Harding was plainly out of his league and out of his depth. In the end the responsibilities of the office he assumed would destroy him precisely because Harding, with his limited horizons, did not understand that the political morality appropriate to the courthouse in Marion, or even to the statehouse in Columbus, did not equip him to discharge his awesome duties as the President of the United States.

By 1920 government in America—even Republican government, which proclaimed *laissez faire*—was big business, replete with titanic possibilities for patronage and misuse of power. Even though by 1920 the entire federal budget was a mere six billion dollars (it would be one-half of that two years later as the effects of the war diminished), still the postwar Veterans' Bureau dispensed half a billion dollars a year after its creation in 1921 and the Department of the Interior had custody of vast natural reserves, ripe for spoliation. Thus there was potentially a giant bag of loot should the federal government ever relax its vigilance.

As for the law enforcement agencies of the federal government, their impact on society had never been negligible. In 1920 the Federal Bureau of Investigation did not exist, but with prohibition in force, the Department of Justice presided over vast opportunities for mischief or good.

For Harding such sober, indeed melancholy, considerations lay in the future. On March 4, 1921, there was the heady experience of the inauguration, an event no doubt marred for the new President by the irksome and probably painful duty of riding to Capitol Hill in the company of a man he not only succeeded but, in the deepest sense, supplanted. His bitterness Wilson scarcely deigned to conceal. But the true source of Harding's well-attested discomfort probably lay elsewhere than in the shallow embarrassment of a good fellow in the presence of tragedy. Harding cannot have enjoyed the experience for the simple reason that he was always in a kind of agony when in the company of extraordinary men.

Harding had asked of the people their friendship and little else. And after his election he had told a newspaperman that if he could not, as he well knew, be the best President of the United States, he might still hope to be the best loved. In the orotund phrases of his inaugural address:

America builded on the foundation laid by the inspired fathers, can be a party to no permanent military alliance. . . . a world super-government is contrary to everything we cherish and can have no sanction by our Republic. This is not selfishness, it is sanctity. . . . Our supreme task is the resumption of our onward normal way. Reconstruction, readjustment, restoration—all these must follow. . . .

Harding was not unaware of the looming problems of the peace treaties with Germany, Austria, Hungary, and Turkey, of the tariff, of the naval arms race, and of mass unemployment. It can be fairly said, then, that Harding saw his administration as something larger than a reflection of small-town provincialism.

There was, for one thing, his pledge to the country to appoint to his Cabinet the "best minds," men who would implicitly make up for the intellectual deficiencies of the chief. In this respect Harding, to a remarkable degree, kept his pledge. In Charles Evans Hughes, his Secretary of State, and Herbert Hoover, his Secretary of Commerce, he appointed men touched by a certain greatness. In Andrew Mellon, his Secretary of the Treasury, and the elder Henry Wallace, his Secretary of Agriculture, he named men of unquestionable competence.

But it was not to the best minds that Harding would in fact turn for advice. He asked visitors to pray for him; he begged a neighbor to "talk to God about me every day by name and ask Him somehow to give me strength for my great task. . . ." Uncomfortable in the presence of excellence, or even competence, he staffed most of his Cabinet and administration with affable nonentities—or worse. This was his "Poker Cabinet" and thus he was to come to ruin.

Who were these men around him?

Item: Harry M. Daugherty, Attorney General of the United States, former courthouse politician and trafficker in liquor permits and immunities from prosecution, who, later evidence was to reveal, had come to Washington in 1920 fully twenty-seven thousand dollars in the red and who, within less than three years, deposited seventy-five thousand dollars in his brother's Ohio bank. Furthermore, in his possession was found forty thousand dollars' worth of bonds, traced by the courts to a bribe, and two thousand shares in an aircraft subsidiary that during the war had bilked the United States government out of three million five hundred thousand dollars in overcharges and had never been indicted.

Daugherty ran the "Little House on H Street," where Warren Harding slipped away of evenings for all-night poker, dirty stories, and, so it was rumored, available girls. Daugherty would boast in after years that nothing had ever been proved against him, that he had escaped court conviction on every charge. But that he did escape, he invariably neglected to add, was solely attributable to the protective umbrella of the Fifth Amendment.

Item: Albert B. Fall, Secretary of the Interior, a man whom Harding had first considered for the Secretaryship of State in preference to the judicious Charles Evans Hughes. A former senator from New Mexico, he had come to his post in 1921 near bankruptcy, the taxes on his Southwest ranch holding nine years overdue. Within two years he had stocked it with blooded cattle and bought adjoining lands to round off his spread at a cost of one hundred and twenty-five thousand dollars—on an official salary of twelve thousand dollars per year. Later exposed as the archmanipulator of the Elk Hills and Teapot Dome scandals, Fall, unlike the luckier Daugherty, would spend a brief time in jail.

Item: Jess Smith, ex-officio member of the Department of Justice and the "man to see" in that aptly named Department of Easy Virtue, the Attorney General's roommate at the Little House on H Street (where both lived rent free at a scale of fifty thousand dollars per year), hanger-on, smalltime sport, slack of lip, invariably greeting callers at his unofficial office with the cry "Whaddaya know?" At last, when the first hints of the corruption in the Harding administration began to come to light, Smith shot himself. Conveniently, most of his and Daugherty's papers had been burned.

Item: Charles Forbes, director of the Veterans' Bureau, onetime Army deserter, professional good fellow, a man whom Harding had picked up one day while on a senatorial junket and had never bothered to investigate. Forbes presided over a department that dispensed five hundred million dollars yearly in pensions, hospital supplies, and construction contracts. In time investigation would bring to light that Forbes in late 1922 had declared surplus several million dollars' worth of government-owned hospital supplies. These were sold, without benefit of competitive bidding, to a Boston firm for about six hundred thousand dollars. One million towels, for example, bought by the government for thirty-four cents each were sold at three cents. Forbes, too, would serve a short time in jail. His chief assistant, Charles F. Cramer, legal counsel to the Veterans' Bureau, would also take his own life.

Item: Thomas W. Miller, alien property custodian, a man who had control over more than thirty thousand active trusts seized as enemy property during World War I. In one instance involving the German Metallgesellschaft and Metall Bank, whose confiscated stock was worth seven million dollars by September, 1921, Miller was brought into contact with the German owners by Jess Smith, acting as intermediary. Effecting the return of the firm's assets within a matter of days, Miller pocketed for his trouble $50,000 out of a total fee of $391,000 in bonds and $50,000 in cash, a sum paid by the German principals, who were apparently more than satisfied that value had been rendered. The rest of the huge fee went to men as varied as Attorney General Daugherty, Jess Smith, and Republican National Committeeman John T. King. Miller, too, would be exposed and go to jail.

Others of Harding's friends were not so much venal as merely fatuous and dim.

The duties of the Presidency weighed on him. Samuel Hopkins Adams, a newsman of the period who made a lifelong calling of writing about the Harding administration and its scandals, wrote:

So he went back to the genial companionship of the Poker Cabinet, where everybody was so comfortable and no questions arose to put a strain on one's mind. He was on first-name terms with the whole bunch, though they maintained the external proprieties by addressing him as "Mr. President." There was . . . Ned McLean, maybe not very strong in the upper story but a millionaire and a society man and not a bit stuck up about it. There was "Doc" Sawyer, who might not be the most scientific guy in the world, having had only a couple of terms in a dubious medical school, but came from the Old Home Town, played a stiff hand of poker, and was good enough for Harding. And how Doc loved the trappings of a Brigadier General which went with his job as the President's personal physician! There was "Mort" Mortimer, a personal friend as well as a reliable bootlegger who knew where the best liquor was to be found and kept his pals well supplied—and to hell with the bluenoses who beefed about the evil example of illegal drinks in the White House! There were those prime Senatorial sports, Joe Frelinghuysen and Frank Brandegee. . . . Harry Sinclair, the big oil man, and Bill Wrigley of the chewing gum family. . . . The President was in his element.

And Alice Roosevelt Longworth, daughter of an earlier President, wrote with distaste of the raffish level to which social life in the White House had dropped: "No rumor could have exceeded the reality; the study was filled with cronies . . . the air heavy with tobacco smoke, trays with bottles containing every imaginable brand of whiskey stood about, cards and poker chips ready at hand—a general atmosphere of waistcoat unbuttoned, feet on the desk, and the spittoon alongside."

Initially, to be sure, the duties were not too stiff, and if Harding had enjoyed his status as senator, how much more did he revel in the pageantry of the Presidency. He was oppressed, however, by a sense of inadequacy. Witness his despairing confidence to a golfing companion, "Judge, I don't think I'm big enough for the Presidency." To David Lawrence, then a young newsman, he admitted, "Oftentimes, as I sit here, I don't seem to grasp that I am President."

But it was no longer easy to get away to the Little House on H Street, let alone to New York for nights of love with Nan Britton. Poor Harding, man of lusts, thereupon smuggled her into the White House, and bedded her down in the coat closet. To such a pass was the President of a mighty nation reduced. Recalled Nan Britton in her best-selling memoirs in after years:

Whereupon, he [Harding] introduced me to the one place where, he said, he thought we *might* share kisses in safety. This was a small closet in the anteroom, evidently a place for hats and coats, but entirely empty most of the times we used it, for we repaired there many times in the course of my visits to the White House, and in the darkness of a space not more than five feet square the President of the United States and his adoring sweetheart made love.

ut he could not conjure away the urgent problems, the crowding events of an era of defiant normalcy: the tax issues, the tariff issues, growing unemployment. A note of desperation began to creep into Harding's voice. William Allen White recalled a talk at the White House with the President's assistant Judson C. Welliver, who quoted the unhappy Harding as crying out: "I can't make a damn thing out of this tax problem. I listen to one side and they seem right, and then—God!—I talk to the other side and they seem just as right, and here I am where I started. I know somewhere there is a book that will give me the truth, but hell! I couldn't read the book."

Nor did he know much more about foreign affairs. America had intervened in a vast European struggle, helping to convert a dynastic and commercial conflict into an ideological crusade that had overturned the established order of things. In the aftermath of that war America's responsibilities were legion. But Harding confided to a visitor: "I don't know anything about this European stuff." Fending off questions, he advised: "You and Jud get together and he can tell me later; he handles these matters for me."

That is to say, Judson Welliver, together with the stately Charles Evans Hughes, one of the few able men in the Harding administration, made the foreign policy decisions for the President. One result was a celebrated international event of the 1920's, the Washington Naval Conference of November, 1921, which set a precedent for disarmament efforts in after years.

The genesis of the conference lay in the fact that World War I had left a legacy of ambitious naval building programs in its wake: the United States alone was engaged in the construction of sixteen capital ships, at the time defined as battleships and battle cruisers (aircraft carriers, which were regarded as peripheral toys, were not included).

Such programs imposed a fiscal burden that even so wealthy a nation as the United States could ill afford, let alone Great Britain, whose economy had been severely damaged by the ordeal of 1914–18. And according to a political belief that has its advocates to this day, the mere existence of these navies, afloat and abuilding, was a potent stimulus to the outbreak of war.

The conference duly convened in Washington on November 12, the day following the entombment in Arlington Cemetery of America's Unknown Soldier. Harding's role in opening the conference was merely ceremonial. The drama of the opening day, shrewdly timed by Hughes to fall on Friday so that world opinion would have time to influence the other delegations before the next workday, lay in the address by the American Secretary of State.

Hughes's proposal was a startling but simple one: let there be disarmament immediately. The United States would scrap—present, building, and planned—capital ships to the number of thirty, with an aggregate tonnage of 845,000; Britain was to scrap nineteen; and Japan, seventeen. All construction of battleships and battle cruisers was to halt for a period of ten years. Restrictions were to be put on the size of aircraft carriers and the total tonnage of such vessels each nation could build. Thus the final ratio of the three fleets was to be fixed at 5:5:3—the discrepancy in favor of the United States and Britain being explained as reflecting their multiocean responsibilities, while Japan needed to guard only her home waters.

Pandemonium thereupon reigned, as if peace had been achieved at one stroke. Wrote William Allen White, who attended: "Hats waved, handkerchiefs fluttered, men shook one another's hands, hugged one another, slapped one another, exhibited every kind of animal delight. . . ."

There was some resentment among the Japanese at taking a lesser role, but Japan was poor and hard pressed to keep pace with the ambitious American naval construction program. What followed, therefore, was some hard diplomatic bargaining in which the Japanese succeeded in exchanging a pledge to abide by the treaty for an American pledge to refrain from further fortifying naval bases west of Pearl Harbor and a British promise not to extend her bases into Asian waters farther north than Singapore.

A jubilant Harding, who believed along with Hughes that the reputation of his administration would stand or fall with the success, or lack thereof, of the naval conference, brought the meeting to a close with his typically orotund rhetoric: "Those of us who live another decade are more likely to witness a growth of public opinion, strengthened by new experience, which will make nations more concerned with living to the fulfillment of God's high intent than with agencies of warfare and destruction. . . . The torches of understanding have been lighted. . . ."

But little more than a decade later Japan's Kwantung Army seized Manchuria, Hitler's brown shirts battled in the streets with a disorganized Left, and in Russia famine, the result of Stalin's drive to abolish private ownership of the land, left windrows of dead throughout the Ukraine. A decade after the conference there was little understanding. Treaties were being honored by those who did not need to be restrained and flouted by those who did.

Harding was a shallow man of small endowments, but on occasion he could show a modicum of political courage. In the climate of wartime political excess Eugene V. Debs, the imposing Socialist leader, had been jailed by the Wilson administration for expressing an opposition to the war that went little beyond classical American noninterventionism, the hallowed doctrine of nineteenth-century isolationist American foreign policy. But Wilson, for all the nobility of his vision of a world cleansed of war and hate, could not rise to conventional compassion after the war had ended and repeatedly refused to pardon Debs. Harding, however, ever of good, if slack, will, sent him home, pardoned, to his family for Christmas, 1921.

Yet easy tears and a congenital inability to say No to old friends (when William F. Anderson, Methodist bishop of Ohio, had objected to the idea of Harry Daugherty's appointment as Attorney General, Harding heatedly replied, "I would not want the country to think me so much of an ingrate that I would ignore a man of Mr. Daugherty's devotion . . .") did not qualify the man to be President of the United States. Already the reek of scandal permeated Washington. If Harding, despite his nights at the Little House on H Street, did not suspect that something was very much wrong, he was shocked into awareness by the suicide of Charles Cramer.

t was "Doc" Charles Sawyer who first brought an intimation that something might not be quite right in the Veterans' Bureau. Hospital administrators and others, disturbed by the way Forbes was selling hospital supplies to a private firm at a fraction of their cost to the federal government, had voiced their misgivings to Sawyer. The doctor spoke to the President, and Harding, perturbed, ordered the sale of surplus hospital supplies temporarily halted. He was soon visited by Forbes, who assured him expansively that everything was in order and that the Veterans' Bureau was being honestly and efficiently operated.

Forbes attempted to lay public suspicions by arranging for a superficial investigation by a War Department official, who, of course, found nothing amiss. At this Harding, gullible to the last, allowed sales to resume, and Forbes was soon doing business again. By this time, though, the hounds were closing in, and Forbes found it wise to go abroad in January, 1923. When Cramer found that there was to be a Senate investigation, he, in March of 1923, shot himself in the head in the house on Wyoming Avenue he had bought from Harding two years before. Before ending his life, Cramer took the trouble to pen a letter to the President, presumably detailing all. This letter a Department of Justice man duly delivered, only to have it refused by the despondent President, who, rather mysteriously, seems to have been aware that Cramer was dead although he had been roused from bed to receive the message. Baffled, the agent turned it over to Harry Daugherty, who arranged for it to disappear. Shortly thereafter Forbes resigned.

Nor was the Forbes scandal all. In May, 1923, Jess Smith put a bullet in *his* brain. Even Harding at last was beginning to realize the dimensions of the corruption. The President, behind closed doors, was heard to whimper to himself, "What's a fellow to do when his own friends double-cross him?"

Thus Harding by the spring of 1923 was a man distraught. He could not bear the duties of the Presidency, and he could not, amiable spirit, truly comprehend the massive venality and faithlessness of those he had put in a position to wield great power in the land.

Harding determined on a trip, a cleansing voyage of the soul. He would go to Alaska. The trip was initially conceived as one more poker-booze-and-girls junket, but as the shadows thickened over the administration, the plans were revised: the journey to Alaska would be a pilgrimage of duty. He would take the Duchess along with him; he would take outstanding men.

And simultaneously in this harrowing spring and summer he sought to pull himself together, to make of himself what he had never been: a self-denying man. If he could not (fatal flaw) quite bring himself to dismiss old friends, he would at least regenerate his own life. The tearful Nan Britton herself proposed that she make a trip to Europe, the all-night poker ended, the booze stopped. Unbelievably, in the Era of Prohibition the nation's White House at last went bone dry, or nearly so. Warren Gamaliel Harding went on the wagon.

But it was too late. Fate, initially prodigal in her gifts to this man of small qualities, now proceeded to destroy him. Harding went to Herbert Hoover for counsel. "Mr. Secretary," he complained, "there's a bad scandal brewing in the administration. What do you think I ought to do?" But advised to make a clean breast of it, to go to the country, Harding faltered. Summoned to the White House on the eve of the Alaska trip, President Nicholas Murray Butler of Columbia University spent hours with the President, treated to a rambling discourse yet momentarily expecting dark disclosures. None came and he returned to New York baffled. What had the President wished to say?

The trip was not a success. How could it have been? Incessantly the President played bridge, dragooning the men of his entourage into marathon sessions that lasted without appreciable break for ten or twelve hours or more. Oftentimes the President would merely sit and stare out the windows of the train, lost in thought. He was visibly depressed.

And in the end, quite simply, he died. On the way back from Alaska he suffered a coronary thrombosis, which, by a supreme irony, was incorrectly diagnosed as acute indigestion by Doc Sawyer, who was, like all the other venal or merely incompetent cronies, as Harding repeatedly asserted, "good enough for me."

The nation mourned Warren Gamaliel Harding as a good man, a giant that day fallen in Israel. The funeral cortege, as the train crossed the land to Washington and thence to the final resting place back home in Marion, Ohio, was hailed at every crossroads by doleful crowds. It was only as the 1920's drew to their close that the true dimensions of the disaster that had been the Harding administration became known. Charlie Cramer had put a bullet in his head; Jess Smith had put a bullet in his head. Forbes went to jail in 1925. Harry Daugherty resigned as Attorney General of the United States in 1924; his records had already been burned and he took the Fifth when he was brought to trial in 1926. But all that was trivial compared to the great Teapot Dome scandal, which shook the nation.

The origins of the case were simple enough. For years the United States Navy, then shifting from a coal to a petroleum navy, had feared for the sufficiency of its oil reserves in the event of war. Over the years, three great oil fields had therefore been set aside: Naval Reserve No. 1 at Elk Hills, California; Naval Reserve No. 2 at Buena Vista Hills, California; Naval Reserve No. 3 at Teapot Dome, Wyoming. These reserve lands, however, had not solved the Navy's problem. Though the government had, by and large, resisted pressure by private operators to lease lands within the reserves, the oil fields were threatened with depletion, for drilling on adjacent privately owned oil lands threatened constantly to drain the oil pools under government control.

How to meet the challenge of oil depletion had vexed preceding administrations ever since 1909. The obvious choices were to drill what was known as offset wells on the government land to match the drainage of the adjacent private wells or to lease the lands to private speculators, who would pay royalties to the Navy either in money or in kind.

The first alternative had been the decision of the Wilson administration, but the Harding administration, true to the Republican doctrines of *laissez faire*, preferred the second one. And very conveniently the second alternative had the advantage of benefiting the oil interests that had backed Warren Harding (more than half a million dollars in oil money was alleged to have been spent in 1920 to elect Harding). The oil interests also liked Albert Fall, who was a good friend to the great oil buccaneers Harry Sinclair and Edward

Doheny. They soon had much more reason to like Fall.

Fall's stratagem was a simple one. The oil reserves were under the jurisdiction of the Secretary of the Navy, an amiable cipher named Edwin Denby. The problem of jurisdiction offered no insuperable obstacles. Less than three months after becoming Secretary of the Interior, Fall induced the trusting President to transfer jurisdiction to the Department of the Interior. A year later, without benefit of competitive bidding, Fall leased Teapot Dome to Harry Sinclair's Mammoth Oil Company. In two separate contracts that same year, 1922, he leased Naval Reserve No. 1 at Elk Hills to Edward L. Doheny's Pan-American Petroleum and Transport Company. The Navy was to receive a moderate royalty, and the two beneficiary companies undertook to build oil storage tanks for the government.

Fall always argued that he had aided the Navy, which, had it received moneys, would have been forced to turn them over to the federal government rather than use them for needed storage construction. No doubt Fall, not to say Sinclair and Doheny, clothed the deal in the raiment of national interest.

But the sordid facts remain: when the scandal broke, Fall was revealed to have received one hundred thousand dollars in cash from Doheny and a cool two hundred and sixty thousand dollars in Liberty bonds from Sinclair. Fall went to jail for accepting a bribe, but by a quirk of justice neither Sinclair nor Doheny was convicted of offering that bribe (". . . the law," as Mr. Bumble puts it in *Oliver Twist*, "is a ass, a idiot"). But Sinclair at least was to serve two terms in prison: three months for contempt of the Senate for refusing evidence and six months for contempt of court for attempted coercion and bribery of his jurors.

Thus the sorry record: suicides, jailings, disgrace. In after years a minor bagman of the Harding administration would spread the story that the President had been murdered by a despairing Duchess, who had put the vexed and troubled man to sleep out of the compassionate desire to spare him disgrace and the concomitant desire to revenge herself for his petty amours. Others speculated that Harding, like Cramer and Smith, had committed suicide.

The soberer verdict will probably stand: Warren Gamaliel Harding may be said to have died of a broken heart in the real sense of the expression.

THE EYES AND EARS OF THE WORLD
2.

Out of postwar Europe emerged a new kind of dictator, the totalitarian strong man. Three great dynasties—the Romanovs of Russia, the Hohenzollerns of Germany, the Hapsburgs of Central Europe—had collapsed, and many of the new parliamentary governments, established during and after the war, were too weak to withstand the rising forces of Communism, Fascism, and Nazism. In Russia, Lenin wrenched control from a duly elected constituent assembly, and after his death in 1924, Stalin took over as dictator, silencing opposition in a series of bloody purges. Benito Mussolini formed his Fascist party in 1919, marched on the Italian capital in 1922, and took up the reins of dictatorship. In Germany the Nazi party was established, and in 1923 a young ex-corporal named Adolf Hitler came to the fore in an abortive but dramatic coup against the constitutional government in Munich. Elsewhere new nations were struggling for survival and democracies were dying in infancy. Against the tide of totalitarianism there seemed little hope for Woodrow Wilson's ideal of "self-determination" for the postwar nations of Europe.

The 1923 Tokyo earthquake killed thousands and left the city (above) a ruin.

enin's death in 1924 set off a Communist power struggle. Stalin (ahead
photograph at right) won; pro Trotsky Zinoviev (at rear) was expelled

In May, 1927, Japan launched the *Myoko* (above). Already she was building her navy, foreboding of things to come.

India's Gandhi is shown in 1924 after his release from prison for civil disobedience, early in the years of the campaign that finally won independence for his country.

Pius XI (above) was elected pope in 1922. A strong peace crusader, he condemned Communism and Fascism loudly during his 17-year reign.

Mussolini (top hat, left) with King Victor Emmanuel in 1923, shortly after assuming dictatorship. Above, he addresses a crowd in October, 1926.

Hitler (right), jailed in an attempted Nazi coup, relaxes in prison, 1924, where he wrote *Mein Kampf*. Three years later he commands a Nazi army (below).

COPYRIGHT © 1927, 1955 BY THE CONDE NAST PUBLICATIONS, INC.; OPPOSITE: LIFE, FEBRUARY 18, 1926, NEW-YORK HISTORICAL SOCIETY

In the short span of a decade the Jazz Age bloomed with a fleeting brilliance and faded. This 1927 Vogue cover is Jazz Age America in full flower: high life, city lights, a defiant and self-assured flapper. The brightness would wane two years later, when the glamour and allure, all the fragile underpinnings of the 20's, would collapse with the stock market crash.

The Great Euphoria

The country mourned Harding, but not for long. Vice President Calvin Coolidge, "Silent Cal," a man who the wits said had "been weaned on a pickle," was now President. He was a no-nonsense sort of man. Had he not dealt firmly with the striking Boston police in 1919? Was he not the proven friend of laissez-faire business, that mighty engine of social betterment through profits?

Coolidge was all these things, and a great deal less as well. A man who raised inertia almost to the level of a way of life, he took pains not to overwork himself, or the government either. Every afternoon he napped in the White House after a grueling four-hour workday. His social life was carried on grudgingly; asked why he continued to dine out, he replied, "Got to eat somewhere." Twitted by a sprightly young dinner partner— "Mr. Coolidge, I've made a rather sizable bet with my friends that I can get you to say three words this evening"—he answered tersely, "You lose."

Of medium height, angular, ungracious, limited in interests and unoriginal in thought, he seemed, as William Allen White put it, constantly "looking down his nose to locate that evil smell which seemed forever to affront him." But his intellectual defects would become apparent only in the aftermath. Not that he, like his predecessor, Harding, permitted sordid enterprises by his Cabinet (though his stately Secretary of the Treasury, Andrew Mellon, it would later be revealed, staggered the imagination of a Harry Daugherty or an Albert Fall by "legitimately" acquiring while a Cabinet officer three billion dollars through stock-market speculation). Coolidge was, as we shall see, a subscriber to the conventional economic wisdom of the time, and as such he paved the way for disaster.

Yet in the eyes of his contemporaries, old Silent Cal was good enough. "The business of America is business," he had said, and he conducted himself in that belief. He was good for business, and in 1923 business was good. The depression of 1921 was nothing more than a distant memory. By 1922 the market had begun to turn upward, and the Big Bull Market was in the making even as Warren Harding died amidst intimations of impending private disgrace.

And take off the market did as more and more people entered the stock market for the first time and began to buy into a steadily, or so it was thought, growing America. By 1925 there were one and a half million active stock market accounts, and of these 40 per cent were wildly speculative and on thin margin. The Dow-Jones industrial average, which had hit a bottom of 63.90 in 1921, soared to around 200 only six years later. The gross national product grew by nearly a third in that same period, coming within sight of one hundred billion dollars for the first time in the history of the nation.

In such a climate of prosperity and optimism, the businessman began to look upon himself as the Lord's Anointed. No longer was the statesman or the priest or the philosopher the spokesman for American society; the businessman, gathered with his fellows in the conviviality of weekly Rotary meetings, became the self-assured seer. Babbitt, as Sinclair Lewis named his caricature of a small-business man, was in the saddle.

Viewed from a vantage point nearly a half-century later, the social and psychological climate of the 1920's seems complex in the extreme. It was a time of ballyhoo and whoopee, overlying a stratum of moral disorientation and cynicism, especially among the young and especially in urban areas. It was a time when all the inherited modes of love, social intercourse, public decorum, dress, and speech were under assault. It was a time of deliberate cultivation of what was new, shocking, and very often vulgar: the stocking rolled below the knee, the four-letter word in the mouths of young debutantes, the hip flask, getting "boiled" or "fried" or "stewed," the scorning of old standards of polite behavior.

But though the stock market was giddy, though young men and women spat in the face of convention, though George Babbitt reigned in Zenith City, nevertheless there was sinew beneath the seemingly flabby surface of American life. Great industrial techniques, which would one day transform the world, were being worked out in Henry Ford's River Rouge and in a hundred other giant manufacturing complexes; and most impressive of all, America was coming of age intellectually. There was much first-class work being done in the arts—in poetry, the novel, painting, and music, and not least of all in the moving pictures. If some of the work seems dated and banal today, much of it stands up as it did in its own day, and a good case can be made that contemporary America is not doing anywhere near as well in its attempts to produce an artistic expression of our own life and times.

The years of the great euphoria were the years when young men and women in vast numbers fled the small towns for the cities—if possible to New York's Greenwich Village, then coming into its own as America's Bohemia, and best of all to Paris. In Paris they swarmed in the cafés, sipping endless espressos and Pernods and soaking up a European past that was in glaring contrast to the American myth of the new. No doubt for every genuine talent, for every novelist like Ernest Hemingway and F. Scott Fitzgerald, every painter like Lionel Feininger, or every poet like Ezra Pound, there were droves of the untalented. But the poignancy of an older European landscape did much to awaken the sensibilities of even these less-talented Americans.

On one level, the great mass of middle-class Americans was hostile to this upward movement in the arts. *The Saturday Evening Post*, then a self-appointed guardian of traditional American values, vented its fury against Greenwich Village repeatedly. "The sad truth is," it pronounced in 1931, "that the Village was a flop." Yet even the *Post*, as Malcolm Cowley has observed, would succumb in the end to the insidious lure of the foreign and the new. "Long before Repeal," he recorded in *Exile's Return*, "it began to wobble on Prohibition. It allowed drinking, petting, and unfaithfulness to be mentioned in the stories it published; its illustrations showed women smoking. Its advertising columns admitted one after another of the strictly pagan products —cosmetics, toilet tissues, cigarettes. . . ." The *Post* even published the short stories of Fitzgerald, thus financing that doomed young man's riotous descent into the pit of exhaustion, heartbreak, and oblivion.

Although books like Hemingway's *The Sun Also Rises* and Fitzgerald's *This Side of Paradise*, which spoke for postwar youth, made the best-seller lists, the public really preferred the faddish and trivial. Its first choices were such works as James Branch Cabell's *Jurgen*, which was dirty enough by the standards of the day to be banned in Boston, or John Erskine's *The Private Life of Helen of Troy*, or "smart" imported novels like Michael Arlen's *The Green Hat*, which gave a spurious introduction to modish London life.

What the general public failed to see was a shift in the intellectual trade between Europe and America. If young Americans flocked to Europe, still for the first time Americans at home were producing a sustained body of work that would export well and export in volume, and Europe became aware of a vital twentieth-century American literature.

In the same way, other artists found their inspiration in native soil. American painters discovered rich themes in the American scene, and American architects developed in the skyscraper an American building form. As for the American cinema, ambitious tragedies such as Erich von Stroheim's *Greed*; spectaculars like King Vidor's indictment of war, *The Big Parade*; and the zany and artful silent comedies starring inspired clowns like Charlie Chaplin, Harold Lloyd, and Buster Keaton proclaimed the birth of an American cinematic art form worthy to rank with the work of Russia's Sergei Eisenstein and Germany's Ernst Lubitsch.

While the new American writers and artists were having an effect on the European scene, their role in American life as transmitters of foreign ideas and values was even more profound. American intellectuals in those years served as popularizers of foreign doctrines: Leninism, Keynesian economics, and most startling of all, the new depth psychology of Sigmund Freud, Karl Jung, and Alfred Adler.

Though these advanced ideas from abroad strikingly affected America, some of them became in this country garbled versions of what the European innovators had intended. Freud, for example, became in popular perception the fomenter of a revolt against all inhibitions. What Freud had sought to do was to explain human motivation as primarily libidinal, that is to say, sexual, in origin and thus to remove from the individual the burden of undeserved guilt, the shackles of excess repression. But he had never championed total freedom: civilization, he would assert until his death, demanded restraint, an accommodation to the reality principle whereby present trivial pleasures were put off in favor of a future larger gain.

It was just this that Freud's followers and pseudo followers chose to misunderstand. Prattling of inhibitions, inferiority complexes, introversion, and libido, a generation of sheiks and flappers asserted that Freud approved of free love—and if some of them could not quite bring themselves to practice what they preached, at least it was possible for them to pet and flirt, all the while anesthetizing their inhibitions with the pocket flask of hootch.

"I've kissed dozens of men," one of Fitzgerald's heroines blandly asserted. "I suppose I'll kiss dozens more." All of which is a pretty tame declaration by today's standards, but an older generation of mothers gasped at licentious youth and sought to lock the doors. It was too late. The young were in automobiles parked in lovers' lanes across the nation. Freud had spoken; no one was going to move against "science" and the new thought.

The effects of this intellectual and moral revolution are with us today, though yesterday's dancing daughters, who wiggled the Charleston on a thousand table tops and passed out at the prom on bad booze, are today's grandmothers, shocked by the new freedom of pot and communal love. But the thinkers of the 1920's transformed American life and left doctrines that are canonical, or nearly so, to this day.

As summed up by Malcolm Cowley, they make an impressive list. There was, first of all, the doctrine of salvation by the child, the notion that a new generation raised with love and permissive understanding was going to transform our society. The world the children made was going to be a better one. (We are living with that world now.)

There was the doctrine of self-expression and its close parallel, the doctrine of paganism, which asserted the Judeo-Christian ethic to be a lot of buncombe. Men and women should do what they wanted; anything that inhibited self-expression was intrinsically bad.

There was the doctrine of living for the moment. No free spirit of the age better summed up the aspiration of a generation of maidens thirsting for sin and experience than the poetess Edna St. Vincent Millay, who boldly proclaimed that though her candle burned at both ends, it shed a lovely light. Ten thousand college girls read that one under the blanket by flashlight and wanted to live, live, live.

There was the idea of liberty, the notion that any law, be it one of art or rhyme or perspective, that limited the freedom of the individual was bad. And there was the idea of feminine equality, not quite brand new, since the mothers had championed votes for women, but equality in the Twenties did not mean the franchise. It meant, the horrified mothers whispered, their daughters' right to take and discard lovers at will.

There was the notion of psychological adjustment—through therapy—which has made psychoanalysis into a major American industry.

What eventually sold *The Saturday Evening Post* and other defenders of the old order, even as they fulminated and thundered, on at least two or three of these articles of faith was that, for all their irreverent treatment of tradition, the doctrines were good for business. The ideas of self-expression and paganism especially brought about not only a shattering of old social institutions but new demands: cosmetics, beach pajamas, holidays in the Florida sun, washing machines, and an automobile in every garage.

The new intellectuals' creed in fact helped transform America from a Puritan-minded, savings-oriented society, worshiping long-held ideals of prudence, self-reliance, and frugality, into a materialist-hedonist producers' and consumers' paradise. People extended themselves beyond all wisdom in their thirst for new toys. Thus the economy was in time subtly transformed by an intellectual revolution.

The new thinkers might have sneered at George Babbitt, but they were his brothers under the skin, essentially pragmatic like most Americans and vulnerable to the lure of material things. Even as they raged, the new generation of editors and writers and university professors was being bought off by creature comforts so that for many their rebellion in a nation where luxuries abounded faded away into a mere sense of grievance that the Joneses had a great many of the good things of life and why shouldn't they?

The increase of material abundance has a way of passing into vulgarity. And in the America of the great euphoria vulgarity was as much a hallmark of the period as were industrial innovation and experimentation in the arts. There was a proliferation of phony Tudor manor houses and imitation Spanish colonials in a hundred burgeoning suburbs from Scarsdale to Shaker Heights to Santa Monica. There was a growing country club morality of necking on Saturday night with one's business partner's wife and becoming drunk, to wake up on Sunday morning and drag oneself to church—there to hear a sermon on Jesus the great booster. Bruce Barton struck the note for the era in his monumentally vulgar *The Man Nobody Knows* when he contended that Jesus had been the first Rotarian, "the most popular dinner guest in Jerusalem," a hardheaded go-getter who had put together the greatest little sales organization on earth. This crass book was so in step with the times that far from being considered vulgar by most people, it was the nonfiction best seller for two successive years, 1925 and 1926.

In prospering urban America no one noticed that the

farmers had suffered the most precipitous price decline in history, with the index of farm prices falling nearly 44 per cent from 1920 to 1921. In that world of the easy dollar it was quite natural to believe that God moved in his heaven and all was right with the world. Religion was a celebration of the existing order. Hardly unprecedented, and hardly remarked upon as bizarre, was the pamphlet issued by the Metropolitan Casualty Insurance Company. "Moses," declared the pamphlet, "was one of the greatest salesmen and real-estate promoters that ever lived."

If the American movie industry, especially in its comedy films, had unwittingly produced a genuine art form, there was plenty of vulgarity ground out in Hollywood, which by the early 1920's had become the new center of the industry. Ballyhoo could, it seemed, do anything in that frenetic time.

 pretty young man of somewhat limited talents, one Rodolfo Alfonzo Raffaeli Pierre Filibert Guglielmi di Valentina d'Antonguolla, known as Rudolf Valentino, troubled the nighttime hours of tens of thousands of disappointed housewives lying in the dark next to snoring husbands. Why could they not be carried off by him to a desert seraglio? What delights might they not rise to if only they could give themselves to him? When Valentino died in 1926, mobs surged in a vast heaving mass of humanity, fighting for a sight of the funeral cortege and injuring dozens in the general melee. And there was Clara Bow, the "It" girl, who certainly had "it" but little else. And a dozen, two dozen, lesser sex pots and sheiks, along with a few rather more admirable figures, who, like Mary Pickford and the athletic Douglas Fairbanks, merely played out the fantasies of ordinary men and women condemned to lives of quiet desperation. Even Babbitt could yearn.

But the pressure for vulgarity pushed the film makers too far. Not only poor taste and sex in motion pictures but several nasty scandals among Hollywood stars eventually produced widespread public protest. To protect itself, the film industry named a morals guardian. This was good, affable Will Hays, Postmaster General in the Harding Cabinet, who, incapable of overseeing the morals of the Ohio Gang, had resigned in good time to oversee the morals of the motion picture industry.

Hollywood had sought to exploit sexiness for its own

sake, unredeemed by any search for form or meaning. Equally devoid of meaning was most of the profusion of fads of those years: the dance marathon, where a hundred unfortunate couples stumbled about a basketball amphitheater hour after hour, day after day; flagpole sitters, like Alvin "Shipwreck" Kelly, who set a record by perching on a staff several hundred feet above oblivion for twenty-three days and seven hours, never sleeping for more than twenty minutes at a time lest he fall to his death; six-day bicycle races; mah-jongg tournaments; the crossword puzzle craze; the contract bridge craze; the miniature golf craze; the Channel swimming craze; the shimmy craze; the Charleston craze.

Only occasionally, as in the case of Charles Augustus Lindbergh, Jr., the first man to fly the Atlantic nonstop and alone, did a figure emerge from the crowd of transitory idols worthy of the national acclaim. For even if Lindbergh's feat was not entirely without precedent (John Alcock and Arthur Brown of England had crossed nonstop from Newfoundland to Ireland eight years before), the young flyer comported himself with a most becoming modesty.

Cheered by thrill-hungry millions were the sports idols of the time: Bobby Jones, the golfer, with his deadly putter, "Calamity Jane"; "Big Bill" Tilden, a giant among the tennis greats; Babe Ruth, of the unbeatable New York Yankees, pounding out his record home runs and worth millions in box-office draw; dangerous Jack Dempsey, the "Manassa Mauler," who had broken big Jess Willard's cheekbone in his fight for the championship and who had in another bout come back to win after being knocked out of the ring by the "Wild Bull of the Pampas," Luis Firpo; Gene Tunney, onetime heavyweight champion of the American Expeditionary Forces, master boxer, dethroner of the great Dempsey, and, on retirement, giver of a special lecture series at Yale on Shakespeare; and many more.

The Twenties was a time of brilliant Irish and Polish middleweights and blazing, fast Jewish lightweights, of men, if the old-timers and the surviving motion pictures are to be believed, who knew the now neglected art of feinting, who fought in tank towns of the West, steel towns in Pennsylvania, the neighborhood fight clubs of Chicago and New York. In those years there were among the disadvantaged many who hungered for fame as athletes, and a lucky few would be richly rewarded. The first Dempsey-Tunney fight paid more than $900,000 to the principals; the second, $1,400,000.

But booming America was afflicted by something worse than either vulgarity or a mindless pursuit of fads and thrills; it was racked by a new upsurge of the violence that has bedeviled this aspiring land regularly through its history, from the Whisky Rebellion through range wars to race riots. In large part the violence of the Twenties was born of the Eighteenth Amendment and the attempt to dictate the drinking habits of an entire nation. An incredible era of lawlessness was the result, and murder became a commonplace as rival gangland mobs contended for the fortunes to be made from assuaging the great American thirst.

Yet at the outset prohibition was supported by an overwhelming majority of Americans. The Eighteenth Amendment had been passed by Congress late in 1917 in the midst of wartime fervor. Drinking interfered with the war effort; moreover, brewing and distilling used up grains needed to win the war. Therefore, liquor had to go; it was that simple. By January, 1919, the necessary thirty-six states had ratified, and the amendment became effective a year later. Enforcement machinery for the amendment was provided by the National Prohibition Enforcement Act (known as the Volstead Act for its author, Representative Andrew Volstead of Minnesota), which was passed over Wilson's veto in October, 1919. It defined intoxicating liquor as anything containing one-half of one per cent or more of alcohol by volume, put the Bureau of Internal Revenue in charge of administering the law, and set penalties for violations.

There was opposition, of course, and there were those who felt unfair advantage had been taken of our fighting men while they were overseas. But by and large the American people believed that a world without liquor, once they got used to it, would be a much better place. Few expected more than trivial opposition to enforcement, let alone real trouble.

"This law," declared the first prohibition commissioner, John F. Kramer, in accents self-assured, "will be obeyed in cities, large and small, and in villages, and where it is not obeyed it will be enforced. . . . The law says that liquor to be used as a beverage must not be manufactured. We shall see that it is not manufactured. Nor sold, nor given away, nor hauled in anything on the surface of the earth or under the earth or in the air."

Brave words, braver hopes, though just what Kramer meant by "hauling under the earth" is not clear. Yet the reality of enforcement was anything but brave. The Anti-Saloon League had estimated that a mere five million dollars yearly would suffice, and Congress took it more or less at its word. To enforce the law—restricting the drinking propensities of better than 105,000,000 people inhabiting a nation with more than 18,000 miles of coast only sketchily guarded by a reluctant Coast Guard and with two very long borders, north and south—fewer than 1,600 agents were authorized to the ebullient Kramer. And they were miserably paid, at a high of something under forty dollars per week in 1920, which was increased to a little better than fifty dollars per week a decade later.

Had America retained its lofty vision of prohibition and its benefits, this thin line of defense against violators of the Volstead Act might have been enough. But after the war came the inevitable letdown. People were weary of sacrifices. Giving up liquor became a reminder of the drab times of doing without, of the war years of meatless and wheatless days and sugar rationing. Besides, the heady feeling of social change and rebellion against old ways was in the air. The Eighteenth Amendment had hardly gone into effect before people started to drink again, though now they had to flout the law to mix a cocktail. What prohibition did accomplish was to make drinking initially a furtive affair, then a defiant practice. And it spread the habit of drinking, along with other contemporary marks of equality of the sexes, to the ladies.

Whether the volume of drinking actually increased, as the drys argued then, or decreased, can never perhaps be known, but the mere existence of the debate is proof that the point was a moot one. What is clear is that the patterns of drinking changed: there was a shift to hard spirits and the increasing consumption of these by the young and the female. And especially among the young the consumption of illicit booze came to be considered a symbol of the defiance of arbitrary authority; drinking and the dogma of self-expression became one.

The law was openly flouted. Tens of thousands of speak-easies sprang up in the cities. At every football game throughout the 1920's the raccoon-coated rah-rah boy and his date could be seen, faces tilted to the autumn sky, guzzling from the ubiquitous hip flask. And though hotels sanctimoniously warned guests that no alcoholic beverages were to be consumed in the rooms, a bla-

tantly common sight was the bellhop in the elevator carrying a tray of setups to Room 417.

Most of all a certain quality of frenzy, of desperation even, entered into the institution of drinking. Among the poor this was particularly pronounced. As the Wickersham Report, the result of Herbert Hoover's later official inquiry into prohibition, told it: "The discussion of prohibition . . . is the general topic of conversation among workers." All agreed, the report went on, that a worker "has to buy a drunk to get a drink . . . he buys a half pint of liquor and he is afraid he is going to lose it, or be arrested or it will leak out of his pocket and he drinks it all at one drink."

The change in the drinking habits of the poor was described by a Croatian immigrant in Cleveland, who told a private board of inquiry:

Now wine and whisky sold in homes. No good for woman to stay and sell liquor to mens all day. They get drunk and say bad things before children and she forget husband and children. Saloons was better; no children could go there and no women. Men who got drunk before prohibition get drunk now, but it costs them more. We want to have wine to drink, but dare not buy it for fear of being raided. Men used to go to a saloon maybe once a week and get a drink. Now go one or two months without a drink. Then meet a friend, go to private home, take one drink, then two, then another because they know it will be long before they can have more, and end by spending their whole pay and then getting very sick.

But if prohibition tended to degrade the poor and foreign, and brutalize the young, its most devastating social effect was on organized crime. Prohibition, whatever the drys may have said, shifted untold millions of dollars from avenues of more or less legitimate trade to channels controlled by the underworld. To be sure, there had been criminal gangs even before the Volstead Act. They had battened on prostitution, on small-scale trade in narcotics, on gambling. But American crime was largely a smalltime operation before 1919. Afterward it ballooned to terrifying proportions, and as it grew, it diversified, spreading into a hundred rackets: by the late 1920's the Chicago mobs had muscled in on everything from cleaning and dyeing to the sale of artichokes, at tremendous profit to themselves and a very considerable cost to the public.

The profits to be made out of booze were staggering. In the early years of organized crime in Chicago, mobster Johnny Torrio, in partnership with the "respectable" socialite brewer Joseph Stenson, amassed more than fifty million dollars over a four-year period. Stenson's take was twelve million dollars, and when the ring was broken up, he was not among those whom the law chastised. Stenson had the best of connections in the mayor's office, in the statehouse, and in the federal government itself.

But the Torrio-Stenson take was hardly unique. Initially evasion of the Volstead Act was attempted by the "legitimate" producers of beer and liquor: just as Stenson employed the services of the Torrio Gang to handle the opposition and ensure deliveries, so dozens of other brewers and distillers from coast to coast hired their gangster protectors. They did so, that is, until they learned the old lesson that if you dine with the Devil, you must bring a long spoon. The mobs had initially cooperated. But the first generation of gangsters, like "Big Jim" Colosimo, who controlled Chicago's South Side, was made up of slow-moving carnivores who were soon pushed to extinction by a newer and much more vicious breed.

olosimo died in 1920 of gunshot wounds at the hand of Frankie Yale and was succeeded by his good right hand, Johnny Torrio. Torrio brought the gangs together to end the senseless warfare, and he was the headman and doing very well until he made some enemies and was gunned down in 1925. He recovered, but prudently retired to Italy, turning his empire over to his first lieutenant, Alphonse Capone, imported from the East to run the mob. So enterprising was Capone that by 1927 he was reaping profits of about sixty million dollars a year, most of it from beer sales alone.

Crime thus became big business, and like all big business of the period it soon learned to form giant combines, to allocate territories, to restrict competition, to make contracts.

Initially the warfare was murderous; in 1924, as Capone built his empire, there were nearly four hundred gang murders in Cook County, Illinois, alone. The sawed-off shotgun, the Thompson submachine gun, or Tommy gun, the corpse weighted in cement in Lake Michigan, the bomb blast that destroyed a gangster's house and family, became everyday items hardly worthy of notice in the tabloids.

So, too, did the gangster funeral—orchids and lilies in overabundance, the great casket of bronze, the long funeral march. Capone, having wiped out Dion O'Banion, sent a giant basket of flowers, touchingly inscribed "From Al," to the obsequies of the victim.

The cooler and wiser heads among the mobsters realized that there were no winners in the murderous gang warfare, and in 1929 there was a "convention" of the mobs in Atlantic City. The results were beneficial, in effect a series of arms control agreements and non-aggression pacts. The rights of the various gangs to the territory they controlled were recognized: Frankie Costello and his friends in New York, Capone in Chicago, Maxie Hoff in Philadelphia, the Purple Gang in Detroit, Solly Weissman in Kansas City, and the Remus Mob in St. Louis. Lesser men had their territories too, but they existed in the shadow of the great.

Big Business in America did not shun the help of organized crime. Henry Ford might have talked of small-town virtues, but his connections with the mobs were uncomfortably close. Nearly eight thousand men who had served time in jail were employed in Ford plants, ostensibly to be rehabilitated, but in fact to intimidate the labor union organizers, who, throughout the decade, were depressingly unsuccessful in their efforts to unionize Ford. Among his concessionaires were two big-time racketeers, one of them Chester LaMare of Detroit, who, the federal government charged, took in over two hundred million dollars in gross bootlegging receipts in 1928 alone.

The mobs were glad enough to sell their talents to business; confronted by the challenge, big labor struck back in kind. During the long struggle in New York between the clothing manufacturers and the unions, the employers called in the notorious "Legs" Diamond and the opposition called in an equally competent band of thugs under Augie Orgen. But the situation became a standoff, and both sides appealed to the underworld notable Arnold Rothstein, who controlled the two gangs, to call the dogs off.

Thus the rackets proliferated amidst a general climate of violence and defiance of law. The drys might have shouted hosannas, as did the head of the Anti-Saloon League in 1924: "Ask the big hotels and restaurants which laughed at the law, whether enforcement is a fizzle. Then hear the doleful chorus. Let the Paradise restaurant on 58th Street, New York, sing bass; let Shanley's, Murray's, and the Little Club sing tenor; let Cushman's and the Monte Carlo sing alto; let Delmonico's sing soprano, and the words of the music are 'We have been padlocked, padlocked, padlocked.' The famous Knickerbocker Grill sings 'Amen, padlocked, amen and amen.'"

But the social landscape about the drys was one of disorder. For every padlocked speak-easy, there were dozens going full blast. Exciting, or seemingly so, were the doings of the mobs: the ingenious assassinations of gangland notables, the hijackings of booze trucks, the great motor cruisers lying off the twelve-mile limit ready to discharge their cargoes by night. More sordid were activities in the slums, where the mobs created cottage industries by organizing thousands of the poor to work part time as alky cookers.

Sordid, too, was the phenomenon of widespread evasion of the law by those who could not afford the good stuff, "just off the boat," from a reliable bootlegger or by those who merely delighted in the trivial defiance of authority. They made their own home-brew or bathtub gin according to frequently ingenious formulas: prune mash, apple cores, corn sugar, lemon extract, or industrial alcohol, sometimes suitably purified and sometimes not.

The better speak-easies – the New York commissioner of police estimated in 1929 that there were thirty-two thousand of all classes in that city alone – operated by paying off the prohibition agents, the local cops, and the mob, and usually protected their investment by serving something like the real thing. However, many an innocent customer woke up quite literally blind the next day, having been served industrial poisons. Again, it was the poor who suffered the most from unreliable rotgut liquor.

And over this frenetic age, these years of euphoria and lawlessness, of experimentation and action, presided Calvin Coolidge, apostle of nonaction.

In 1929, after Silent Cal did "not choose to run," his place was taken during the last days of this strange decade by a conservator of the frontier virtues, Herbert Hoover, the "Great Engineer," who for all his humanity really did not like change or know what to do about it. Hoover would prove a better President than Harding, a better President than Coolidge, too. But if he was touched by a certain greatness – he had been in turn the organizer of wartime production under Wilson, then a capable feeder of the war-torn and starving, and finally an able Cabinet member in two administrations – still he was limited in his vision, conservative in his mold.

The decade danced on to its close. The great euphoria seemed never to end. Stocks, said Professor Irving Fisher of Yale in a celebrated *gaffe* to be regretted later, had reached, it seemed, a "permanently high plateau." But the nation, caught up in its round of joy and violence and incessantly searching for new thrills, was nearing the edge of an abyss.

The New Morality

It was the Roaring Twenties, the Jazz Age, the Age of Ballyhoo, and the golden age of sports, speak-easies, and easy money. It was also an age of discontent: there were periods of serious unemployment, and farmers were generally outside the pale of the Coolidge Prosperity. There was the Lost Generation, described by Gertrude Stein and epitomized by the alienation of young writers like Hemingway, Fitzgerald, Sinclair Lewis, and John Dos Passos. And there was a moral breakdown, not just of outdated social and sexual mores but of more meaningful standards—a willingness to overlook corruption in government (disclosure of the Teapot Dome scandal, for example, brought more wrath upon the investigators than upon the defrauders) and a nonchalance about organized crime that amounted almost to approval. It began as a reaction to war and a rejection of prewar values, but the pendulum swung far the other way. Flappers, like the seven above, staged Charleston marathons down New York's Fifth Avenue; young men donned raccoon coats, swilled bathtub gin, and raced Stutz Bearcats; the public made demigods of its heroes and chased overnight sensations of crime, sex, and scandal. For better or worse, Americans threw off the shackles and in one brief decade attempted to rewrite the rules.

The passing of Warren G. Harding was more than the death of a kindly President betrayed by the perfidy of corrupt friends and counselors. It was the end of any pretense of "normalcy." The longing for normality that had helped to elect Harding was superseded, during his administration, by a

mania for the new and exciting. Hemlines were rising, speak-easies flourishing, autos proliferating. The Coolidge prosperity was just around the corner, and Americans were ready for it. Meanwhile they paid their last respects to the exemplar of small-town philosophy and virtues (the Harding

End of Normalcy

scandals had not yet come to light). As he lay in state (above) in August, 1923, the nation mourned; it was a truly heartfelt expression of grief, and Harding's secretary, George Christian (right, escorting Mrs. Harding), spoke for many when he said, "I have lost the best friend I ever had. . . ."

President Coolidge took the philosophy of laissez faire literally. He simply propped up his feet on his White House desk and let the nation run itself. "Coolidge's chief feat," wrote H. L. Mencken, "was to sleep more than any other President. . . . The itch to run things did not afflict him. . . ." Whether from an honest conviction that the least government was the best or from a fear of making himself unpopular, Coolidge refused to pull the bit on a runaway economy, and for five years the country indulged in a mindless spree of easy credit, unchecked speculation, and high living. He appeared as the champion of business (caricatured below opposite as accompanist to a freewheeling Charleston by Big Business), but he was less a patron than a passive spectator. Yet with all his free time (it is estimated that he averaged a four-hour workday as President), he seemed to derive

Jazz Age President

little enjoyment from his leisure. While the rest of the country frolicked in prosperity and new-found freedoms, Coolidge remained the picture of restraint. Shunning society and "the affectations of the drawing room," the President preferred the simple pleasures and was an avid fisherman (below opposite) all his life. He was shy and introverted and appeared both in cartoons and in photographs (opposite, with Mrs. Coolidge and Mr. and Mrs. Tom Mix) with the same dour expression. He was a basically joyless soul, and there was something very incongruous in the picture of "Silent Cal" as the unwitting midwife of the high-living Age of Ballyhoo.

"In building our cities we deflowered a wilderness," wrote the critic Lewis Mumford in 1922. The industrialization and urbanization that had been growing since the Civil War took a giant step during World War I. Not only was over half the population living in cities by the mid-1920's but it was

Concrete Wilderness

in this "deflowered wilderness" that new trends and opinion were being formed. Georgia O'Keefe's smog-choked New York (above) and Reginald Marsh's jackhammer men and derrick loaders (opposite) were part of the trend. H. L. Mencken, that master opinion maker, could rant against the

"appalling desolation" of industrial towns, but where did *he* live? In Baltimore, a metropolis that, in 1920, was among a dozen leading industrial cities on the Eastern seaboard churning out manufactures of over $200,000,000 annually. Like it or not, America was creating a new wilderness.

Times Square, New York's gaudy Great White Way, was the capital of America's amusement world. Howard Thain's 1925 painting, above, evokes the excitement that Broadway's lights always give.

Rollin Kirby's 1927 drawing of a New York subway (left) speaks for itself—and things have not changed much since.

Chicago was also booming in the 20's. At right, the Wrigley Building towers over the never-ending flow of traffic.

94

Los Angeles' Broadway, above, did not hesitate to advertise its attractions. The far banner boosts the movie industry, while the near, less legible, one plugs the stage drama Life of the Christ.

Martin Lewis' etching The Glow of the City *suggests a mood of loneliness amidst the throng of urban dwellers.*

"the advertisements of Jesus"

Among the true believers in the 20's Cult of Business few were more dedicated than Bruce Barton, a founder of the advertising firm of Batten, Barton, Durstine and Osborn. In 1924 Barton wrote a book called The Man Nobody Knows, *tracing his profession to "the founder of modern business," Jesus. Below is an excerpt.*

It has been remarked that "no astronomer can be an atheist," which is only another way of saying that no man can look up at the first and greatest electric sign—the evening stars—and refuse to believe its message: "There is a Cause: A God." I propose in this chapter to speak of the advertisements of Jesus which have survived for twenty centuries and are still the most potent influence in the world.

Let us begin by asking why he was so successful in mastering public attention. . . . In the first place he recognized the basic principle that all good advertising is news. He was never trite or commonplace; he had no routine. . . .

Take one single day as an example. . . . see how it bristles with front-page news.

The activity begins at sunrise. Jesus was an early riser; he knew that the simplest way to live *more* than an average life is to add an hour to the

All my life I had been interested in books, but somehow I had overlooked books on salesmanship. Literally hundreds of them, it appears, are now on the market, and used by our colleges, universities and Y.M.C.A. night schools in the laudable business of giving hope and cheer to the overworked and underpaid. . . .

Among the first things which attract attention in this literature is the fact that a prospective purchaser is not regarded simply as a human being, or even referred to in terms of his occupation or social position. For the salesman all men are Prospects. It seems to me only fair, then, that we look upon every one who attempts to sell anything as a Prospector.

Obviously, if a Prospector is to be successful, he must prepare himself for his arduous life of gold-digging. All the books thus start out with chapters on the general subject: "How to Get Ready and Why." The first thing the aspiring salesman must do, it appears, is to develop the physical basis for the combative spirit necessary in forcing a Prospect to buy:

Many young men are not highly developed in the faculty of combativeness and in order to become good salesmen they require this faculty brought into positive function, that they may not give up or become undecided and discouraged. Combativeness functions through the shoulder and arm muscles as shown by the soldier, prize fighter, athlete, etc., and, well developed, it imparts a feeling of enthusiasm, physical vigor and power of decision that no other faculty can give; the best way, then, of bringing it into proper function is to take up some form of exercise that will call into use the shoulder and arm muscles, each morning immediately upon arising, devoting ten or fifteen minutes to this. . . .

But this is not enough. No ambitious salesman will be content with the development merely of his physical powers. He will also cultivate his spiritual gifts for the contest. Thus he is instructed to say to himself: "I *will* succeed. I will *awaken* tomorrow feeling good. . . ."

It is a good idea, we are informed, to keep on repeating this formula until one falls asleep. . . .

An example of one of these bedtime incantations reads as follows:

At 2 P.M. tomorrow, precisely, I will walk into Hornyhand's office. I am not afraid of him. I am as good as he is. I will be absolutely confident. . . . I *will* be confident.

. . . All this mental discipline, of course, is possible only if the salesman has some training in and understanding of psychology. . . .

When the Prospector gets well in touch with his Prospect then all his learning in psychology is called into play. To persuade or hypnotize the Prospect, it is of first importance to get his attention. This does not mean that he merely listen politely, but that he give Real Attention to the salesman. Giving him a mental shock is sometimes valuable.

This you can do by dropping your pencil or striking the table. The effect of this is very good providing that the instant you have his attention you drive home some selling point.

. . . One book tells of excellent success following making the Prospect angry.

It was up to me to get their attention. What did I do? I tramped on their corns. I reached over and plunked down on their corns. I really did this; I am not stuffing you. When they got red and mad all over, I knew that I had their attention. . . .

After the salesman gets the attention of the Prospect, he is ready to unlimber all of his psychological artillery. Of course, he understands that no sale can be made unless he first induces a Desire to Buy. . . .

There must be enough desire in any particular instance to over-balance all obstacles and make the man desire to do the thing more than for some reason—either concealed or expressed—he desires not to do it. . . .

Nothing could be clearer than this. Contrary to the political economists, fresh end of the day. At sunrise, therefore, we discover a little boat pushing out from the shore of the lake. It makes its steady way across and deposits Jesus and his disciples in Capernaum, his favorite city. He proceeds at once to the house of a friend, but not without being discovered. The report spreads instantly that he is in town, and before he can finish breakfast a crowd has collected outside the gate—a poor palsied chap among them.

The day's work is at hand.

Having slept soundly in the open air he meets the call with quiet nerves. . . . [and] stoops down toward the sufferer.

"Be of good cheer, my son," he cries, "your sins are all forgiven."

Sins forgiven! Indeed! The respectable members of the audience draw back with sharp disapproval. "What a blasphemous phrase," they exclaim. . . .

Jesus sensed rather than heard their protest. . . .

Bending over the sick man again he said: "Arise, take up thy bed and go unto thine house."

The man stirred and was amazed to find that his muscles responded. Slowly, doubtingly he struggled to his feet. . . .

Can you imagine the next day's issue of the *Capernaum News*, if there had been one?

PALSIED MAN HEALED

JESUS OF NAZARETH CLAIMS RIGHT
TO FORGIVE SINS

PROMINENT SCRIBES OBJECT

"BLASPHEMOUS," SAYS LEADING
CITIZEN.

"BUT ANYWAY I CAN WALK,"
HEALED MAN RETORTS.

Front page story number one and the day is still young.

---

sales are not made because the purchaser needs the article and wants to get it, but because the Prospector creates a Desire to Buy in him—a desire which the Prospect never had before, or which at least lay dormant in his unconscious. . . . it is easier to make a sale if you are sitting in a semi-dark room than if you are in one brightly lighted. Impressionability and sensitiveness are apt to be overcome by bright lights. . . .

The whole procedure may be summed up in one sentence, taken from a leading textbook: *Do not permit the Prospect to reason and reflect.* A scientific salesman must always bear in mind that it is his first duty to get control. . . .

No matter how good an approach you have made, regardless of how clever or how perfect your Selling Talk may be, it is all of no avail unless you close the sale. Therefore, you should have a Reserve Talk in readiness if the need should arise. In large letters the salesman is told that "many Prospects must be led; others driven. The closing argument must be directed at the Prospect's *weakness.* Tie your Prospect up so that he must act. The majority of salesmen make it too easy for their Prospect to slip away. Tie him up so that he cannot *possibly* back down."

Just as important as advertising was the fine art of salesmanship. In 1925 the brilliant attorney Clarence Darrow made a study of the proliferating books on the subject and published the results, excerpted here, in a devastating satire "Salesmanship" in the August, 1925, issue of The American Mercury *magazine.*

"all men are Prospects"

Oliver Herford caricatures the vulgarity of business in his cartoon "The Window Shopper."

Town and Country

In contrast to the rapid growth of urbanization, change came slowly to the outposts of small-town America. The corner drugstore (shown in George Wright's painting below) had not altered much since 1910, and its patrons tended to cling to mores and moral codes that, after all, had been good enough for grandma. Farm life (left) changed even less, for farmers did not share in the general Coolidge prosperity. At the same time "country living" was taking on a new meaning as urbanites discovered Long Island and other accessible rural areas. Lavish estates like the one opposite were the country houses of the new rich, where harried corporate executives could "get away from it all" and play the country squire in grand style.

VOGUE

The 20's Look

Fashions of the 20's reflected the tenor of the era: a combination of affluence and abandon. Furs were much in evidence and worn with studied casualness. There was an air of escape from prewar confinements, and it was the women in whom the change was most striking. Skirts rose (from a few inches above the ankle in 1919 to a daring inch above the knee), chests and hips were flattened to effect a carefree, little-boy look, and locks were sheared. Emphasis was on sleek sophistication, and then, as now, it worked best on the young.

The Sealskin of Swimming Apparel

Proud of their athletic prowess — their graceful suppleness — their clear bronzed skin! — The modern man! — The modern girl! In whatever sport they engage, this out-of-doors age demands that they look the part. If swimming, they must be as trim coming out of the water as before getting wet. Since every eye is a searchlight, an ill-fitting water garment, though a bargain, is no longer tolerable. To appear on the beach today as a Raggedy Andy or Raggedy Anne is unpardonable.

Attitude was as much a part of fashion as the hemline. A slight slouch, languorous gaze, and air of world-weariness was what the lady in Vogue (opposite) was wearing in 1929. Miss Sunshine (above) represented the modern outdoor girl, while the flapper at right preferred a more exotic backdrop (possibly inspired by E. M. Hull's popular sex-in-the-desert romance, The Shiek). Men, too, were becoming more clothes-conscious, and both sexes were increasingly aware of "accessories," like the 1929 Chrysler "75" roadster below. Anyone who could wear that was definitely ahead of the game.

NEWPORT HISTORICAL SOCIETY

CHRYSLER CORPORATION

HART SCHAFFNER & MARX

BLVE MOON
FULL FASHIONED
Silk Stockings
$1.65 to $1.95
AT THE FINER STORES

LONGER WEAR IN EVERY PAIR

LARGMAN-GRAY COMPANY
SALES OFFICES
389 FIFTH AVENUE, NEW YORK
MILLS AT CROYDON, PA

OUR BLUE MOON GIRL FOR YOUR AUTO WINDOW
OR RAIN SLICKER WILL BE SENT UPON REQUEST.

UNDERWOOD & UNDERWOOD

With more leg exposure, women were forsaking the old black cotton stocking for the more alluring legwear of the Blue Moon Girl, at left. Fashions were, of course, an important element of the movie industry: above, a fashion still from the 1926 movie Irene; at top, Clara Bow introduces a two-piece henna crepe affair; and at right, Joan Crawford models a cozy fur-trimmed evening wrap.

Turning Off the Tap

Prohibition may have been a lost cause from the beginning; certainly it was not helped by the general caliber of its enforcement agents. As the journalist Stanley Walker attests in his book *The Night Club Era:* "The dry agent . . . by his duplicity, his bad manners, his cheapness and his occasional brutality, made himself the symbol of all that was wrong with the law." While there were displays of enforcement fervor (opposite, axemen dispose of $1,000,000 worth of liquor, and at top, border police nab a rumrunner), the agent often took advantage of his position to milk a hapless speak-easy proprietor of whatever he could extort. Not that the agent's lot was an easy one. Salaries ranged from about $1,200 to $2,800, and there were never more than three thousand men to control all the illicit traffic. There were, of course, a few dedicated agents, such as the ingeniously disguised Izzy Einstein and Moe Smith, above, but it was a thankless task and a losing battle.

Hip Flasks and Peepholes

The Leading **Mineral Water**

Pale Dry **Ginger Ale**

THE night club . . . sophisticated enjoyment for those who know life . . . captivating rhythm of the orchestra . . . spotlights playing on accomplished entertainers whirling to the strains of the music . . . beautiful women . . . jewels . . . lovely gowns . . . laughter . . . the smart world at play . . . In the midst of it all, the brown

bottles of White Rock Water and the green bottles of White Rock Pale Dry Ginger Ale are taken for granted . . . quenching thirst after the dance . . . stimulating conversation . . . bottles of sparkling deliciousness attuned to every occasion . . . their circle of friends as broad as the land . . . the standard of smart America!

Perhaps no law in history did more for the cause of drinking than the Volstead Act. During Prohibition the hip flask (above), the converted brownstone hideaway (opposite), and the female drinker all made their appearance. In New York, it is estimated, 32,000 speak-easies replaced 15,000 pubs, and the speak-easy proprietor was a popular man. One of the best-loved, reported journalist Stanley Walker, was Barney Gallant, whose spot in Greenwich Village attracted large crowds and ultimately a federal agent. As Walker told it, Barney's arrest made life miserable for a number of people, including the harried prosecuting attorney: "May it please the Court," he pleaded at Barney's trial, "since this man was convicted I have not had a moment's peace or pleasure. I have been besieged with pleas to let this man go. Even a police captain and a priest have come to me." The judge was lenient, and Barney was soon back in business. Extravagant claims were made for mineral water and ginger ale (left), but no one missed the point that those night club sophisticates were not drinking that White Rock straight.

*Texas Guinan, the wisecracking night club propri-
etress, strikes a jaunty pose, above, and one can
almost hear her famous greeting, "Hello, Sucker."*

*The seedier side of the Village speak-easy is shown
in Reginald Marsh's etching of Julius' Annex, left.*

During Prohibition many of New York's finest hotels — the Knickerbocker, the Buckingham, the Manhattan — went under as their bars were closed and their dining rooms dried up. The Lafayette (in John Sloan's 1928 painting above) was one of the few to survive the drought.

Dion O'Banion's funeral (top) brought an $8,000 floral display from rival Al Capone (above). It is not recorded what, if any, tribute Al paid victims of the 1929 St. Valentine's Day massacre (right).

The Gangs

PHOTOWORLD

Johnny Torrio (above) was Chicago's first, and for five years leading, bootleg racketeer. A former member of New York's infamous Five Points Gang, he imported a fellow member, Al Capone, as his right-hand man and made him his heir.

November 10, 1924—Three men walked into the floral shop of Dion O'Banion, orchid lover and gangland rival of Alphonse Capone; one gripped O'Banion's hand in "friendship" while the others pumped six bullets into the florist's head and body.

September 20, 1926—Eight touring cars paraded single file through the streets of a Chicago suburb in broad daylight, spraying machine gun fire into Al Capone's Hawthorne Hotel headquarters and nearby buildings (miraculously killing no one), and then disappeared into traffic.

February 14, 1929—Three men in police uniforms drove up to a garage where the O'Banion gang was awaiting a shipment of booze, lined them up against a brick wall, noses to, while two men in civilian clothes mowed them down with machine guns; then the "policemen" marched the two civilians out in mock arrest, and drove off.

Those were three of the more notorious vendettas of the Prohibition era; by the time it was over there were some five hundred gang murders in Chicago alone, and few slayers were ever tried. And so the gangs continued. They were, for the most part, just protecting their corner of an illegal and highly profitable booze market created by the Eighteenth Amendment.

INTERNATIONAL NEWS PHOTO

The notorious gunman Jack "Legs" Diamond (below) survived numerous attempts on his life, including, in one assault, five bullet wounds, before his enemies finally put a fatal shot through his head. At bottom, his body is removed from an Albany, New York, boardinghouse, where he was "rubbed out" in 1931. By that time, gang warfare was rampant, and relatively smalltime operators were getting into the act. At right, policemen inspect the body of a New York racketeer killed in a petty beer rivalry.

LOU GEHRIG

BIG LEAGUE CHEWING GUM

Age of Sports

UPI

PHOTOWORLD

Every age needs its heroes, but the Twenties seemed to need them more than most. They got them too, and the popular figures of the era constituted a sort of pantheon of demigods. Nowhere was this as true as it was in the field of sports, where a generation of superheroes created what old-timers still call the Golden Age. And what an age it was! Baseball's fabled "Murderers' Row," a New York Yankee line-up that ruthlessly shattered enemy pitching, pivoted on the peerless Babe Ruth, the most awesome slugger the game has known and one of its most colorful figures. In the prize ring the merciless Jack Dempsey, who had written a prologue to the decade by bludg-

eoning huge Jess Willard into submission in 1919, fought epic brawls with Georges Carpentier and Luis Firpo before Gene Tunney, a Shakespeare scholar with an educated left jab, put a definitive end to his murderous endeavors. In football it was the time of the legendary Knute Rockne, Red Grange, and the "Four Horsemen." Men's tennis was dominated by "Big Bill" Tilden, and the women's game by Helen Wills. Golf produced the redoubtable Bobby Jones and the imperiously brilliant Walter Hagen. And even names that are forgotten today—names like Jim Londos, "Strangler" Lewis, and "Torchy" Peden—were household words to Americans.

OPPOSITE: *New York Giant Casey Stengel beats the Yankees at their own game with an inside-the-park homer in the '23 Series.*

Big-bellied Babe Ruth (left) was abetted considerably by Lou Gehrig (top), who was next up in the Yankee batting order.

Six-foot-six-inch champion Jess Willard was flabby when he fought at Toledo, Ohio, in 1919 (below) against young Jack Dempsey. Dempsey put him down seven times and out in the third round. The detail from George Bellows' painting (inset opposite) depicts the moment when Dempsey was knocked out of the ring by Luis Firpo, the Argentinian "Wild Bull of the Pampas." He was pushed back by sports writers in ringside seats and won by a knockout. The most controversial knockdown of the era occurred in the second Tunney-Dempsey fight, when Tunney was down for fourteen seconds (opposite) but came back to win. Light heavyweight Jack Delaney (right), like many athletes of the time, was pictured on a *Police Gazette* cover. Though one of the great fighters in his weight class, Delaney is largely forgotten today by all but fight buffs.

J. HOCHMANN 1926

JACK DELANEY

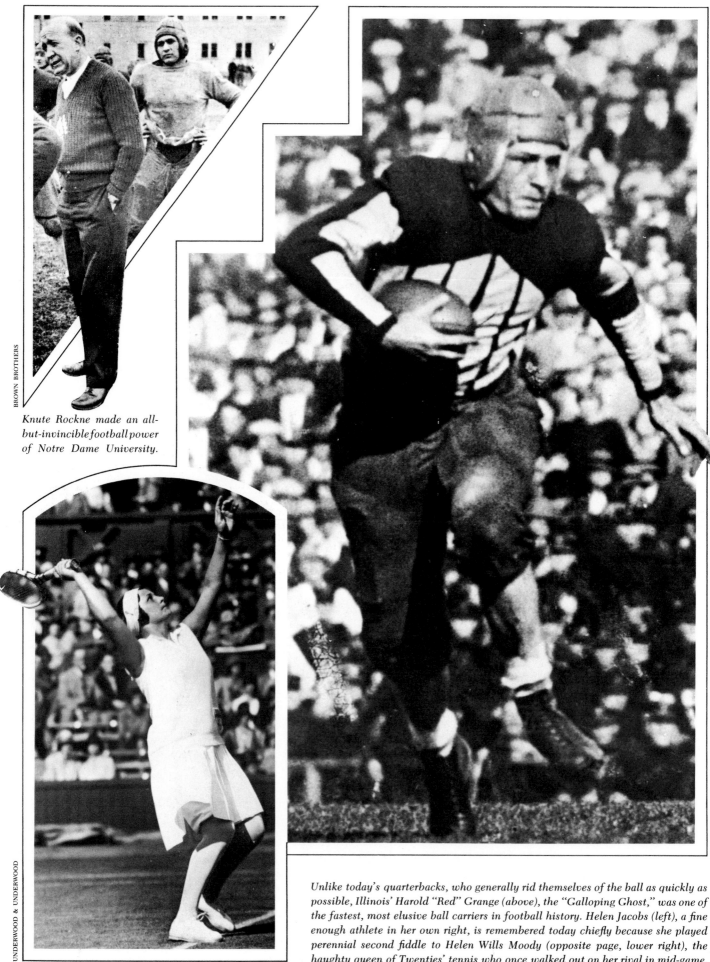

Knute Rockne made an all-but-invincible football power of Notre Dame University.

Unlike today's quarterbacks, who generally rid themselves of the ball as quickly as possible, Illinois' Harold "Red" Grange (above), the "Galloping Ghost," was one of the fastest, most elusive ball carriers in football history. Helen Jacobs (left), a fine enough athlete in her own right, is remembered today chiefly because she played perennial second fiddle to Helen Wills Moody (opposite page, lower right), the haughty queen of Twenties' tennis who once walked out on her rival in mid-game.

118

Johnny Weismuller, later to win fame as Tarzan, was the swiftest swimmer of the 20's.

Robert Tyre "Bobby" Jones, Jr., above, was the dominant golfing figure of the Twenties. Winner of his first U. S. Open in 1923, he went on to win two more during the course of the decade, along with a pair of British Open championships and no fewer than four U. S. Amateur titles. In 1930 Jones capped a brilliant career with his famous Grand Slam, which consisted of winning performances in the U. S. Open, the British Amateur, the British Open, and finally the U. S. Amateur. After capturing these top honors that the golfing world had to offer, Jones retired from competition.

Sports writing of the 1920's was a particular breed of journalism. At its best, it was pithy, inventive, and vigorous. At its worst, it was horrible. Grantland Rice and Heywood Broun, quoted on these pages, were of the former category, and their colorful verbiage delighted sports fans. So did the blow-by-blow broadcasts of such announcers as Graham McNamee (at microphone below). The Grantland Rice story excerpted below appeared in the New York Herald and Tribune, October 19, 1924, and is one of his most memorable sports accounts.

"the Four Horsemen rode again"

Outlined against a blue-gray October sky, the Four Horsemen rode again. In dramatic lore they are known as Famine, Pestilence, Destruction and Death. These are only aliases. Their real names are Stuhldreher, Miller, Crowley and Layden. They formed the crest of the South Bend cyclone before which another fighting Army football team was swept over the precipice at the Polo Grounds yesterday afternoon as 55,000 spectators peered down on the bewildering panorama spread on the green plain below.

A cyclone can't be snared. It may be surrounded, but somewhere it breaks through to keep on going. When the cyclone starts from South Bend, where the candle lights still gleam through the Indiana sycamores, those in the way must take to storm cellars at top speed. Yesterday the cyclone struck again, as Notre Dame beat the Army, 13 to 7. . . .

The Army had great backs in Willson and Wood, but the Army had no such quartet, who seemed to carry the mixed blood of the tiger and the antelope. . . .

We doubt that any team in the country could have beaten Rockne's array yesterday afternoon, East or West. It was a great football team brilliantly directed, a team of speed, power and team play. The Army has no cause for gloom over its showing. It played first class football against more speed than it could match.

Those who have tackled a cyclone can understand.

CULVER PICTURES

Good evening, Ladies & Gentlemen of the Radio Audience.

This is a big night. Three million dollars' worth of boxing bugs are gathering around a ring at Soldiers' Field, Chicago. . . .

Here comes Jack Dempsey, climbing through the ropes . . . white flannels, long bathrobe. . . . Here comes Tunney. . . . The announcer shouting in the ring . . . trying to quiet 150,000 people. . . . Robes are off. . . .

Jack leads with a long left and misses. . . .

Gene is stabbing Jack off . . . oh-o . . . Dempsey drives a hard left under the heart. . . . Gene beginning to wake up . . . like a couple of wild animals . . . Gene's body red . . . hits Dempsey a terrific right to the body. . . . Jack leads hard left. . . . Tunney seems almost wobbling . . . they have been giving Dempsey smelling salts in his corner.

. . . Some of the blows that Dempsey hits make this ring tremble. . . . Tunney is DOWN . . . down from a barrage . . . they are counting . . . six—seven—eight —NINE and Tunney is UP . . . backing away . . . now outboxing Dempsey . . . Jack trying to get Tunney where he can hit him . . . motions Gene to come in and fight . . . Dempsey comes in like a wild man. . . . Dempsey is DOWN from a hard left to the jaw. He is UP . . . Dempsey's eyes are getting worse. . . . TUNNEY LOOKS MAD . . . drives hard on

Dempsey's eye, and it is a very, very bad eye. Dempsey is very, very tired . . . Dempsey is almost down. . . . FIGHT IS OVER.

I think Tunney is still champion. . . .

One of boxing's most controversial bouts was the Dempsey-Tunney "Long Count" of 1927. Dempsey downed Tunney in the seventh and should have walked to a neutral corner for the count to begin. Instead he hesitated for five seconds, and Tunney was actually down for 14 before he rose on the count of 9 to beat Dempsey. Graham McNamee's vivid account is from a Time transcript of October 3.

"Tunney is still champion"

The Ruth is mighty and shall prevail. He did yesterday. Babe made two home runs and the Yankees won from the Giants at the Polo Grounds by a score of 4 to 2. . . .

Three of the Yankees' four runs were the product of homers. . . . but yesterday's show belonged to Ruth.

For the first time since coming to New York, Babe achieved his full brilliance in a World's Series game. Before this he has varied between pretty good and simply awful, but yesterday he

is supposed to pretend he is merely glancing around to see if the girl in the red hat is anywhere in the grand stand, although all the time his eyes are intent on McGraw.

Of course the nature of the code is secret, but this time McGraw scratched his nose, to indicate: "Try another of those shoulder high fast ones on the Big Bam and let's see if we can't make him break his back again."

But Babe didn't break his back, for he had something solid to check his

base. By every consideration of prudent tactics an intentional pass seemed indicated.

Snyder jerked his head around and observed that McGraw was blowing his nose. The Giant catcher was puzzled, for that was a signal he had never learned. By a process of pure reasoning he attempted to figure out just what it was that his chief was trying to convey to him.

"Maybe he means if we pitch to Ruth we'll blow the game," thought

In 1923 Heywood Broun, well-known columnist of sports, drama, and general affairs, covered a World Series game at the Polo Grounds. The story, extracted here from the October 12 issue of the New York World, *is one of baseball's best.*

"The Ruth is mighty and shall prevail"

was magnificent.

Just before the game John McGraw remarked:

"Why shouldn't we pitch to Ruth? I've said before, and I'll say it again, we pitch to better hitters than Ruth in the National League."

Ere the sun had set on McGraw's rash and presumptuous words, the Babe had flashed across the sky fiery portents which should have been sufficient to strike terror and conviction into the hearts of all infidels. But John McGraw clung to his heresy with a courage worthy of better cause.

In the fourth inning Ruth drove the ball completely out of the premises. McQuillan was pitching at the time, and the count was two balls and one strike. The strike was a fast ball shoulder high, at which Ruth had lunged with almost comic ferocity and ineptitude.

Snyder peeked at the bench to get a signal from McGraw. Catching for the Giants must be a terrific strain on the neck muscles, for apparently it is etiquette to take the signals from the bench manager furtively. The catcher

terrific swing. The ball started climbing from the moment it left the plate. It was a pop fly with a brand new gland and, though it flew high, it also flew far.

When last seen the ball was crossing the roof of the stand in deep right field at an altitude of 315 feet. We wonder whether new baseballs conversing together in the original package ever remark: "Join Ruth and see the world."

In the fifth Ruth was up again. . . . McGraw blinked twice, pulled up his trousers and thrust the forefinger of his right hand into his left eye. Snyder knew that he meant, "Try the Big Bozo on a slow curve around his knees and don't forget to throw to first if you happen to drop the third strike."

Snyder called for the delivery as directed and Ruth half topped a line drive over the wall of the lower stand in right field. With that drive the Babe tied a record. Benny Kauff and Duffy Lewis are the only other players who ever made two home runs in a single World's Series game. . . .

In the ninth Ruth came to bat with two out and a runner on second

Snyder, but he looked toward the bench again just to make sure.

Now McGraw intended no signal at all when he blew his nose. That was not tactics, but only a head cold. On the second glance, Snyder observed that the Little Napoleon gritted his teeth. Then he proceeded to spell out with the first three fingers of his right hand: "The Old Guard dies, but never surrenders." That was a signal Snyder recognized, although it never had passed between him and his manager before.

McGraw was saying: "Pitch to the big bum if he hammers every ball in the park into the North River."

And so, at Snyder's request, Bentley did pitch to Ruth and the Babe drove the ball deep into right centre; so deep that Casey Stengel could feel the hot breath of the bleacherites on his back as the ball came down and he caught it. If that drive had been just a shade to the right it would have been a third home run for Ruth. As it was, the Babe had a great day with two home runs, a terrific long fly and two bases on balls.

The Silent Screen

Like the gods of sports, the heroes of the silent screen reached new pinnacles of idolatry in the postwar decade: Rudolph Valentino, the Great Lover; Douglas Fairbanks, swashbuckling adventurer; and Charlie Chaplin, the great comedian. There was Mary Pickford, America's Sweetheart; Gloria Swanson, society sophisticate; sultry Pola Negri; and Clara Bow, the "It" girl. With these and other stars, Americans could enjoy, as one film plug put it, "all the excitement you lack in your daily life. . . ." That excitement generally reflected the "new morality" of the Jazz Age, thus such films as *Flaming Youth* (billed as "bold, naked, sensational"), *Alimony* ("champagne baths, midnight revels, petting parties in the purple dawn"), Chicago gangster movies, and society romances with sophisticated heroines enjoying the sophisticated pleasures of country clubs and cocktail parties. Rudolph Valentino made hearts throb in the desert romance *The Sheik* and came back as his own progeny in *Son of the Sheik* (below with Vilma Banky) in 1926; Greta Garbo and John Gilbert thrilled audiences in a horizontal love scene (opposite)—one of the first—in the 1927 *Flesh and the Devil*. But titles often promised more than they delivered: Hollywood did have a certain moral responsibility. As William C. De Mille, brother of Cecil B., put it: "It would never do to have the Virgin Mary getting a divorce, or Saint John cutting up in a night club." Even the Jazz Age had its limits.

Mary Philbin calms disfigured Lon Chaney in scene from chiller Phantom of the Opera.

John Barrymore was the epitome of sartorial elegance in his 1924 role as Beau Brummel. *Below, a scene from Cecil B. De Mille's extravaganza* The Ten Commandments, *with cast of thousands.*

Douglas Fairbanks in flamboyant posture in the 1924 spectacle The Thief of Bagdad.

Tom Mix takes a flying leap off a moving flatcar in one of his many Western thrillers.

Mary Pickford fends off villain with pitchfork in the 1926 tear-jerker Sparrows (above). At right, handsome Ramon Novarro (on white horse right of center) is surrounded by a bevy of bare-breasted beauties in his 1926 role as Ben Hur. Such scenes were soon censored, and movie audiences would not see flower children so briefly attired until restrictions were lifted in the 60's.

PICTURE COLLECTION, NEW YORK PUBLIC LIBRARY

*The great comedians of the 1920's
needed no words to get across the
message. In a hilarious scene from
The Gold Rush (above) a famished
Charlie Chaplin picks at a plate of
boiled shoe leather with the relish
of a true gourmet. At right, Harold
Lloyd tackles a tricky tooth extrac-
tion in Why Worry; below, Buster
Keaton has a shipboard problem in
Joseph Schenck's The Navigator.*

COLLECTION OF LESTER GLASSNER

The sets built for David Griffith's Orphans of the Storm *(left) sprawled over some thirteen acres and cost more than box-office sales could offset. Nonetheless, it was a critical success, with Dorothy and Lillian Gish in starring roles.*

The movie goddesses of the Twenties had a beauty that suffused the silent screen, but did not always carry over to the talkies. Some casualties: Clara Bow (top right), who definitely had "It" while it lasted; elegant Norma Talmadge (middle right) in The Dove; *and Pola Negri in the 1925* Woman of the World.

Al Jolson's The Jazz Singer, *1927, right, ushered in the talkies. It was the beginning of a new era—good-bye to all those mimes, comics, enigmatic beauties, with gestures so often worth thousands of words.*

127

It was November, 1920, when KDKA broadcast the Harding-Cox election returns to a few receiving sets; by 1925 some fifty million Americans were tuning in on $50 Crosleys, on sets made from do-it-yourself mail-order kits, and on inlaid consoles. And what was Radioland listening to? Just about everything: the hotcha rhythm of the Cliquot Club Eskimos (above), Agnes Moorehead (opposite, right of mike) in *Real Folks*, Graham McNamee's sports casts, Floyd Gibbons' rapid-fire newscasts, crooning Rudy Vallee, wisecracking Jack Pearl, morning exercises, Sunday sermons, and talks on baby care, auto repair, and the Dawes Plan. It was the Twenties' ear to the world.

RADIO NEWS

H. GERNSBACK, Editor and Publisher
SYLVAN HARRIS, Managing Editor

EDITORIAL AND GENERAL OFFICES, 53 PARK PLACE, NEW YORK

Vol. 8   SEPTEMBER, 1926   No. 3

NATIONAL BROADCASTING COMPANY

HARPER'S MAGAZINE, JULY, 1950

Held's Hellions

"In America," according to William and Mary Morris' *Dictionary of Word and Phrase Origins,* "a *flapper* has always been a giddy, attractive and slightly unconventional young thing who, in [H. L.] Mencken's words, 'was a somewhat foolish girl, full of wild surmises and inclined to revolt against the precepts and admonitions of her elders.'" She was also, according to the same source, not averse to drawing attention to her somewhat unconventional manner of dress, particularly her penchant for galoshes, worn, like John Held's young thing above, with buckles unfastened so as to create the greatest possible "flap"—thus the definition reinforced. Whatever the definition, the flapper would not have been quite what she was without the sharp eye and keen wit of John Held, Jr. Like that other "creator" of the Jazz Age, F. Scott Fitzgerald, Held portrayed the flapper as he saw her, and she, in turn, became the flapper he portrayed. His widely published drawings of flat-chested lovelies in rolled-down hose, living it up at house parties, in secluded corners, and in the back seats of roadsters, inspired many a young lady to ape the manners and gestures of Jazz Age sophisticates like the finger-snapping Held hellion opposite.

SHE LEFT
HOME UNDER
A CLOUD

The cartoons on these pages show John Held's sheiks and shebas engaged in two popular pastimes—petting (with more or less success) and smoking. A master cartoonist, Held sold his first cover to Judge *in 1922 and was soon contributing regularly to* Life, McClure's, Collier's, *and* College Humor. *"I've always looked for success," he wrote a friend after the* Judge *cover, "now I've found it." Indeed he had.*

133

Crossword puzzles, dance marathons, and the Charleston were three big 20's crazes. At left, a crossword puzzle costume designed by John Held for a Ziegfeld Follies number (note instructions to wardrobe department). Below, a dance marathon intermission; and middle page, dancers demonstrate the Charleston.

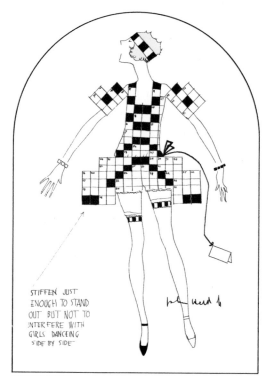

STIFFEN JUST ENOUGH TO STAND OUT BUT NOT TO INTERFERE WITH GIRLS DANCEING SIDE BY SIDE

At left, a mah-jongg tournament in Greenwich Village, New York, complete with Oriental atmosphere. The game was played with colored tiles, shown in the inset above. The raccoon coat (above) was another big fad.

Fads and Fancies

The era that went mad for silent stars, baseball, Stutz Bearcats, and radio lost its head completely over the fads that were sweeping the country. Mah-jongg, crossword puzzles, dance marathons, and flagpole sitting all had their day in the public arena. Most of the fads were harmless, and most were dropped as quickly as they had been taken up, but all were embraced with an enthusiasm that amounted to mass mania. Marathon dancers might drag themselves around the floor for days, blistering their feet and aching from fatigue. What matter if they finally dropped over from utter exhaustion? It was all just part of the Twenties' madness, and madness is always exhausting.

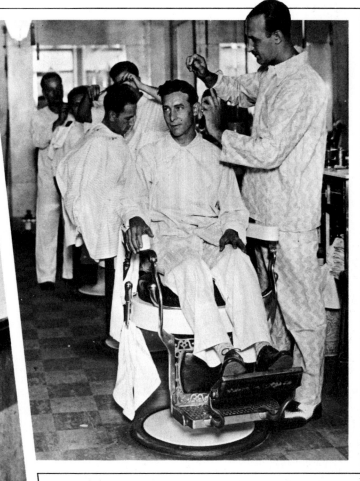

The pajama-wearing craze (above) was mercifully short-lived. "Shipwreck" Kelly also had his day. At left, his wife hoists a newspaper after 24 hours of planned 8-day flagpole perch.

The Sound of Jazz

Nothing caught the spirit of the 20's quite so expressively as the syncopated beat of jazz. Essentially a Negro creation, it spread across the country in many forms. There were legendary instrumentalists like Jelly Roll Morton, Louis Armstrong, Bix Beiderbecke; blues singers like Bessie Smith (left) and Ma Rainey; and of course the Big Bands—the great ones of Duke Ellington and Fletcher Henderson and of popularizers like Paul Whiteman, Cab Calloway (cornballing it above), and Ted Lewis. In whatever form, it had its buffs, high- and low-brow. As Leopold Stokowski put it: "Jazz has come to stay because it is an expression of the times, of the breathless, energetic, superactive times in which we are living. . . ."

136

Composer, arranger, conductor, and keyboard king, Duke Ellington (at top with his band) was in a class of his own. So was that dazzling trumpeter Louis Armstrong (left). Above, Ted Lewis (in top hat) and his band in 1921.

The Bible Thumpers

Not even the pulpit was immune to the temptations of the Twenties. Publicity, sensationalism, and the almighty dollar were prime movers in the spiritual zeal of such evangelists as Billy Sunday (driving home a point at right) and Aimee Semple McPherson (at top opposite). While Billy packed them in at revival meetings like the one commemorated in the post card below, golden-haired Sister Aimee wowed them with a combination of sensualism and splendor from her $1,500,000 Angelus Temple in Los Angeles. There were, of course, a good many dedicated community preachers of the "old time religion," as portrayed in John Steuart Curry's *Baptism in Kansas* (opposite). But for big-time operators, the technique was hard-sell showmanship, mass soul-saving, and massive profits.

Sunday telling the story of the preacher praying on the steeple top imploring God to come down

138

New York's Greenwich Village was the Twenties' Bohemia—its artistic center, intellectual haven, and general refuge for the disaffected and nonconformist. Theodore Dreiser, Willa Cather, and Sherwood Anderson were among its foremost literary figures; John Sloan, George Luks, William Glackens, and Maurice Prendergast among its painters. The sculptor Jo Davidson had a studio in MacDougal Alley not far from that of Gertrude Vanderbilt Whitney. Allen Churchill in his book *The Improper Bohemians* tells the story of one of Mrs. Whitney's posh painting exhibitions, at which George Luks would not leave the lady alone. "Mr. Luks, why do you keep following me?" she finally asked. "Mrs. Whitney," Luks replied, "because you are so God damn rich." Most Villagers were not. Actors, dancers, musicians, hopefuls, and hangers-on were attracted to the Village not only for its aura but for its low rents. There one could live cheaply, anonymously, and uninhibitedly. And many did.

Greenwich Village had a quiet side, as John Sloan's etching of Washington Square (above) indicates. It had absorbed its share of prewar immigrants, and to them it had truly become their village. Wood Gaylor's Bob's Party Number One *(below) shows another side: the uninhibited amusements of its Bohemian colony.*

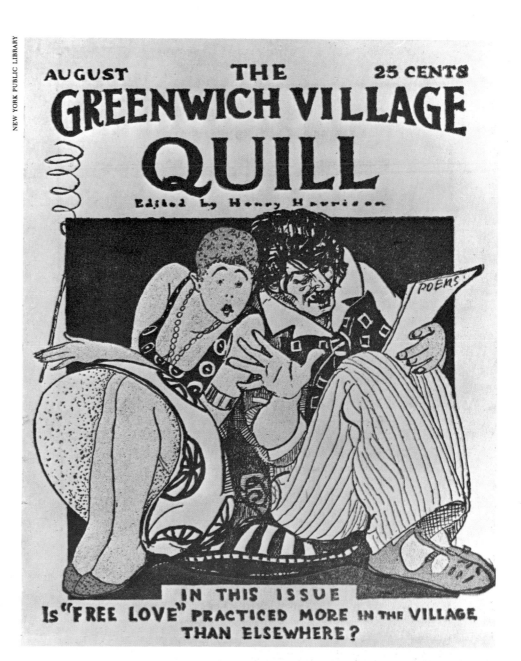

The Quill was the Greenwich Village house organ and intellectual outlet, often satirizing (as above) its own sinful image. At right, a Village intellectual with a sinful image of her own: the poetess Edna St. Vincent Millay.

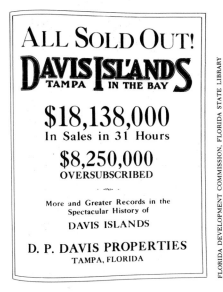

Florida Frenzy

"Bronzed, erect old men. Women delighting in new cream-and-rose complexions. Round and brown children. . . ." These were the attractions of Coral Gables, according to a 1920's promotion piece. Spurred on by the Coolidge prosperity and the general climate of speculation, people were buying up Florida real estate, sight unseen, hoping for a quick killing—or at very least a spot in the sun for their old age. Everybody was going: business executives and pensioners, the couple next door and the rich and famous. William Jennings Bryan ran a Bible class for tourists in Miami, and Gilda Gray shimmied in the sun. All you needed was a little cash and you could forget Wisconsin snows and join the well-born in America's winter playground. Of course, there was the danger of getting stuck with a plot of desert or mangrove swamp, but it could always be resold to another sucker. By 1925 the boom had reached its frenzied peak. In a year it was over. Sales began to drop, and a hurricane in September, 1926, did the rest. Not everything was rosy, even in sunny Florida.

The cartoon at top right gives a picture of Palm Beach during the boom, when real-estate offices like the one at right promoted Florida. Opposite, above: an ad for Miami's "Riviera," Coral Gables; below, a Miami street after the hurricane of 1926.

Sex and Sensation

In an era that craved sensationalism there was plenty of it in the luridly detailed tabloids of the 20's. For murder connoisseurs there were the Leopold and Loeb and the Hall-Mills trials. The first involved the thrill murder of a little boy named Bobby Franks by two young postgraduate students, Nathan Leopold and Richard Loeb, in 1924. They had done it, they confessed, for a lark, in an attempt to commit the "perfect crime." Only their penalty was in question. Pleading mental illness, the crack defense lawyer Clarence Darrow saved them from the gallows (thwarting public blood lust), and the boys were given life terms. In the Hall-Mills case the defendants were acquitted, but not before their names were smeared enough by stories of passion, murder, and intrigue to satisfy the most depraved reader.

Chicago's top criminal lawyer, Clarence Darrow, left, saved Richard Loeb and Nathan Leopold (above left and right) from the death penalty. Opposite, Mrs. Jane Gibson, "The Pig Woman," testifies from a bed in the 1926 Hall-Mills trial. It concerned the murder of a balding rector, Reverend Hall, and a choir soloist, Mrs. Mills, whose bodies were found in a compromising pose in a deserted lane. Mrs. Hall and her two brothers and cousin were accused of the crime but acquitted.

BROWN BROTHERS

The aging Edward "Daddy" Browning and his sixteen-year-old bride, "Peaches," were not quite as compatible as the photograph at right suggests. Newspaper coverage of the marriage and divorce brought journalism to a new low. (The composograph below was a crude attempt to illustrate the intimacies of their bed chamber.) Floyd Collins received slightly more dignified but no less detailed treatment (opposite) when he was trapped in a cave for eighteen days and died before rescue workers could reach him.

WOOF! WOOF! DON'T BE A GOOF!

HONK! HONK! IT'S THE BONK!

COURTESY SY SEIDMAN

FINAL EDITION

DAILY MIRROR

FINAL EDITION

Vol. 1. No. 205. * *   Copyright, 1925, by the Public Press Corporation. Registered U. S. Pat. Off.   New York, Tuesday, February 17, 1925   Entered as second class matter Post Office, New York, N. Y.   2 Cents   IN CITY LIMITS | 1 CENTS Elsewhere

COLLINS DEAD IN CAVE; ROCK HOLDS BODY FAST

Story on Page 3

CAVE EXPLORER FOUND DEAD. Floyd Collins's body was found yesterday in the narrow passage where he was held 17 days by a boulder which fell on his leg. The victim, the cave entrance, the rescue shaft and the rescuers are in the diagram above which shows how the body will be removed.
Story on Page 3   (Mirror Photo-Diagram)

COLLINS'S LAST PICTURE. This photograph of Floyd Collins (under arrow) was taken as the cave victim and his friends were exploring Crystal Cave, near Sand Cave in which he perished, a few days before he was trapped.

FACING DEATH for the murder of her escort on an all-night party, Mrs. Maria Zelio, 19, went to trial yesterday in Jersey City with her husband and baby in the courtroom. She's shown (centre) with officer and matron on way back to jail after the court session.   Story on Page 2

Two front-page stories involving neither sex nor murder were the Scopes trial of 1925 and the execution of Sacco and Vanzetti in 1927. The trial of John T. Scopes for teaching the theory of evolution in Tennessee (illegal by state law) was really a battle between Fundamentalists and scientifically oriented "modernists." Were we created by the hand of God, as the Bible claimed, or were we descended from the apes, as Darwin had it? On the side of God stood volunteer prosecutor William Jennings Bryan; on the side of the apes stood Clarence Darrow. Battling it out in Dayton, Tennessee, Darrow (clenched fist, below right) made mincemeat of Bryan (seated, below left) as the latter claimed as literal every biblical story from Eve and the apple to Jonah and the whale. In the end Scopes was found guilty, but Bryan had lost the larger cause: Fundamentalism had been dealt an irremediable blow.

There was no comic relief in the Sacco-Vanzetti case. Arrested in 1920, during Attorney General Mitchell Palmer's Red raids, two Italian anarchists, Bartolomeo Vanzetti and Nicola Sacco (at top, left and right), were convicted of a holdup murder and thrown in prison in spite of copious evidence of their innocence. (The presiding judge, the Honorable Webster Thayer, a rabid antiradical, had, in fact, tried Vanzetti on an earlier holdup charge, unabashedly instructing the jury that "although he may not actually have committed the crime attributed to him [he] is nevertheless morally culpable,

because he is the enemy of our existing institutions....") The case aroused revulsion at home and abroad, but Judge Thayer remained adamant; in 1927 the last appeal was denied and the death sentence pronounced. An irate public forced the governor of Massachusetts to review the case, but his advisory committee (the lily holders in Ben Shahn's painting above) turned thumbs down. On the appointed day thousands of demonstrators lined the streets of Boston; with the electrocutions of Sacco and Vanzetti their faith in American justice was badly shaken.

In the spring of 1927 the country again lost its head, but this time over a clean-cut, all-American boy named Charles A. Lindbergh. On the morning of May 20 Lindbergh took off from Long Island in his monoplane, *The Spirit of St. Louis,* for a nonstop trip to Paris. He was not the first to make a transatlantic flight (Alcock and Brown had beaten him by eight years), but Lindbergh was handsome, young, and daring—and he was making it *alone.* His success was greeted with hysteria. Some 100,000 Frenchmen met him at the field, and Paris lauded him as a hero.

But it was his return that broke all records for celebration. In Washington President Coolidge presented him with the Distinguished Flying Cross (opposite below); in New York he was greeted by 200 boats and 75 planes (some of which are shown below), then showered with 1,800 tons of paper in a superspectacular ticker-tape parade. A new dance (the Lindy Hop) was named for him and the song "Lucky Lindy" celebrated his "peerless, fearless" feat. And through it all Lindbergh maintained an uncorrupted modesty and quiet dignity uncommon in the Age of Ballyhoo.

Wild speculation in stocks, as Reginald Marsh suggests in his lithograph of the Stock Exchange, led to the crash. But the real cause of the nation's troubles was an economic system badly out of order.

The Great Crash

ON THE FLOOR — N.Y. STOCK EXCHANGE   REGINALD MARSH

Popular belief is that the Great Bull Market finally broke October 24, 1929, the day the Wall Street brokers lost their minds and small investors wept. But the cold light of history reveals that the stock market boom of the Twenties did not come to an abrupt end in late October, but had begun its demise more than a month earlier.

September 2, 1929, was a Monday and Labor Day and a holiday. The stock market was closed. The next day, Tuesday, was noteworthy in two respects. The first quickly became apparent: it turned out to be the hottest day of the year and set a record high temperature for the date. The second would not become known until much later and after detailed analysis: September 3 was the final day of the Great Bull Market.

When the market opened that morning, the trend of stock prices continued upward, as it had for many days and weeks and months. There was nothing spectacular, just a general inching upward of prices that brought the Dow-Jones average to its highest point yet. The next morning the *Wall Street Journal* saw fit to comment on the activities of the first day of the new season and on the general financial situation and found the outlook for earning on shares to be "extremely promising."

But in spite of the *Wall Street Journal's* optimism, prices slipped that day somewhat from their high of the previous day. It was nothing frightening, and the so-called market experts called it a technical correction, but the tide had started to ebb. And on the following day, September 5, came the famed Babson Break. Roger Babson, a well-known economist, that day told the Annual National Business Conference, "Sooner or later a crash is coming, and it may be terrific." He predicted that "factories will shut down . . . men will be thrown out of work . . . the vicious circle will get in full swing and the result will be a serious business depression." Word of Babson's talk reached the floor late in the afternoon and prices at once tumbled. But Wall Street spokesmen were unanimous in attacking Babson for his pessimistic views, and Professor Irving Fisher of Yale, an economist, carefully explained why there was no danger of anything upsetting the stock market.

The market climbed on September 6, but the week of the ninth prices became erratic again. There were days when the market was strong; there were other days when it was weak. But the trend was down.

October 4 was bad, but three days later there was a sharp rise, evident in those market indicators Radio Corporation of America, Westinghouse, United States Steel, and American Can. On the whole, opined the *Wall Street Journal*, it was the bulls who had had much the best of it since early September. "Stocks are now 10, 20, and 30 points above where they were a week ago, and optimism again prevails."

As before expert opinion agreed. There had been bad stock market breaks in 1873, 1893, and 1907, but each time the market had recovered. America was not to be sold short, not its immense productive capacity, its great inventiveness, its vast hunger for luxury goods. Ignored in the general optimism was the warning signal sales departments had begun to whisper six or seven months earlier that inventories were swollen and that America seemed to have bought most of the automobiles, the radios, the purple silk shirts, that it would need for a while.

The market break, so rumor had it (and the *Wall Street Journal* again affirmed), was little more than a battle between the bulls and the bears, not a symptom of underlying unsoundness at all. In 1873 it had been the fall of the House of Jay Cooke that had broken the market, twenty years later it had been railroad speculation, and in 1907, the collapse of the Knickerbocker Trust. This time things were fundamentally sound: was not the Hoover administration a businessman's administration, wedded to the notion of sound money and balanced budgets?

On October 21 prices again fell sharply. Professor Fisher, however, remained imperturbable: the decline would only have the effect—the salutary effect—of "shaking out the lunatic fringe" of investors. The smart money seemed to agree. Who was selling out? The truth seems to be that in these early weeks of the slump most of the selling was the result of calls on luckless speculators for more margin. Everywhere there was a

will and a desperate need to believe. R. W. McNeel, the director of McNeel's Financial Service, advising his clients, said: "Some pretty intelligent people are now buying stocks. Unless we are to have a panic—which no one seriously believes—stocks have hit bottom." And the Boston News Bureau affirmed that the tremors on the market were only "those of the runner catching his breath. . . . The general situation is satisfactory and fundamentally sound." Yet belief scarcely veiled the slowly building anxiety of the nation, and the mood of Wall Street visibly darkened. The calming predictions of the financial soothsayers, the incantations of the big-money men, could not conjure away the underlying anxiety. On Tuesday, October 22, the market rallied, only to close somewhat shakily. Wednesday was worse: there was a paper decline of four billion dollars, and American Telephone & Telegraph, General Electric, Westinghouse, and Hershey were definitely down. Adams Express, as well-managed an investment trust as any in the country, lost 96 points.

On October 24, Black Thursday, the vast jerry-built structure that was American finance and industry fell down. Nothing would be the same again.

The first few minutes of trading that day seemed normal enough. Yet by midday the ticker, overwhelmed by the volume of selling, was running more than an hour and a half behind. A mad, jostling crowd on the Exchange floor fought to unload; telephone switchboards were swamped as frightened investors, fearing that the actual value of their stocks might be 10, 15, or 20 points below the ticker-tape reading, called their brokers to sell, sell, sell, or were in turn called to put up more margin.

There was a brief moment of hope. At noon Charles E. Mitchell of National City, Albert H. Wiggin of Chase National Bank, William Potter of Guaranty Trust, Seward Prosser of Bankers Trust, and George F. Baker, Jr., of First National met at the offices of J. P. Morgan and Company with Thomas W. Lamont, senior Morgan partner. The Street was hysterical with rumors: the big money was banding together to save the market. As old J. P. Morgan had sought to stem the tide in 1907, propping up the Trust Company of America, so now, the story ran, the new consortium would defend United States Steel.

At about one thirty Richard Whitney, vice president of the Exchange, did stride briskly across the floor through the watchful throng and in a loud, firm voice bid

205, the price of the last sale — though the bidding at the moment was considerably less — for ten thousand shares of steel. He did the same for several other stocks. There were scattered cheers; perhaps the worst was over. But nearly thirteen million shares were unloaded that day; at closing time the ticker was four hours late. Brokers slept fitfully at their desks waiting fearfully for what the morning would bring.

Friday's events seemed a harbinger of better things: prices were up a bit. On Saturday they were down again, but Saturday was a short session, only two hours. No one could be quite sure what the day meant. No doubt that Sunday there were fervent prayers for the market, but the Deity turned a deaf ear to the importunities of a financial America long sunk in self-congratulation and pride. Monday brought not bread but a stone both to the sober money men and the "lunatic fringe." Before the end of trading General Electric fell 48 points, AT&T 34. Again the ticker was swamped.

The next day was even worse. By nine thirty, three million shares had been traded. By noon, eight million had been dumped, not only by the little speculator forced to sell by his broker's urgent calls for more margin but in blocks of five and ten thousand shares at a time by panicky institutional and big investors as well. By the close of business the volume of trading had gone somewhat above 16,400,000 shares, a record that would stand for more than thirty years. It was equivalent to the market of 1969 or 1970 registering a volume of one hundred million shares traded in a single day.

In one day the value of stocks listed on the Exchange had dropped fourteen billion dollars. By then no one, not even Yale's ever-optimistic Professor Fisher, truly believed that the body blow America had received was only a minor market adjustment. The sense of doom over Wall Street was almost palpable.

Two years later the value of all the shares on the New York Exchange had fallen a total of thirty-seven billion dollars since the morning of Tuesday, October 29, 1929. Financial America — and the America of small-town spinster choir singers, automobile tycoons, iron puddlers, sharecroppers, corner druggists, chain-store executives, and college professors — had edged over into the abyss.

Yet how could it have happened? The initial reaction of Americans to the collapse was a dull and uncomprehending disbelief, a state of shock. After a time the American spirit of the eternal booster and unkillable optimist asserted itself again. There had been financial troubles before, idle factories, jobless men, ill-fed children, even if there had been nothing on this tremendous scale. Eventually the dimensions of the disaster would overwhelm the first optimism, and men would come to question the system, but in these early days the jokes appeared as if by magic once the first shock had passed. Comedian Eddie Cantor brought down the house on Broadway (though the joke does not seem that funny today) with his story of the room clerk's query of the registering guest: "Do you want a room for sleeping or jumping?" By November everyone was desperately singing "Happy Days Are Here Again," though it would be many long years before prosperity truly proved to be "just around the corner," as Hoover proclaimed in March, 1931.

he grim humor of the masses expressed the toughness of the American psyche. Myth to the contrary, the suicide rate did not climb after Black Thursday; it remained essentially what it had always been, but now any suicide was blamed on the crash. But the official optimism, of business and government, had a hollow ring. New York's jaunty Mayor Jimmy Walker, soon to be swept away by financial scandals that even his quips could not divert attention from, argued that the movies ought always to be cheery. "Forward, America! Nothing Can Stop U.S.!" billboards proclaimed. And well they might, since no one was leasing billboard space anyway. "Just grin," ordered Charles M. Schwab of United States Steel. "Keep on working." Buttons appeared on lapels throughout the Midwest to announce: "I'm sold on America. I won't talk depression."

Henry Ford, dour old champion of independent virtues, backed his beliefs by raising wages in November, 1929, though there were a million unsold second-hand cars on dealers' lots and no one was buying autos that winter. Eventually even he admitted defeat; wages at River Rouge were cut 10 per cent in September, 1931.

Senator James Couzens of Michigan estimated that there were more than three million out of work (up from a mere seven hundred thousand) in the two weeks following the crash. His figures are open to some question, but that unemployment increased catastrophically is beyond argument. Unwilling to talk depression, Julius Rosenwald of Sears, Roebuck announced that he feared an impending labor shortage. Other businessmen took turns proclaiming an early end to the Depression.

In a dogged attempt to belie the reality of bankruptcy and fear, the New York Stock Exchange determined to see the old year out with a bang and a whoop rather than a whimper. *The New York Times* reported on New Year's Day, 1930:

The celebration at the Stock Exchange started at 1:30 with the arrival of the 369th Infantry Band, thirty Negro musicians under Lieutenant J. W. Porter. A stand had been erected in the center of the trading floor and the music started with still an hour and a half of trading scheduled for 1929. Confetti started flying immediately, solo dances were given at almost every trading post and soon the brokers had forgotten trading for sport. Dances were interrupted to close trades which had to be made, but the main endeavor of those around each post was to originate some form of impromptu entertainment that would surpass that given at other posts. . . .

E. H. Simmons, president of the Exchange, personally sounded the gong at 3 o'clock to announce the end of trading for 1929. As the gong was still reverberating, the members broke into a pandemonium of noise, everything in the Exchange that had noise-making possibilities being utilized. The din could be heard as far away as Broadway. This outbreak in celebration of the passing of the year lasted over five minutes, members yelling until they were hoarse.

It became fashionable to show the flag, to keep a stiff upper lip, to brag about one's losses rather than to moan. George F. Baker, chairman of the board of the chronically scandal-ridden First National Bank, allowed that he had dropped a cool fifteen million dollars. Perhaps his sorrow was offset by the knowledge that he could afford it: during one good day of the Great Bull Market Baker had taken twenty-two million dollars in profits. If fifteen million dollars was all he had dropped, he was still, on the two transactions alone, seven million dollars to the good.

There were others less lucky, and to them the traditional business community gave short shrift. Most businessmen and economists still believed firmly in unrestrained competition. Government intervention, the purists argued, would court disaster and ruin the morals of the nation. Even the editorial page of *The New York Times*, which ought to have known better, pontificated that there were still "the fundamental prescriptions for recovery . . . such homely things as sav-

ings, retrenchment, prudence, and hopeful waiting for the turn." The president of the National Association of Manufacturers, John E. Edgerton, was less sentimental. However sad it might be that the unemployed suffered, it was crucial to remember, he said, that their suffering was the result of moral infirmity, not of the economic infirmity of the nation.

Some observers disagreed. Winston Churchill, no sentimentalist, defending his nation's program of helping those out of work through unemployment insurance, a program the American business community referred to with distaste as the dole, said: "I do not sympathize with those who think that this process of compulsory mass saving will sap the vitality and self-reliance of our race. There will be quite enough grindstone in human life to keep us keen."

But he was an Englishman and, for all his mother's blood, not truly heir to the creed of the American frontier, which demands self-reliance or voluntary community action in the face of outside threat. It was a creed that was to cost the Hoover administration, and the nation, dear.

And why had there been a crash? As always in human affairs the causes were complex; indeed the roots of disaster lay not in the events of September and October, 1929, nor even in the recent giddy years of the intoxicating Coolidge prosperity. The truth was that by October, 1929, the crash was long overdue. American business for more than a decade had teetered on the verge of disaster, for while American productivity and real wealth grew, beneath the surface prosperity there lurked cancerous economic weakness in the form of continuing farm depression, unequal distribution of personal incomes, shaky credit, and speculative practices bordering on outright fraud by the great men of Wall Street.

Pre-World War I America had been a mighty work horse; in those years it had been a debtor nation, steadily selling its products abroad because Europe, by virtue of its investments in the United States, had the dollars to buy what American workers made and American farmers grew.

World War I changed all that, converting a debtor nation into a creditor and demanding too that the United States, if it was to discharge its new duties in international affairs, adjust its ways. But the United States preferred to believe that its new-found prosperity was a part of the divine order of things and paid little heed to the needs of its European trading partners. This refusal to adjust ensured that one day Europe could no longer buy America's products and made it certain also that the effects of the American economic disaster would be felt world-wide.

Her neutrality during the first years of the war had benefited America, even as it had been good for American self-esteem. "Do you want to know the cause of the war?" Henry Ford had asked, in counseling strict neutrality. "It is capitalism, greed, the dirty hunger for dollars. Take away the capitalist and you will sweep war from the earth." Strange words for Henry Ford, for long before the United States entered the war he and his fellow capitalists in America had booked orders from abroad running into many hundreds of millions of dollars.

When the Wilson administration broke with the ancient American policy of isolation from the world, it did nothing to slow the American boom. The Allies continued to buy, and so did the American government. America, holding Europe's gold hoard, sent to this country for safekeeping, lent Europe its own money back at interest to spend in American factories. These loans to the Allies were funded by Liberty bond issues. The volume was immense: loans from such sources reached a figure of more than nine billion dollars by 1919—three times the American national debt two years earlier. Most important, the experience of those years— the buying of Liberty bonds—conditioned the general public to the securities market. Men and women who had never aspired to more complex acts of finance than depositing their mite with the small-town banker now learned about bonds.

From Liberty bonds to corporate bonds to common stocks was but two short steps. So the state of mind that led to the Bull Market of the Twenties, and the money earned to finance it, came into being. And so it was that behind the apparent good times of the booming Twenties lay the dark experience of the Great War—which seemingly had benefited America, but in reality had twisted world economics out of shape.

The character of the Stock Exchange was radically changed too by the war. Once it had been a rich man's preserve, but in the Twenties file clerks, taxi drivers, barbers, and housewives all talked knowingly of American Can or RCA, buying five or ten shares on the thinnest of margins. Such smalltime investors had few reserves to withstand disaster. If the market fell, they were ruined, losing all their small savings.

And ruined they would be because they were playing at roulette with a fixed wheel. In the Wall Street of prewar days, great banking houses like J. P. Morgan and Company and Harriman Brothers, to say nothing of such conservative edifices as the Jewish-German House of Kuhn, Loeb, had played an inside game; great fortunes were won and lost, and though the rules were often rough, a kind of honor held the greed of such men in check. The government, however, floated its Liberty bond issues not through the stately old houses, which thereby lost ground, but through channels of its own. New firms broke into Wall Street—and with them a new breed of men, rapacious, devoid of conscience, rigging the market for the big kill and the innocent be damned.

There were men like Mitchell of National City Bank, who in the spring of 1929 defied the Federal Reserve's halfhearted efforts to tighten credit by coolly announcing that his bank had twenty million dollars on hand available for the call money market. It was Mitchell who rejected a rebuke from the Morgans and pushed a package of worthless Peruvian bonds on the market, blithely asserting it was his bank's business to sell, sell, sell, as if the notion of a fiduciary relationship between banker and public had never been born.

There was Wiggin of Chase National. In July, 1929, suspecting that his bank's future was dim, he sold 42,500 shares of Chase short, thereby neatly evading the consequences of the October, 1929, crash. His supreme act of faith would go undetected for years.

There was the famed band of Irish buccaneers—men like Mike Meehan, Esmonde O'Brian, John Myland, and, not the least, Joseph Patrick Kennedy of Boston, who would later join the forces of the Roosevelt administration, oversee the new Securities and Exchange Commission as chairman, gain respectability and an ambassadorship, and sire future statesmen. But in those years Kennedy was no more a statesman than were the others. He defended the stock of John D. Hertz's Yellow Cab Company against a celebrated bear raid in 1924, but when Yellow Cab stock went down again a few months later, Hertz accused Kennedy of being the bear raider. No one ever proved anything, but a Kennedy biographer noted that "it would not have been unthinkable" for Kennedy to engage in such double-dealing.

Mike Meehan was more flamboyant still—a garrulous, high-living man who made a specialty of the speculators' delight, Radio Corporation of America, and earned over and over again the title of greatest manipulator of them all. For the market was not what it seemed to be, and the technique of manipulating it was simple. A band of speculators would pool their resources and hire as "floor manager" a specialist in the selected stock. The manager would begin a flurry of trading to bring the stock to notice, even though the initial trades might be with thinly disguised confederates, and thus would reflect no real advance. The stock would begin to nose upward, accompanied by shrewdly timed and worded publicity. Then as the peak was reached, just as all threatened to collapse, the pool would sell out and take its profits, leaving the luckless taxi drivers and housewives to lick their wounds and count their losses.

So adept at this kind of near larceny was Meehan that he drove Radio Corporation of America up from a low point in 1928 of 85¼ to a high in 1929 of 549 — and this despite the fact that RCA had declared no dividend at all for longer than anyone cared to count. The financial morals of the time were thoroughly lax and mercenary. Even the vice president of the New York Stock Exchange, Richard Whitney, was involved in shady financial operations that would later land him in jail.

et if America of the boom years seemed prosperous, and if that prosperity seemed divinely ordained and eternal, there was nevertheless a skull beneath the skin. Farmers had never shared in the wartime prosperity. Afterward it was worse: when in the spring of 1920 the Harding administration withdrew agricultural support, there was a crash among those who in the wartime years had mortgaged their futures to buy land and equipment to increase their production for war. Bankruptcies and foreclosures multiplied disastrously: a total of 435,000 farmers lost their land and stock in the 1920–21 recession. Others survived, but only on the margin of the economy, wholly without reserves, ready to be cut down by any further stroke of ill luck.

And as the farmers had expanded plant and output far beyond their real ability to sell at profit, so had many industrialists, likewise caught up in the wartime excitement. When the farmers could no longer buy, when Europe, hard hit by the war and no longer supported by American loans, could no longer buy, the American industrialist could not sell.

Some industries, like many farmers, never recovered from the 1920–21 depression, and others recovered only in part, to limp through the years of Coolidge prosperity without sharing in the general gains. Throughout the next decade, the cotton and wool industries, as well as bituminous coal, would be classified as chronically sick. Such industries were vulnerable targets, to be knocked down by the first Depression winds eight years later.

How spotty was the alleged "Coolidge prosperity" is attested over and over again. In Gastonia, North Carolina, where a bloody textile workers' strike broke out in 1928, workers earned a weekly wage of only eighteen dollars for men and nine dollars for women — and this for a seventy-hour week! Children of fourteen worked in the mills too, an eleven-hour day, for trivial wages. In all, something less than one-half of the labor force bettered its condition during the Twenties. Many parts of New England, the Midwest, and the Mountain States also failed to share in the prosperity.

Merger after merger squeezed the small-business man. For the Harding and Coolidge administrations the antitrust laws were virtually a dead letter. Owners of businesses increased their earnings two and three times faster than their employees' wages rose. Yet no one, least of all the New York Federal Reserve, then under the direction of Benjamin Strong, a man more concerned with easy credit for Britain than with tighter money at home, acted to challenge the irresponsible business practices of the time. Labor was weak, farmers were weak, politicians were venal. Most of all, the businessman, according to the gospel of the boosters, sat at the right hand of God. Could it be expected that someone like Andrew Mellon, Harding's and Coolidge's Secretary of the Treasury, who made hundreds of millions during the decade, would act to curb business? Mellon, and nearly everyone else in the Treasury Department and on Wall Street, felt that tight money and high corporate taxes were not only unsound economics but morally wrong.

The result of such a moral position was that in the great boom decade business ran riot, ignoring the needs of the nation; so unequally distributed was income on the eve of the crash in 1929 that the sixty thousand families at the top of the economic pyramid controlled as much wealth as the twenty-five million families at the bottom.

Collapse was long overdue. The Great Bull Market

had been sustained for months, even years, on dreams and promises of wealth. It was a jerry-built structure, a slapdash creation of admen's hard sell, stock pushers' fraud and near fraud, business self-complacency, do-nothing government, economic nationalism, high tariffs, and an unregulated market place. It could not last, and it did not last. One humid autumn, in October, 1929, it all fell down.

If the initial crash was purely a stock market phenomenon, the months that followed were to provide practical lessons in abstruse economics, demonstrating beyond all question the close relationship between working capital and jobs.

National income plummeted after 1929: from $87,800,000,000 that year to less than $75,700,000,000 in 1930, and down to $40,200,000,000 in 1933, the low point. National wealth shrank from a pre-Depression $439,000,000,000 to $330,000,000,000 in 1933. In the three years 1930–32 eighty-six thousand businesses failed. Nine million savings accounts were wiped out. Wages fell by an average of 60 per cent.

Factory girls in Chicago in 1932 were earning an average of twenty-five cents an hour; live-in maids got ten dollars per month; in New York a top-flight executive secretary was paid sixteen dollars per week, down from forty-five dollars only three years earlier. Even the great Babe Ruth of the Yankees took a ten-thousand-dollar annual salary cut and for once did not fight back.

In April, 1930, the Hoover administration summoned its courage and ordered a sample house-to-house census to discover the extent of unemployment. The estimate was three million out of work, but by January of the new year the Department of Commerce believed the number had doubled. Both estimates were much too low.

Individuals were bankrupt, but so was local government. As property owners defaulted on taxes, hundreds of small towns found themselves unable to pay their teachers or garbage men, so that schools closed down and refuse rotted in the streets. In Chicago teachers went unpaid for months and were forced to borrow to exist. By 1932 seven hundred and fifty of them had lost their homes through mortgage foreclosures.

For a little while the building trade staggered on, carried by the momentum of previously planned construction. Expressing the ebullient confidence of the years before the crash, a New York syndicate had planned the Empire State Building, a vast edifice soaring to one hundred and two stories and surmounted by a dirigible mooring mast. It was to be, in effect, the incarnation of the majesty and wealth that were America. Two years after the crash the work was done, but the Empire State Building by then had become a monument to vanished glory and would stand largely untenanted through the Depression.

So too would the vast, echoing Waldorf Astoria Hotel on Park Avenue, which opened its doors to an uncaring public in 1931. And so too Rockefeller Center, that handsome essay in modern urban design, eleven of whose fifteen buildings were completed during the period 1931–37.

In the autumn of 1930 the International Apple Shippers' Association, saddled with a vast crop surplus, dreamed up a scheme offering its fruit on credit to the jobless who would peddle it on street corners. By November six thousand unemployed had taken up the offer in New York alone, and the nation hailed this new experiment in capitalist self-help. But by spring of the next year the novelty had long since worn off, and there were countless complaints that the apple peddlers were an insufferable nuisance. In New York, City Hall ordered most of them off the streets.

Desperate and ugly was the mood of the farmers. A. N. Young of the Farmers' Union of Wisconsin testified before a Senate committee:

They are just ready to do anything to get even with the situation. I almost hate to express it, but I honestly believe that if some of them could buy airplanes they would come down here to Washington to blow you fellows all up. . . . The farmer is naturally a conservative individual, but you cannot find a conservative farmer today. . . . I am as conservative as any man could be, but any economic system that has in its power to set me and my wife in the streets, at my age—what can I see but red?

His testimony was an understatement. In the Midwestern Corn Belt, in the parklike dairy country of Pennsylvania, in the Cotton South, gangs of angry farmers gathered at mortgage foreclosure sales brandishing pitchforks, clubs, and shotguns to threaten the sheriff and save the land. Backed by his neighbors, who prevented others from bidding, the desperate farmer could redeem his forfeited land for a few dollars.

Probably the most tragic event of this season of discontent was the routing of the bonus army in Washington. In 1924 Congress had voted to give the veterans of the World War a bonus, payable in 1945, but many destitute former servicemen began demanding immediate payment, and in the spring of 1932 Congressman Wright Patman of Texas introduced a bill that would have made the bonuses payable at once.

It occurred to Walter W. Waters, an unemployed cannery worker in Oregon and former sergeant, that the presence of a few hundred veterans in Washington might influence some members of Congress to support the Patman Bill. Leading three hundred like-minded recruits, Waters left Portland early in May, traveling by boxcar. By the time they reached Washington at the end of the month the news of the Bonus Expeditionary Force, as the men mockingly called themselves, had spread over the nation, and twenty thousand veterans were pouring into the Capital.

The government ignored them; their only friend in any place of power was the Washington police chief, who more than once spent his own money to buy them food. The bonus army settled down, some in abandoned government buildings, most in ramshackle camps, of which the largest by far was on the flats of the Anacostia River. There they built a pitiful collection of shacks out of anything available, from tar paper and straw to cardboard and old auto bodies. Among them were seven hundred women and four hundred children.

On June 17 the Senate overwhelmingly defeated the Patman Bill. A few of the veterans went home but most stayed on, though Hoover refused to meet with any of them or even to acknowledge their presence. Much later Hoover was to describe the army as "mixed hoodlums, ex-convicts, Communists and a minority of veterans." Actually there were very few Communists present, and they were very unpopular with the majority. Also the crime rate fell in Washington during the time the bonus army was there, belying the claim that it included many criminals.

On July 28 the Washington police moved to clear out the men who were living in abandoned government buildings. During a scuffle jittery police started shooting, killing two men. Hoover immediately called out Army forces: four troops of cavalry, a column of infantry, and six tanks, under the command of General Douglas MacArthur, whose second-in-command was Major Dwight Eisenhower. After giving the veterans and their families an hour to move out, the cavalry charged through the shacks by the Anacostia River with drawn sabers. The infantry with fixed bayonets followed them, throwing tear gas bombs into groups of veterans. One seven-year-old boy, turning back for his pet rabbit, was bayoneted in the leg. A veteran lost his ear to a cavalry saber, another was stabbed in the hip with a bayonet. An eleven-week-old baby, overcome by tear gas, later died. As night fell over the scene, the bonus army's shantytown went up in flames, reddening the sky. The bonus army straggled out of Washington and disintegrated in the next few days and weeks.

General MacArthur was much satisfied with his evening's work. He observed that action had been taken in the nick of time, for the "mob" was about to seize control of the government. "I have released in my day more than one community in the grip of a foreign enemy," the general said. Not all Americans were as proud of the triumph. Many citizens considered it the most shameful episode of Hoover's administration: that the Army should be used against unarmed, peaceful men, women, and children.

By the summer of 1932 the onetime Great Engineer—the man whom the young Franklin D. Roosevelt, then assistant secretary of the Navy under Wilson, had hailed as a "wonder"—was the object of hatred and contempt. Old newspapers became "Hoover blankets." Jack rabbits, mighty tough eating, were known throughout the Southwest as Hoover hogs.

The transformation of the quality of national life within a matter of months after the crash beggars description. Not only poverty stalked America. The crash worked vast social change. There were bread lines on ten thousand street corners, where desperate and homeless men, once employed and self-respecting, their shabby overcoats lined with newspaper against the cold, cardboard insoles covering the holes in their worn-through shoes, stamped their feet idly waiting for a handout meal. Women were abandoned, by design or not, as their men hit the road.

Homeless boys and girls, many in their teens, the victims of families disintegrated by unemployment and near starvation, squatted around fires in hobo jungles, and begged and stole in the towns to which they drifted aimlessly. The economic status of Negroes, marginal even in the boom economy of the past decade, plummeted like a stone. Racial tensions deepened in an already racially riven America.

Factories lay idle. The dust blew over the land.

Famous Faces
of the Twenties

The Jazz Age produced more than flappers,
the Charleston, and bathtub gin. Out of it also
came a number of the most memorable
characters of this century.

F. Scott Fitzgerald

It was Francis Scott Key Fitzgerald—he was named for a forebear—who called the decade the Jazz Age, and the label is as descriptive as any that has been attached to the frantic, mindless, pleasure-seeking Twenties. But Fitzgerald did more than give the era a name; he was its spokesman and one of its typical products, and he took part in its excesses until both his health and talent were spent.

Fitzgerald had come to Princeton in 1913 from St. Paul, Minnesota, largely, he said, after hearing about its Triangle Club, which produced a musical comedy annually. This and other extracurricular writing activities during the week, and theater and debutante parties in New York on weekends, badly interfered with his studies, and in the autumn of his third year he left to avoid failing. He returned to Princeton, but the war came and he left for good.

To his lifelong regret, he never got overseas, but he served in the Army in the South as a second lieutenant. While stationed near Montgomery, Alabama, he met and fell in love with blonde, popular Zelda Sayre. Zelda returned his love but refused to marry him until he could assure some financial stability, so after the war he went to work in a New York advertising agency. He was not very good at writing advertising copy, and in desperation he quit and went home to St. Paul to finish a novel he had been working on for some time.

The novel, *This Side of Paradise*, was published in 1920 and won Fitzgerald almost immediate fame. It contained the first description of the flapper and of disillusioned postwar youth looking for meaning in a world where the old verities had vanished. As Fitzgerald put it in one of the last paragraphs of *This Side of Paradise*, his was "a new generation, dedicated more than the last to the fear of poverty and the worship of success; grown up to find all Gods dead, all wars fought, all faiths in man shaken. . . ."

Scott and Zelda were married in St. Patrick's Cathedral in Manhattan and at once began to live at the extravagant, high-speed, hard-drinking, party-going pace of the Jazz Age. Zelda danced on tables and drove their new Marmon into a fire hydrant; Scott rode down Fifth Avenue atop a taxi in some drunken hour after midnight and on another occasion was thrown out of a theater when he began disrobing. The couple waded in the fountain at the Plaza, passed out at parties, greeted the dawn in all-night cafes. ". . . from that period I remember riding in a taxi one afternoon between very tall buildings under a mauve and rosy sky," Fitzgerald wrote later. "I began to bawl because I had everything I wanted and knew I would never be so happy again."

Fitzgerald received eighteen thousand dollars from his book, which was a very good return indeed from a first novel, especially in that day, before the devaluated dollar. And in three months it was all gone, spent on fun and frolic. But now magazines were clamoring for stories and ready to pay good prices. There were complications, though, for Zelda soon found herself pregnant, and even the pleasure-obsessed couple felt that the liquor-sex-and-party atmosphere of New York was not the place to bring a baby into the world.

The two went to the Fitzgerald home in St. Paul, and there their daughter, Frances Scott ("Scottie"), was born. During this period Fitzgerald finished his second book, *The Beautiful and Damned*, a story of a wealthy young couple spending their lives in dissipation, a tale somewhat reminiscent of the Fitzgeralds' manner of living. The book, published in 1922, was only moderately successful.

St. Paul proved too quiet; the couple returned east and rented a large house on Long Island. Their friends from Manhattan soon found them, and life was again a round of parties, booze, and whoopee. In 1923 Fitzgerald wrote a play, *The Vegetable*, which opened and quickly closed in Atlantic City. But he kept writing short stories and managed to pay most of their creditors—but not all. When he took stock he found that they had spent one hundred and thirteen thousand dollars in four years and had little more than memories to show for it—and some of those very foggy. In the last year of the four, they had spent thirty-six thousand dollars and were still five thousand dollars in debt.

In 1924 they moved to Europe, and there they remained, except for brief intervals, until 1931. They found the Jazz Age flourishing among the expatriates, and the endless round of parties went on. The two wandered about the Continent, enjoying Paris one week, the Riviera another, then going on to Spain when the whim moved them. During the first year in Europe Fitzgerald found enough time from partying to write and publish another novel, *The Great Gatsby*, the story of a Long Island bootlegger who finds that money cannot buy quite everything he wants (specifically, a place in upper society and one of its girls, whom he loves). Though most critics agree that it is his best book, the public was not greatly impressed. For Fitzgerald it marked the high point after which his talent began to ebb. The carefree life of jazz and whoopee and endless parties was not really carefree after all; it was dissipation, and no finely tuned talent can stand such mistreatment indefinitely without losing some of its keenness.

But the couple were on a treadmill, and the frantic search for pleasure went on. Fitzgerald was drinking far too much and was often drunk during the day as well as at night. He was able to do little work. As for Zelda, her preoccupation with gaiety and alcohol gave way in 1928 to a burning passion for ballet. She studied day and night, but by 1930 it was clear that she lacked any real talent for success. That same year she had a nervous breakdown. After a year in a Swiss sanatorium she was well enough to return to the United States, but there was another breakdown, and she never completely recovered again.

The Depression was on, the parties were over, the flappers and sheiks were gone. Scott Fitzgerald settled for a time in Baltimore, trying to cope at once with his continuing debts, his drinking, Zelda's sickness. "I left my capacity for hoping on the little roads that led to Zelda's sanatorium," he said.

In 1934 he finished *Tender Is the Night*, his first novel in eight years. The critics had little good to say about it, and the public was not much interested. The disappointment sent Fitzgerald back to steady drinking again, until in 1935 he went to a small Southern town to dry out and take stock of his prospects. He concluded that his talent as a writer was dead and decided that he would write for the movies, where little talent was needed.

In 1937 he moved to Hollywood, where he worked hard, stayed sober, paid off most of his debts, and even sent his daughter, Scottie, to college. He fell in love for the first time since leaving Zelda and her wrecked mind. Then, when a producer rewrote his scripts, he went back to the bottle again and was fired. But it was not the end. He found his talent returning and started work on another novel, *The Last Tycoon*. It was a worthy work and might have been his best book, but when it was half finished, he suffered a heart attack. He was soon

NEW-YORK HISTORICAL SOCIETY

sitting up in bed and working again, but a second attack a month later, in December, 1940, took his life at the age of forty-four.

He had wanted to be buried by his father in the Catholic cemetery in Rockville, Maryland, but the church authorities ruled that he had strayed too far from the faith of his childhood. His grave,

consequently, is across the road from where his father lies.

Zelda, who had once danced on tables and waded in the fountain at the Plaza, died in 1948 when fire swept an Asheville, North Carolina, sanatorium, the last of the series of institutions in which she had spent the final fourteen years of her life.

bar

163

The Great Lover

Many years have passed, but Rudolph Valentino remains the Great Lover. Other actors have brought women moments of emotional fantasy, but none approached Valentino's ability to make them shiver and grow weak. Yet his depiction of physical passion was rather comical. Producer Adolph Zukor once described it as "largely confined to protruding his large, almost occult eyes, until vast areas of white were visible, drawing back the lips of his wide, sensuous mouth to bare his gleaming teeth, and flaring his nostrils." But it was good enough for millions of women, who sighed, twisted handkerchiefs, and often actually swooned as they watched his flickering figure go through its charade of love and passion on the silent screen.

Rudolph Valentino started life in Italy as Rodolpho Alfonzo Raffaeli Pierre Filibert di Valentina d'Antonguolla. He was educated well enough to receive a degree as an agriculturist, but decided that the soil was not for him and in 1913, at the age of eighteen, came to the United States. Things were not easy for a boy who knew little English; he was by turns a gardener on a Long Island estate, a New York parks worker, and a polisher of brass in front of the houses of the rich. More than once he slept on a bench in Central Park because he was broke.

Then, because he was young and handsome, he found a job in a restaurant as a dancing partner—a gigolo—for lonely matrons. Within a year he was half of a dance team, then joined a musical road show that went broke on the West Coast. He eventually found bit work in the movies, and was noticed in time, given a screen test, and won a principal part in *The Four Horsemen of the Apocalypse*. The film, which appeared in 1921, was an instant success, and Valentino stole the picture.

The young man with the regular profile, pointed sideburns, and slicked-down hair was a star. Next there was a forgettable picture called *The Conquering Power*, then Valentino appeared opposite Nazimova in *Camille*. After that came *The Sheik*, the desert picture that made him a sex symbol for an untold number of yearning women. Nationwide swooning reached its peak at the moment when Valentino, as the desert sheik overcome by lust for the Englishwoman he holds captive, sweeps the fearful maiden up in his arms and pops his eyes, bares his teeth, and flares his nostrils as the scene fades out. No woman had any doubts about what went on in the tent after the fade-out, and suddenly rape did not seem a fate worse than death.

There were other pictures, some empty bits to exploit his sex appeal, others, like *Blood and Sand*, that demanded real acting ability. For while he was no great actor, he was better than most Americans of the period. Had he been given more time than his scant six years, he might have developed into an artist.

Even during the years when he was the supreme idol of womankind his life was not easy. At the outset of his career he married Jean Acker, an actress of some note at the time. It was a mistake; they left each other in 1922, she charging that he had struck her, he accusing her of having deserted him.

Almost immediately he married Winifred Shaunessey, stepdaughter of Richard Hudnut, the cosmetics magnate. She was dancing with a Russian ballet and called herself Natacha Rambova. A very domineering woman, she took charge of her husband's career, so often insisting on changes in story line, setting, or costume, that soon studios inserted clauses in Valentino's contracts barring her from sets. In time the marriage wore thin and Miss Rambova went to France for a divorce.

The Great Lover was never much appreciated by men. Many of them might have slicked their hair down and let their sideburns grow in hopes of emulating his success with the ladies, but they accused him of effeminacy. When he loyally wore a slave bracelet that Miss Rambova had given him, there were hoots of derision from hairy-chested American males. He was blamed for things with which he had nothing to do: when an editorial writer for the Chicago *Tribune* found pink talcum powder in a men's room in a hotel, he connected it with the Great American Lover and called him a bad influence on American youth. The piece was written with tongue in cheek, but Valentino was deeply wounded, and when he passed through Chicago soon after, he challenged the newspaperman to a duel with any weapons, even fists. He got no satisfaction, and was accused of being a publicity seeker.

The Chicago incident was one of the last of many in Valentino's short and

MIGUEL COVARRUBIAS, *THE PRINCE OF WALES AND OTHER FAMOUS AMERICANS*, 1925

quite unhappy life. In August of that same year, 1926, he was taken to a New York hospital, violently ill. Doctors who operated for an inflamed appendix also found a perforated ulcer. Peritonitis developed, an infection against which medicine of the time had few effective weapons.

For two days he hung on to life by a thin margin, then rallied and was improving until the end of the week, when pleurisy further taxed his weakened body. On August 23, the eighth day, the New York *Daily News* rose to noteworthy heights of overripe reporting when it announced the coming end: "The Great Director today stood ready to call Rudolph Valentino off the screen of life." The Great Director did, shortly after noon that same day.

For sheer ghoulish bad taste, the honors went to the New York *Evening Graphic*. A reporter and a photographer from that paper went to Frank E. Campbell's Funeral Church, where the reporter posed in an empty coffin while his picture was taken. The paper superimposed a photo of Valentino's head on the picture, which was published in the *Graphic* and was on the streets even before the body of the actor reached the funeral parlor.

Though Campbell's did not plan to open its doors until four in the afternoon so the public could pay homage, the crowds began to collect before dawn. As the crush developed, police had to charge the mob again and again to keep it from storming the chapel. More than a hundred were injured. Campbell's had a skilled publicity man; Valentino's manager, S. George Ullman, was just as able and was equally interested in publicity for there were films of the Great Lover, particularly *Son of the Sheik*, still not released. At first Ullman had planned to have the actor lie in state in an open coffin, but he gave thought to souvenir hunters, who might well strip the Great Lover naked, and the bronze coffin was sealed so that only Valentino's face

showed. Thereupon the souvenir collectors turned on the furnishings of Campbell's magnificent Gold Room until the owner had the body moved to simpler quarters.

The second day fifty thousand showed up in the rain to file past the coffin. Jean Acker, the Great Lover's first wife, called in reporters to tell how she had been spirited into Valentino's hospital room during his last hours. But the show was stolen by Pola Negri, last of Valentino's heart interests. She had been too busy to come to New York when the actor was fighting for his life, but after his death she hastened east in a private railroad car, reportedly on the verge of collapse, but somehow finding the strength at Kansas City and Chicago to talk to reporters. In New York, in a sterling performance, she collapsed before Valentino's bier. And at the funeral at St. Malachy's, "the actors' church," which was attended by most of Hollywood's greats, among them Douglas Fairbanks, Mary Pickford, Gloria Swanson, William S. Hart, Bebe Daniels, and Marilyn Miller, Miss Negri sobbed the loudest in a congregation where many wept.

There was more outpouring of emotion and more display of bad taste and clamoring for personal publicity on the funeral train west and at the burial in Hollywood. Ullman revealed several years later that the publicity had been effective. Valentino had died half a million in debt; his films shown after his death left his estate seven hundred thousand to the good.

The early life and times of Alphonse Capone were the American dream come true, 1920's fashion. Capone was washing dishes in a cabaret in 1920; half a dozen years later he was head of an organization grossing around a hundred million dollars a year. It was not always easy—hazards such as machine gun and pistol fire, for one thing, made it difficult to keep fully staffed—but what business does not have its problems?

But Al Capone did not make it entirely on his own. His great friend and mentor was Johnny Torrio, who had been brought to Chicago from Brooklyn in 1910 by "Big Jim" Colosimo, Chicago's vice king. Big Jim had needed someone to manage his booming brothel business as well as to take care of certain people who were bothering him. He heard good things about Torrio on both counts. Under Torrio's management Colosimo's business expanded into new territory, and Torrio's hoods were diligent about persuading people to let Colosimo alone.

Then Prohibition came. Torrio realized that much money could be made quenching the American thirst, and he spoke of this to Big Jim Colosimo. But Big Jim was not interested; they had done very well with the women, he said, and besides, bootlegging would never amount to anything. Torrio was very persuasive, however, and one day Big Jim was shot down as he was about to enter his office. Nothing was ever proved, but the police said that Torrio's former partner in Brooklyn, Frankie Yale, had arrived in town shortly before Colosimo passed on and had received ten thousand in cash from Torrio. One thing was clear: Torrio now ran Colosimo's empire.

Torrio's first interest was to surround himself with dependable men. It is very probable that when Frankie Yale was in Chicago, he told Torrio about a likely young fellow then working in Yale's Brooklyn cabaret as a dishwasher and part-time bartender. The youth, twenty-three-year-old Alphonse Capone, had a very fine reputation as a handler of pistol, blackjack, knife, and other implements of the sort. Torrio wired Capone to come to Chicago at once.

Capone was given a tryout as a bouncer in an outlying bordello. He did so well that Torrio made him manager of his Four Deuces, which combined cabaret, gambling rooms, and brothels into one pleasure dome. Capone was very assiduous as a manager and zealous in eliminating those whose existence was irksome to Torrio. Within little more than a year, young Al Capone had become Torrio's chief lieutenant.

Torrio called the gang chiefs together. Why should they—good friends and gentle fellows all—fight one another, he asked, when there were millions in bootlegging, enough for all? He proposed that they divide the area among them, that they form a syndicate with himself as general manager, and that he and Capone supply beer and hard liquor at fair prices to those who wanted them. The chiefs agreed, and gangland settled down to a period of relative peace and prosperity.

Only one bit of trouble marred the early months of the syndicate. For complex reasons the South Side O'Donnell mob had been ignored when the territorial division was made. As a result the four O'Donnell brothers and their henchmen began to run beer into sections of the city allocated to others. Johnny Torrio told Capone to talk sense to the O'Donnells.

In the resulting debate, seven of the O'Donnell mob went to glory, and their leader, Spike O'Donnell, finally quit. Later he made his peace with Capone and did well in the organization, though he confessed that he felt he was made for finer things and that he secretly yearned to be an actor.

In the division of territory Torrio had kept for himself a piece of the South Side and a part of the West Side, including the suburban towns. When he set out to take over Cicero, the largest city in Cook County after Chicago, he handed the job over to Capone. As his first move, Capone campaigned for the re-election of Mayor Joseph Klenha and his slate by intimidating voters, slugging and kidnapping election workers, and raiding polling places. Klenha, of course, won, and Capone turned Cicero into a kind of playground for weary gangsters. Saloons ran openly, and the nearly two hundred gambling houses were so competitive that they had barkers in front. Capone made Cicero his headquarters and ruled so completely over the city that once when Mayor Klenha said something that annoyed Capone, the gangster knocked the mayor down in public on the steps of city hall. Another time, when the city council met to consider an ordinance Capone did not like, some of his hoods came to the council meeting, cracked a head or two with blackjacks, and sent the council members home.

Things were going smoothly for the mobsters. Chicago police were on their payrolls; patrolmen were seen riding guard on truckloads of beer. Then trouble came. Dion O'Banion, lord of the North Side, involved himself in a dispute with the six Genna brothers—called the

Al Capone and His Pals

Terrible Gennas—of the West Side. He accused them of selling alcohol in his territory; in retaliation he hijacked a few loads of their beer. When he was warned by his lieutenant Hymie Weiss that it was not a good thing to irritate the Terrible Gennas, he responded, "To hell with them Sicilians." It was an unwise thing to say, considering the number of Italians and Sicilians in the mobs. O'Banion was committing suicide, and two or three other indiscretions made his end certain.

Dion O'Banion loved flowers and ran a florist's shop as a hobby. In November, 1924, while he was happily making up a wreath, three men came in and gunned him down. It is said that the job was done by two Genna gunmen and possibly Frankie Yale, brought from Brooklyn for the event. O'Banion was given a funeral to be proud of, and Torrio, Capone, and at least one of the Gennas were there, looking quite mournful.

Less than three months later Torrio himself was shot outside his apartment. Though doctors shook their heads, he was soon up and about in spite of having absorbed five slugs. However, he did consider it a good time to serve out a nine-month jail sentence he owed the state, while outside O'Banion's heirs worked devotedly, laying to rest, among others, three of the six Terrible Gennas. Torrio thought over the situation and then called Capone. "It's all yours, Al," he said, and left for Europe when his nine months were up.

Al Capone, at twenty-eight, was now gangland's number-one big shot. But Torrio's syndicate was shattered, and Chicago echoed to the rattle of Tommy guns for four years, during which some five hundred mobsters were killed. Capone led a charmed life. More than once the steel armor and the bullet-proof glass of his limousine saved him. When Hymie Weiss ran eight cars full of gunmen past Capone's Cicero headquarters and raked the building with shotgun and machine-gun fire, Capone hugged the floor unharmed.

Two weeks after Hymie Weiss refused a peace offer, he was machine-gunned by Capone's boys. Leadership of his gang eventually passed to Bugs Moran, who made his headquarters in a North Side garage. There, on St. Valentine's Day in 1929, a car drove up and four men, two of them in police uniform, got out and entered the garage. The seven men inside were lined up against the wall and shot down. Bystanders who saw the four leave again assumed two policemen were making a routine arrest.

The massacre not only shocked a nation that had tended to glamorize gangsters, but it worried mobsters across the country. A conference was held in Atlantic City, where the Capone-Moran and other Chicago difficulties were settled and boundaries were laid out for the domains of all the Eastern big-city mobsters.

While Capone was on his way home, the unbelievable happened. He was arrested in Philadelphia for carrying concealed weapons and for the first time in his life went to jail, where he stayed for ten months, until March, 1930. By then public opinion had changed, and he was no longer a hero. In the fall of 1931 the federal government sent him to prison for income tax evasion. He was released in 1939, a sick man, and died in Florida in 1947.

A bemused Al Capone appears in a detail from artist Ben Shahn's symbolic Prohibition Alley.

Aimee Semple McPherson

As an evangelist, Aimee Semple McPherson brought something new to the art of saving souls. While her fellow workers in the vineyard, including the great Billy Sunday, depended mainly on threats of hell-fire and damnation to frighten sinners back to God, Aimee dispensed only love and sunshine. For her it was enough that heaven was lovely; why talk about that other unpleasant place?

Aimee Kennedy was a seventeen-year-old Ontario farm girl in 1907 when she met and married Robert Semple, an itinerant preacher and missionary, who soon left her a widow in China, a month before her daughter was born. She returned to the United States, and in time married Harold McPherson, who fathered her second child, a son, but restlessness so overcame her that she packed up her

mother, two children, and a tent in a car and started out as a traveling revivalist.

At first the little troupe traveled up and down the East coast; in 1918 they went to California for the first time. Aimee's talents were maturing; within a week after arriving in Los Angeles she rented an auditorium seating thirty-five hundred and filled it to overflowing. Thereafter she returned to southern California each year. In 1921 she went to San Diego, then a town with a huge population of invalids, and while she was speaking at an outdoor rally, an event occurred that made her famous. An overwrought crippled woman rose from her wheel chair and tottered toward the platform, to be followed by hundreds of others of the infirm as the hysteria spread. Aimee became known as a faith healer, but she modestly refused any credit. "I am not a healer," she once said. "Jesus is the healer. I am only the little office girl who opens the door and says 'Come in.'"

That same year, 1921, McPherson divorced her, charging desertion and complaining that her "wildcat habits" in their

home were such that he would rather give up ever seeing his son again than have the slightest thing to do with her.

After the San Diego episode, Aimee decided to settle permanently in southern California, and little more than a year later, on New Year's Day, 1923, she dedicated Angelus Temple in Los Angeles. It was an ugly structure, topped by a large rotating illuminated cross visible for fifty miles, but Aimee kept its five thousand seats filled, for her services were described by one critic as "supernatural whoopee" and they gave Angelinos, most of them transplanted Midwesterners, just what they wanted. Instead of the old gospel of fear, acceptable in more rugged climes, she substituted a sunnier religion, which she called the Foursquare Gospel. Worship was fun. Instead of the dolorous hymns of Wesley, she had her flock sing of a heaven rather like a block party, with music, dancing, and milk and honey.

Sister Aimee always put on a good show. In her throw-out-the-lifeline number a dozen imperiled damsels clung to a storm-lashed Rock of Ages, while special-effects men worked heroically with thunder, lightning, and wind. Just when all seemed lost, Sister Aimee in admiral's uniform appeared and ordered a squad of lady sailors to the rescue. They tossed out the blessed lifeline while the male chorus, dressed as coastguardmen, swept the mechanical waves with searchlights. The virgins were saved, trumpets blared, and an inspired congregation cheered the triumph of good as the American flag waved over all. Sister Aimee alone was also worth seeing, garbed in a white robe for her sermon and with skillful lighting setting her tawny hair aglint.

Aimee's sense of the dramatic was sure and her use of publicity almost unerring. Angelus Temple boasted a huge choir, a brass band, and a pipe organ. A broadcasting station sent the Foursquare Gospel story to the world. A "Miracle Room" displayed stacks of crutches, wheel chairs, and braces from faith cures. Aimee was famous and the money was rolling in. Then in 1925 things began to come unglued.

She was thirty-five that year, divorced four years, lonely, a vulnerable woman, when Kenneth G. Ormiston, operator of the temple's radio station—but not a member of her cult—came into her life. At first he was only a voice from the control room, commenting to Aimee that she had sounded weary that night or that she had done well. Before long the curious evangelist drove him home in her car, and soon the temple community was buzzing that the two were meeting regularly.

In mid-May of 1926 Sister Aimee drove to an ocean beach, changed into a swimsuit, and sat on the sand for a time working on a sermon. Her secretary left her for a short while, and when she returned Aimee was gone. The supposition was that the evangelist, a strong swimmer, had gone out, suffered a cramp or other mishap, and drowned.

Thousands of the faithful camped on the shore. Boats patrolled the water. One heartbroken girl committed suicide. A young man plunged into the ocean crying, "I'm going after her," and was drowned. A diver died of exhaustion.

Officials and newsmen delving into circumstances surrounding her disappearance found that Ormiston had left the temple at a time that had a curious relation to Aimee's movements. When further revelations seemed imminent, Aimee, missing for thirty-two days, came out of the dark to knock on the door of a cottage in Agua Prieta, Mexico, just across the Arizona border. She told of having been kidnapped from the beach by a trio she called Steve and Jake and Rose, who took her to a shack in the Mexican desert, whence she finally escaped and stumbled for miles to safety over the burning sands. Skeptics noted that the long, hot walk had left her shoes unscuffed and that she had not even perspired. But Los Angeles gave her a tumultuous welcome, and the faithful of the temple greeted her as one risen from the dead.

Aimee, beyond doubt, had first hoped to disappear permanently. Ormiston was married, and she might as well have been, for she had once proclaimed that no member of the Foursquare faith could remarry while his former spouse lived. As a way out of this dilemma she contrived her disappearance, then had to devise a reappearance when gathering events made it plain that it was impossible to give up all for love and live in secret sin.

The affair would likely have blown over had not Aimee insisted that her kidnappers be brought to justice. The ensuing investigation dragged out the dirty linen: chambermaids, room clerks, hotel registers, and scraps of paper in Aimee's handwriting gave eyewitness or circumstantial evidence that Sister Aimee and Ormiston had had many hotel room trysts over several months and had been together in a seaside cottage during the month she claimed to have been a prisoner in the desert.

Though the evidence was conclusive, the investigation was suddenly terminated in January, 1927. Aimee at once set out on a rehabilitation tour, but something was missing. In cities where crowds had once thronged to hear her, the halls were half empty. The great faith healer had become a woman with a somewhat dubious past. Then the stock market crash and the Depression further turned people's minds to other things.

Love came again to Aimee (Ormiston had simply faded away) at the age of forty, and this time she forgot her strictures against a divorced member of her cult remarrying. But two days after her wedding to roly-poly Dave Hutton, he was sued by another female for breach of promise. Aimee fainted, cracked her skull on the flagstones, and after her recovery, the couple were divorced.

Though attendance had dwindled, the Foursquare faithful stood by Sister Aimee, and her services at Angelus Temple were still worth seeing. Lawsuits deviled her: for unpaid bills, broken contracts, false arrest, a dozen other legal tangles. Despite changing times, she not only outlasted the Twenties but was active into the Forties.

On a September evening in 1944 Aimee spoke to a warm and receptive crowd in Oakland, California. The next morning she was found unconscious in her hotel room and died soon after. The coroner's verdict was "an overdose of barbital compound," that is, sleeping pills. Very likely Aimee went to glory by her own choice.

Joseph Golinkin's drawing of Texas Guinan's Portable Night Club shows Texas atop the piano, holding police whistle and noisemaker.

Texas Guinan and the 1920's were made for each other. She was not much of an actress, as her few tries at the stage proved, and her singing voice was no great shakes, but she had a personality that made the customers in her night clubs willing to be overcharged and happy to be greeted with "Hello, Sucker" as they entered the smoky, crowded room where she held court. And in the Twenties laughs and fun were very important.

Texas Guinan was originally Mary Louise Cecilia Guinan from a ranch near Waco, Texas, who disappointed her parents' hopes for a musical career by leaving home to become a cow girl in a circus. From the circus she went to vaudeville and then to Hollywood, where her skill at riding and roping won her some renown in Westerns and the sobriquet "the female Bill Hart." But New York called and in 1922 she answered. She was no spring chicken at the time: a ripe thirty-eight. Her

first job—or one of her first—was as a substitute singer in a place called the Café des Beaux Arts. She set no worlds afire with her voice, but she did so impress the owner with her ebullient manner that he hired her as mistress of ceremony; she delighted the customers with her salty repartee and boisterousness and was observed by one Larry Fay, a horse-faced gentleman of many interests, some legitimate, some not.

Fay hired Miss Guinan for his own club, El Fey. It was the start of a long and profitable relationship between the two, and though they eventually parted, the partnership enabled Texas to establish herself as one of the brightest lights on the Great White Way. With Fay and alone, she was hostess in a succession of night clubs whose names bring a nostalgic tear to the eye of anyone who knew Manhattan in that long-ago dry era: El Fey, the Rendezvous, the 300 Club, the Argonaut, the Century, the Salon Royal, the Club Intime,

and a number of Texas Guinan Clubs.

Miss Guinan was involved in so many night clubs in those relatively few years for a good reason: such places of relaxation were raided and padlocked by prohibition agents with disturbing frequency. But Texas had no hard feelings against the dry agents. When the Feds flashed their badges and announced that a raid was on, she sometimes had the band strike up "The Prisoner's Song." She was smart enough to see beyond the temporary inconvenience. "Where the hell would I be without prohibition?" she would say. She capitalized on the publicity value of raids, took to wearing a necklace strung with little gold padlocks, and had a diamond bracelet from which a small gold police whistle dangled. Though arrested several times, she never spent a minute in jail.

Miss Guinan presided from atop a piano, booming out "Hello, Sucker" at every arriving customer and keeping up a running fire of wisecracks. In one hand she

"Hello, Sucker!"

held a police whistle and in the other a clapper-type noisemaker for use in the rare but unbearable moments when relative quiet fell on her clamorous domain. Writer Edmund Wilson, who knew New York of the Jazz Age well, described her as "this prodigious woman, with her pearls, her glittering bosom, her abundant beautifully bleached yellow coiffure, her formidable trap of shining white teeth, her broad bare back behind its grating of green velvet, the full-blown peony as big as a cabbage exploding on her broad green thigh."

Miss Guinan made the shallow pretense that she sold no liquor, only setups for customers who brought their own. Some idea of her scale of prices can be gathered from her two-dollar charge for a pitcher of plain water. But she did a brisk business in booze whenever it was reasonably certain that there were no Feds on the premises, which was most of the time, for the dry agents were badly overworked. Her liquor was not for the indigent: twenty-five dollars for a fifth of mediocre Scotch and a like amount for a bottle of champagne of dubious vintage. No wonder she said "Hello, Sucker." There was also a cover charge of from five to twenty-five dollars, depending on business at the time, and to make sure she did not miss a penny, Texas packed them in like sardines, a custom still followed happily by night clubs.

Her language was colorful, and at least two of her phrases are still current. One night a big spender not only insisted on paying the cover charge of everyone present but also gave fifty-dollar bills to each of the performers. The man would identify himself only as being in the dairy produce business, whereupon Miss Guinan dubbed him a "big butter-and-egg man."

The phrase is still used to refer to a big spender from out of town. After one of her performers finished a number, Miss Guinan would call out, "Give the little girl a great big hand"; now masters of ceremony everywhere use the same exhortation to wring applause from apathetic audiences. One time a dry agent stood up in the audience, put his hand on Miss Guinan's shoulder, and called to a fellow agent, "Give this little girl a great big handcuff." Miss Guinan took it in good grace.

The one night club entertainer who rivaled Texas Guinan in popularity was Helen Morgan. Both perched on pianos, but there the similarity ended. The customers went to Miss Guinan's club for laughs and horseplay; they visited Miss Morgan's to weep. Helen Morgan had a low, husky singing voice, and when she gave out with "Bill" or "Can't Help Lovin' Dat Man," the combination of sentiment, liquor, dim lights, and smoke-filled air was too much for many of the customers and tears rolled down their cheeks. Miss Morgan in time wearied of being raided and padlocked, and so gave up the game before the Twenties were over.

Another of Miss Guinan's rivals—and her good friend—was Belle Livingston, who entered the night club field late in the 1920's. During her show-girl days, back in the early 1890's, Belle had billed herself as the Kansas Sunshine Baby, but that time was long past. She was six feet tall and during her career as a night club queen weighed about one hundred and seventy-five pounds. She usually acted as her own bouncer and once tried to throw out a squad of dry agents who were raiding her club. Unlike Texas Guinan, who tried to get along with the Feds, Belle fought them and got into trouble.

Texas favored crowded, intimate, noisy spots; Belle tried to give the customers everything. Her Fifty-eighth Street Country Club was a pleasure palace that offered, among other things, bars, grillrooms, private rooms, a miniature golf course, and ping pong. One floor was decorated in a Japanese motif; the customers sat on cushions on the floor while they quenched their thirst. Belle thought it a practical arrangement. "A man could get hurt falling off a bar stool," she said.

Texas Guinan, despite her apparent irreverence, was devoted to family and friends. She brought her father and mother to New York and lived with them. And she watched over her girls—at one time there were as many as seventy-eight—with the protectiveness of a mother lion. Her attitude toward husbands was more casual; there were three in her life.

The end of the Volstead Act put a period to her way of living, and she turned to a new career and went on the road with a troupe of dancing girls. It had been a good ride while it lasted, and it lasted a long time. Texas Guinan had loved the fun and excitement, to say nothing of the money; she is said to have put seven hundred thousand dollars in the bank during one ten-month period in the mid-Twenties. What happened to it and her other earnings no one knows, for when she died her entire estate amounted to only $28,173.

Prohibition made Texas Guinan famous; it was very fitting that they went out together. She died on November 5, 1933, at the age of forty-nine, at Vancouver, British Columbia, where she was appearing with her dancing girls. One month later, to the day, the Twenty-first Amendment was ratified, legally canceling the Eighteenth Amendment and prohibition.

When the nation went dry in 1920, all that stood between millions of thirsty Americans and alcohol, besides their consciences, was a thin line of prohibition enforcement agents, only fifteen hundred strong. And since the dry agents were paid the noble sum of about $2,500 a year, it is not surprising that many soon lost their sense of dedication and could be induced, for a consideration, to look elsewhere when beer or liquor was being moved or served in their vicinity.

But there were exceptions, and none more outstanding than a pair of agents whose appearance and names seemed better fitted for a vaudeville team than for a couple of gumshoes: Isadore Einstein and Moe Smith—Izzy and Moe. If all agents had shown as much energy and initiative as they did, even the small band of fifteen hundred might have done much toward drying up the country. Izzy demonstrated his unorthodoxy on his very first assignment, a suspected speak-easy in Brooklyn, which other agents had been unable to enter. He knocked boldly on the door, and when the peephole was opened, loudly demanded a drink, identifying himself as a newly appointed prohibition agent sent by his boss. The door swung open, and the doorman guffawed and slapped Izzy on the back in appreciation of his sense of humor. But then the new agent made a mistake. When the bartender poured him a drink, he downed it before trying to make the arrest. The bartender grabbed the bottle and escaped out a back way, and Izzy was left without evidence. Thereafter he carried a small funnel in a vest pocket, from which a rubber tube ran to a flask inside his clothing. On future raids most of his drink would go there, to be used as evidence.

Both Izzy and Moe were rotund men. Izzy was not quite five and a half feet tall and weighed two hundred and twenty-five pounds; he was forty years old and was almost bald when he became a liquor snooper. Moe outweighed his partner by about ten pounds but did not look as fat because he was a couple of inches taller. Izzy was the more talented of the two.

In addition to English, he spoke Yiddish, Polish, German, and Hungarian fluently, French, Russian, and Italian well enough to get along, and even a bit of Chinese. And he played the violin and the trombone.

Izzy had entered the prohibition service first. He had been trying to feed a family of six on the meager salary of a postal clerk when the country went dry, and the forty-odd dollars a week being paid to prohibition agents was decidedly an attraction. After he had been an agent a short time, he induced his old friend Moe Smith, owner of a cigar store on New York's East Side, to join up. Thereafter the pair usually worked as a team, although Izzy often made raids singlehandedly. Their ingenuity was endless. To get into a speak-easy whose cautious owner refused to open to anyone he did not know personally, they waited until a cold night. Then after Izzy had stood outside in light clothing until he was blue and his teeth were rattling, Moe pounded on the door and shouted, "Give this man a drink! He's been frostbitten." The owner, caught off guard, let Moe drag his partner inside and came forward with a bottle of reviving whiskey, which Moe grabbed and then made the arrest.

The stories about the pair multiplied, especially the tales about Izzy, who became a master of disguises. More often than not his principal concealment was that he looked too ingenuous and amiable to be a dry agent. On more than one occasion he repeated the stratagem that had worked on his first assignment: he would demand admittance to a speak-easy, crying out, "How about a drink for a tired prohibition agent?" And because fat little Izzy did not look at all like a Fed, he would be served a drink, which went into the funnel in his pocket before he made the pinch.

Once he gained admittance to several bars by carrying a large pail of dill pickles. "Who would ever think a fat man with pickles was an agent?" he asked. At Sheepshead Bay in Brooklyn, a mecca for fishermen, he was admitted without question to several speak-easies because he carried a string of fish. And more than

once he entered a place with the musicians, carrying his trombone or violin.

At one time Izzy was called upon to raid a soda fountain on the edge of a New York park, which was dispensing something besides sundaes and lime phosphates, but whose wary proprietor made it difficult to obtain evidence. He borrowed half a dozen dry agents, dressed them and himself in football uniforms, smeared some dirt on all faces, and then, with a football under his arm, led them whooping into the soda fountain, where he shouted that they had just won their last game of the season and wanted to celebrate by breaking training. The proprietor obliged without question; he sold each man a pint of booze.

The pair was sometimes borrowed for difficult raids in other cities. During his travels Izzy made a survey of the relative difficulty of obtaining a drink in various cities. It took only thirty-five seconds in New Orleans; he got into a taxi at the railroad station, asked the driver where he could buy a drink, and the driver at once produced a bottle. In Pittsburgh he had to wait eleven minutes, in Atlanta he found hard liquor in a candy store seventeen minutes after he got off the train. In other cities theater ushers, streetcar conductors, and other helpful souls saw that he did not have to wait more than half an hour before finding a drink. Washington was more difficult. There he could not find a speak-easy or anyone to direct him to one. As a last resort he asked a policeman, who gave him precise directions. Time, one hour.

Izzy and Moe served for a little more than five years, and in that time they made 4,392 arrests, of which more than 95 per cent resulted in convictions. They seized fifteen million dollars' worth of hard liquor and beer, and a tremendous quantity of stills and bar fixtures. It would seem that they would have been valuable men to retain in the prohibition service. But Izzy and Moe had a failing in the eyes of their superiors. They were not only effective but they were interesting and amusing. Their exploits made good newspaper stories, and the two agents were co-

Izzy and Moe

Dry agents Moe Smith (top) and Izzy Einstein, caricatured in a rare moment out of disguise.

operative enough to give reporters advance notice of many of their raids. Once they even staged a raid for the benefit of a well-known pastor and his Baptist congregation, timing their descent on a small speak-easy near the church so that the worshipers, leaving church, were edified to see dry agents removing barrels of liquor from the speak-easy and smashing them in the gutter.

This sort of thing enchanted the public, but it did not charm prohibition officials. In early 1925 Izzy was called to Washington by a high official of the enforcement service, who put into a few words the

complaint of the higher-ups: "You get your name in the newspaper all the time, whereas mine is hardly ever mentioned. I must ask you to remember that you are merely a subordinate and not the whole show."

Izzy and Moe tried to be self-effacing, but it was no longer possible. If they failed to give the reporters a story, the newsmen would concoct one. On November 13, 1925, they were dismissed "for the good of the service." "The service must be dignified," an official said in explaining the firing. "Izzy and Moe belong on the vaudeville stage." They probably

would have been a fair success in vaudeville; as dry agents they were superlative and no other pair of agents equaled their record of arrests, convictions, and seizures of bootleg booze.

Both men went into the insurance business and did well. Izzy wrote a book about some of the episodes that had so caught the fancy of the public and had kept reporters on their heels. It was published as an autobiography and was called *Prohibition Agent Number 1*. The public, which had once hung on his every exploit, had turned to new interests, and the book sold only five hundred and seventy-five copies.

Will Rogers

"**I** never met a man I didn't like," Will Rogers once said, and it was probably just as true that there was no one who did not like Will Rogers. The rope-twirling humorist hardly seemed to belong in the Jazz Age, but probably that era of glibness and glitter accepted a drawling cowboy as its political pundit because it desperately wanted someone who represented the honest, homespun virtues.

Will was a real small-town boy. He was born in 1879 in Indian Territory (now Oklahoma) four miles from a place called Oologah. There he grew up in what was still pretty much frontier country, riding horses, learning something about ranching, and becoming expert in handling a rope, an art that would later open the way to fame for him. His father was one-eighth Cherokee Indian and his mother one-quarter, and he was extremely proud of

his Indian blood. "My forefathers didn't come over on the *Mayflower*, but they met the boat," he once said.

Will's schooling, in a succession of Indian Territory schools, was somewhat erratic, and he claimed he never got past McGuffey's Fourth Reader, though he went to school until he was past eighteen. However, there is good evidence that his careless grammar and spelling were deliberately contrived to strengthen his image as a common man, for he was much more literate in private. After a year in a military school in Missouri, he quit school for good in 1898.

He was a cowboy in Texas for three or four years, traveled a little, and in 1902 entered show business for the first time

when he joined a Wild West show as a rider and rope expert. The folksy Rogers came into being by accident three years later, on the occasion of his first announcement of his next trick. The audience laughed at his Southwestern drawl and idioms, and Will became so angry that it was a long time before his manager was able to convince him that he should do it again. "And that's how I got to putting talk into my act."

As he developed a patter, he learned that he could take advantage of his mistakes: "A rope ain't bad to get tangled up in if it ain't around your neck" or "Well, got all my feet through but one." He began to chew gum as part of the characterization he was working for. A

174

shock of hair hung over his forehead, and from under it he would look up quizzically at his audience and make his shrewd comments in drawling, ungrammatical English. Before long the rope became secondary.

Soon he reached Broadway, and by 1915 was with the Ziegfeld Follies, then the aspiration of most entertainers. Not long after starting there and after his wife suggested he talk about what he had read, he developed his style of using topical jokes. "So I started reading about Congress," he wrote, "and believe me, I found they are funnier three hundred and sixty-five days a year than anything I ever heard of." Thereafter, his monologues always opened with a line that became famous, "Well, all I know is what I read in the papers."

Almost anyone or anything was a fair target for his wit, which was often trenchant but equally as often was based on a broad pun or similar bit of humor that failed to throw light on a problem. On five occasions President Wilson was in his audience, and he did not spare the President in his sallies, though Will admitted he was scared to death the first time. Wilson laughed heartily at jokes against himself; not so tolerant was Warren G. Harding, who grew so nettled over the humorist's remarks about his golf that he had a secretary ask Rogers to let up on it.

In the summer of 1918 Will became a movie actor with a film called *Laughing Bill Hyde* and followed this over the next two years with a dozen more, but they were not great successes and he was let go. Thereupon he made three pictures on his own and went broke. He returned to the Follies to pay off some of his debts, was back in Hollywood in 1923 making short comedies (an art form forgotten today) for Hal Roach, and spent a final season with the Follies in 1924.

In the meantime he had begun writing a weekly column for a number of newspapers in 1922. But Will had a tendency

to ramble on in print as he did when he was talking, and it was not until he was sent abroad in 1926 that he discovered his journalistic forte. In preparing his first dispatch home from London he was inhibited from wordiness by high cable rates, and he sent a message of only fifty-six words, telling in homely terms of the coming visit of Lady Astor to New York. As news it was not very important, but it set his style, and thereafter he submitted only one brief paragraph to the newspapers every day. That paragraph was soon syndicated to three hundred and fifty newspapers, with an estimated forty million readers.

Will Rogers seldom took sides, except that of the underdog, and his political and social philosophy was somewhat vague, something that bothered ardent admirers, who wanted to put him in the long tradition of incisive American humorists that included, among others, Artemus Ward, Mark Twain, and Mr. Dooley. In his first years on the stage Will had looked on the news strictly as a source of laughs, but in time, and especially after the Depression had set in, he found it less humorous. He shared the bewilderment of millions that America could go broke in the stock market crash although nothing had really changed. "Well, if somebody lost money there, why somebody else must have made it. You can't just lose money to nobody, unless you drop it somewhere and nobody ever finds it."

Politics was his favorite subject, although — or because — he once expressed his opinion by writing, "I tell you folks, all politics is applesauce." But during the 1932 campaign between Hoover and Roosevelt he became so disgusted at the way the contest was being conducted that he took a trip to South America and advised both candidates to go fishing until after election day.

Nominally a Democrat because "it's funnier to be a Democrat," he was impartial in twitting both parties for their foibles. "There is something about a Republican that you can only stand him for just so long," he wrote. "And on the other hand there is something about a Democrat that you can't stand him for quite that long."

Probably the nearest he came to being strongly partisan in his support of the Democratic party was during the first months of the Roosevelt administration, when the country felt that something was at last being done about the Depression. "The Republicans think the boat shouldent be rocked. The Democrat says, 'Rocked bedambded, why sit here and starve in it? Go ahead and turn it over, maby the bottom side has got some barnacles on it we can eat.'"

Despite his newspaper writings, Will Rogers made his greatest impact on the public as a movie actor. He returned to the screen in 1929, after pictures had learned to talk, and was an immediate hit. Among his better-known films were *State Fair*, *A Connecticut Yankee*, and *David Harum*. It is somewhat misleading to call him an actor, for in all his pictures he was Will Rogers, ducking his head, saying "Shucks," and chewing gum.

He made good-will trips abroad, wrote three or four humorous books, and was generous with both his time and money in many charitable causes. He refused ever to tell an off-color joke or to use even mild swear words in his act, and he was happily and faithfully married in an era that had begun to sneer at fidelity.

In the summer of 1935 he set out on a flight to Alaska and the Orient with his good friend aviator Wiley Post. In northernmost Alaska, near Point Barrow, the single engine of their plane faltered, and with a lone Eskimo as witness, they crashed. Both men were killed.

Isaac Soyer, in his Employment Office, *aptly portrays the apathy, during the Depression, of job seekers, who had become resigned to finding no work. On opposite page Hoover is caricatured with symbols of his two fields, engineering and government. However, when the Depression came, his expertise entirely failed him and he waited for economic forces to save the nation.*

Roots of Disaster

HERBERT HOOVER

A prevalent belief is that President Hoover had no plan to counter the effects of the Wall Street crash, that he was a do-nothing President who believed the best course was to sit and wait for normal economic forces to bring back prosperity, even though millions might suffer in the meantime. To be sure, his public statements appeared to show a blind optimism. He persisted far into the Depression in telling the country that the "fundamental business of the country . . . is on a sound and prosperous basis." What did he have in mind on March 7, 1930, when he assured the country that the crisis would be over in another sixty days? And what was he thinking, well after those sixty days had passed and the unemployment figures, even by the most optimistic estimates, had climbed to four or five million, when he assured the country that the crisis was indeed over?

But Hoover was no naïve optimist, nor was he a bland liar. The President considered the psychological state of the country of paramount importance to recovery, and he was determined to bolster confidence. Soon after the crash he told his secretary, "Ninety per cent of our difficulty in depressions is caused by fear." Throughout his Presidency Hoover tried, within his personal limitations, to dissipate this fear and to cheer up his people. In October of 1931 he went to the World Series in Philadelphia, largely because he felt that his presence there would indicate to the nation that he was unconcerned and that there was nothing for the people to worry about. When the national economy remained stagnant in spite of all his encouraging statements, he told newsman Raymond Clapper in February, 1931: "What the country needs is a good big laugh. There seems to be a condition of hysteria. If someone could get off a good joke every ten days, I think our troubles would be over." In 1932 he asked Will Rogers to think up a joke that would make people stop hoarding. And to crooner Rudy Vallee he made a promise: "If you can sing a song that will make people forget their troubles and the depression, I'll give you a medal."

But a joke or a song was very cold comfort to some of those badly hit by the Depression. Consider a typical item from the pages of *The New York Times* in September of 1932. It appeared nineteen months after Hoover had observed that the country needed a good laugh, almost a full year after he had attended the World Series to show that all was serene. The news story was brief:

DANBURY, CONN., Sept. 6. Found starving under a rude canvas shelter in a patch of woods on Flatboard Ridge, where they had lived for five days on wild berries and apples, a woman and her 16-year-old daughter were fed and clothed today by the police and placed in the city almshouse.

The woman is Mrs. John Moll, 33, and her daughter Helen, of White Plains, N. Y., who have been going from city to city looking for work since July, 1931, when Mrs. Moll's husband left her.

When the police found them they were huddled beneath a strip of canvas stretched from a boulder to the ground. Rain was dripping from the improvised shelter, which had no sides.

The President made no mention of such grim evidence that the national economy was sick, but in private he put aside his surface optimism and revealed a darker view of the nature and duration of the crisis. In November, 1929, he had told a conference of industrial and labor leaders that he viewed the crisis as being more serious than just another stock market crash, that no one could "measure the problem before us or the depth of the disaster," and that the Depression would last for some time.

Despite what his critics say, Hoover did have a specific plan for dealing with the Depression. He told the conference that steps must be taken to prevent suffering and to maintain social order and industrial peace. Labor, he said, should not be required to bear the burden of the sagging economy through wage cuts because such cuts would reduce purchasing power and would also cause labor troubles. Instead, said the President, wages should be maintained until increasing competition and lowered demand forced price levels down. And when the time did come to reduce wages, they should not be brought down faster or lower than the cost of living.

Hoover believed that if his plan were adhered to, production costs would be lowered to a point where profits could again be made. Capital values, which had been so badly inflated in the previous few years, would be brought into line with their true worth, and then the national economy could resume its progress forward and upward. "We have come out of each previous depression into a period of prosperity greater than ever before," Hoover told the group in concluding his expo-

sition. "We shall do so this time." This was his faith.

But many citizens, though they may not have lost faith, were having difficulty sharing in the American dream. One among many was Karl Monroe, a reporter looking for work in New York City early in 1930. Almost out of money and with no job in sight, he began to save the price of lodging by riding the city's subways and found that hundreds of others were doing the same thing. He discovered that he could get the most for his money — subway fare was then a nickel — on the B.M.T. trains running from Times Square to Coney Island and back in a loop, the round trip taking two hours and costing only a single fare. Repeating this ride three or four times, and napping in a corner seat, he got a tolerable night's rest. In the morning, after washing up in the men's room at Grand Central Terminal for another nickel, he was ready to join the growing army of job hunters for the new day.

When President Hoover appeared before a joint session of Congress on December 3, 1929, to deliver his State of the Union message, he elaborated upon what would in retrospect prove to be his first theory of the cause of the Depression: it was a homemade phenomenon. The President began by assuring Congress that "during the past year the Nation has continued to grow in strength. . . . The problems with which we are confronted are the problems of growth and of progress." He discussed the various other concerns of the government — foreign relations, defense, reduction of taxes, government finances, debts owed by foreign nations, and even alien government property — before he turned to the stock market crash, the business slump, and unemployment. He echoed economists and businessmen of his day in seeing business cycles as natural and inevitable: "The long upward trend of fundamental progress . . . gave rise to over-optimism as to profits, which translated itself into a wave of uncontrolled speculation in securities, resulting in the diversion of capital from business to the stock market and the inevitable crash. The natural consequences have been a reduction in the consumption of luxuries and semi-necessities by those who have met with losses, and a number of persons thrown temporarily out of employment. Prices of agricultural products dealt in upon the great markets have been affected in sympathy with the stock crash."

He called the attention of the senators and representatives to his plans for expanding public construction and to the encouragement he had given to business in its voluntary efforts to ease misery. He assured the anxious members of Congress that "we have re-established confidence." The measures taken, he said, would be "vigorously pursued until normal conditions are restored." If in hindsight the plan seems woefully inadequate, at the time it jibed with the best judgment of such pundits as economist Irving Fisher of Yale as well as with the prevailing opinion of those who exercised actual economic power in the nation: the Mellons, Thomas W. Lamont of J. P. Morgan and Company, Henry Ford, and others of that stripe.

At first there was a feeling that the brakes would hold, that optimism would help to raise the economy out of its doldrums, and that business through its voluntary and unselfish efforts could help to put things in order again. The utter failure of these first moves proved not that Hoover was incompetent but rather that his analysis was wrong and that the Depression had deeper causes than the collapse of the stock market. The truth is that production and trade in the America of the expansive Coolidge years had not been basically sound. American factories could not keep producing at a high rate because they could not sell all that they made. As a result men were laid off their jobs and wages were cut. The domestic market for durable items such as automobiles, houses, and radios shrank because sales, especially the great rise in installment sales, took away much of the purchasing power of consumers. And a program of public works within the balanced budget that Hoover insisted upon as a matter of principle was much too small to get the economy moving again. In the remaining years of his Presidency, Hoover's steadfast faith in the self-healing ability of the economy and the socially cooperative spirit of business to help relieve the Depression would meet disappointment again and again.

The government did very little during the first year or so of the Depression. Its public works program included only a few items, such as half a billion dollars for new federal buildings and sixty-five million for the construction of Boulder Dam. And there was some aid to farmers in drought areas, but only as loans to buy cattle feed. More, much more, was needed. In February, 1932, Oscar Ameringer, a Socialist publisher, appeared as a witness before a House labor subcommittee conducting hearings on the Depression and related what he had seen of the impact of the Depression during a trip through twenty states. He had been told in the state of Washington, he said, that the numerous forest fires in that region the previous summer and fall had been set largely by out-of-work lumbermen and bankrupt farmers wanting to earn a few dollars as fire fighters. His testimony contained graphic descriptions of how farmers let cotton, wheat, apples, and other crops rot in the fields because it would not pay to harvest them, while at the same time armies of ragged and hungry unemployed moved across the land looking for work.

The last thing I saw on the night I left Seattle was numbers of women searching for scraps of food in the refuse piles of the principal market of that city. . . . I talked to one man in a restaurant in Chicago. He told me of his experience in raising sheep. He said that he had killed 3,000 sheep this fall and thrown them down the canyon, because it cost $1.10 to ship a sheep, and then he would get less than a dollar for it. He said he could not afford to feed the sheep, and he would not let them starve, so he just cut their throats and threw them down the canyon.

The roads of the West and Southwest teem with hungry hitchhikers. . . . Between Clarksville and Russellville, Ark., I picked up a family. The woman was hugging a dead chicken under a ragged coat. When I asked her where she had procured the fowl, first she told me she had found it dead in the road, and then added in grim humor, "They promised me a chicken in the pot, and now I got mine."

It was natural that Hoover, faced with an increasingly angry and restless nation as the Depression grew deeper, should try to shrug off the responsibility for national misfortune. The calamity was not his fault, but to a distressed people who recalled his campaign promise of two chickens in every pot and his assurances that poverty would soon be abolished, the contrast between Coolidge prosperity and Hoover collapse was a profound one, and Hoover seemed the obvious person to blame it on. At the same time it was not politically possible for Hoover to put the blame on the two previous administrations without indicting his own Republican party—and indeed himself since he had served both Harding and Coolidge.

Toward the end of 1930 Hoover therefore advanced his second theory of the cause of the Depression: the ills of the United States derived from causes outside its borders. On October 2 of that year he addressed the American Bankers Association. "This depression is world-wide," he assured his listeners, who were themselves only too glad to be relieved of blame. "Its causes and effects lie only partly in the United States. . . . A perhaps even larger immediate cause of our depression has been the effect upon us from the collapse in prices following overproduction of important raw materials, mostly in foreign countries. . . . Their collapse has reduced the buying power of many countries. . . ." And this, the President said, resulted in "slowed-down demand for manufactured goods from Europe and ourselves, with inevitable contribution to unemployment." But, said Hoover, though the world got us into this mess, we can get out by ourselves: "Because the present depression is world-wide, does not require that we should wait upon the recovery of the rest of the world. . . . We are able in considerable degree to free ourselves of world influences and make a large measure of independent recovery because we are so remarkably self-contained."

So eagerly did Hoover follow this argument that by June, 1931, he would assert that "the main causes . . . came not from within but from outside the United States." This view, however, was blind to the fact that the Wall Street collapse had inflicted much additional pain on a Europe still struggling to recover from the physical damage and economic dislocation of the war; it refused to recognize how the Hawley-Smoot Tariff of 1930 had only caused more financial havoc. The tariff was a typical example of the self-centered, short-range thinking of the time. Early in 1929, before Hoover became the President, the House of Representatives had already begun to hear arguments for increasing the tariff, something certainly not needed during those boom days. After the crash Congress was handed a tariff bill drawn up by two extreme protectionists, Senator Reed Smoot of Utah and Congressman Willis C. Hawley of Oregon. More than one thousand members of the American Economic Association signed a statement warning the President that he must veto the bill if it was passed by Congress. If he did not, the Hawley-Smoot import duties (the highest in American history) would force the prices of foreign goods so outrageously high that Americans would stop buying European goods, with adverse effects on the entire international trade situation. But Hoover ignored the warning and gladly signed the tariff into law, using six golden pens for the ceremony.

The Hawley-Smoot Tariff just about finished off a European economy that was already faltering from the effects of the boom and the Wall Street crash. Early in

the boom large American investments abroad had played a big part in European recovery. But as the speculative frenzy on Wall Street increased, American investors preferred to use their money at home to get rich quick gambling in common stocks, and this source of funds for European growth tapered off. Even Europeans sent their money to New York on the promises of big and quick profits. Thus gold reserves in Europe were lowered, currencies were weakened, and industrial growth was hampered.

While the European economy was in this vulnerable state, the Wall Street crash came, drying up the remaining American credit and investments. A second, and equally serious, blow came a year later with the passage of the Hawley-Smoot Tariff. Unable any longer to sell to the United States, European countries could not earn the dollar exchange needed to buy farm products and other items from the United States. Most countries hastened to protect themselves by setting up their own tariff barriers.

he country hardest hit by the Hawley-Smoot Tariff was Germany, deep in debt because of huge war reparations and heavy borrowing. No longer able to borrow abroad or to sell to other countries, she tried to make one breach in the tariff barriers around her by forming a customs union with Austria in 1931. This set off a chain of reactions. The French, still bitter toward Germany, opposed even this hint of a move toward union between Austria and Germany, and demonstrated their hostility by demanding the payment of short-term credits by Austrian banks. Unable to meet the demands, the great Vienna bank the Austrian Kreditanstalt collapsed.

On the heels of this, foreign investors began a run on German banks, and at the same time the German people withdrew their savings and stored them away in the traditional cookie jar. President Hoover, to ease some of the pressure, in June, 1931, proposed a one-year moratorium on all international debts, especially the war reparations installments that Germany paid Britain and France and that those countries in turn used to make payments on their war debts to the United States. It was a wise move, but it came late, and the French backed and filled before accepting the plan, fearful that it might mean giving up reparations permanently. By that time the panic in Germany, which had subsided, had renewed, and on July 15 the German banks closed their doors.

Austrian and German currencies dropped in value as the financial systems of the two countries collapsed; as a result investors became jittery and suspicious of every national currency. Even the pound sterling of Great Britain fell under the cloud; the Bank of England had to ship large amounts of gold out of the country to those who wanted to convert their notes into yellow metal. The pound sterling, which for generations had been the very symbol of monetary stability, began to shake, and on September 20, 1931, Prime Minister Ramsey MacDonald, openly weeping, announced that Great Britain had left the gold standard. Forty countries linked to Great Britain in the sterling bloc and dependent on British trade followed England off the gold standard.

There was one more act in the drama, a wholesale rush by European countries to devaluate their currencies in order to obtain an advantage in selling abroad. Hoover blamed European countries for the Depression. He ignored that the Depression had started in the United States with the Wall Street crash and that European nations were virtually forced by high American tariffs to devaluate their currencies.

Hoover's strongest weapon for fighting the Depression—besides the voluntary cooperation among businessmen in which he believed fervently—was public works to prime the economic pump. But the President could never quite commit himself to a meaningful program of public construction. His first request for an appropriation for such a purpose, in December, 1930, had been for a maximum of one hundred and fifty million dollars, not enough to do any economic pump priming. His reluctance to resort to public works stemmed, for one thing, from his slowness to admit that the Depression was there to stay. When a delegation of citizens came in June, 1930, to ask him to increase the amount of federal public works at once, Hoover assured them that nothing of the sort was needed because unemployment was dropping and business improving. "Gentlemen," he said, "you have come sixty days too late. The depression is over." Furthermore, he was obsessed with a balanced budget. As the national economy became more and more sluggish, tax income became less and less. The deficit for 1931 was very near a billion dollars. Under such conditions the President considered

it almost heresy to borrow money for public works or any kind of relief. "Prosperity cannot be restored by raids upon the public treasury," he said in December of 1930.

Hoover was at last forced to some dramatic action, and in December, 1931, he proposed to Congress the creation of the Reconstruction Finance Corporation (R.F.C.), a government institution to lend money to banks, railroads, and industries. Its aim was to help businesses get their affairs in order and hire back workers, and thus to help set the economy moving once more. Hoover did not like the idea of the government's lending money on a large scale, but he had been argued into it by Eugene Meyer, governor of the Federal Reserve Board. The R.F.C. was approved by Congress in January, 1932. Peppery little Congressman Fiorello La Guardia of New York was skeptical; he promptly named the operation "millionaire's dole."

 nder its chairman, Eugene Meyer, and its president, Charles G. Dawes, the R.F.C. moved rather cautiously; in its first year it used only three-fourths of its two billion dollars. It showed a partiality for banks and trust companies over industries, and it favored large enterprises, though Hoover had specified the reverse at the signing of the bill: it was not, he said, "created for the aid of big industries or big banks." But the worst aspect of the R.F.C. operations was that favoritism, and worse, was being shown in the granting of loans. In June, 1932, Dawes suddenly resigned as president of the R.F.C. to return to his own bank; a few weeks later his bank received a loan of ninety million dollars. John Nance Garner, Speaker of the House, proposed a resolution requiring the R.F.C. to name the banks it had given loans to. Both bankers and Republicans argued that when the public learned that a bank had asked for a loan, its credit would be hurt. To which Garner replied, "If the truth scares people, let it come."

Though the R.F.C. propped up railroads teetering on the verge of bankruptcy and staved off a number of bank failures, it did very little to prime the economic pump. For bankers the R.F.C. was a way to save themselves, not to help others. Railroads and utilities cut operations despite promises to the R.F.C. to the contrary. The industries that might have employed large numbers of men remained idle. The economy continued to stagnate.

Hit worse than industry or commerce were the farmers because their depression dated back to 1921. Congress had tried to give the farmer a leg up in 1924 and again in 1928 with the McNary-Haugen Farm Relief Bill, which would have empowered the government to buy up farm surpluses in years of heavy production and either hold them until prices rose or sell them abroad. Both times Coolidge vetoed the bill; among his reasons was that it legalized price fixing. Overproduction and low prices continued; the farmer felt none of the prosperity of the Twenties, and when the Depression came, he was one of the first and worst sufferers. Farm prices fell much faster and further than the prices of the things the farmer had to buy. Wheat prices dropped below forty cents a bushel and corn almost to thirty, cotton was down near a nickel a pound, and beef at the Chicago stockyards brought only a bit more than five cents a pound. Farmers who had borrowed when prices were three times as high could not possibly pay off their mortgages; very often they did not get enough to make harvesting crops worthwhile or to pay the expense of shipping livestock to market. Many Corn Belt farmers used their crop for fuel as the only way to get some return out of it.

he Federal Farm Board, set up by Hoover in 1929 before the crash to help farmers market surpluses, had begun in January of 1930 to urge a program of reduced production as a way of forcing farm prices up. Plant less wheat, plant less cotton, raise fewer cattle, the board urged. But the program was purely voluntary, and most farmers, fearing that others would not reduce their planting, planted as much as before. Indeed, some increased their acreage on the chance that they might cash in if others planted less and prices went up. In any event, the President did not like the idea of federal control over farm production, and by the middle of 1931 attempts to help the farm economy were all but abandoned.

Friends urged the President to strike a better public pose. "I can't be a Theodore Roosevelt," he said, or "I have no Wilsonian qualities." The White House usher, Ike Hoover, noted, "There was always a frown on his face and a look of worry. . . ."

Former President Calvin Coolidge was occupying some of the hours of his retirement by writing a syndicated newspaper column, and one of his more trenchant observations on the Depression was, "When more and more people are thrown out of work, unemployment results." And unemployment was certainly resulting: an estimated four and a half million persons out of work in 1930, as against one and a half million in 1929. However, the fact that one and a half million workers had no jobs in a boom year like 1929 shows how false is the belief that everyone in America (except possibly the farmers) was prosperous and busy until the crash came. On the contrary, considerable segments of labor were having it none too good during the era of hip flasks and whoopee. Industrialization and technological change had thrown many men out of work. The short skirts and skimpy clothing that meant emancipation to young females in the Twenties brought deep trouble to the textile mill towns of the South. Even during the best of the boom times there was much unemployment in the mill towns, and textile workers lived in conditions of almost unbelievable squalor. Unemployment was not limited to the South; in Philadelphia, to name just one place, more than 10 per cent of the city's wage earners were unable to find jobs. So when the crash came and layoffs started, there were many who had worked only fitfully and had scant savings to fall back on. It did not take long for serious hardship to become widespread among such vulnerable people.

Coolidge had explained what caused unemployment; from his retirement he also proclaimed the cure. "The final solution of unemployment," he said in 1931, "is work." But there was no work. From almost four and a half million in 1930, the number of unemployed jumped to eight million in 1931, twelve million in 1932, and almost thirteen million the following year. And Hoover did virtually nothing to provide work for the jobless, who were queuing up in soup lines and sleeping in doorways across the nation. Nor did he believe in direct relief; he felt that it would somehow injure the spirit of the recipient. His action after the 1930 drought in the Southwest was typical. He approved a congressional appropriation of forty-five million dollars to be used for loans for cattle feed but opposed the appropriation of only twenty-five million to feed farmers' families because, he said, it was the duty of the Red Cross to do that. When Congress did vote twenty million dollars for the relief of farm families, the President, though a kind man, made the condition that the money should go as a loan rather than a gift because, he said later, if the federal government had given the money as a dole it "would have injured the spiritual responses of the American people. . . . We are dealing with intangibles of life and ideals. . . . A voluntary deed is infinitely more precious to our national ideals and spirit than a thousandfold poured from the Treasury."

Hoover appears to have overlooked the other side of the coin: how poverty and joblessness and the loss of hope can sear the human soul. A newspaperman, left without a job or money at the age of fifty-five, described his feelings in the May 13, 1931, issue of the *Nation:*

I should like to find out at what stage of your poverty other people realize or sense it, and pass you by as one no longer interesting or useful to them. You wear the same suit, more carefully brushed and pressed than ever before to conceal your poverty. You walk just as cockily. You know as much; you know a lot more, in fact—things you didn't suspect or believe before. I guess, after all, it's the droop in the shoulders, the look in your eyes—furtive, expectant, resentful.

The nights are the worst; the time when all you can see is the unseen. You've done everything humanly possible to avert the inevitable. You've gone over your life-insurance policies, to be sure they are all incontestable after the first year. You've taken out additional accident insurance. You realize that for the first time in your rather carefree, indifferent life you are worth more dead than alive—a good deal more.

Yet slowly and reluctantly Hoover was forced to recognition; finally, in 1932, against all his instincts he compromised. For by the summer of 1932 masses of desperate citizens, as well as local and state governments, were imploring Washington for aid.

John Garner of Texas demanded federal loans for the needy. The American Federation of Labor wanted appropriations to pay teachers in bankrupt cities. A chorus of voices urged revival of the United States Employment Service, defunct since the war. Hoover looked coldly on these proposals, but he was driven in July, 1932, to accept a bill that authorized the Reconstruction Finance Corporation to lend $300,000,000 to states for relief and to make $1,500,000,000 available for public works.

But though Hoover approved the bill, his comments on it proved that he had not changed his basic philosophy. "These loans," he said, "are to be based upon absolute need and evidence of financial exhaustion. I do not expect any state to resort to it except as a last extremity." Governor Gifford Pinchot of Pennsyl-

vania asked for forty-five million dollars for his state after pointing out that even sixty million would give each of the million jobless persons in Pennsylvania only thirteen cents' worth of food a day for a year. The R.F.C. granted a loan of eleven million dollars.

Governor Pinchot knew firsthand what happened when people went absolutely stone-broke. In the spring of 1932, only a few months before the governor applied to the R.F.C. for a loan, private relief had broken down in Pennsylvania's largest city. On May 9, 1932, the executive secretary of the Community Council of Philadelphia told a subcommittee of the Senate Committee on Manufactures what had occurred when relief funds in Philadelphia were completely used up:

On April 11 we mailed to families the last food orders which they received from private funds. It was not until April 22 that the giving of aid to families from public funds began, so that there was a period of about 11 days when many families received nothing. . . . We made an intensive study of 91 families to find out what happened when the food orders stopped. . . .

One woman said she borrowed 50 cents from a friend and bought stale bread for 3½ cents per loaf, and that is all they had for eleven days except for one or two meals. . . .

One woman went along the docks and picked up vegetables that fell from the wagons. Sometimes the fish vendors gave her fish at the end of the day. On two different occasions this family was without food for a day and a half.

One family had nothing the day the food order stopped until 9 o'clock at night. Then the mother went to a friend's house and begged for a loaf of bread. This woman finally got two day's work at 75 cents a day. She bought a little meat and made a stew from vegetables picked up which they cooked over again every day to prevent its spoiling. . . .

Still another family thinking to get as much as possible with their last food order bought potatoes and for 11 days lived only on them. . . .

I should also like to say that when we talk to people who ask about unemployment they say, "Well, people manage to get along somehow or other, don't they? You do not have very many people who really drop dead of starvation." That is perfectly true. Actually, death from starvation is not a frequent occurrence. . . . This is because people live in just the way that I have described. They live on inadequacies, and because they live on inadequacies the thing does not become dramatic and we do not hear about it. Yet the cost in human suffering is just as great as if they starved to death overnight.

The stories from Philadelphia were not unique. There were hungry people everywhere, like the Kentucky miner who in June of 1932 related that since the previous January he and his family had been living mainly on wild greens: wild onions, violet leaves, forget-me-nots, and the like. Yet with hunger so pervasive, after a year the R.F.C. had lent out only thirty million of the three hundred million dollars made available in July, 1932, to supplement local relief. The agency's slow pace was a reflection of the President's own dark and gloomy forebodings about anything that smacked of relief or that made demands on the federal treasury for individual needs.

Also—and this seems very hard to understand— there is some evidence that the President just was not aware of the dimensions of the national tragedy. On several occasions he made public letters from his Surgeon-General that appeared to show that the American people were healthier than they had been during the years of prosperity. And yet in December, 1932, Grace Abbott, chief of the Children's Bureau of the Department of Labor, reported that 20.5 per cent of the school children in New York City who were examined were found to be suffering from malnutrition and that in the South there was an increase in pellagra because the people could not buy proper food. When these and other accounts of the effects of hunger were brought to the President's attention, he would not even discuss them.

However, Hoover deserves better of history than he has received. Viewing the world as he did, against the background of the rising despotisms of Italy, Germany, and Russia, he sought in the midst of the maelstrom to preserve the true features of American political democracy. Though a Republican and a businessman's President, he was concerned with political rather than economic issues, with moral survival rather than material gain.

Hoover exhausted every traditional remedy, and then in a desperate attempt to relieve the distress about him he acted counter to his most cherished beliefs. He failed because he was inherently unable to take any really new and bold steps. His principal innovation, the R.F.C., was sound and would not only prove to be a major precedent for the New Deal, which followed, but would be continued by the Roosevelt administration in substantially the same form. But even the R.F.C. accomplished only a small part of what it might have done to loosen the cold grip of the Depression during Hoover's administration. It was a good weapon, but it needed to be wielded forcefully, and Hoover, by temperament and philosophy, was unable to be forceful.

Decisively defeated at the polls in November, Hoover left the national scene four months later. Millions who scorned and ridiculed him during those last months had voted for him as the prosperity President in 1928.

After the Crash

The Roaring Twenties did not quite make it through the decade. In October, 1929, the bottom fell out of the stock market, and within months the Coolidge Prosperity was all but forgotten. Banks failed, mortgages were foreclosed, and unemployment was rampant; bread lines formed throughout the country in grim testimony to the state of the economy. While President Hoover clung stubbornly to his policy of noninterference and reiterated assurances that "with continued unity of effort we shall rapidly recover," the nation sank ever deeper into the pit of depression. By 1931 over eight millions were jobless, and the President did nothing. Any direct federal relief, he asserted, would have "injured the spiritual responses of the American people." To men without jobs, without food, clothing, or shelter for their families, that could hardly have been a very comforting philosophy. Their "spiritual responses" were written on the faces of men like the one above.

The Happy Warrior

Alfred E. Smith was urbane, witty, honest, progressive, and (unfortunately for his presidential aspirations) Catholic. Running against Republican Herbert Hoover in 1928, "the Happy Warrior" (in motorcade left) fought valiantly for the Democratic party and for repeal of prohibition. But his campaign appealed mainly to the urban population (he carried the nation's twelve largest cities) and left most of the country cold. As H. L. Mencken put it: "Those who fear the Pope outnumber those who are tired of the Anti-Saloon League." And Smith had other things working against him: his connections with the machine politicians of Tammany Hall, his association with the flamboyant, none-too-scrupulous New York Mayor Jimmy Walker, and the Republican prosperity. As Will Rogers observed: "You can't lick this Prosperity thing; even the fellow that hasn't got any is all excited over the idea."

ART YOUNG, *NEW LEADER*

Prosperity's Heir

Herbert C. Hoover was conservative, Protestant, Middle Western, and the man America wanted. He was, as he described himself, just "a boy from a country village, without inheritance or influential friends" (the inheritance and influence of the Coolidge prosperity notwithstanding). Campaigning in his home state of Iowa (below) or whistle-stopping with his wife (opposite), he told the people what they wanted to hear: "Given a chance to go forward with the policies of the last eight years . . . poverty will be banished from this nation." There were a few skeptics (the cartoon above is a 1928 gibe by the Socialist party), but most Americans were optimists, and Hoover rode the crest of prosperity into the White House.

Black Tuesday

The Panic began on Thursday, October 24. The scene at the Stock Exchange was pandemonium: brokers swamped the floor with heavy orders to sell, hysterical spectators mobbed the visitors' gallery (among the calmer observers was Winston Churchill, passing through New York), and crowds gathered outside in utter disbelief (above). The market steadied somewhat on Friday and Saturday, but on Monday it dipped again. By Tuesday, the twenty-ninth, there was no longer any doubt about the extent of the damage. Opposite, lights burned late on Wall Street (J. P. Morgan offices are at bottom center) as employees worked through the night to record the disastrous transactions of that Tuesday.

Christmas Greetings
New Years Joy
But Buy Some Apples
And Help This Boy

The Face of Hunger

As the ranks of the unemployed grew, President Hoover remained adamant in his refusal to provide emergency relief. It was, he believed, strictly a state and local responsibility. Local organizations, however, could not begin to cope adequately with the situation. In many cities only the most destitute families were accepted for welfare, and the childless or single were ineligible altogether. Some of the jobless managed to earn a few cents a day shining shoes or selling apples. However, Hoover later said, and possibly believed: "Many persons left their jobs for the more profitable one of selling apples." Still, it saved a few from the humiliation of charity. As Joseph Heffernan wrote of his observations as mayor of Youngstown, Ohio, ". . . I have seen thousands of these defeated, discouraged, hopeless men and women, cringing and fawning as they come to ask for public aid. It is a spectacle of national degeneration."

Louis Ribak's Home Relief Station *(above) shows the degradation of private charity and the humiliating interrogation imposed upon relief applicants. Since there was no federal relief program, local organizations depended on posters like that of Rollin Kirby, right, to prick the consciences of the more fortunate. The apple seller (opposite) became a symbol of hard times.*

OVERLEAF: *A settlement of unemployed in Seattle, Washington. Dubbed Hoovervilles, such shantytowns became common in large cities during the Depression.*

In 1930 Bruce Bliven, a reporter for *The New Republic*, described a scene at the Municipal Lodging House in New York City: "There is a line of men, three or sometimes four abreast, a block long, and wedged tightly together—so tightly that no passer-by can break through. For this compactness there is a reason: those at the head of this grey-black human snake will eat tonight; those farther back probably won't." Similar lines formed daily in almost every American city. Those who did not make it to a shelter slept in doorways, on park benches, or in subways. On October 7, 1932, *The New York Times* reported the arrest of fifty-four men for idling in a subway. Most considered their arrest a stroke of luck—free food and lodging for at least a night. There were other lines: queues of the still hopeful at employment agencies, where there might be dozens of applicants for a single job. (In 1931 Russia advertised in the United States for skilled workers—there were over 100,000 applicants for 6,000 jobs.) The unlucky joined bread lines. The photograph below shows the bleakness of a soup line in Kansas City, Missouri, and Reginald Marsh's *Holy Name Mission*, right, suggests the meager camaraderie of the down-and-out.

"when you can't get out from under"

George Grosz's Shoeshine, *above, evokes the despondency of the Depression.*

Perhaps no one has captured the spirit of the Thirties with such immediacy and poignancy as the author and radio commentator Studs Terkel. Using the technique he developed in his book Division Street: America, *Terkel has interviewed people from all walks of life and recorded their memories and impressions of the chaotic and painful years of the Depression in* Hard Times: An Oral History of The Great Depression, *published in 1970, from which the following selections are taken.*

One of the people Terkel interviewed was Oscar Heline, seventy-eight, who owned a farm in northwestern Iowa.

The struggles people had to go through are almost unbelievable. A man lived all his life on a given farm, it was taken away from him. One after the other. After the foreclosure, they got a deficiency judgment. Not only did he lose the farm, but it was impossible for him to get out of debt.

The farmers became desperate. It got so a neighbor wouldn't buy from a neighbor, because the farmer didn't get any of it. It went to the creditors. And it wasn't enough to satisfy them. . . . First, they'd take your farm, then they took your livestock, then your farm machinery. Even your household goods. And they'd move you off. The farmers were almost united. We had penny auction sales. Some neighbor would bid a penny and give it back to the owner.

Grain was being burned. It was cheaper than coal. Corn was being burned. A county just east of here,

they burned corn in their courthouse all winter '32, '33. You couldn't hardly buy groceries for corn. It couldn't pay the transportation. In South Dakota, the county elevator listed corn as minus three cents. *Minus* three cents a bushel. If you wanted to sell 'em a bushel of corn, you had to bring in three cents. They couldn't afford to handle it. Just think what happens when you can't get out from under. . . .

For some, there was nothing to do but move on. Cesar Chavez, today leader

198

of the United Farm Workers of America, recounted what happened when his family lost their farm in the North Gila Valley in southwestern Arizona.

We all of us climbed into an old Chevy that my dad had. And then we were in California, and migratory workers. There were five kids—a small family by those standards. It must have been around '36. I was about eight. Well, it was a strange life. We had been poor, but we knew every night there was a bed *there*, and that *this* was our room. . . . But that all of a sudden changed. . . .

When we moved to California, we would work after school. Sometimes we wouldn't go. "Following the crops," we missed much school. Trying to get enough money to stay alive the following winter, the whole family picking apricots, walnuts, prunes. We were pretty new, we had never been migratory workers. We were taken advantage of quite a bit. . . .

Anywhere we stopped, there was a labor contractor offering all kinds of jobs and good wages, and we were always deceived by them and we always went. Trust them.

Coming into San Jose, not finding—being lied to, that there was work. We had no money at all, and had to live on the outskirts of town under a bridge by a dry creek. That wasn't really unbearable. What was unbearable was so many families living just a quarter of a mile away. You know how kids are. They'd bring in those things that really hurt us quite a bit. Most of those kids were middle-class families.

Even the middle classes often had to scrape. Robert Gard, a professor at the University of Wisconsin, recalled his college years during the Depression.

I set out for the University of Kansas on a September morning with $30 that I'd borrowed from my local bank. I had one suit and one necktie and one pair of shoes. . . . My father, a country lawyer, had taken as a legal fee a 1915 Buick touring car. It was not in particularly good condition, but it was good enough to get me there. It fell to pieces and it never got back home anymore.

I had no idea how long the $30 would last, but it sure would have to go a long way because I had nothing else. The semester fee was $22, so that left me $8 to go. Fortunately, I got a job driving a car for the dean of the law school. That's how I got through the first year. . . .

One friend of mine came to college equipped. He had an old Model T Ford Sedan, about a 1919 model. He had this thing fitted up as a house. He lived in it all year long. He cooked and slept and studied inside that Model T Ford Sedan. How he managed I will never know. I once went there for dinner. He cooked a pretty good one on a little stove he had in this thing. He was a brilliant student. I don't know where he is now, but I shouldn't be surprised if he's the head of some big corporation. . . .

The weak ones I don't suppose really survived. There were many breakdowns. From malnutrition very likely. I know there were students actually starving.

Some of them engaged in strange occupations. There was a biological company that would pay a penny apiece for cockroaches. They needed these in research, I guess. Some students went cockroach hunting every night. They'd box 'em and sell them to this firm.

I remember the feverish intellectual discussion we had. There were many new movements. On the literary scene, there was something called the Proletarian Novel. There was the Federal Theater and the Living Newspaper. For the first time, we began to get socially conscious. We began to wonder about ourselves and our society.

We were mostly farm boys and, to some extent, these ideas were alien to us. We had never really thought about them before. But it was a period of necessity. It brought us face to face with these economic problems and the rest. . . . All in all, a painful time, but a glorious time.

New York's Broadway was not so glorious in those days. The producer and director Herman Shumlin, whose works include Grand Hotel, The Little Foxes, The Children's Hour, *and* Inherit the Wind, *described the scene to Terkel in poignant and vivid detail.*

Two or three blocks along Times Square, you'd see these men, silent, shuffling along in line. Getting this handout of coffee and doughnuts, dealt out from great trucks, Hearst's New York *Evening Journal*, in large letters, painted on the sides. Shabby clothes, but you could see they had been pretty good clothes.

Their faces, I'd stand and watch their faces, and I'd see that flat, opaque, expressionless look which spelled, for me, human disaster. On every corner, there'd be a man selling apples. Men in the theater, whom I'd known, who had responsible positions. . . .

One man I had known lived in New Rochelle. Proud of his nice family, his wife and three children. He had been a treasurer in the theater which housed a play I had managed in 1926. . . .

It was in 1931 that I ran into him on the street. After I had passed him, I realized who it was. I turned and ran after him. He had averted his eyes as he went by me. I grabbed hold of him. There was a deadness in his eyes. He just muttered: Good to see you. He didn't want to talk to me. I followed him and made him come in with me and sit down.

He told me that his wife had kicked him out. His children had had such contempt for him 'cause he couldn't pay the rent, he just had to leave, to get out of the house. He lived in perpetual shame. This was, to me, the most cruel thing of the Depression. Almost worse than not having food. Accepting the idea that you were just no good. No matter what you'd been before.

TOO MUCH OIL

TOO MUCH WHEAT

TOO MUCH POVERTY

FREE SOUP

Coming north during the Depression, the young novelist Thomas Wolfe was repelled by the "scenes of suffering, violence, oppression, hunger, cold, and the filth and poverty going on unheeded in a world in which the rich were still rotten with their wealth. . . ." Perhaps the most discouraging thing about those years was the picture of dire poverty in a land of plenty. As Daniel R. Fitzpatrick suggests in his cartoon above, vast stores of food and resources went to waste as the hungry stood in bread lines. Men cried for work, but industry could not provide jobs when there was no profitable market for the goods. The economy stagnated, no one could get the wheels turning, and men like the unemployed hand opposite sank ever deeper into despair.

A Few Brave Buildings

Not everything came to a halt in the 30's. In New York, Rockefeller Center rose across from St. Patrick's Cathedral (above), and the Empire State Building (opposite) opened in 1931. The George Washington Bridge linked New York and New Jersey in a graceful span of the Hudson River, and on the Colorado, Boulder Dam (later renamed Hoover) was completed in 1936. But these and other scattered projects were not enough to lift America out of the doldrums.

PIERCE ARROW

SURVIVAL VALUE • A PIERCE-ARROW FUNDAMENT.

ASK THE MAN WHO OWNS ONE

End of Elegance

The automobile industry continued to produce luxury models in the early 30's, though there were few who could afford them. The gold-trimmed Packard, bottom left, was advertised as a paragon of "practical usefulness," while the $3,650 Pierce-Arrow, left, was touted for its "survival value." The public, however, was far more practical and survival-conscious than the industry might have wished. While there were still some who could afford the 1932 Chevrolet sedan, above, or the six-cylinder Oldsmobile touring car, below, others were settling for a modest tin lizzie (in 1931 the twenty millionth Ford rolled off the assembly line) or, more often, making their old car do. It was not a time for luxury, and many of the elegant brands of the 20's (Stutz Bearcat, Marmon, Pierce-Arrow, the air-cooled Franklin) did not survive the Depression.

Hollywood Finds Its Voice

Hollywood continued to make pictures as the Depression settled in, experimenting with the possibilities of sound and other new techniques. And the public still went to the movies, one place where they could escape from bleak reality for only twenty-five cents. Opposite is Marlene Dietrich in *Blonde Venus*, a glamour film of 1932. Above is a scene from *The Gold Diggers of Broadway*, a musical made in 1929 on the eve of the crash; its production numbers were filmed in Technicolor. Below left are Harry Carey, Duncan Renaldo, and Edwina Booth in *Trader Horn* (1931), the first sound picture made on location in Africa. Below are Charles Farrell and Janet Gaynor in *The Man Who Came Back* (1930); the pair were a popular romantic team of the silents who bridged the gap to talking pictures.

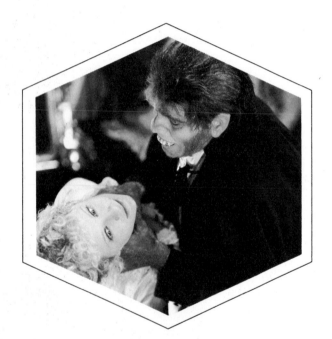

Movies offered hours of diversion (the double feature was introduced in 1931) and plenty of variety. Above, Wallace Beery and Marie Dressler (with Marjorie Rambeau in background) play a brawling, boozy couple in the 1930 comedy Min and Bill, and opposite, Joan Crawford is Clark Gable's mistress in Possessed, 1931, a rags-to-riches romance of high life and martyrdom designed to please the ladies. Gangster movies and horror films were popular; at left, Frederic March forces his attentions on Miriam Hopkins in the 1932 thriller Dr. Jekyll and Mr. Hyde, and at top, James Cagney dodges a bullet as Edward Woods gets it in The Public Enemy, 1931. Below, Paul Muni heads the line-up in I Am a Fugitive from a Chain Gang, 1932. Muni's portrayal of a jobless veteran framed for robbery was a forceful indictment of some of the abuses of the Southern penal system.

All's well on the Ark in a scene from Marc Connelly's hit Green Pastures, *below.* At left, Ethel Merman and Al Siegal rehearse a number from Girl Crazy, *and above,* Alla Nazimova and Earle Larimore in O'Neill's Mourning Becomes Electra.

Joyce Carey, Dorothy Mathews, and Katharine Cornell played in the highly successful The Barretts of Wimpole Street.

The Broadway Season

Broadway had its hits, too. *Green Pastures* and *Of Thee I Sing* were the big successes of 1930 and 1931. The latter, a biting political satire (with Victor Moore as Vice President solemnly proclaiming, "Posterity is just around the corner"), was awarded the Pulitzer Prize for drama in 1932. Katharine Cornell packed them in at the Empire Theatre as the sweetheart of poet Robert Browning (played by Brian Aherne) in *The Barretts of Wimpole Street* in 1931. In October of that year Eugene O'Neill's lengthy but highly acclaimed trilogy, *Mourning Becomes Electra*, with Alla Nazimova, Alice Brady, and Earle Larimore in the leads, was presented by the Theatre Guild.

Diversions

Even the worst years of the Depression were not without fads and diversions. Miniature golf swept the country in 1930; vacant lots (and the roof of at least one skyscraper, at left) blossomed with courses, and a miniature golf tournament was held in Chicago (above). Card playing was popular—card sales rose during the Depression—and a national craze for the relatively new game of contract bridge led to a match (opposite) between Ely Culbertson (left) and his wife on one side and Sidney Lenz (center) and Oswald Jacoby on the other. The Culbertsons won the match, which was broadcast nationwide. Jigsaw puzzles also were highly popular in the early 30's, and at parties people hunched over tables chatting and fitting little pieces together. It was an inexpensive way to entertain.

212

Farmers in Revolt

Farmers were among the hardest hit by the Depression. In 1932, when the national agricultural income had dropped to less than half of what it had been in 1929, farmers began to take action. In Iowa a robust sexagenarian Milo Reno organized the Farmers' Holiday Association, whose aim was to withhold produce until prices rose to reasonable levels. Wielding clubs and pitchforks, they set up roadblocks and turned back cars and trucks bound for market (opposite above). Strikes spread to other areas. Dairy farmers took more aggressive action, seizing milk shipments, prying open the cans, and dumping them along roads or railways (left). Meanwhile, hundreds of farmers were losing everything they owned as banks foreclosed on mortgages and homesteads were auctioned off. It was not uncommon for friends and neighbors to converge on such a sale, scare off any outsiders, and buy back the farmer's holdings for him—a quarter for a horse or cow, a dime or a nickel for a hog. Judges and local authorities in foreclosure cases were sometimes threatened with violence, and in one instance an Iowa judge was dragged from the courtroom by an angry mob, choked, and forced to kiss the American flag (above). It was perhaps unfair to blame a judge or sheriff for simply doing his duty, but where else could a distressed farmer direct his rage?

216

The People Protest

Anger and frustration over the deepening Depression became increasingly evident in outbursts of violence. To be sure, they were sporadic; most people took their plight stoically, but occasionally resentments — the bitterness of being thrown out of work after years of dedicated service, indignation over lack of adequate relief programs — were too much to be contained. Citizens began to demonstrate, and riots sometimes ensued. One of the worst occurred in March, 1932, when some three thousand men marched on the Ford plant in Dearborn, Michigan, to demand jobs. Armed only with a petition, the men were met at the city limits by policemen with guns and tear gas and Ford firemen with high-pressure hoses. When the protesters refused to turn back, the authorities opened up — first with tear gas, then with torrents of icy water, and finally with revolvers and a machine gun. The toll was four dead and many wounded. Two days later thousands of Detroit workers marched in the victims' funeral parade behind a red banner with the slogan "Ford gave bullets for bread." As early as March, 1930, a confrontation in New York's Union Square (depicted by Peter Hopkins, left) had broken out between police and Communist-organized protesters demanding unemployment relief. According to the New York *World*, women were "struck in the face with blackjacks, boys beaten by gangs of seven and eight policemen, and an old man [was] backed into a doorway and knocked down time after time. . . ." The scene was becoming familiar in almost every major American city, and people were talking uneasily about Communism and revolution.

Clockwise: veterans on the Capitol lawn awaiting news of the bonus bill; commanding General Douglas MacArthur (foreground) and U. S. Army troops; troops and veterans in gas barrage; veterans and mock graves of former Secretary of the Treasury Andrew Mellon, Hoover, and the bonus.

The Bonus Army

In the early summer of 1932 some 20,000 jobless veterans descended on the nation's Capital. Setting up a makeshift camp on the mud flats of the Anacostia River, the Bonus Expeditionary Force, as they called themselves, settled in to dramatize their plea for immediate payment of a bonus due them in the year 1945. An orderly group, they maintained a strict military discipline (bugle calls, chow lines, K.P.'s, liaison officers) and had no use for Communists ("Eyes front—not left!" was their motto). But neither determination nor discipline helped their cause. On June 17 the Senate killed a bonus bill designed to meet their demands. Some of the veterans left, but the majority, many with families and nowhere to go, stayed on. Their presence, however, was something of an embarrassment to the administration, and on July 28 President Hoover called in the United States Army, which forced out the ragged bonus army with cavalry, tanks, bayonets, and tear gas and set fire to its encampment. It was a tragic and shameful episode.

In the three years following the stock market collapse, nearly a quarter of the nation's banks were forced to close. Scenes like the one above were commonplace as rumors of bank failures sent depositors rushing to withdraw their savings. Often it was too late.

The reporter Marquis W. Childs described one such closing: "There was no warning; in the middle of the banking day the doors were closed by the examiners. . . . Depositors, stunned and disbelieving, gathered in small groups to read the notice on the door. . . ."

Enter
Roosevelt

An astute strategist and campaigner, Roosevelt
(with nonvoter, top) managed to bury his rivalry
with Al Smith (speaking at 1932 Democratic rally
above) long enough for a show of solidarity. An
apple vendor and a vacant shop flanking the
Hoover Club of Eastern Pennsylvania (at left)
help to explain the crushing Republican defeat.

After three years of Herbert Hoover and depression, the country, in 1932, was decidedly ready for a change. Yet the Republicans renominated the President; they could hardly do otherwise without discrediting the party's leadership and formula for recovery. It was not, however, an optimistic campaign. Hoover recognized the problem as well as anyone. "We are opposed," he told his secretary on election eve, "by six million un-employed, ten thousand bonus marchers, and ten-cent corn." The Democrats, on the other hand, had a clean slate and a new face: the smiling, confident New York governor, Franklin Delano Roosevelt. Roosevelt promised action and a change of direction. In a campaign speech in Georgia he said that "the country demands bold, persistent experimentation. . . . Above all, try something." The voters apparently agreed.

The ride of Franklin Roosevelt and Herbert Hoover from the White House to the inauguration at the Capitol in 1933 was certainly one of the gloomiest on record. Machine guns lined the route, and the defeated Hoover repulsed Roosevelt's attempts to make conversation and stared glumly at his hands. On opposite page is the cover from a less-than-memorable 1933 campaign song.

"Hunger Is Not Debatable"

The morning of March 4, 1933, twelve years after the invalid Woodrow Wilson had escorted Warren Harding to his investiture, an emotionally shattered and wholly discredited champion of Republican normalcy sat beside a joke-cracking, self-confident Democrat who had struck down the pretension to normalcy. Herbert Hoover — his works, his ideals — had been blown away by the cold Depression winds that had swept the world; Franklin D. Roosevelt, apostle of action, of the new, inherited the nation.

The two rode along in the black limousine under clearing skies, but the mood of the city was somber and exactly matched the temper of the nation: dull, devoid of hope, confidence in the future apparently gone beyond recovery. Within the official car conversation, for all Roosevelt's jaunty style, soon lapsed into silence. There was great bitterness between the two men, at least on the loser's side. When Roosevelt had called on Hoover the day before, after previously refusing to endorse Hoover's policies by uniting with the lame-duck President in joint proclamations on the growing financial crisis, he remarked amiably that he would understand it if the outgoing President, with so much to do, did not return the call. "Mr. Roosevelt," Hoover snapped, "when you have been in Washington as long as I have been, you will understand that the President of the United States calls on nobody."

Security precautions along the route were especially stringent. Roosevelt, though coming to office with the promise of change and betterment for the country, had been the target of a would-be assassin's bullet only three weeks before in Miami, where the crazed assailant, an unemployed bricklayer, had tried to shoot the President-elect and instead had mortally wounded Anton Cermak, the mayor of Chicago.

In this America, though the inaugural ritual seemed comfortingly normal and traditional, things had become badly unglued. America, for so long fortune's darling, for more than a century hope and refuge of the teeming wretched of the earth, had at last run out of luck. The gross national product, worth $104,400,000,000 in 1929, had skidded to $60,000,000,000 in 1932. American Telephone and Telegraph had fallen too, from a high of $310\frac{1}{4}$ to $69\frac{3}{4}$. Sears, Roebuck was down from 181 to $9\frac{7}{8}$, reflecting the catastrophic slide of the purchasing power of the bankrupt farmers.

The outgoing President could speak of a mere crisis of confidence, eternally voicing the litany of hope, that prosperity was just around the corner, but the nation had made a favorite song of a gloomier refrain, "Brother, Can You Spare a Dime?"

Few could. By that Saturday, March 4, 1933, bank holidays had been declared in more than half of the states and now virtually all the other banks were closing as panicky depositors demanded their savings, often the fruits of a lifetime of toil, and the bankers ran out of money. The American banking system was on the verge of total collapse. Where would men find the cash to tide themselves over until Monday? And on Monday, what then?

Arriving at the inaugural stand, Roosevelt was helped forward on the arm of his son James. The poliomyelitis that had struck him down twelve years before had left his legs too withered to carry his leonine head and mighty torso unaided.

The distinguished Chief Justice of the United States, Charles Evans Hughes (a moderate on the Supreme Court, who would nonetheless clash with the President before long), duly administered the oath, which Roosevelt repeated with his hand on an old Dutch Bible, an heirloom in his family.

Then Roosevelt, hatless and coatless in the chill wind, as if to emphasize to the nation that despite his infirmity he remained in the soundest health, began his inaugural address. He spoke to the thousands jostling before the Capitol steps and to the millions more who sat before their radio sets waiting to hear something new.

"This is a day of national consecration," Roosevelt began. "I am certain that my fellow Americans expect that on my induction into the Presidency I will address them with a candor and a decision which the present situation of our Nation impels." Thus far a formal beginning, and thus far the crowd stood listlessly.

". . . So, first of all," the new President continued, "let me assert my firm belief that the only thing we have to fear is fear itself—nameless, unreasoning, unjustified terror which paralyzes needed efforts to convert retreat into advance."

At last the crowd stirred. The man on the rostrum, whatever he was, could turn a phrase. This speech, unlike most of those during the campaign, was Roosevelt's

own work. A few nights before he had been glancing at the *Journal of Henry D. Thoreau,* and the happy phrase "Nothing is so much to be feared as fear" leaped from the page.

The sonorous voice, its accents the legacy of Groton, Harvard, and a half-dozen or more generations of Hudson Valley patroons, went on: "This Nation asks for action, and action now. . . . We must act and act quickly. . . ." Here for the millions who heard him was reason at last to hope. Do-nothing government and mere moral exhortation to end the Depression were at an end.

But now the tone darkened. "If I read the temper of our people correctly," the new President warned, "we now realize as we have never realized before our interdependence on each other; that we can not merely take but we must give as well; that if we are to go forward, we must move as a trained and loyal army willing to sacrifice for the good of a common discipline, because without such discipline no progress is made, no leadership becomes effective."

The crowd, as a whole, evidently approved of the words. But what precisely did they mean? What was this stress on collectivity and discipline? Some who listened—and the former President and the bewhiskered Chief Justice were certainly among them—were disturbed. That very winter across the sea in Germany another leader, Adolf Hitler, was on the verge of coming to power by legal means and of imposing a new and savage discipline on his people. And did not the phrase "we can not merely take but we must give as well" disconcertingly echo the old Marxist adage "From each according to his ability"?

Those who doubted were not reassured by the words that followed. "It is to be hoped," the President declared, "that the normal balance of executive and legislative authority may be wholly adequate to meet the unprecedented task before us. But it may be that an unprecedented demand and need for undelayed action may call for temporary departure from that normal balance of public procedure. . . . in the event that Congress shall fail . . . and in the event that the national emergency is still critical, I shall not evade the clear course of duty that will then confront me."

The President moved to summation: "The people of the United States have not failed. . . . They have asked for discipline and direction under leadership. They have made me the present instrument of their wishes. In the spirit of the gift I take it."

As the President ended, there was a roar from the crowd. The nation at large, in its desperate situation, did indeed want discipline and direction. But there were those who wondered if the cure Roosevelt proposed might not destroy the essential values that were America. An issue had been joined, one that within a short while would divide the nation and keep it split through the twelve years that would constitute the Roosevelt era. "The thing that emerges most clearly," wrote the *New Republic*'s correspondent Edmund Wilson, no old fogy, "is the warning of a dictatorship."

The official party then went directly to the reviewing stand in front of the White House, driving through streets lined by generally sober crowds. "It was very, very solemn, and a little terrifying," the President's wife, Eleanor, said. "The crowds were so tremendous, and you felt that they would do anything—if only someone would tell them what to do."

That evening the entire Cabinet was sworn in at a simple ceremony at the White House before the liberal Justice Benjamin Cardozo of the Supreme Court. All took the oath in unison, then filed from the room to turn to urgent tasks at hand. That night there was an inaugural ball at the Washington Auditorium. There was an outcry when the President and the First Lady announced that they would not attend, and Mrs. Roosevelt relented when the large number of cancellations threatened to ruin the ball and agreed to go. Roosevelt remained at home and went to bed after dinner, but he did not go to sleep. His good friend and adviser Louis Howe sat by his bed, and the two men talked over the problems and challenges facing the new administration. Keyed up by the exciting events of the day and the prospects ahead, they were still wide awake when Mrs. Roosevelt returned from the ball.

To that moment Franklin Roosevelt had enjoyed what some would have termed a distinguished career. But there was nothing that smacked of inevitability about his rise to greatness. As a boy he had been rich, amiable, and not especially outstanding. He served as assistant secretary of the Navy under Wilson, ran unsuccessfully as the vice-presidential candidate with James M. Cox against Harding in 1920, and introduced Al Smith's name in nomination in 1924, where he coined the felicitous phrase for Smith "the happy warrior." But his only

true achievements prior to the victory over Hoover in 1932 were his feat in the elections four years before, when, while Smith failed even to carry his own state of New York in the presidential election, Roosevelt sneaked in as governor of New York by a narrow margin of 25,000 votes out of more than 4,200,000 cast, and again in the 1930 gubernatorial election, when he scored a genuine triumph by running well ahead of his party, which could not, despite his success, capture either the upper or lower house in Albany.

By the end of 1930, as the nation skidded toward bankruptcy, it was clear that a Democrat, perhaps any Democrat, could beat any Republican in the upcoming national elections. (And, be it noted, it was not going to be *any* Republican the Democrats had to beat; it was going to be the discredited Herbert Hoover, for to nominate anyone but him would have been a suicidal admission of responsibility for the economic collapse.)

Roosevelt was a strong contender for the Democratic nomination. He had demonstrated impressive practical political abilities, plus a winning charm. Significantly, he had money and, perhaps more important, connections to money. And he could, so it was thought, deliver New York's powerful bloc of votes at the convention.

But there were problems too. Other contenders for the nomination were legion. Al Smith was Roosevelt's strongest rival; John Nance "Cactus Jack" Garner of Texas, who was then Speaker of the House, and Newton D. Baker, who had been Wilson's Secretary of War, also had impressive backing. Furthermore, Roosevelt was making enemies, despite the flashing smile. Al Smith, Roosevelt's former mentor, had brooded over Roosevelt's failure to consult him after the latter became governor of New York; this was probably Smith's principal reason for opposing Roosevelt for the nomination. Moreover, the investigation led by Samuel Seabury in New York City, which probed into the financial scandals involving the playboy Mayor Jimmy Walker and Tammany Hall and which forced Roosevelt to take sides either with the reformers or the machine, threatened to undercut Roosevelt's New York City voting base.

But in the 1930 elections in New York Roosevelt had defeated the Republicans by 1,800,000 to 1,000,000. He carried 41 out of the 57 upstate counties, a feat unmatched by any Democratic candidate for governor in history, since upstate New York was traditionally Republican.

The day after his gubernatorial victory, Roosevelt's

long-time political confidant James Farley, an Irish politician of unrivaled gifts for intrigue and the trading of favors, announced his boss's national candidacy. "I do not see how Mr. Roosevelt can escape becoming the next presidential nominee of his party," he loftily declared, adding, "even if no one should raise a finger to bring it about." But Farley had every intention of raising a finger. Roosevelt had a superlatively astute supporter in Farley, and in retaining him Roosevelt demonstrated an invaluable attribute that was to mark the rest of his political years: he knew how to attract able men, of every stripe and quality, to serve under him in a loyal band.

Besides Farley there was grim-faced Louis McHenry Howe, a man dour and jealous but fanatically loyal to his "Franklin" and immensely combative on his behalf.

There was Harry Hopkins, a young social worker imported by Roosevelt during the winter of 1931–32 to head up the New York State temporary emergency relief program. Hopkins immediately demonstrated that he was a hardheaded organizer who knew how to get things done. He would go on, one day, to play a role on the international stage, winning the regard of men like Winston Churchill for a mind that quickly pierced to the core of a problem.

There was an able young lawyer, Adolf Berle, Jr., who had a gift for phrasing and a receptivity to ideas. And there were idea men, like Raymond Moley and Rexford Tugwell, two Columbia University professors, who at the outset gave an academic tone to the Roosevelt administration, which it would never lose, a departure in politics that would often reduce practical businessmen to impotent fury.

But at the moment, with the nomination still to be won, it was not ideas Roosevelt needed as much as votes and money. Thanks to Farley and Howe, the money was found — in the pockets of "renegade" bankers, industrialists, and financiers, among them Herbert H. Lehman, Henry Morgenthau, Sr., William H. Woodin, and Joseph P. Kennedy.

As the Democratic convention approached, the Roosevelt candidacy was far from assured. His backers were a variegated lot: labor organizers; big financiers; Deep South magnates; Midwestern bosses, like Thomas J. Pendergast of Missouri; Irish city politicians, like James M. Curley of Boston; and that ebullient demagogue and proto-Fascist, leader of the unwashed common man, Huey "Kingfish" Long of Louisiana. The sources of

Roosevelt's strength were so diverse that the alliance threatened constantly to come apart at the seams. All these men and forces might support Roosevelt, but could they support one another? Sometimes they did not even suspect that hated enemies were working with them on the Roosevelt team. Later, when they awoke to the truth, the discovery left much bitterness in its wake.

Thus, as the delegates met in Chicago that hot June of 1932, the Roosevelt strategy was to steam-roller the convention, smashing through to a first or at most second ballot victory before the inevitable splintering of the coalition began. The Roosevelt task was made all the harder because the Democrats then still retained the archaic two-thirds rule; no simple majority would win for Roosevelt.

There was a check to the Roosevelt drive almost at once. The Democrats were scenting victory, and thereby behind the façade of elaborate convention tomfoolery and turgid speechifying they indulged themselves in the near-suicidal luxury of indiscipline and bloody, internecine warfare. It was not until four thirty A.M. on July 1 that the nominations came to a vote before the exhausted delegates. The Roosevelt forces were talking — at least for publication — of a stampede on the first ballot. It did not work out that way.

The balloting, proceeding amidst confusion, was interrupted by challenges from unhappy minorities. On the first ballot Minnesota's delegation demanded to be polled. A majority of its 24 delegates chose Roosevelt, and under the state's unit rule, he thus won all 24. New York, badly split also, demanded to be polled as well; $28\frac{1}{2}$ votes went to Roosevelt and, nasty shocker, $65\frac{1}{2}$ to Al Smith.

Roosevelt polled $666\frac{1}{4}$ on the first roll call to Smith's $201\frac{3}{4}$ and Garner's $90\frac{1}{4}$, seemingly an impressive showing, though 104 short of victory. But no band-wagon rush developed, and on the second ballot, which lasted two hours and fifty minutes, he picked up only $11\frac{1}{4}$ votes, and only an insignificant 5 more on the third.

By this time it was clear that the Roosevelt threat had been stopped. For the Roosevelt men, it was plainly time to shift strategy, to play for time. Farley did just that. The exhausted delegates agreed to adjourn. At this juncture the astute Farley played his last trump card — pressure on the Texas delegation, which until then had been solidly ranked behind its native son, Cactus Jack Garner.

Farley and others had previously tried the tactic of

calling publisher William Randolph Hearst in California, warning him that in a protracted deadlock the convention might well swing to Newton D. Baker, whose Wilsonian internationalism was anathema to Hearst. As a result Hearst put feelers out to the Texas delegation about switching its vote, but with no apparent effect. Now Farley strongly hinted to the Texans that the Vice Presidency might be available for their favorite son. The log jam broke. Texas swung to Roosevelt. Soon thereafter California followed, beginning the victory roll. There were angry accusations, holdouts, but most of the rest followed.

Roosevelt won. There were a few shortsighted prognosticators who predicted defeat for him in the coming election. H. L. Mencken, whose political vision had already begun to cloud as the 1920's were supplanted by the grimmer 1930's, opined:

The great combat is ending this afternoon in the classical Democratic manner. That is to say, the victors are full of uneasiness and the vanquished are full of bile. It would be hard to find a delegate who believes seriously that Roosevelt can carry New York in November, or Massachusetts, or New Jersey, or even Illinois. . . . Meanwhile the Southern and Middle Western delegates are going home with a tattered Bible on one shoulder and a new and shiny beer seidel on the other, and what they will have to listen to from their pastors and the ladies of the W.C.T.U. is making their hearts miss every other beat.

"It's a kangaroo ticket," a sullen Texan, still faithful to Garner, complained after the convention, "stronger in the hindquarters than in the front."

Newsman Walter Lippman had done his wrong guessing even before the convention: "Franklin D. Roosevelt is no crusader. He is no tribune of the people. He is no enemy to entrenched privilege. He is an amiable man who, without any important qualifications for the office, would very much like to be President."

But these and the other discomfited failed to see the great new fact of American politics: Depression. Before the mighty economic glacier then moving down over America, as banks failed and the dispirited bread lines formed, mere regionalism and the prayerful entreaties of the Women's Christian Temperance Union alike would have to give way.

Roosevelt moved to the attack.

It was a campaign cautious in substance though aggressive in style. Roosevelt dealt with a broad range of issues, but was vague about exactly what action he meant to take on any of them. He made the traditional demand for economy in government, and he depended, in time-honored politician's fashion, on letting the cold facts of national distress drive the lesson home that it was indeed time for a change. Republicans had been in office for twelve years, for at least the first ten of these loudly proclaiming that they had made prosperity, had invented, as it were, the chicken in the pot, the car in the garage, silk stockings, silk shirts, and the Dow-Jones average soaring out of sight. Now they were hoist with their own petard: prosperity had collapsed during their administration.

The people that year, Roosevelt proclaimed, wanted a "real choice," and he would give it to them. Not content with that empty affirmation, he advised the nation that his was a "party of liberal thought, of planned action, of enlightened international outlook, and of the greatest good to the greatest number. . . ."

"You could not quarrel with a single one of his generalities," a disappointed newsman, Elmer Davis, reported. "You seldom can. But what they mean (if anything) is known only to Franklin D. Roosevelt and his God."

But the campaign, if windy, was conducted in an extraordinarily vigorous fashion. The new candidate, acting to belie his infirmity, made three regional speaking tours and twenty-seven major speeches, whistle-stopping through towns and villages, everywhere radiating confidence and charm.

One of his memorable speeches, foreshadowing the course he would pursue, was to the Commonwealth Club of San Francisco on September 23. Surveying the economic history of America, Roosevelt asserted that with the Great Depression a new era had opened: "The day of the great promoter or the financial Titan, to whom we granted anything if only he would build, or develop, is over." Echoing the discouragement of those who had witnessed fiscal and industrial contraction without real precedent in history and who now believed that equitable distribution of existing goods rather than new production was the imperative, he asserted:

Our task now is not discovery or exploitation of natural resources, or necessarily producing more goods. It is the soberer, less dramatic business of administering resources and plants already in hand, of seeking to reestablish foreign markets for our surplus production, of meeting the problem of underconsumption, of adjusting production to consumption, of distributing wealth and products more equitably, of adapting existing economic organizations to the service of the people.

And he concluded, ominously for those who still worshiped the gods of nineteenth-century America: "The day of enlightened administration has come. . . ."

Thus he sounded the keynote of the 1930's, a doctrine not to be changed until the coming of World War II. Then America, as the arsenal of democracy, would once again emphasize unrestricted output.

Roosevelt probably would have won had he made no speeches at all. On November 2, sitting with his confidants at election headquarters in New York, he counted the late returns from across the nation: 22,800,000 for the victor, a sour 15,800,000 for Hoover. The electoral vote for Roosevelt was massive—472. Only six states, four of them in New England, held out for Hoover. And though Roosevelt ran ahead of his party, he had a solidly Democratic Congress at his back. The Senate went Democratic 60 to 35, the House 310 to 117.

oover was left to the agony of nearly four months of lame-duck Presidency, still stoutly maintaining, as before, that the roots of disaster lay abroad. Prosperity, he continued to argue desperately, demanded a sound currency and faith in individual action. But the President-elect refused, time and again, to join in cooperative measures with the discredited old. Roosevelt wanted a free hand when he took power. To Hoover's frantic appeals to Roosevelt's headquarters in New York for common policies to "restore confidence" to the business community and the masses, Roosevelt always sent back the same answer: Hoover had sufficient power to act.

There was to be a new broom, a clean sweep. Meanwhile the problems came crowding. The banks failed, the lines before the soup kitchens grew, so that in the waning hours of his administration the worn Hoover, his task done except for the ordeal of the inauguration, rose from his desk and wearily said to his advisers: "We are at the end of our string."

But the national paralysis that the outgoing President had found so soul-destroying was to the incoming man an exhilarating challenge. The pace of Roosevelt's first full day in office was frantic. After worshiping with his family and lunching with friends, he plunged into a feverish round of official duties. As he recorded in his diary (begun that day and abandoned, to the regret of historians, two days later):

Two-thirty P.M. meeting in Oval Room with all members of Cabinet, Vice-President and Speaker Rainey, outlining banking situation. Unanimous approval for Special Session of Congress Thursday, March ninth. Proclamation for this prepared and sent. This was followed by conferences with Senator Glass, Hiram Johnson, Joe Robinson and Congressmen Steagall and Byrnes and Minority Leader Snell—all in accord. Secretary [of the Treasury] Woodin reported bankers' representatives much at sea as to what to do. Concluded that forty-eight different methods of handling banking situation impossible. Attorney General Cummings reported favorably on power to act under 1917 law, giving President power to license, regulate, etc., export, hoarding, earmarking of gold or currency. Based on this opinion and on emergency decided on Proclamation declaring banking holiday. . . . Talked with Professor Warren in evening. Talked with representatives of four Press Associations explaining bank holiday Proclamation. Five minute radio address for American Legion at 11:30 P.M. Visit from Secretary of State [Cordell Hull]. Bed.

Altogether a busy day. The bank holiday took effect at one o'clock in the morning of Monday, March 6. The country at large learned the news when it woke up. America had gone off the gold standard (only temporarily, to be sure, but it would go off it for good by act of Congress in June), and all banks across the land were shut tight. The emergency banking bill of March 9 permitted them to open and dispense cash only as they were deemed capable of meeting their obligations against assets that were certified sound by Treasury officials.

What going off the gold standard meant could be argued endlessly, but what closing the banks meant became clear at once. What to do without cash was the paramount topic of the day as friends borrowed from one another, fathers broke open their children's piggy banks, and mothers raided cookie jars. That Monday a good many men walked to work for lack of fare, if they went to work at all. A bizarre atmosphere of carnival gaiety prevailed across the land. Edward S. Robinson, a Yale professor, had asked Thurman Arnold of the university's law school: "Do you think that when the banks all close people will climb trees and throw coconuts at each other?" Arnold offered the opinion that there would probably be rioting and revolution. "I will venture a prediction," Robinson replied. "When the banks close, everyone will feel relieved. It will be a sort of national holiday."

Robinson was proved right. A few moss-grown bankers of the old school muttered darkly that the government had no right to shut them down, but most bankers felt relief at having been ordered to do what they had to do anyway. Merchants took IOU's; prize fight tickets at Madison Square Garden were exchanged for shoes, canned goods, frankfurters, foot ointment; in Salt Lake City transit fares went for tubes of toothpaste, silk stockings, or other items; and a Midwest newspaper advertised a year's subscription for ten bushels of wheat or two years for eighteen bushels. The ingenuity of citizens in filling the vacuum left by the sudden removal of the currency on which they had always depended was amazing. Barter became popular, impromptu credit systems were organized, various articles were adopted as emergency currency. The *Princetonian* printed scrip for students, pesos circulated in the Southwest, a chemical company paid its workers with coins stamped from a metal alloy that was one of its principal products. Possibly, had the bank holiday lasted long enough, the people would have permanently adopted some new medium of exchange.

he bank holiday proclamation, later ratified by Congress, together with the President's emergency bank legislation of March 9, which was debated hardly forty minutes in the House and not much more than four hours in the Senate, initiated a furious round of executive and legislative activity that was to dominate newspaper headlines for three months to come. This period, March 9–June 16, during which Congress was in special session, later came to be called the Hundred Days. It was a frantic time, in which a nation suddenly lifted out of despair saw translated into action the President's call in his inaugural for "action, and action now."

And through all the hectic activity Roosevelt, always the master politician, buttressed his support among the great mass of voters by taking the people into his confidence, or at least giving the appearance of doing so. He was the first President to exploit the potentialities of radio, and he took to the air frequently, not to give a speech but to talk to the people; he emphasized the difference by calling his talks fireside chats to create the illusion that they were intimate, folksy affairs. Millions tuned in to his familiar "Good evening, my friends," and the chats played an important part in maintaining his popularity.

On March 10 the President caught off guard a Congress more economy-minded than he by sending a message demanding stringent restrictions on government spending. During the campaign Roosevelt had promised economy in government. And if few Republicans had taken him seriously, surprisingly he had meant it. "Too often in recent history liberal governments have been wrecked on rocks of loose fiscal policy," he intoned.

The broad executive powers he demanded, the President asserted, would be used in "a spirit of justice to all." But some of the effects of this power were savage: a veteran totally disabled had his pension slashed from a meager forty dollars per month to a cataclysmic twenty dollars. By contrast, the salaries of senators and congressmen were cut back a mere 15 per cent.

In his steadfast refusal to nationalize the banks, and in his insistence on government economy and financial contraction, Roosevelt seemed to be reassuring the conservative sectors of society. He seemed to be protecting those all too likely to have voted against him rather than those who had turned to him for help and had elected him by a landslide.

On March 13 the President called for the legalization of beer, a move that cheered up everyone, except the bootleggers and the W.C.T.U., immensely. On February 20, before Roosevelt was inaugurated, Congress had already passed a resolution asking for an end to the Eighteenth Amendment, but that would have required another amendment to the Constitution and would have taken time. In the interim Prohibition could be eased considerably simply by modifying the Volstead Act, and this Congress did in a bill, which the President signed on March 22. Any beverage with 3.2 per cent or less of alcohol by weight was to be considered nonintoxicating and hence legal. The act went into effect April 7 and let Americans drink beer and light wines openly for the first time in more than a dozen years.

On March 16 the President dropped a bombshell—in effect initiating the true New Deal. This was a call for comprehensive agricultural legislation, long overdue, to refinance farm mortgages in order to relieve debt pressures and save the land from foreclosure and also to raise farm income by restricting production and paying farmers not to produce. The measure, to be passed on May 12 as the Agricultural Adjustment Act, was a departure from traditional economics indeed and, what is more, from traditional American work ethics, which, for more than three centuries, had enshrined the full granary as a measure of the farmer's merit. The bill, with its seeming absurdity of paying the farmer to loaf, would prove one of the most controversial measures of the New Deal. It would be struck down by the courts, only to prevail two years later with its invalidated sections modified.

The Agricultural Adjustment Administration (A.A.A.) would catapult into national prominence Secretary of Agriculture Henry A. Wallace, former Republican turned Democrat, son of the Secretary of Agriculture in Harding's Cabinet, a visionary and a mystic. It would do the same for one of the original "Brain Trusters" (those young men who had helped spark the New Deal), Assistant Secretary of Agriculture Rexford Tugwell. Tugwell, along with Assistant Secretary of State Raymond Moley and Adolf Berle, who refused any position but served as a special adviser during the early months of the New Deal, would do as much as anyone to give the new administration a reputation for intellectualism by flouting the inherited dogmas of old-time America.

In this case it was largely in the cities that the conservatives demanded the frontier virtues; the A.A.A. had the wholehearted support of the bankrupt farmers themselves.

On March 21 the President asked for authorization and funds for the Civilian Conservation Corps (C.C.C.), a plan to employ more than a quarter million out-of-work youths between the ages of eighteen and twenty-five in damming streams, seeding forests, building dust storm barriers, on the economy salary of one dollar per day plus board and lodging in Spartan work camps. It was to prove a productive program, both in terms of work accomplished and young men employed; by the end of 1941 more than two million youths had been given work.

The same day, the President asked for legislation leading to what would become the Federal Emergency Relief Administration (F.E.R.A.), authorized to spend half a billion dollars in direct aid to state and local relief agencies. By granting such aid, the federal government, in the traditional view, encroached on the freedom of the states, something Hoover had refused to do. The agency came under the direction of the able Harry Hopkins, who curtly dismissed the controversy that immediately raged about the F.E.R.A. with the observation, "Hunger is not debatable."

On March 29 the President proposed legislation to supplement state blue-sky laws. Passed on May 22 as the Federal Securities Act, it required all new stock issues sold through interstate commerce to be registered with the Federal Trade Commission. Full and fair disclosure by those who floated new securities was demanded, under severe penalty of law. "The money changers," Roosevelt had declared in his inaugural address, "have fled from their high seats in the temple of our civilization." He would now act, as he had promised, to "restore that temple to the ancient truths."

The money-changers moaned, but there had been too many scandals. They involved even great lending institutions like the National City Bank, whose chairman of the board, Charles E. Mitchell, had resigned under fire after he confessed in February, 1933, before a Senate investigating committee that he had permitted officers in his bank to use two and a half million dollars of stockholders' money to speculate on the stock market and then had not required them to make full repayment when they had lost money. Two weeks later Mitchell was arrested on income tax evasion charges.

On April 10 the President demanded one of the most far-reaching of all the New Deal measures, legislation authorizing a government-owned corporation to build dams, develop electric power, sell electricity in direct competition with private firms, produce nitrogen fertilizers, conserve soil, and promote social welfare throughout the entire seven-state drainage basin of the Tennessee River. Here, in the Tennessee Valley Authority (T.V.A.), was a departure from tradition indeed, an example of government in business, pure socialism, for which the initial legislation had been the dream of Senator George W. Norris of Nebraska, who had been fighting for more than a decade to have the government operate the hydroelectric plants it had built on the Tennessee River during World War I.

The T.V.A. would later prove one of the most brilliant conceptions of the New Deal. But though brilliant in both the conception and the execution, the T.V.A. has remained a curiously ignored precedent for America. Though widely imitated abroad, there has been no other undertaking of the same kind here, unless one excepts the Atomic Energy Commission, established at the end of World War II.

As the reopened banks, seeking assets, foreclosed in increasing numbers on defaulters, the President on

232

April 13 sought legislation to protect small-home owners from eviction. To accomplish this, he proposed not to cancel mortgages, as more radical contemporary social theory would have had it, nor even to guarantee them, but to reduce interest rates and provide liberal conditions for postponement of interest and principal payments. The legislation was passed on June 13, creating the Home Owners' Loan Corporation (H.O.L.C.).

On May 17 the President proposed what would become the National Industrial Recovery Act, a sweeping conception that sought to regulate cut-throat competition within industry and commerce, to improve working conditions for labor by various means, including a guarantee of the right to organize, as well as to administer a vast program of public works designed to turn unemployed men into producers and consumers once again. The legislation was authorized by a somewhat wary Congress on June 16, the final day of its special session and the end of the Hundred Days. The National Recovery Administration (N.R.A.) was without doubt the broadest invasion of the traditions of American free enterprise in the years of the republic before or since.

The fundamental notion of the N.R.A. was simply that each separate business sector should more or less divide the total business among its members, under government regulation, for its own and the public good. To this end, each industry or trade was required to draft codes of fair competition. In effect, this was to authorize legal transgressions of the trust-busting Sherman Antitrust Act, which had until then prohibited combinations in restraint of competition on the theory that such competition produced the greatest public good.

The man that Roosevelt chose to head this vast social engineering combine was no doctrinaire Democrat but a curiously enigmatic, or at least unclassifiable, personality, a weather-beaten former cavalryman and West Pointer, General Hugh S. Johnson, former industrialist, flamboyant swearer, rough of voice, and emotionally unstable. Johnson was a classic example of the military ideological mind—and a mind fascinated by Raffaelo Viglione's work *The Corporate State*. During the two years the N.R.A. functioned under Johnson, his imperious manner gave it more and more an authoritarian stamp. Johnson had come to Washington on the recommendation of that perennial elder statesman Bernard Baruch, though his mentor mistrusted him even while he valued Johnson's energy and superficial brilliance. "I think he's a good number-three man," he opined.

"Maybe a number-two man. But he's not a number-one man."

It may, in fact, have been in shrewd anticipation of Hugh Johnson's weaknesses that the astute and pragmatic Roosevelt made a last-minute alteration of plans. The N.R.A., initially conceived as a giant and self-contained governmental effort designed to regulate production at the same time as it worked through a formidable public construction program to stimulate an ailing economy, had been drafted as a single piece of legislation. But that summer, just before leaving on a fishing cruise, the President summoned his Cabinet. The huge public works program would be a separate venture, he announced. Pending a decision on who should head it, a board was put in charge, but when the President returned, the program, totaling in all $3,300,000,000, was put under the aegis of Harold Ickes, that irascible but fanatically honest Secretary of the Interior. Ickes, in his insistence on honesty, would prove to spend too slowly for Johnson's conception of an explosive effort to push the economy into activity again.

"It's terrible, it's terrible," a broken Johnson wept to Frances Perkins, Roosevelt's female Secretary of Labor, after learning of the President's decision. But driving for miles through the Washington dusk, pleading with the badly shaken Johnson, Miss Perkins persuaded him to stay on.

Bitterly in after years, when he had broken with Roosevelt, Johnson was to recall, ". . . very fatuously, I did."

As the President departed that summer for a well-deserved rest, the first phase of the New Deal drew to a close. The nation had demanded action; action there had been. Roosevelt had undeniably pierced the gloom that had, in the desperate last Hoover years, settled like a palpable shroud over America. He had put the country on the move again, but to where?

Gradually, as the ebullience and vigor of the new administration lightened the darkness, the alienated—the fifteen-million-odd who had voted for Hoover, the myriad bankers cast out of the temple, the vast host of small-business men beaten down by the failure of the economy but unable to break with old political allegiances—began to ask what it was that the nation, by exercising its constitutional liberties, had bought.

And no one could truly say. Because the truth, it seemed, was that the President himself did not know where he was headed.

There were a few clues, but even these were contradictory. Roosevelt had spoken at his inauguration like an incipient dictator, but proved that very weekend to be strangely tender of the sensibilities of the banking structure of the nation. He rammed through a deflationary government spending cut on March 15, and then just as inconsistently, the next day, asked for an inflationary spending program like the A.A.A.

Even his Cabinet gave no real clue. His Secretary of State, Cordell Hull, was a southern Bourbon of conservative Democratic stripe, a free trader, though the President had spoken of protecting American trade. His Secretary of Agriculture, Henry Wallace, was an ex-Republican, a reputed visionary who dabbled in astrology and had raised the production of hybrid corn to a science. His Secretary of the Treasury, William Woodin, was an industrialist but a Democratic industrialist who, in moments of acute stress, strummed a guitar. His Secretary of the Interior, Harold Ickes, who ran the Public Works Administration (P.W.A.), was tightfisted and an implacable curmudgeon, but the F.E.R.A., the parallel spending program that Harry Hopkins ran, stressed jobs, jobs, jobs and higher efficiency be damned. "Ironbottom" Johnson, Czar of the sprawling N.R.A., was that contradiction in terms—a highly emotional general. What did it all mean?

What it meant, Roosevelt himself did not know—or care. His was a flypaper mind, enormously receptive to the new, appreciative of the old, little troubled by inconsistencies. Above all, what emerged from the Hundred Days was the picture of a man totally at peace with himself in the Presidency, enjoying the tension, the at-mosphere of perpetual crisis, running, ever questioning, exulting in a battle with poverty and despair that had struck his predecessor down.

The supreme irony of the Hundred Days was that, repudiating Hooverism, it succeeded in carrying into practice what Hoover had always preached as the remedy for economic stagnation, but what he had been unable to carry off himself. This was to reassure the nation, to bring back "confidence."

If state of mind could have combated a shrunken economy, if good will and returning confidence could have exorcised bread lines and set the wheels of production moving, Roosevelt by the summer of 1933 would have won—and by a curious twist of history, Hoover would have been vindicated.

By the summer of 1933 almost everybody did believe the worst was over, that prosperity was just around the corner. Business confidence had revived, and with it the all-but-unkillable urge to speculate in the market.

The Stock Exchange showed life. The Dow-Jones index swung upward; a mild bull speculation broke out. In June and again in July the volume of trading topped the level of any single month during the Big Bull Market of 1929. And just as abruptly, late in July, the market collapsed. American Commercial Alcohol fell from $89\frac{7}{8}$ to $29\frac{1}{8}$ in four days.

The poor, it seemed, were eternally present. The shrunken faces of the unemployed still reproached the less-than-affluent passer-by. The factories still stood idle. The inventories still gathered dust.

Apparently there was more to fear than fear.

THE EYES AND EARS OF THE WORLD
3.

Rivalries and power struggles abroad intensified during the mid-30's. As early as 1931, Japan began an aggressive campaign against Manchuria; by 1935 she had advanced across the Great Wall, and by 1937, was embroiled in an undeclared war against China. Italy's Fascist regime strengthened its position, and Mussolini's imperialistic ambitions culminated in the conquest of Ethiopia in 1936. That same year a revolt of army officials against the leftist government in Spain, spurred on by General Francisco Franco, led to full-scale civil war. The most alarming threat to peace, however, was Nazi Germany. In 1935 Hitler denounced the Versailles Treaty arms limitation agreements and re-established universal conscription. Then, in quick succession, he reoccupied the Rhineland (1936), invaded Austria (1938), absorbed Czechoslovakia (1939), and looked menacingly toward Poland. His intent was clear. "Upon the careless and imprudent world . . . ," Churchill had warned in 1935, "Hitler, casting aside concealment, sprang forward armed to the teeth."

A touch of romance provided distraction from graver matters on the international scene when, in December of 1936, King Edward VIII renounced England's throne for the woman he loved, an American divorcée, Mrs. Wallis Simpson. Above, the newlyweds, as Duke and Duchess of Windsor, enjoying their honeymoon on Venice's Grand Canal. At left, Edward's brother and successor, the former Duke of York, after his coronation as King George VI.

Advance troops of Spanish Loyalists (left) rout Fascist insurgents on the Saragossa front in 1936. An attempt at a coup (which was started by army officials in Spanish Morocco and soon spread to Seville, Saragossa, and other Spanish towns) failed but plunged the nation into civil war. Below, Germany's new chancellor, Adolph Hitler, rides with President von Hindenburg in Berlin's May Day parade in 1933; the next year, Hitler took advantage of Von Hindenburg's death to seize dictatorial power. Italy's dictator, Mussolini, had his own designs for power. At bottom, Ethiopian cavalry line up for review in August, 1935, two months before the Italian invasion.

BROWN BROTHERS

DEM DEUTSCHEN VOLKE

The bitter enmity between the Communist and Nazi parties in Germany reached a climax during a 1933 election campaign, when fire broke out in the *Reichstag* (above) on February 27. The blaze had been set by the Nazis in a plot to discredit their enemies. Hitler had some 100 Communist members of the *Reichstag* arrested and used the incident as an excuse to suspend such constitutional guarantees as freedom of speech and press. A nationwide man hunt followed in which hundreds of Nazi opponents were thrown into concentration camps and many executed.

At right, a happier occasion: the birth of the Dionne quintuplets in Callander, Ontario, on May 28, 1934.

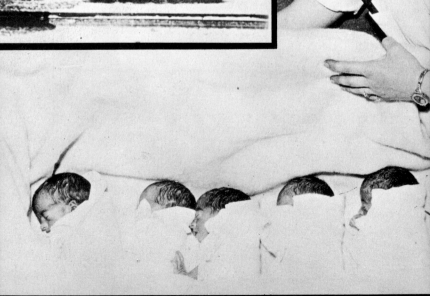

At left, Japanese troops celebrate victory atop th
Wall after taking the city of Chuyungkuan in Nor'
Repeated acts of Japanese aggression agains'
brought about an unofficial war that lasted from 1'
World War II. Below, German troops reoccupy th
land at Cologne in March, 1936; at bottom, the
chancellor, Dollfuss, assassinated by Nazis in an
attempt to annex Austria, lies in state in 1934.
Anschluss was finally accomplished by invasion

The art program of the Works Progress Administration gave employment to an army of hungry artists and at the same time adorned public buildings across the land with allegorical art. These are two of twelve panels by Henry Varnum Poor in the Justice Department Building: TVA Worker and Family (at left) and Surveying New Lands. On the opposite page, W.P.A. artists prepare a mural for use at the 1939 World's Fair.

Half Turn Left

There was poverty in the land, but for all the fury of action, the President's purpose in the first half of his first term was a curiously moderate one: to preside over a national consensus, a coalition of Left and Right, in an attack on disaster. To the despair of his supporters in the Democratic party, a fundamentally conservative Roosevelt, conditioned by the patrician family tradition of public service, steadfastly refused through 1933 and 1934 to allow his name to be more than perfunctorily invoked at those party jamborees the annual Jefferson Day dinners.

Early in 1934 he rebuked a supporter who had asked him to speak at a Jefferson Day function: "Our strongest plea to the country in this particular year of grace is that the recovery and reconstruction program is being accomplished by men and women of all parties—that I have repeatedly appealed to Republicans as much as to Democrats to do their part."

Nor, initially at least, did this impartial approach appear fatuous or doomed. The majority of the country seemed to respond to the appeal. "The New Deal is Christ's Deal," the Detroit "radio priest," enormously popular Father Charles E. Coughlin, intoned from his Shrine of the Little Flower in Royal Oak, Michigan, to more than twenty million listeners. The President's backing came from diverse sources. William Randolph Hearst was a guest at the White House, and Roy Howard of the conservative Scripps-Howard newspaper chain was a strong supporter. William Green, president of the American Federation of Labor, and organized labor adored Roosevelt. That rugged liberal and former Bull Mooser Governor Alfred M. Landon of Kansas in 1933 waxed eloquent in un-Republican fashion: "Even the iron hand of a national dictator is in preference to a paralytic stroke. . . ." Warming to his case, he concluded: "If there is any way in which a member of that species, thought by many to be extinct, a Republican governor of a Midwestern state, can aid in the fight, I now enlist for the duration of the war." Old Republican Senator George W. Norris could not say enough good for the man who had rammed through the T.V.A. Liberal financiers and industrialists like Robert Lovett, Averell Harriman, and James V. Forrestal rallied "respectable" support for the man who had come to the White House.

Yet there was a false note in this unusual chorus of unity. If success came, and came early, the Democrats, however nonpartisan the President might pretend to be, could not fail to win the national gratitude and go on to win and win and win. On the other hand, if the campaign against poverty were to prove long, then the Democrats might become vulnerable, but a loyal opposition of Republicans, who had cooperated whole-heartedly with the administration, could hardly use continuing hard times as an election issue against the Democrats. In the congressional elections of 1934 what would be the fate of a party that had proclaimed Harding-Coolidge normalcy (and brought on Hoover disaster) if it now tamely served as tail to the President's kite? Nor were the Republicans, who had for nearly a century since Abraham Lincoln's success in 1860 been conditioned to think of themselves as the majority, likely to take kindly to a continuing subordinate role.

And party politics aside, there were the social realities of the early 1930's. Franklin Roosevelt had, however reluctantly, cast himself in the role of reformer and crusader. He had assaulted the class, his own class, that had for generations symbolized public virtue in American life. The President's attack on the "money changers" at his inauguration affronted those who saw themselves as the true makers of America. As one shrewd foreign observer put it, Roosevelt succeeded in separating the idea of wealth from the idea of virtue in the public mind; this was a revolution in American thinking, and never again in this country would merely being wealthy be synonymous with being good.

The result was that bitterness welled up, as Harold Ickes later put it, from the grass roots of every country club in America. Helpless and angry in the wind-storms of 1933, as the country settled into the New Deal, the bankers, businessmen, leading industrial-ists, important financiers, gathered their wits. In August, 1934, the first fruit of the new bitterness of the up-rooted conservative forces was the American Liberty League. Chartered to "teach the necessity of respect for the rights of persons and property," it drew the support of great industrialists like the automobile maker William S. Knudsen, oil millionaires like J. Howard Pew, merchant-adventurers like Sewell L. Avery of Montgomery-Ward, and renegade old Demo-cratic politicos like Jouett Shouse and the erstwhile Happy Warrior, Al Smith.

Licking his wounds in semiretirement, Smith, who had seen his onetime disciple administer a bad beating to him at the Democratic convention of 1932, warned of Communism, thundering, "There can be only one capital, Washington or Moscow." Sadly listening to the harangues of the old battler, now the friend of the very rich, liberal columnist Heywood Broun reported from Washington of a Liberty League dinner during the 1936 presidential campaign:

The whole thing seemed unreal. Certainly it was surprising to hear Al Smith begin a speech with a reference to his wife and end it with the Bible and the American flag. . . . "I talked to my workers, 900 of them," said the gray-haired man behind me, "and I told them just what Al is saying tonight. I told them that they'd have to work their fingers off for every last nickel they ever earned, that it always had been so and it always would be so and, by gad, sir, I made them like it."

Later events of those New Deal years might raise doubts as to whether they liked it.

Among those hysterically weeping when the Happy Warrior had ended, Broun sardonically noted, were Felix A. du Pont, Jr., A. V. du Pont, Emile F. du Pont, Eugene E. du Pont, Henry B. du Pont, Mrs. H. B. du Pont, Irenee du Pont, Mrs. Irenee du Pont, Miss Octavia du Pont, Pierre S. du Pont, and Mrs. Pierre S. du Pont.

It is normal in American politics for an incumbent party to lose strength in mid-term elections. Not so in 1934. The Democrats, already in commanding control, upped their number in the House from 313 to 322 and in the Senate from 59 to 69.

The forces of conservatism, let alone reaction, were badly beaten. But victory did little to strengthen Roosevelt's resolve to govern as father of all the people. A new note of rancor crept into his discourse. Big business, he told Ickes, was bent on sabotaging his administration. In the fall of 1934 he told reporters: "I would now say that there is a greater thing that America needs to fear, and that is those who seek to instill fear into the American people."

The lines on the right were being drawn.

The Depression had done more than cast doubts on the motives of the leaders of the financial world; it had called into question for many the very soundness of the economic system itself. In America Marxism was in the air in the early 1930's. A doctrine that preached that the capitalist system was doomed, that greed and starva-tion and scarcity were inherent in the very structure of capitalism, could not fail to gain ground in an environment in which between eight and twelve millions were unemployed year after year.

True, in those years the outright converts to Communism were few, and most of them were not proper proletarians, the workers who theoretically formed the backbone of the movement, but rather intellectuals: authors, artists, teachers, movie directors, journalists, and New Dealing bright young men. The party in the United States in the early 1930's probably numbered fewer than fifteen thousand card carriers, but those who met in dozens of little cells in Hollywood or Washington's Georgetown or New York's Greenwich Village for heated discussions—of the Decline of Capitalist Culture and How Things Were Better Done in Moscow and Was Trotsky Really a Dirty Wrecker?—were usually the best of the country, the talented and committed and influential.

The names of those who flirted with doctrinaire Marxism during the 1930's read like a *Who's Who* of the arts and letters, though the arguments they put up in defense of Stalin's terror machine, then cranking into high gear, seem, in retrospect, hopelessly naïve. When *The New Masses* published a symposium early in the Depression years entitled "How I Came to Communism," the contributors included the author Sherwood Anderson, the critic Edmund Wilson, the political muckraker Upton Sinclair, and the editor Clifton Fadiman, though none of these contributors were literal Communists, either then or later.

Thus, though there were few card-carrying Communists (less than one-hundredth of one per cent out of a national population of some one hundred and twenty-five million), their influence spread wide. The eminent philosopher John Dewey felt called upon in this climate of opinion to defend himself in an apologia, "Why I Am Not a Communist," without finding it necessary to explain why he was not for free silver or the single tax. He noted sensibly: "Were a large-scale revolution to break out in highly industrialized America, where the middle class is stronger, more militant and better prepared than anywhere else in the world, it would either be abortive, drowned in a blood bath, or . . . a Pyrrhic victory. The two sides would destroy the country and each other. For this reason . . . I am not a Communist."

Yet the very elitism of the Communist party of the 1930's was a bar to mass expansion: however much the isolated and doctrinaire intellectuals might talk of an alliance with the toiling masses, they seldom understood or really liked the workingman, who returned the dislike full measure. It was largely because of this antagonism that the party's efforts at militancy usually backfired. When on March 7, 1932, the Communist party in Detroit led three thousand hunger marchers against Henry Ford's River Rouge Plant, violence erupted. The municipal police and the Ford "security force" of former mobsters and thugs left four marchers dead and fifty hospitalized—with sobering effect on those who had rallied to the party's call. Ford, for years to come, would prove a tough opponent of radical labor.

Thus, though the Communists were a noisy and sometimes influential minority, within the New Deal their influence was slight and was pretty well limited—when it was felt at all—to the middle and lower echelons of the rapidly expanding New Deal bureaucracy. Far more potent a threat to the New Deal was the almost formless yearning of millions of citizens deprived of adequate food or shelter or clothing, to say nothing of medical care or education, and with scant prospect of improving their lot.

To lead this potentially powerful force of the semi-literate and dispossessed, a number of demagogues appeared. Capitalizing on the troubled times, these rabble rousers and peddlers of social salvation by 1935 had Franklin Roosevelt's New Deal the next thing to running scared.

Least threatening of the snake-oil merchants was perhaps the elderly Dr. Francis E. Townsend of Long Beach, California, though for a time his devoted band of ten million Townsendites resolutely demanding theirs in an age of handouts seemed threat enough to the New Deal. Dr. Townsend had moved to California in the 1920's for reasons of health. The Depression treated him no more kindly than it did many others. He was out of a job one bleak day when he looked out his bathroom window to see three old women poking for salvageables in trash cans in the alley.

For Townsend the sight of these women, discouraged, old, and discarded, like so many of his generation, by a society that needed them no more, was the moment of epiphany. The god of the Townsend Plan appeared, fully accoutered, before him. Why be old and forgotten? asked the good doctor. A nation that cared for its aged would never have to be poor. What was called for, he saw with a new certainty, was a plan: two hundred dollars per month, the bare decent minimum, for all over sixty, provided—and here was the magnificent simplicity of it all, the stroke of genius that lifted it above the host of mere pleas for help that had multiplied over the Depression-ridden land and gave it the status of a social panacea—each sexagenarian plus would spend his two hundred dollars within thirty days and within the United States. The good doctor conjured up a vision of contented oldsters, their honest work done, priming the pump of prosperity simply by living it up in their last days.

It was potent, magnificent nonsense. No one stopped to worry that giving the oldsters their two hundred dollars per month would take a full half of the national income. A sales tax would magically provide all the necessary money.

Townsend's aide Robert L. Clements had organized Townsend clubs throughout the nation, and they were said to hold the balance of political power in eleven states by 1935. Clements put forward a claim of ten million supporters by mid-1935, and even conservative reports conceded a figure of three million.

"Onward, Townsend soldiers, / Marching as to war, / With the Townsend banner / Going on before," the old folks sang lustily at their rallies. Hearing their thunder, Jim Farley, looking forward to the 1936 elections, scratched his bald pate and wondered where the 3,000,000 votes would go.

Father Charles E. Coughlin, the radio priest, who had hailed the New Deal as a Christian coming, warning of "Roosevelt or Ruin," was another powerful force of the mid-Thirties. But Coughlin did not remain a Roosevelt backer for long. His entry into politics had been accidental. An Irish-Canadian by birth, with the merest trace of a brogue and a magnificent radio delivery, Coughlin had begun in the mid-1920's as a kind of spiritual uncle ministering to an audience of kiddies over radio station WJR in Detroit. But he was not content to preach to five-year-olds forever, and on October 30, 1930, as the Hoover Depression deepened, he took the plunge. That Sunday Coughlin sternly warned the mothers and fathers of America against that perennial target the money-changers and, with a magnificent disregard for consistency, against "subversive socialism" as well. International bankers had ruined America, and the Reds now wanted to pick up the pieces.

The response was overwhelming. Letters poured in.

By the end of January, 1931, their number had swelled to fifty thousand a week. Coughlin's bishop, the Right Reverend Michael Gallagher of Detroit, was delighted. A potent political star was born.

Moving cautiously in the beginning, Coughlin took on no dangerous foes. In Depression America tilting with Herbert Hoover was hardly a perilous sport—or a novelty. But the mob enjoyed hearing the message yet one more time. Warning against Hoover in a talk immoderately titled "Hoover Prosperity Means Another War," Coughlin drew fully 1,200,000 letters in response, most of them hysterically approving.

From that point forward there was no stopping Father Coughlin, though William Cardinal O'Connell of Boston assailed him as disseminating "demagogic stuff to the poor" and that eminent Catholic layman Al Smith hurled barbs as well, dismissing him and his theories as "crackpot." But when Catholics denounced him, Father Coughlin merely broadened his appeal by arguing that this was positive proof that the simple priest of the Shrine of the Little Flower was no minion of a Roman pontiff five thousand miles away. Lower-class Protestants of America accordingly joined his army. Even the *Literary Digest*, a leading political commentary of the day, could piously note that Father Coughlin's politics were evidently "beyond the gates of creed."

Father Coughlin was a radical of a curiously inconsistent sort, and though he had backed Roosevelt in 1932, by 1935 he was denouncing the New Deal and terming Franklin Roosevelt a "liar." At the same time, he was praising Huey Long for his "soak the rich" schemes and Benito Mussolini for the true progressivism of the corporate state and organizing the "nonpolitical" National Union for Social Justice. All this was being done over a coast-to-coast radio hookup that by 1936 included thirty-five stations.

The New Deal, thundered Coughlin, was an old deal. In a manifesto he demanded that private banking be abolished and called for the nationalization of "resources too important to be held by individuals"— resources he carefully left undefined—and he violently attacked the T.V.A. as "socialism." There was to be a "just, living, annual wage for all labor," he assured his faithful, even as his weekly sermons were being printed in a nonunion shop. He was apparently for big government of some kind, for the "use of private property" was to be "controlled for the public good" but by whom he did not say. In the case of the cost of living and "the value of money" the answer was easy. They would be controlled by a central government bank, though, Coughlin assured his listeners, there would be "simplification of government" and "lightening taxation" on the working class.

Snake oil surely, but potent snake oil too.

But Father Coughlin could never aspire to the Presidency. The Constitution limits the office to the native-born, and the priest had been born in Canada. That alone, if nothing else, would bar him from the White House. Father Coughlin was ambitious, but his ambitions had to be limited to the role of being the power behind someone else's throne.

ot so Huey Long, the Kingfish, senator from Louisiana, ruthless ruler of a quasi duchy all his own, who recognized no limits on how far he might go. Long had come up the hard way, being born in a log cabin, the eighth child of nine, to the wife of a farmer in northern Louisiana. From his earliest days Long displayed a driving ambition and formidable talents to match it. He toured the northern backcountry parishes of his native state as an itinerant peddler, learning the moods and prejudices of the dirt farmers and poor Negroes who made up the region's neglected rural poor. One term at Oklahoma University Law School and then only eight months at Louisiana's Tulane Law School were enough to earn him a law degree. Admitted to the Louisiana Bar by a special session of the state supreme court, he "came out of that courtroom running for office," as his campaign autobiography put it later, and had been running ever since.

The war years came, but Long had no intention of dying in a trench in France. In case marriage and fatherhood would not be enough to get him excused, he claimed that he was an essential "public official"; Long was a notary public when America went to war.

But he was more than a draft dodger and country buffoon. Behind the small eyes and sunburned brow there lay a cunning and powerful mind. And Long was a genuine champion of the poor and dispossessed. Elected railroad commissioner at twenty-four, he at-

tacked the oil interests of Louisiana, developing the style of slangy, earthy oratory that delighted the rednecks and would later attract millions on the national scene. In 1924, not yet thirty-one years old, he ran for governor in a three-cornered race and finished a mere 11,000 votes behind the winner, and then only because rainy weather had kept many of his farmer supporters from voting.

Sweet victory was only four years off. Stumping up and down the rural parishes, he alternately hurled scurrilous charges at his enemies and waxed rhapsodical, promising good country roads, low utility rates, and free schoolbooks for the children, all at the expense of the rich. The dirt farmers loved him. Standing beneath the Evangeline Oak, he assured the rednecks:

And it is here that Evangeline waited for her lover Gabriel who never came. . . . But Evangeline is not the only one who has waited here in disappointment. Where are the schools . . . that have never come? Where are the roads and highways . . . ? Where are the institutions to care for the sick and disabled? Evangeline wept bitter tears . . . through only one lifetime. Your tears in this country, around this oak, have lasted for generations. Give me the chance to dry the tears of those who still weep here.

They gave him the chance. No rain fell on election day to turn dirt roads to mud and bar the farmers from the polls. At thirty-five Huey Long sat in the statehouse and kept his promise to the poor. "Every man a king," he proclaimed, "but no man wears a crown." No man, to be sure, but the Kingfish, who proceeded to build within his domain the nearest thing so far to an American version of a police state.

Opponents were first cajoled and offered bribes, but if they remained obdurate, they were threatened and sometimes beaten by the state police and their places of business destroyed. When Long first became governor, he fired every state employee who had not supported him, dealt out patronage to the faithful, and starved those who had presumed to attack. He beat back an attempt to impeach him by bribing a number of state senators to announce in advance that they would vote for acquittal regardless of the evidence. Within two years he owned Louisiana. He could buy a legislator, he chortled, "like a sack of potatoes."

"I'm going to be President some day," he boasted, and he meant it. The Depression was rocking America, and the Kingfish sensed in the despair of millions a sounding board that would respond to his give-'em-hell oratory of easy social salvation. Running for senator in 1930 against the incumbent, a gentle, fatuous septuagenarian caricature of the Southern colonel, Joseph Ransdall, Long won in a walk.

Long went to Washington in 1932 and helped elect Franklin Roosevelt, but quickly decided the New Deal was not for him. The enigmatic, affable Roosevelt and the coarse, virulent redneck could find no common political ground. Storming out of the President's office after a fruitless attempt to obtain patronage, an angry Long hurled at Farley: "What the hell is the use of coming down to see this fellow? I can't win any decision over him!"

Not on the President's home territory but among the Depression-ridden masses Long moved to the attack. "Hoover is a hoot owl. Roosevelt is a scrooch owl," he told a radio audience later. "A hoot owl bangs into the roost and knocks the hen clean off and catches her while she's falling. But a scrooch owl slips into the roost and scrooches up to the hen and talks softly to her. And the hen just falls in love with him, and the next thing you know, there ain't no hen."

By early 1935 Long's "Share Our Wealth" program was in high gear. Unlike Coughlin's and Townsend's panaceas, Long's proposals have a strangely modern ring: fortunes were to be limited to $5,000,000 and annual incomes to $1,800,000; there would be a guaranteed annual income of $2,500 and a homestead grant of $6,000 to every family; there would be free education for all, kindergarten through college, old-age pensions, veterans' bonuses, and cheap food through government purchases and storage of farm surpluses. Though crack-brained by the standards of the time, a good many of the Kingfish's social engineering schemes would re-emerge as orthodox policy three or four decades later.

The movement grew. "Prince Franklin," Long assured his adoring followers, was ready to be taken, and he jeered at the New Deal's lesser men, like "Lord Corn Wallace," the "Chicago Chinch Bug" (Harold Ickes), and "Sitting Bull" (General Hugh S. Johnson). Federal agents roamed Louisiana seeking evidence of tax evasion and fraud in Long's own back yard. New Deal patronage went consistently to Long's enemies.

But in the end it was not classical politics that brought Long down. Living by violence, he was struck down by violence. "Good God, I wish somebody would kill the son of a bitch," newspaperman Hodding Carter recalled someone exclaiming at the conclusion of a secret hotel conference of Long's foes. The wish was granted.

Long never moved without a bodyguard. But on the evening of September 8, 1935, thin, bespectacled Dr. Carl Austin Weiss—a man whose family had been ruined by Long's political enmity—stepped out from behind a pillar in the statehouse and put one shot into the victim's belly. The guards, impotent to save the governor, riddled the killer with sixty-one bullets.

By June, 1936, the three crackpot movements on the New Deal's left had coalesced. The Union party backed Congressman William Lemke of North Dakota, a Populist who walked with the long stride of a prairie farmer. Pursuing that perennial dream of the underdog, Lemke hoped for an election in which no candidate would receive a majority of electoral votes and the final decision would be thrown into the House of Representatives. The Reverend Gerald L. K. Smith, organizer of Share Our Wealth clubs for Huey Long, pledged Lemke the votes of the dead Kingfish's three million backers. Father Coughlin promised that the Union party would receive a vote of nine million or he would leave the air forever.

In the spring of 1935, when a well-wisher had asked the President to keep before the country a "vision of high moral purpose," Roosevelt answered that public opinion could not "because of human weakness, be attuned for long periods of time to a constant repetition of the highest note in the scale. . . . If . . . I had tried to keep up the pace of 1933 and 1934, the inevitable histrionics of the new actors, Long and Coughlin . . . would have turned the eyes of the audience away from the main drama itself!"

If the gathering forces to the left of the New Deal demanded some effective response, the truth is that just as surely the President's ties to the right were dissolving. Roosevelt had begun his Presidency with the lofty conception of a President something like a constitutional monarch, serenely presiding over all the people. But the sniping of the small-town businessmen in a thousand country-club locker rooms across the nation, the fulminations of big business and the Liberty League, and the desertion of essentially conservative minds like Al Smith, Hugh Johnson, and Raymond Moley from his camp had all convinced him that reconciliation, or peace, with the Right was impossible.

The President had begun the year 1935 in a remarkably conciliatory mood. His State of the Union message of January contained little that was startling, or threatening, to those who had weathered the Hundred Days. "We can, if we will," he assured the Congress, "make 1935 a genuine period of good feeling. . . . The Federal Government must and shall quit this business of relief." His request to Congress for $4,880,000,000, shocking as it must have seemed by the standards of the time, fell far short of the relief measures his radical supporters wished of him.

Yet as winter turned to spring, the New Deal, it seemed, could do nothing to appease the forces of conservatism. The legislation of the Hundred Days had been a mixed bag, measures borrowing from the most diverse sources, from right, left, and center. On May 27 the Supreme Court struck down the N.R.A., that mighty government scheme designed to sustain and regulate business, over the mere complaint of a Brooklyn poultry dealer that his constitutional rights had been infringed upon by his being forced to comply with the Live Poultry Code, which set standards for wages, hours, and quality of goods in the chicken business. The federal government, the conservative Court stated, had no right to control the business practices of commercial poultry butchers, even though the sick chicken involved in the Schechter case had manifestly traveled far in interstate commerce. The Court ignored the Depression and was unmoved by the government brief, which pointed out that well over 90 per cent of the chickens, ducks, and turkeys consumed in New York came from thirty-five states, most of them located in the Middle West and the South. According to Chief Justice Hughes, reading the majority opinion: "Extraordinary conditions do not create or enlarge constitutional power. . . . Congress cannot delegate legislative power to the President to exercise an unfettered discretion to make whatever laws he thinks may be needed or advisable for the rehabilitation and expansion of trade or industry." As for the assertion that Schechter's poultry dealings were in interstate commerce, and thus regulable by Washington, Hughes stated: "So far as the poultry here in question is concerned, the flow in interstate commerce had ceased. The poultry had come to a permanent rest within the state."

This was a construction of the commerce clause of the Constitution so narrow that Chairman Donald Richberg of the National Industrial Recovery Board observed (General Hugh Johnson had been asked to leave the N.R.A. months before and had been replaced by a five-member board headed by Richberg): "This deci-

sion of the Supreme Court makes all codes of fair competition unenforceable as a matter of law."

Nor did it end there. In the lower courts the A.A.A. was already under attack—with a predictable outcome when the case reached the "Nine Old Men" in Washington in December, 1935. "The big issue," said the President to the assembled news corps four days after the Supreme Court had struck down the A.A.A.—the First Lady sat nearby knitting a blue sock—"is this: Does this decision mean that the United States Government has no control over any economic problem?" His conclusion was an ominous one: "We have been relegated to the horse-and-buggy definition of interstate commerce." But in the end it would be the people who would decide.

And so, beset by his enemies to the right and the left, Franklin Roosevelt signaled a second Hundred Days.

For months Senator Robert Wagner of New York had been pushing for an expanded labor protection law. Section 7a of the National Industrial Recovery Act (N.I.R.A.) had guaranteed labor the right to organize, but its ambiguities were legion. Shot through with loopholes, the law permitted industrialists to organize docile company unions even while employing thugs to police the assembly lines and cow the organizers of the American Federation of Labor, the United Mine Workers, and the rest of the militant unions.

Roosevelt, though initially no friend of big labor, nonetheless had been depicted by labor as such. The N.I.R.A.'s Section 7a permitted unions, and therefore the administration was taken by the union bosses as giving its blessing to unions. Posters appeared everywhere—"President Roosevelt Wants You To Join the Union." Suddenly unionism became good Americanism, something it had not been since before the years of the Big Red Scare.

Realizing the value of the Wagner Bill (which established a National Labor Relations Board and required employers to bargain with the unions in good faith), the President, three days before the *Schechter v. United States* decision, announced his support of the bill. The legislation passed before June, 1935, ended.

Pressuring Congress, issuing thinly veiled warnings,

firing off dozens of two- and three-line notes to balky legislators, the President next pushed through the first social security legislation. By today's standards it was only a faltering first step, and it was weak by comparison with Bismarck's social legislation in Germany half a century earlier, but for America, citadel of rugged individualism, it was revolutionary.

The T.V.A. was broadened; the A.A.A. was revised in an effort to stave off the disapproval of the Nine Old Men. A holding company act struck at the utilities. And there was a Huey Longish "soak the rich" tax bill designed to make exceedingly difficult the passing of large family fortunes from one generation to the next. To accomplish this the President demanded an increase in taxes on inheritances to a scale sufficient to ensure that few fortunes could survive beyond two or three generations. To plug any loopholes the inheritance tax left, the President requested and, after two months of debate, got a gift tax, greatly increased income taxes on exalted incomes, and, most shocking of all, the first graduated income tax on corporations, the last a clear infringement of business' sacred right to amass unlimited profits free of government inspection.

And, of course, as his political enemies were beginning to learn, Franklin Roosevelt was indeed the grand wizard. Lacking in ideological constancy, "appallingly open-minded" as one critic put it, he was a master of political psychology. By his support of the Wagner Bill he had recruited millions of laboring men to his cause, to join him with a fervor quite different from their numb acquiescence in the 1932 election. In that election Roosevelt had won merely because he was not Hoover. This time, in 1936, the nation turned to him with a perfervid will to believe.

The Liberty League thundered, but such voices of conservatism and inherited wealth merely shored up the President's popularity. The Republicans put up in honest Alf Landon an unassuming but not entirely unimposing former Bull Mooser, no friend to robber barons and unregenerate business, and the *Literary Digest*, on the basis of a straw vote among readers, predicted a heavy Republican victory in the autumn. But the average voter was not listening to Alf Landon.

Only four days before the election Herbert Hoover reviewed and denounced the record of the New Deal: Freedom does not die from frontal attack. It dies because men

in power no longer believe in a system based upon liberty. . . . I gave the warning against this philosophy of government four years ago from a heart heavy with anxiety for the future of our country. . . . Those ideas were not new. Most of them had been urged upon me.

I rejected the notion of great trade monopolies and price-fixing through codes. . . . I rejected the schemes of "economic planning" to regiment and coerce the farmer. That was born of a Roman despot 1,400 years ago and grew up into the A.A.A.

I refused national plans to put the government into business in competition with its citizens. That was born of Karl Marx.

I vetoed the idea of recovery through stupendous spending to prime the pump. That was born of a British professor.

I rejected all these things because they would not only delay recovery but because I knew that in the end they would shackle free men.

But few were listening to Hoover. And few followed the hysterical gaggle to the President's left that confidently predicted nine million votes for William Lemke, who was striding into battle with the joint blessings of Townsend, Coughlin, and the ghost of Long.

Three days before the election the President answered the attack from the business community. Forgotten was the old dream of national reconciliation. The appeal was now frankly to partisanship and class. Reviewing the phalanx of his enemies, he lifted his voice in challenge: "Never before in all our history have these forces been so united against one candidate as they stand today." And the patrician voice grew threatening and grim. "They are unanimous in their hate for me—and I welcome their hatred." The audience roared approval for its man.

On election night the returns came in—the greatest landslide in history: forty-six of forty-eight states, 60.7 per cent of the popular vote, 523 electoral votes out of a possible 531.

The Republican hopes were shattered. The President's enemies on the left likewise were broken. Lemke's Union party polled a mere 882,000—less than one-tenth of Father Coughlin's boast. Earl Browder and the Communist party received a minuscule 80,000 votes.

An old political maxim, based on the supposed accuracy of Maine's September elections as a political barometer, had it, "As Maine goes, so goes the nation." On the evening of November 4, 1936, a happy Jim Farley chortled: "As Maine goes, so goes Vermont."

New Deal Upbeat

In mid-March, 1933, at the request of President Roosevelt, Congress legalized the sale of light wines and beers, not to exceed 3.2 per cent in alcoholic content. Considering the innocuous nature of the brew that was liberated, the resultant celebration (above) seems immoderate in retrospect. However, it was one small token that happy days were here again, as a popular song heralded—or were on their way at least. For conservatives, the rapid succession of new legislation passed during the first Hundred Days of the new administration to alleviate the Depression carried the threat of revolution. Actually, much of what was done was rooted in precedents, both here and abroad, or had earlier been considered. It was the enormously accelerated rate of such developments that, in contrast to the leisurely pace of reform in the past, was truly revolutionary. The social tensions that were created or released by the succession of events, then and during the rest of the decade, gave a distinctive character to those years. Seldom has the nation changed so much in so short a time.

Person to Person

The advent of national network radio broadcasting in the 1920's had given a new, far-reaching immediacy to reports of daily developments throughout the land. A week after his inauguration Roosevelt delivered over the air the first of what were to be called his fireside chats. In those overtly informal talks, addressed to millions of his fellow citizens, the President discussed the grave problems of the time and the steps he was taking to meet them. Invariably starting with the words "My friends," a salutation Roosevelt had used since his earliest days in politics, and delivered in a relaxed, intimate voice, those talks made the mass of the people feel they were closer to their President than ever before in history. In that first "chat" he emphatically reminded his listeners that the problems of the day were theirs no less than his to meet and solve, and asked for their participation in the common cause of national rehabilitation. "Let us unite in banishing fear," he counseled. Even the "forgotten man," to whom Roosevelt alluded in one of his addresses, felt he was remembered. As one workman remarked, "It's the first time in my recollection that a President ever got up and said, 'I'm interested in and aim to do something for the working man.'"

To many the early projects sponsored by the New Deal seemed to promise relief from despair. The short-lived National Recovery Administration (N.R.A.) was launched in the summer of 1933 with all the fervor of a wartime campaign. Supporters of that new expedient marched in a long procession up Fifth Avenue in New York (above left) and in other places; movie starlets stenciled their bare backs with the Blue Eagle, symbol of the N.R.A., and let the sun burn its outline on their skin (top). Earlier that year the Civilian Conservation Corps (C.C.C.) had been organized to provide meaningful paid work for the youth of the land and, incidentally, to help conserve the country's natural resources (above right).

In some areas the soil produced far more than impoverished consumers could purchase, except at prices ruinously low for farmers. Under the Agricultural Adjustment Administration (A.A.A.) cotton farmers (right), among others, were paid for plowing under surplus crops. Elsewhere the land was pitifully blighted. The Tennessee Valley Authority (T.V.A.) undertook to develop an emaciated region almost as large as England. Below, left and right, are two of the twenty-six major dams that are part of this huge system for the development of the land and the betterment of the welfare of its people. The Civil Works Administration (C.W.A.) put four million men to work on highways (bottom) and other projects.

BROWN BROTHERS

UNDERWOOD & UNDERWOOD

BROWN BROTHERS

BROWN BROTHERS

In 1935 the Works Progress Administration (W.P.A.) sponsored the Federal Theater Project to employ jobless performers and to bring entertainment to the country (above). Some W.P.A. clerical workers in Washington even found themselves "on stage" in improvised quarters (below).

The host of federal agencies, designated by initials, was the butt of cartoonists and satirists. Critics complained that the New Dealers had brewed up an "alphabet soup."

Dust and Drought

In May, 1934, the vital topsoil of a large portion of the Great Plains was lifted off the earth and forced upward in wind-driven, opaque clouds of dust. Dust storms had swept over large sections of the West before, but never on such a devastating scale as those that came with the droughts of the early 1930's. Also, by then the nation had become painfully conscious of its land problems and witnessed this phenomenon with an almost morbid fascination. In *Drought Stricken Area* Alexandre Hogue painted his grim impression of the desolation that followed the dust storms.

Early farmers in the Great Plains had abused the soil with poor farming practices from the time they settled the land. The tragedy of this misuse could now be read with a new and poignant understanding. As cattle gathered thirstily about water holes almost filled with shifting soil (opposite), the streets of cities were darkened by the wind-borne dirt (above). Some roads were blocked, railroad schedules were disrupted, and in the wake of the storm came "dust pneumonia." To one observer it seemed that civilization was retreating before an advancing wilderness of wind-driven, parched sand and weeds.

Soil erosion was bad enough; human erosion was worse. For those whose land was skinned there was little to do but move on. The migrant hordes that took to the roads, with their meager belongings packed in jalopies (below), camping now and then to look for work (right), formed the long procession that John Steinbeck described with such compassion in *The Grapes of Wrath*. "In the daylight they scuttled like bugs to the westward; and as the dark caught them, they clustered like bugs near to shelter and to water . . . lonely and perplexed." Their abandoned fields were in time combined into large tracts where power farming plowed over their tragic failures (opposite below).

The Ill-Starred

The temper of the times was tried by other tragedies, which came impartially from the air, from the high seas, and from beneath the earth itself. In 1933 an earthquake brought death and destruction to Long Beach, California (above). A year later the liner *Morro Castle* was suddenly swept by flames and beached, with a loss of about 130 lives, at Asbury Park, New Jersey (opposite). In 1935 the dirigible *Macon* (opposite above), commissioned in 1933, broke up off Point Sur, California. A similar disaster had plunged her sister ship, the *Akron,* into the Atlantic in 1933.

Above: an architect's rendering of the U.S. Government Building; left: the fair at night; below: the Midget City Village. Opposite above: an official poster; opposite below: Sally Rand poses pensively with her bubble.

Like two earlier American world's fairs—the Centennial International Exhibition held at Philadelphia in 1876 and the World's Columbian Exposition at Chicago in 1893—the Century of Progress Exposition of 1933, also staged at Chicago, opened during a great depression. However, on May 27 of that year a beam of light from the star Arcturus actuated the switch that turned on the lights of what proved to be a highly successful venture. It was the biggest show of its kind up to that time. More than twenty million visitors from all points of the compass thronged through the gates. Profits ran to six figures. It was a spectacular rebuke to the Depression, so successful it was held over a second year. There was diversion for people of every stripe—from the most current wonders of science to a reconstruction of a Mayan temple and, along the Midway, Miss Sally Rand, apparently stark naked with, first, her huge fans and, then, her outsize bubble, which she manipulated with titillating grace.

265

Thomas Wolfe, shortly after publication of his second novel.

His first novel, Look Homeward, Angel, *introduced Thomas Wolfe to the reading public in 1929, and his second,* Of Time and the River, *published in 1935, confirmed his place as an author of importance. Wolfe had an almost mystical love for the variety and vastness of America, and he became lyrical when he wrote of his country. The excerpt here, from* Of Time and the River, *consists of musings of the young protagonist, Eugene Gant, about the autumn land as he lies abed in his home, to which he has returned from college because of his father's death.*

"Now October has come again which in our land is different from October in the other lands. The ripe, the golden month has come again, and in Virginia the chinkapins are falling. Frost sharps the middle music of the seasons, and all things living on the earth turn home again. The country is so big you cannot say the country has the same October. In Maine, the frost comes sharp and quick as driven nails, just for a week or so the woods, all of the bright and bitter leaves, flare up: the maples turn a blazing bitter red, and other leaves turn yellow like a living light, falling about you as you walk the woods, falling about you like small pieces of the sun so that you cannot say

where sunlight shakes and flutters on the ground, and where the leaves.

"Meanwhile the Palisades are melting in massed molten colors, the season swings along the nation, and a little later in the South dense woodings on the hill begin to glow and soften, and when they smell the burning woodsmoke in Ohio children say: 'I'll bet that there's a forest fire in Michigan.' And the mountaineer goes hunting down in North Carolina, he stays out late with mournful flop-eared hounds, a rind of moon comes up across the rude lift of the hills: what do his friends say to him when he stays out late? Full of hoarse innocence and laughter, they will say: 'Mister, yore ole woman's

goin' to whup ye if ye don't go home.'"

Oh, return, return!

"October is the richest of the seasons: the fields are cut, the granaries are full, the bins are loaded to the brim with fatness, and from the cider-press the rich brown oozings of the York Imperials run. The bee bores to the belly of the yellowed grape, the fly gets old and fat and blue, he buzzes loud, crawls slow, creeps heavily to death on sill and ceiling, the sun goes down in blood and pollen across the bronzed and mown fields of old October.

"The corn is shocked: it sticks out in hard yellow rows upon dried ears, fit now for great red barns in Pennsyl-

"a cry, a space, an ecstasy!"

vania, and the big stained teeth of crunching horses. The indolent hooves kick swiftly at the boards, the barn is sweet with hay and leather, wood and apples — this, and the clean dry crunching of the teeth is all: the sweat, the labor, and the plow is over. The late pears mellow on a sunny shelf; smoked hams hang to the warped barn rafters; the pantry shelves are loaded with 300 jars of fruit. Meanwhile the leaves are turning, turning, up in Maine, the chestnut burrs plop thickly to the earth in gusts of wind, and in Virginia the chinkapins are falling.

"There is a smell of burning in small towns in afternoon, and men with buckles on their arms are raking leaves in yards as boys come by with straps slung back across their shoulders. The oak leaves, big and brown, are bedded deep in yard and gutter: they make deep wadings to the knee for children in the streets. The fire will snap and crackle like a whip, sharp acrid smoke will sting the eyes, in mown fields the little vipers of the flame eat past the black coarse edges of burned stubble like a line of locusts. Fire drives a thorn of memory in the heart.

"The bladed grass, a forest of small spears of ice, is thawed by noon: summer is over but the sun is warm again, and there are days throughout the land of gold and russet. But summer is dead and gone, the earth is waiting, suspense and ecstasy are gnawing at the hearts of men, the brooding prescience of frost is there. The sun flames red and bloody as it sets, there are old red glintings on the battered pails, the great barn gets the ancient light as the boy slops homeward with warm foaming milk. Great shadows lengthen in

the fields, the old red light dies swiftly, and the sunset barking of the hounds is faint and far and full of frost: there are shrewd whistles to the dogs, and frost and silence — this is all. Wind stirs and scuffs and rattles up the old brown leaves, and through the night the great oak leaves keep falling.

"Trains cross the continent in a swirl of dust and thunder, the leaves fly down the tracks behind them: the great trains cleave through gulch and gulley, they rumble with spoked thunder on the bridges over the powerful brown wash of mighty rivers, they toil through hills, they skirt the rough brown stubble of shorn fields, they whip past empty stations in the little towns and their great stride pounds its even pulse across America. Field and hill and lift and gulch and hollow, mountain and plain and river, a wilderness with fallen trees across it, a thicket of bedded brown and twisted undergrowth, a plain, a desert, and a plantation, a mighty landscape with no fenced niceness, an immensity of fold and convolution that can never be remembered, that can never be forgotten, that has never been described — weary with harvest, potent with every fruit and ore, the immeasurable richness embrowned with autumn, rank, crude, unharnessed, careless of scars or beauty, everlasting and magnificent, a cry, a space, an ecstasy! — American earth in old October.

"And the great winds howl and swoop across the land: they make a distant roaring in great trees, and boys in bed will stir in ecstasy, thinking of demons and vast swoopings through the earth. All through the night there is the clean, the bitter rain of acorns,

and the chestnut burrs are plopping to the ground.

"And often in the night there is only the living silence, the distant frosty barking of a dog, the small clumsy stir and feathery stumble of the chickens on limed roosts, and the moon, the low and heavy moon of autumn, now barred behind the leafless poles of pines, now at the pinewoods' brooding edge and summit, now falling with ghost's dawn of milky light upon rimed clods of fields and on the frosty scurf on pumpkins, now whiter, smaller, brighter, hanging against the steeple's slope, hanging the same way in a million streets, steeping all the earth in frost and silence.

"Then a chime of frost-cold bells may peal out on the brooding air, and people lying in their beds will listen. They will not speak or stir, silence will gnaw the darkness like a rat, but they will whisper in their hearts:

"'Summer has come and gone, has come and gone. And now — ?' But they will say no more, they will have no more to say: they will wait listening, silent and brooding as the frost, to time, strange ticking time, dark time that haunts us with the briefness of our days. They will think of men long dead, of men now buried in the earth, of frost and silence long ago, of a forgotten face and moment of lost time, and they will think of things they have no words to utter.

"And in the night, in the dark, in the living sleeping silence of the towns, the million streets, they will hear the thunder of the fast express, the whistles of great ships upon the river.

"What will they say then? What will they say?"

Circus in Jersey

Early in 1935 a swarm of newsmen set up headquarters in Flemington, New Jersey, to cover the circuslike trial of Bruno R. Hauptmann for the abduction and murder two and a half years earlier of the infant son of Charles A. and Anne Morrow Lindbergh (at right, the baby with his mother and two grandmothers). No crime of the century had so deeply affected the American public at large. The enormity of the deed was compounded by several cruel hoaxes, played by those hoping to profit by supplying false leads. After exhaustive detective work, Hauptmann was brought to justice. The evidence against him was overwhelming. Ransom money paid by the Lindberghs was found when Hauptmann's garage was demolished; a farm couple (above) identified his photograph as the man they had seen near the Lindbergh home just before the crime; the kidnap ladder was traced to him. Found guilty, Hauptmann was executed.

INTERNATIONAL NEWS PHOTO

Above, wreckage of the Hauptmann garage, where ransom money was found; left, defense lawyer, Edward J. Reilly, and Hauptmann (right) during trial; below, photographers, reporters, and the curious await verdict outside courthouse.

LEFT AND BELOW: BROWN BROTHERS

Public Enemies

The crime wave that had mounted to such ominous heights during Prohibition rolled on after repeal. In 1934 the F.B.I. was given the equipment, the trained personnel, and the authority to take effective action. Dauntless G-men were matched against the criminal elite, nominated by Director J. Edgar Hoover as Public Enemies with numbers to indicate their relative status. For a while John Dillinger (below), wanted for sundry murders, bank robberies, and jail breaks, was clearly Number One. G-men gunned him down on July 22, 1934—a melodramatic event that moved Reginald Marsh to reconstruct the scene (opposite). "Pretty Boy" Floyd (below left) and a sordid couple named Bonnie and Clyde (above left) were among the Public Enemies shot down by law officers.

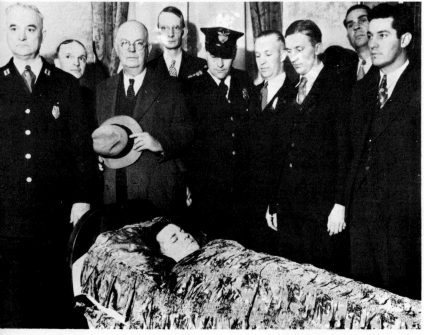

Above: George Burns and Gracie Allen. Opposite, top: One Man's Family, *a program that featured domestic chatter in a typical American family; middle: the* WLS Barn Dance; *bottom: the quiz show* Information Please, *with sports writer and naturalist John Kieran answering a question.*

On the Air

Even in the worst years of the Depression people purchased radio sets in great numbers. For one thing, there was more time to kill; for another, the national networks were providing entertainment such as had never before been accessible to the Middletowns and Main Streets of America. Back in the Twenties, Secretary of Commerce Hoover had warned that the newly opening air waves must be controlled for the public benefit—must not be choked by "advertising chatter." By the Thirties, however, radio had become the most pervasive and persuasive advertising medium ever realized. To associate a product with glamourous performers of Broadway and Hollywood, name bands, famous newscasters, and the like was considered an incomparable commercial advantage to any merchant.

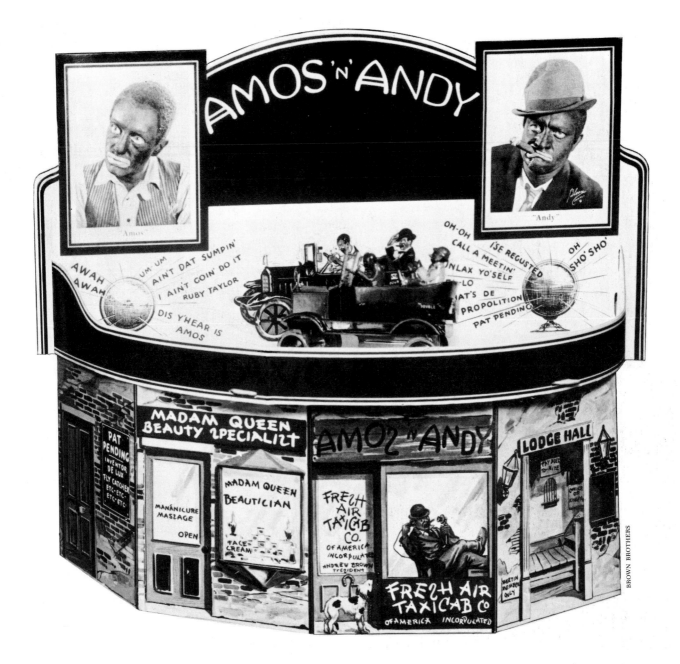

Between the decline of vaudeville and the advent of television, radio provided the greatest variety show of all time. Every conceivable type of entertainment, from symphony to jazz, from drama to *Amos 'n' Andy*, competed for higher ratings to attract more extravagant sponsors. Among the great shows (opposite, by the numbers): (1) Fibber McGee and Molly, (2) the dummy Charlie McCarthy with ventriloquist Edgar Bergen and guests Carole Lombard and Don Ameche, (3) Fred Allen (right) with John Brown and Portland Hoffa, (4) Jack Benny and Mary Livingstone, (5) *The Goldbergs*, (6) singer Jessica Dragonette. Above: a display advertisement for the *Amos 'n' Andy* show. Right: the first broadcast (in 1931) by Kate Smith, soon to become the First Lady of Radio.

Art in the Depression

During the 1930's the W.P.A. paid thousands of artists to produce works ranging from huge murals for public buildings to meticulous renderings of early American artifacts. In those years many who would form the avant-garde in postwar America—Jackson Pollock, Willem de Kooning, Ad Reinhardt, among others—had unprecedented opportunities to develop their talents. However, vintage artists and their followers continued to celebrate the traditional aspects of their native scene with unchanging, more or less realistic styles. Charles Burchfield found poetry in the very drabness of inland American towns, as in his *Six O'Clock* (opposite above). In *Line Storm* (opposite below) John Steuart Curry typically pictured daily life on the plains of his beloved Kansas. In *The Bowl* (above) Reginald Marsh took his theme, as ever, from the turbulence of metropolitan life, in this case Steeplechase Park at Coney Island.

277

In High Yaller, *above, painted from memory after a trip through Harlem, Reginald Marsh has captured the prevailing style of 1934.*

As the Thirties emerged from the Twenties the physical shape of womankind was remodeled to meet the critical demands of the new decade. Her waist was returned to the place where nature had originally planned it. Although her legs almost vanished behind descending hemlines, she was once again permitted to have hips of normal contours. Her corsage assumed new prominence. (Occasionally, it was said, mountains were made of molehills.) Her hair was allowed to grow again, proudly, and the tight helmets, or cloches, of yesteryear were replaced by rakishly tilted, or slouched, headgear that amply framed her hair. Her feet were refashioned into new silhouettes. A whole new species had been created.

"the luckiest generation ever"

You who are crossing forty may not know it, but you are the luckiest generation ever. The advantages you are about to enjoy will soon be recited, with a sincere undertone of envy. The whole world has been remodeled for your greater glory. Ancient philosophies and rituals are being demolished to clear the ground for whatever you choose to erect upon their sites. Every day brings forth some new thing that adds to the joy of life after forty. Work becomes easy and brief. Play grows richer and longer. Leisure lengthens. Life's afternoon is brighter, warmer, fuller of song; and long before the shadows stretch, every fruit grows ripe.

Best of all, though, is your inner deliverance. A better age has delivered you from the Conviction of Incompetence, that curse of the middle years. The men of old believed that life was ended at forty, and for them, alas, it often was. So, as the thirties slipped by, their spirits flagged; they grew disconsolate, embittered, hard; and they looked upon the young with an envy that built a wall of hate between the generations. But this wall is crumbling under the blasts of a new trumpet. Year by year the line between youth and age thins and fades. Already the patriarchal family has vanished. Parents and children are simply human beings of the same blood under one roof; they are not hostile clans. Grandfather dances a jig at little granddaughter's birthday.

The ancient clash of interests is succeeded by a division of labor. For youth the tasks of youth; for age the tasks of age. And for every man his own life, to be ordered and adorned as he will. Man is no longer slave to man; but

---

Books that tell how to be popular, beautiful, healthy, or rich always find large audiences, but few have had such a tremendous reception as Dale Carnegie's How to Win Friends and Influence People, *the leading nonfiction best seller of 1936. The book's appeal lay not only in its promise to the reader of friends, popularity, higher salary, and just about everything else, but also in the way it made their attainment appear to be a matter of following a few simple rules.*

The following selection is the beginning of a chapter in which Carnegie reveals the secrets of "How to Make People Like You Instantly."

I was waiting in line to register a letter in the Post Office at Thirty-Third Street and Eighth Avenue in New York. I noticed that the registry clerk was bored with his job—weighing envelopes, handing out the stamps, making change, issuing receipts—the same monotonous grind year after year. So I said to myself: "I am going to try to make that chap like me. Obviously, to make him like me, I must say something nice, not about myself, but about him. So I asked myself, 'What is there about him that I can honestly admire?'" That is sometimes a hard question to answer, especially with strangers; but, in this case, it happened to be easy. I instantly saw something

Norman Rockwell's The Gossips *shows a kind of human interaction of which Carnegie would not have approved.*

I admired no end.

So while he was weighing my envelope, I remarked with enthusiasm: "I certainly wish I had your head of hair."

He looked up, half-startled, his face beaming with smiles. "Well, it isn't as good as it used to be," he said modestly. I assured him that although it might have lost some of its pristine glory, nevertheless it was still magnificent. He was immensely pleased. We carried on a pleasant little conversation and the last thing he said to me was:

In 1932 Walter Pitkin, a professor of journalism at Columbia University, produced a book called Life Begins at Forty. *Some of its reasoning was rather fuzzy, but its main theme, that a person over forty during the 1930's was fortunate indeed, must have had wide appeal, for the book became a best seller.*

all men pull together to enslave atoms and molecules. Where of old the growing boy had to drudge his years away, now an engine turns the trick. The Machine Age emancipates muscle first, then mind also; and, as we shall try to show, makes it possible for all men to be men as long as they live.

High excitements lie ahead of you now turning forty. The race has nibbled the fruits of wisdom and found them both sweet and sustaining. Thus far it has turned to account almost nothing of its inventions and discoveries. The world is still to be civilized; and, in your day, this supreme process will begin. Were you to be no more than idle spectators, all other ages, past and future, would envy you. But you will be more than that: you will eat the meat of giants and overtop all your ancestors. You will soon look through a 200-inch telescope and scan the back yards of the moon as if they were at the bottom of a little hill. You will remodel your frames and your temperaments with cunningly concocted foods and pills. You will have little cause to worry over the price of clothes and rent. Or, if you do not live to see such wonders, you will at least behold them drawing near. . . .

You will, in a subtle fashion, be even luckier than your descendants; for they will be born in civilization and find all its splendors commonplace. But you, who have known the barbarians and have been choked by the stench of diseased millions and have watched fifty million wretches die in a dirty brawl called war, under the lead of gangsters, will taste the full, tingling bouquet of a wine which, made of a million years of human vintage, is about to be tapped for the first time.

"radiate a little happiness"

"Many people have admired my hair."

I'll bet that chap went out to lunch that day walking on air. I'll bet he went home that night and told his wife about it. I'll bet he looked in the mirror and said: "It *is* a beautiful head of hair."

I told this story once in public; and a man asked me afterwards: "What did you want to get out of him?"

What was I trying to get out of him!!! What was I trying to get out of him!!!

If we are so contemptibly selfish that we can't radiate a little happiness and pass on a bit of honest appreciation without trying to screw something out of the other person in return—if our souls are no bigger than sour crab apples, we shall meet with the failure we so richly deserve.

Oh yes, I did want something out of that chap. I wanted something priceless. And I got it. I got the feeling that I had done something for him without his being able to do anything whatever in return for me. That is a feeling that glows and sings in your memory long after the incident is passed.

Carnegie's book is largely a collection of anecdotes to dramatize the points he wants to make. The following story is meant to prove that if you wish to win men of mettle to your way of thinking, you must throw down a challenge to them.

Charles Schwab [of Bethlehem Steel] had a mill manager whose men weren't producing their quota of work.

"How is it," Schwab asked, "that a man as capable as you can't make this mill turn out what it should?"

"I don't know," the man replied, "I've coaxed the men; I've pushed them; I've sworn and cussed; I've threatened them with damnation and being fired. But nothing works. They just won't produce."

It happened to be the end of the day, just before the night shift came on.

"Give me a piece of chalk," Schwab said. Then, turning to the nearest man: "How many heats did your shift make today?"

"Six."

Without another word, Schwab chalked a big figure six on the floor, and walked away.

When the night shift came in, they saw the "6" and asked what it meant.

"The big boss was in here today," the day men said. "He asked us how many heats we made, and we told him six. He chalked it down on the floor."

The next morning Schwab walked through the mill again. The night shift had rubbed out "6," and replaced it with a big "7."

When the day shift reported for work the next morning, they saw a big "7" chalked on the floor. So the night shift thought they were better than the day shift, did they? Well, they would show the night shift a thing or two. They pitched in with enthusiasm and when they quit that night, they left behind them an enormous, swaggering "10." Things were stepping up.

Shortly this mill, that had been lagging way behind in production, was turning out more work than any other mill in the plant.

282

The Breath of Romance

NOW AT NEW
LOW PRICES

At times it appeared that the most menacing threats to the national well-being were bad breath, unpleasant body odors, pyorrhea ("pink toothbrush"), and poor complexions. Out of delicacy, it seems, even one's very best friends hesitated to mention such intimate afflictions—afflictions that no romance could hope to survive. Fortunately for unwitting offenders, the producers and promoters of toiletries and cosmetics felt no such compunctions and proclaimed the unmentionable, without reserve, to a nationwide audience.

283

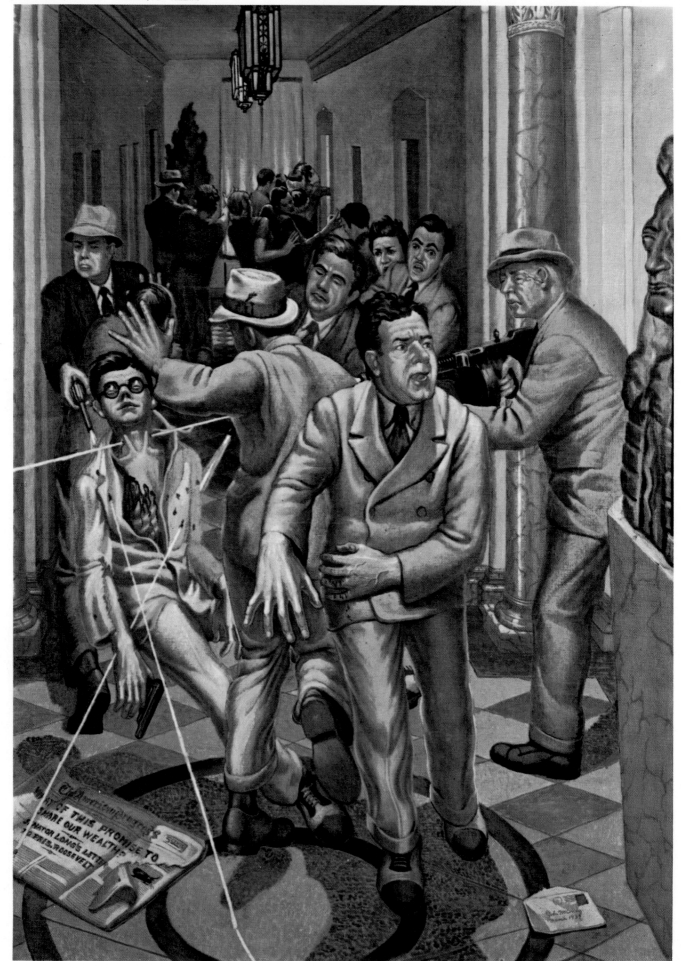

Dixie Dictator

Senator Huey P. Long made himself absolute dictator of Louisiana before advancing on Washington with dreams of greater power. An early supporter of the New Deal, he soon became Roosevelt's most voluble critic. With loud, incontinent rhetoric and a demagogue's eye on the Presidency, he proclaimed his cures for the nation's ills. He attracted followers among the gullible and fellow demagogues before he was shot by an assassin (opposite) in 1935.

The Rabble Rousers

A motley assortment of other would-be reformers offered panaceas to the indigent, the anxious, and the credulous. There were more old people in America than ever before and to them Dr. Francis E. Townsend (right) addressed a beguiling promise of old-age pensions— and to this crusade his followers pledged their allegiance (below). The Reverend Gerald L. K. Smith (opposite left) carried on the dead Huey Long's program, adding anti-Semitism and pro-Nazism to his ranting message. With more piety but with similar prejudices the Michigan priest Father Coughlin (opposite right) immoderately challenged democratic approaches to social justice. A coalition party formed by these three nominated William Lemke (opposite below) for the Presidency in 1936, but garnered few votes.

OVERLEAF: *presidential contender Governor Alfred M. Landon of Kansas at Republican National Convention in Cleveland, 1936. Landon lost to Roosevelt by a wide margin.*

Famous Faces of the Thirties

The Depression cast a dark shadow
over the 1930's, stifling gaiety and causing
the courage of men to flag. Nevertheless, the
decade produced a full quota of heroes, artists,
clowns, and villains.

Comedians in Blackface

Freeman F. Gosden (Amos), left, and Charles J. Correll (Andy) applied plenty of burnt cork before they posed for publicity pictures.

The program was called *Amos 'n' Andy*; tens of millions of Americans religiously tuned it in on their radios five times a week during the 1930's, and a great many of those onetime listeners still remember it with nostalgia. Yet today it is doubtful whether such a show would last beyond its first episode in the face of the torrent of protests it would receive from Negroes and civil rights groups. Not that there was anything at all vicious about *Amos 'n' Andy*; on the contrary, it was engaging and humorous in its own way. But the climate of feeling has changed since the Thirties, and the black man refuses to let white actors depict him as a bumbling, amusing refugee from a minstrel show.

Amos and Andy were, respectively, Freeman F. Gosden, formerly a salesman in Virginia, and Charles J. Correll, onetime Peoria bricklayer. Both men had had the urge to be actors, and each had acquired—largely self-taught—such artistic talents as clog dancing, singing, and ukulele playing. They became amateur entertainers, and both—Correll in 1918 and Gosden in 1919—eventually gave up their regular jobs to go to work for the Joe Bren Company, an organization that went about the country supplying direction, script, music, and costumes for lodges and other organizations wishing to put on home-talent shows. The two men met in Durham, North Carolina, when both were sent there to produce a show for the Durham Elks Club.

After that their paths crossed from time to time as each traveled about the country for the Joe Bren Company, and when they were both given managerial jobs at the home office in Chicago in 1924, they shared an apartment. They worked out a song-and-patter routine, took it on the radio once a week for eight months, tried a bit of vaudeville, and then quit the Bren Company and joined radio station WGN in Chicago. They were asked to work out a radio serial, and the result was *Sam 'n' Henry*, a dialect comedy series about two Negro boys.

They moved to station WMAQ, and since their contract did not permit them to take *Sam 'n' Henry* along, they created a new blackface show, *Amos 'n' Andy*, which first went on the air in March, 1928. It was heard live over WMAQ and was broadcast over another fifty stations through recordings. Then, a little more than a year later, a couple of months before the Wall Street crash, Gosden and Correll, as Amos and Andy, went on the NBC network. From then until 1943 the American listeners heard the adventures of Amos and Andy as a continuing serial, five times a week, in fifteen-minute installments, beginning at seven o'clock in the evening.

At the outset, Amos and Andy were depicted as two young colored men just up from Atlanta and out to make their way in Harlem. They started a taxi business; their only capital asset was a decrepit automobile without a top, whence the name Fresh Air Taxicab Company. The taxi company thereafter remained a central focus throughout the series. Amos was the steady one of the pair and did all the work. Andy, lazy, always making elaborate plans that went awry, was too busy to do any work. The Fresh Air Taxicab Company, although a shoestring operation, managed to support a secretary, and Andy, whenever he wanted to play the executive, would command, "Buzz me, Miss Blue."

As the show continued, the number of characters proliferated until, when it was finally concluded in 1943, there had been more than five hundred and fifty in all. Some of these had been merely bit parts, but many were continuing roles. The remarkable thing is that Gosden and Correll played every male part, and in addition,

wrote every single episode.

It was inevitable that steady, gravel-voiced Amos should marry his sweetheart, Ruby Taylor, and in time they had a daughter, Arbadella. Andy, on the other hand, was susceptible to every likely filly that crossed his path, a weakness that got him into endless trouble, but he did maintain a more or less steady relationship with Madame Queen, a "beauty specialist." One episode that delighted fans of the series was a trial that resulted when Madame Queen grew impatient with Andy's perennially roving eye and sued him for breach of promise. The two had been engaged 147 times in one year, she testified at the trial, "an' it would been more dan dat if we'd been goin' steady."

Among other characters on the program was the Kingfish, who was willing to obtain something in a straightforward manner only if it was impossible to get it by conniving. There was Brother Crawford, henpecked and complaining, "I want you to know that my wife is very unhappy." There was Sapphire, wife of the Kingfish, and Lawyer Calhoon, who usually met his clients behind the jail, and Needle Nose Fletcher, and slow-moving, dim-witted Lightnin', and a host of others. As they multiplied, the Fresh Air Taxicab Company offices became too confining a stage, and Gosden and Correll created a lodge, the Hall of the Mystic Knights of the Sea, to which all the male members of the cast belonged.

All these people spoke a curious dialect full of malapropisms. "I'se regusted," they would say when something went wrong, and the expression became part of the American language. So did "Check and double check," and "Ow wah! Ow wah!" a groan of misery. "Sho', sho'," "Onlax yo'self," and "What's yo' propolition, stranger?" were typical expressions in the dialogue of the show.

This oddly assorted collection of characters and their misadventures struck a response in an enormous number of Americans. In the early 1930's at seven in the evening the strains of "The Perfect Song," the *Amos 'n' Andy* theme song, could be

heard coming from one open window after another, down neighborhood streets throughout America. Department stores open on weekday evenings broadcast the show on every floor so that potential customers would not stay home to listen. The New York Telephone Company found that calls fell off sharply during the fifteen minutes the program was on the air. Calvin Coolidge, an early fan, left instructions that he should not be disturbed while listening to the program. Henry Ford was another ardent fan, as were author James Thurber and G-man J. Edgar Hoover. Huey Long took his nickname, the Kingfish, from the *Amos 'n' Andy* character.

Though the program reached the height of its popularity in 1930, its decline was so slow as to be almost imperceptible for several years. It was not until 1943 that it was considered necessary to discontinue the long-running serial story of Amos and Andy and their friends. In that year it became a half-hour show once a week, with guest stars, an orchestra, and a studio audience. And Gosden and Correll at last gave over to others the arduous task of writing the show.

There was one part of the population to whom the charm of burnt-cork humor was less than overwhelming. After World War II Negroes, backed by civil rights groups, were at last becoming heard in their protests against making colored people objects of ridicule. As a matter of fact, many of the characters created by Gosden and Correll were sympathetic, and the program itself was warm and witty, but the 1930's were long past, and the social climate was no longer hospitable to blackface humor, even when it was free from malice.

The Columbia Broadcasting System, which had taken over *Amos 'n' Andy*, reduced the emphasis on racial humor and even used Negro actors when a television *Amos 'n' Andy* series was started. Although Negro protests were denied as a reason, the radio show was ended in 1958, and in 1965 the TV series was concluded, laying Amos and Andy to rest at a venerable age.

John L. Lewis

If John L. Lewis was a nightmare to management, he was a political cartoonist's dream, with his baboon's mane, eyebrows like the pelts of two small animals, broad-brimmed fedora, omnipresent stogie, accusatory forefinger, and slumped jowls quivering in righteous umbrage. With all stops out, his bass-baritone had the plangency of a cathedral organ, but its range was limitless; it could rumble like distant thunder or shrivel the marrow of an adversary by fading to a ghostly whisper. His prose was majestic, and never more so than when he was venting his hyperactive spleen. When John L. Lewis characterized a hapless opponent as "a liar by the clock," the alleged liar had been called a liar eloquently, definitively, and with finality. As he himself put it, Lewis spoke for America's mine workers "not in the quavering tones of a mendicant asking alms, but in the thundering voice of the captain of a mighty host."

Lewis had reached the nadir of a promising career in 1932, by which time his mighty host had undergone "an unbroken series of defeats" in the twelve years of his stewardship, and had dwindled from a force of four hundred thousand men to an embattled contingent of one hundred and fifty thousand, many of whom were out of work and most of whom were agreed that "Lewis must go." From this unenviable position Lewis fought his way up (with the help of some providential legislation) to an almost godlike dominance of the American labor movement. As *The New York Times* was later to sum up what

Lewis achieved during the Thirties: "With the exception of President Franklin D. Roosevelt, there were few in those years who exerted more influence in shaping the economic face of the United States."

John L. Lewis was (again in the words of the *Times*) "born to coal mines and to unionism." That birth occurred on February 12, 1880, in Lucas, Iowa. Lewis' father, Thomas, was a miner who had immigrated to Lucas from Wales, as had Lewis' mother, herself a miner's daughter. By the age of twelve, John L. had dropped out of school and followed in his father's coal-smudged footsteps. Those footsteps were more vagrant than those of most miners; Tom Lewis had been active in a workmen's organization called the Knights of Labor and, as a consequence, had been blacklisted by the mine operators around Lucas. John L. was a truculent, sharp-tongued, burly young tough and was perfectly capable of adding injury to insult when exception was taken to his sarcasm.

At twenty-six, Lewis was back home in Lucas after knocking around various mine fields and taking an active role in the affairs of the United Mine Workers' local. The next year, 1907, he married a schoolteacher, Myrta Bell, who took it upon herself to smooth a few of her spouse's rougher edges. John L. had always had a literary bent, and Myrta supplied him with books, charted a systematic course for his self-improvement, and eventually converted him into a man who was as handy with a literary allusion as he was with his fists.

During the next few years, Lewis moved

to another mining town, Panama, Illinois, assumed the presidency of the United Mine Workers' local, became the union's Illinois lobbyist, and in 1911 was appointed by Samuel Gompers to the post of general field agent for the American Federation of Labor. In the course of his subsequent travels Lewis built up a substantial and devoted personal following among the nation's mine unionists. Then in 1920, at the age of forty, he took over as president of the U.M.W., a post he was to occupy, with varying degrees of distinction, for the next four decades.

Lewis set about consolidating his position by excommunicating any union officials who looked even remotely like trouble. Lewis thus made enemies in fairly high places, but his "mighty host," the union rank and file, stood solidly behind him—up to a point. That point was reached when the economic slump following World War I led to a drastic cut in national coal consumption and the laying off of many miners. Other complications, such as the opening of new non-union mines in the South, exacerbated the situation, and Lewis in no way ingratiated himself with his followers by calling a strike that kept union wages up but cut union employment even further. The mine workers were so chronically unemployed that, in effect, they had almost a ten-year head start on the Depression.

By the time the Depression hit the general populace, Lewis' fortunes were at a low state indeed. They took a sudden upturn in 1932, however, with the passage of the Norris-La Guardia Anti-Injunction

Act (which forbade injunctions to prevent peaceful strikes or to enforce yellow dog contracts) and again in 1935 with the Wagner Act (which gave workers the "right to organize and bargain collectively through representatives of their own choosing").

With the passage of the Wagner Act union enrollment increased nearly five-fold, many mine operators realized they were beaten, and wages and employment rose. As Roy Cook put it in his book *Leaders of Labor:* "Lewis' self-confidence, scarcely dented during his years of adversity, gleamed more brightly than ever. With some justice, he saw himself as the savior of the entire working class. Coal was just one link in a great industrial chain. Now was the time to 'organize the unorganized' and bring the auto, aluminum, steel, rubber, and other large industries into the labor movement."

Conservative craft-union-oriented elements within the labor movement were not altogether enchanted with Lewis' grandiose vision of the millennium, and battle was joined at the 1935 A.F. of L. convention at Atlantic City. The debate was heated, acrimonious, and unresolved. In the end, Lewis and a group of seven union leaders founded the Committee for Industrial Organization. Taking the C.I.O.'s case to the nation via radio, Lewis was in fine oratorical fettle when he declaimed: "Let him who will, be he economic tyrant or sordid mercenary, pit his strength against this mighty upsurge of human sentiment now being crystallized in the hearts of thirty million workers who clamor for the

establishment of industrial democracy and for participation in its tangible fruits." By September, 1937, the C.I.O. had a whopping 3,718,000 membership. It was "the greatest mass maneuver of organized industry and organized labor in all history," Lewis said with becoming modesty. "Its results will affect the lives of thousands yet unborn."

If he came off with fewer laurels in his next campaign (ten strikers and union sympathizers died in a losing cause during the Little Steel Strike of 1937), his rhetorical talents remained unimpaired. Hearing that F. D. R.—whose 1936 campaign fund had been enriched to the tune of five hundred

thousand dollars by the C.I.O.—had wished a plague on the houses of both labor and management, Lewis bellowed: "It ill behooves one who has supped at labor's table and who has been sheltered in labor's house to curse with equal fervor and fine impartiality both labor and its adversaries when they become locked in deadly embrace."

John Llewellyn Lewis served organized labor for another twenty-two years, and died within hailing distance of his ninetieth birthday in 1969. He was part and parcel of the Thirties, though, and neither the era nor the man would have been quite the same without the other.

Mae West

It is not accurate to call Mae West a celebrity of the 1930's, for her career began before the turn of the century, and at this writing she has not yet called it quits. But it was in the Thirties that motion pictures first brought her and her free, easy, and exuberant attitude toward sex to a nationwide audience, and made her famous, rich, and something approaching a legend.

Mae West was born in Brooklyn in 1892 (she says 1893) and, like many other actresses-to-be, was on the stage at an early age. In 1897 she appeared in something called *Little Nell the Marchioness*

with a Brooklyn stock company, and during the next half dozen years or so, she had parts in such tried and true favorites as *East Lynne, Ten Nights in a Barroom,* and *Mrs. Wiggs of the Cabbage Patch.* At fourteen she left Brooklyn to go on the national vaudeville circuit. There she teamed up with Frank Wallace to form a song and dance team, and when Miss West was eighteen, the two were secretly married. The union was a failure; the partners separated in every way after a very short time, but it was not until 1943, thirty-two years later, after Wallace had toured the country billing himself as "Mae West's

Husband," that Mae finally got a divorce. She has never tried marriage a second time.

From vaudeville she moved to Broadway and played in a number of revues and dramas. In 1926 she first achieved celebrity with *Sex,* a play she wrote herself. In it Mae played the part of a waterfront prostitute, and the drama was an immediate success, even though the New York newspapers refused to carry advertisements for it. The professional moralists finally brought pressure on the police, who closed *Sex* after a very respectable run of 375 performances, or eleven months. Miss West was found guilty of corrupting the morals of youth after a police officer testified that he had observed her do a belly dance, in which she "moved her navel up and down and from right to left." She spent eight days in the city prison, thoroughly enjoying the immense amount of free publicity.

In 1928 she wrote and produced her greatest stage success, *Diamond Lil*, a humorous melodrama set in New York's Bowery during the Gay Nineties. Miss West played Diamond Lil, a saloon singer, but it was a case of Mae West playing Mae West in the manner that later became so famous. There was the famous hourglass figure clad in long, tight gowns, the piled-up blonde hair, the nasal, sexy voice that was able to turn innocent remarks into double-entendres, the walk that was halfway between a wiggle and a swagger. It was in *Diamond Lil* that she made her famous invitation to a Salvation Army captain, "Come up and see me sometime." A typical Westian touch: in one scene an admirer, overcome by her beauty, exclaims, "Your hands, your lips, your hair, your magnificent shoulders——" She cuts him off with a drawled, "What're you doin', honey, makin' love or takin' inventory?"

After nine good months in New York, Miss West took *Diamond Lil* on the road, and the next year revived *Sex* and took that on the road. In her spare time she wrote *The Constant Sinner*, a novel about a woman whom Miss West described as "an amoral lady of pleasure, whose career takes her from the dives of Harlem to the smart circles of New York and Paris." And, of course, she turned that into a play, with herself in the lead role, which had a successful 1931–32 run. Miss West had only one string, sex, to her violin, but it played a clear tune.

In 1932 she made her first motion picture, a drama about speak-easy life called *Night After Night*. She insisted upon, and got, the unusual right to write her own dialogue. Her opening line set the tone not only of her role in the picture but of every part she would ever play. As she

swept into a speak-easy, glittering with jewelry, an impressed hat check girl remarked, "Goodness, what beautiful diamonds." Miss West turned and drawled, "Goodness had nothin' to do with it, honey." Her costar in the picture, George Raft, recalled her constant upstaging with something less than complete fondness. He commented sourly that she "stole everything but the cameras."

In 1933 *Diamond Lil* was made into a movie called *She Done Him Wrong*, and Mae West became nationally known. The picture broke box office records everywhere. There is a legend that Cary Grant, Miss West's leading man, had never made a picture until she noticed him standing around and picked him. Actually, he had had the lead in four or five pictures, but had never caught the public's fancy till Mae gave him the role of the undercover agent acting as a Salvation Army captain. It was through this picture that her "Come up and see me sometime" invitation became a national catch phrase, and it was also here that she uttered her axiom "When women go wrong, men go right after them."

She played a lion tamer in her next picture, *I'm No Angel*, a circus drama, and actually went into the cage with boots and whip. She admitted that she had had a compulsion toward lion taming since childhood. In the picture she tossed off another line that became famous, "Beulah, peel me a grape." The picture was even more of a money-maker than *She Done Him Wrong*, and by the time her fourth, *Belle of the Nineties*, came out in 1934, she was the highest paid star in Hollywood, receiving three hundred thousand dollars per picture and another one hundred thousand for the story.

The motion pictures had forced her to change her style somewhat. "There were a lot of things censors wouldn't let me do in the movies that I had done on the stage," she wrote later. "They wouldn't even let me sit on a guy's lap—and I'd been on more laps than a napkin. I had to do something different, so I put in some humor. That way I could get away with

more things. I never meant 'Come up and see me sometime' to be so sexy, but I guess I was thinking about sex all the time. . . . It was always natural for me, it was never a strain. I guess that's why it goes over so well."

In spite of her imposing figure, Mae West is not a large woman—up and down. She is only five feet two, but at the peak of her career she measured 36–26–36—a very impressive set of statistics for a woman so short. She has never lost her Brooklyn accent and still comes out with pronunciations like "pernt." She does not drink and she does not smoke.

In 1937 she was a guest star on the Edgar Bergen-Charlie McCarthy radio show, and the emphasis she put on some of her exchanges with the ventriloquist's dummy McCarthy were considered too suggestive by a great number of listeners, who lit up the network switchboard to complain. As a result, it was a dozen years before nervous program officials asked her to appear on the air again.

Her one movie in which she shared top billing was *My Little Chickadee* with W. C. Fields in 1940. It is considered a classic as a comedy, but she found working with the comedian distasteful because of his drinking habits. In spite of her dislike for liquor, many of her plays and movies centered around saloons or speak-easies.

Miss West returned to the stage in 1944 and went on tour occasionally, but over the passing years her activities diminished. Then, in 1969, at the age of seventy-seven (or seventy-six) and after twenty-six years away from movies, she returned to play a leading part in *Myra Breckinridge* and to talk of future movies beyond that.

Mae West has left a great store of observations on many subjects. "I used to be Snow White but I drifted." "The best way to hold a man is in your arms." "It's not the men in my life, but the life in my men that counts." And, "These days I think love is being kicked around . . . it ain't lofty enough."

Public Enemy Number One

A big-time gangster of Prohibition days—a man like Al Capone—was a man of substance. Aldermen and judges showed him respect, politicians and patrolmen were on his payroll, and headwaiters bowed him and his expensive blonde women to the choice tables. He ran his rackets like a business, and he seldom knew the inside of a jail. But the public enemy of the Depression years was an outlaw, a bank robber, hunted, in and out of prisons, hardly daring to show his face in public, and as often as not ending up filled with slugs on a morgue slab. He and his kind were punks

and killers, yet many of them were glorified by victims of the Depression and bank closings as modern Robin Hoods. And the greatest myths of all clustered around the name of John Herbert Dillinger.

John Dillinger gave no early promise as a boy most likely to succeed, but on the other hand he hardly seemed a killer. He was raised in a good Indianapolis neighborhood, but his youthful misdeeds led his father to move to Mooresville, Indiana, in the hope that a rural atmosphere would straighten out his son. Instead, young John got into trouble by stealing a car, joined the Navy, deserted when discipline be-

came too onerous and returned to Mooresville, and at the age of twenty-one married an empty-headed sixteen-year-old, who kept wheedling him to move to the bright lights and fun of the big city, Indianapolis. To get money to satisfy her whims, Dillinger joined a pool hall hustler in an attempt to rob a Mooresville store. They were caught in the act. The other man pleaded not guilty, was tried, and got two years. Dillinger admitted his guilt and was sentenced to ten to twenty years.

Dillinger brooded on the injustice during the nine years he spent behind bars.

"They should never have hit me with that rap," he once said. "That's what started me off." When he came out of the Michigan City Prison in May of 1933 he had a dream of getting rich quick with a series of bank robberies carried out by a gang of professionals. The only hitch was that the professionals he had in mind were still in the prison, but he quickly set about remedying that. With Homer Van Meter, a cold-eyed ex-convict who was to become his right-hand man, he robbed several small banks to obtain some working capital. Then he smuggled guns and money into the prison, and in September his four recruits—Harry Pierpont, Charles Makley, John Hamilton, and Russell Clark—escaped, killing a guard on the way. In the meantime Dillinger had been captured after another bank job and locked up in Lima, Indiana. Very shortly the four recruits went to the Lima jail and presented themselves as deputies come to take Dillinger back to the Michigan City Prison. When the sheriff asked for identification, Pierpont pulled a gun and mortally wounded him, and Clark and Makley killed a deputy who ran in. After freeing Dillinger, they got away without incident.

The gang embarked on a series of bank robberies that was to range from Pennsylvania into South Dakota. To replenish guns and ammunition, they simply raided police stations. Once Dillinger and Van Meter visited the Peru, Indiana, police station posing as coauthors doing a story for a detective magazine. The flattered officers showed them the police arsenal and revealed their plans for roadblocks and the like. Thoroughly briefed, the two cleaned out the place a day later: guns, ammunition, bulletproof vests.

Similar icy-nerved daring marked Dillinger's other operations. Once he posed as a salesman for a device to pump oxygen to persons accidentally locked in bank vaults. He so impressed the bank president with his description of the agonies of suffocation that the latter let Dillinger make a careful preinstallation inspection of the bank vault. Dillinger promised to return in a few days. He did, with his

gang, and cleaned out the vault.

To rob a bank at Greencastle, Indiana, Dillinger rigged out the gang like a movie crew, complete with director with megaphone, cameraman with cap on backward, and actors in make-up. Curious townspeople were told that the crew was from Hollywood, come to film a bank robbery on authentic location. After a couple of rehearsals, the "actors" entered the bank for another shot while the cameraman got ready to record the action. Very shortly the actors ran out of the bank and jumped into the getaway car, the rest of the phony crew jumped on the running boards, and all sped out of town while the spectators watched slack-jawed.

But more often than not robberies were carried out at gun point, and frequently there were killings. Early in 1934, when things got too hot, the gang went to Arizona, and there they were spotted and most of them taken prisoner without a fight. Pierpont, Makley, and Clark were taken back to Ohio and eventually sentenced to death; Pierpont was killed in an escape attempt but the other two died in the chair. Dillinger was locked up in the Crown Point, Indiana, jail but defied rigid security precautions by breaking out. The story was that he used a pistol carved from wood, and this became part of the growing legend of a modern Jesse James. Poor people in 1934 were not kindly disposed toward banks and were all too ready to glorify a man who got the best of them. The truth, though, is that Dillinger's lawyer bribed someone to smuggle a real gun to him; the authorities concocted the wooden gun to hide the evidence of collusion and corruption.

The jail break, early in March, 1934, set off one of the greatest man hunts in history. Every police department in the Midwest had its plans for dealing with a visit by Dillinger. The Federal Bureau of Investigation was in the case for the first time because the outlaw had crossed a state line in a stolen car after getting out of jail. And Dillinger and his re-formed gang continued to hit banks, and innocent bystanders were shot with alarming fre-

quency by trigger-happy police.

The F.B.I. found Dillinger hiding out in a resort in northern Wisconsin in April, but with forty-eight G-men and a dozen local law men staked out around the place, someone blundered and started shooting at a man and his two companions who, completely oblivious, had wandered onto the scene. The gang, alerted by the shots, fought its way out. The toll: three innocent bystanders wounded by the law, two agents killed by the gang.

Dillinger's dream of quick riches had long since gone glimmering. He was spending money as fast as he got it, huge quantities for bribes and living expenses. Plastic surgery on his face was a failure as far as altering his appearance was concerned. His only aim now was to get enough money to get to Mexico, but a big robbery that was to provide it was a fiasco when spirited townspeople killed one outlaw and wounded Dillinger, Van Meter, and a third bandit.

On July 21 a woman, Anna Sage, came to Melvin Purvis, head of the Chicago F.B.I. office. She was almost certain, she said, that the "Jack Lawrence" brought home the night before by her roommate, Polly Hamilton, was John Dillinger. She believed she could get "Lawrence" to take her and Polly to the movies the next night, Mrs. Sage said. If she did, would Purvis put in a good word for her with the immigration people, who were trying to deport her for a record of prostitution?

The next evening a quick call told Purvis that the trio was on its way to the Biograph Theater. Purvis sat in a parked car and watched them enter the movie house. Pairs of agents were stationed along the street. Six went inside. When the picture ended and Dillinger and the women left, the six agents followed. Outside Purvis signaled to them to close in. Two other G-men approached from the front to block escape. Suddenly sensing danger, Dillinger leaped toward an alleyway and grabbed for his gun. Then bullets tore into him, and he fell dead instantly.

The man who was going to make it big had exactly $7.87 in his pocket.

Dorothy Parker

The times, as a contemporary troubadour has pointed out, they are a-changing, and with the passage of time, the bright one-liners and mordant verse that Dorothy Parker rapped out during the Twenties and Thirties seem just a bit tarnished. "Men seldom make passes / At girls who wear glasses" provided a chill sort of comfort for myopic wallflowers four decades ago. The couplet might as well be written in Etruscan, though, for all the sense it makes at a time when girls with 20/20 vision shop for glasses in high-fashion boutiques and remove them from their pert noses only to facilitate bedroom romps that seldom are prefaced by anything so square as a "pass." As Mrs. Parker herself put it some years after her salad days: "Let's face it, honey, my verse is terribly dated."

Much of that verse was written in the Twenties, but in retrospect Dorothy Parker really seems to have been a decade ahead of her time; unlike most of her contemporaries, she appears to have sensed the imminence of an era when personal tragedy was not so much the result of an innate character flaw as of unpredictable external events. "Three be the things I shall have till I die: Laughter and hope and a sock in the eye," she wrote.

She was born Dorothy Rothschild in 1893, the daughter of a Scotswoman and a Jew—a circumstance that some three decades later was to provide an opening for one of George Kaufman's better moments. Feigning anger at an anti-Semitic remark, Kaufman threatened to abandon the assembled company, then added: "And I'll expect Mrs. Parker to accompany me halfway." In 1916, after an education of sorts absorbed at a convent boarding school, she landed her first job, writing picture captions for *Vogue*. A year later she was taken on as a staff writer at *Vanity Fair*, where she shared an office with the humorist Robert Benchley and the playwright-to-be Robert Sherwood, two charter members of the Hotel Algonquin's legendary Round Table, a daily lunch time exercise in one-upmanship whose off-and-on participants included Kaufman, Frank Crowninshield, Alexander Woollcott, Heywood Broun, Marc Connelly, Edna Ferber, Franklin P. Adams ("F. P. A."), George Jean Nathan, and just about any other literary light who did not object to having his chicken à la king liberally seasoned with arsenic.

With the passage of time, the Round Table has acquired the dimensions of the original Arthurian legend. Nostalgic hangers-on have portrayed it as a perpetually scintillating affair made up of constant verbal swordplay, inexhaustible wit, and dazzling spontaneity. Never one to leave a legend unpunctured (even when she was its heroine), Dorothy Parker later recalled that the Round Table "was no Mermaid Tavern, I can tell you. Just a bunch of loudmouths showing off, saving their gags for days, waiting for a chance to spring them." Disillusioning as the Parker evaluation may be to romantics, it has a ring of truth about it; one can almost imagine George Kaufman forcing aspersions on his faith in order to get off his well-rehearsed riposte. "These were no giants," Mrs. Parker summed up. ". . . only a lot of people . . . telling each other how good they were."

If she herself was no giant, Dorothy Parker was a dedicated bringer-down of those who imagined they were. A favorite target was Clare Boothe Luce, who was outbitched superbly when her "Age before beauty" was countered by Mrs. Parker with "And pearls before swine" as the two women collided at a doorway. Told that Mrs. Luce was habitually gracious toward her inferiors, Parker meowed: "And where does she find them?" Katherine Hepburn, she said, "runs the gamut of emotions from A to B." Informed that Calvin Coolidge was dead, she asked: "How can they tell?"

Her self-criticism was no less barbed than that which she reserved for others. "I was following in the exquisite footsteps of Miss Edna St. Vincent Millay," she said of her verse, "unhappily in my own horrible sneakers."

If Dorothy Parker was not another Edna St. Vincent Millay (and another would have been supererogatory indeed), it was not for lack of technical ability, but because of an inability to take herself or life as seriously as it usually is taken by major poets. "Laughter and hope and a sock in the eye" were her attributes and these, for better or worse, are the stuff of light verse, however exquisitely they may have been combined. Socked in the eye, she could only respond with an insouciant gesture:

> But I, despite expert advice,
> Keep doing things I think are nice,
> And though to good I never come—
> Inseparable my nose and thumb.

In a way, Dorothy Parker epitomized the transition between the Twenties and Thirties, between romanticism and reality, between Boom and Bust. Her best work incorporates the sentimentality of the Twenties and the rude awakening undergone by all Americans during the next decade—a decade when most of us were willing to forego the *beau geste* for tangible assets:

> A single flow'r he sent me,
>   since we met.
> All tenderly his messenger
>   he chose;
> Deep-hearted, pure, with scented dew
>   still wet—
> One perfect rose.
>
> Why is it no one ever sent me yet
>   One perfect limousine,
>   do you suppose?
> Ah no, it's always just my luck
>   to get
> One perfect rose.

Dorothy Parker herself attempted to forego the *beau geste* for tangible assets by moving with her on-again-off-again second husband, Alan Campbell, to Hollywood, where she collaborated with him on several screenplays. But Hollywood money, she found, was little more satisfactory than that single perfect rose. "It's congealed snow," she said, "it melts in your hand."

During the Forties she was an ardent supporter of left-wing causes, and in the Fifties she worked on *The Ladies of the Corridor*, a play about the loneliness of female hotel residents. Again, she seemed to be looking ahead to a bleaker future, for Campbell died in 1963 and Dorothy, in failing health, moved to a New York hotel, where she died in 1967.

Years earlier, she had written her own epitaph, "Excuse my dust." Whatever dust Dorothy Parker stirred up has long since settled.

New York's Little Flower

Fiorello La Guardia was five feet two inches tall, but he was the biggest thing that had happened to New York City in a long, long time. The city had had reform mayors from time to time in the past, when graft and corruption became too rampant even for the tolerant and long-suffering citizenry, but they tended to be colorless men in frock coats whom the bored voters let go after a single term. Not La Guardia. He was a case of perpetual motion, a delight for newsmen, a constant reminder to honest people that campaign promises of reform had not been conveniently forgotten the day after he was elected.

La Guardia is not easy to classify. He was a Republican in a city that had been controlled by the Democratic Tammany machine for longer than many citizens liked to remember. His father was a lapsed Catholic and his mother a Jew whose religious convictions did not run deep; the couple sent their children to the Episcopal Church as a compromise between their divergent faiths. When La Guardia married, new ingredients were added to this melting pot mixture: his wife was a Lutheran of German ancestry. (There had been a first marriage, but his wife and their small daughter had both died.)

He was born in New York City, but his father was an Army musician, and Fiorello —the name means "Little Flower"—grew up on military posts in the West and the Southwest, where he absorbed Populist ideas. While he was a boy in Arizona Territory, he read the newspaper accounts of current investigations being made into graft and corruption in Democratic machine politics in New York City, and the revelations gave him a lifelong dislike for Tammany. So when he later entered politics in New York, there was only one party open to him, and he became a Republican. However, he was an unorthodox member of his party. "I stand for the Republicanism of Abraham Lincoln," he once said, "and let me tell you now that the average Republican leader east of the Mississippi doesn't know any more about Abraham Lincoln than Henry Ford knows about the Talmud."

On his return to New York in 1907 (he was twenty-five years old at the time) he worked as an interpreter at Ellis Island—he spoke six languages besides English—while he went to law school at night. In 1914 he first ran for Congress. He lost, but he cut so deeply into a strong Tammany district that he was appointed deputy attorney general for New York State. In 1916 he again ran for Congress from the same district and won. The next year he became a lieutenant in the United States Air Service and commanded a bombing squadron in Italy. He proved to be a very effective propagandist among the Italians, and since he was still a congressman, he often ignored the military chain of command to get things done, intimidating superior officers who did not know just how strong his political connections were.

After his term in Congress ended he served on the New York board of aldermen for a year, then was re-elected to Congress in 1922 and served five terms, from 1923 to 1933. In the House of Representatives his record was consistently liberal; he deserted the Republicans and allied himself with the progressive bloc.

In 1929 La Guardia ran for mayor of New York against the flashy incumbent, James J. Walker. Walker was a playboy, who carried on an open amour with an actress mistress, spent much of his time on vacations, and was a frequenter of

night clubs, race tracks, and Broadway bright spots. He neglected the duties of his office while Tammany hacks filled administrative offices and sat in the courts, plundering the city mercilessly. When a somewhat naïve lady commiserated with him on the burdens of his office, Walker wisecracked, "Ah, yes, you can often see the lights burning in my office long after I'm gone for the day."

La Guardia fought a hard and scrappy campaign and uncovered some of the rot and graft in the Walker administration. But Walker only made wisecracks and refused to answer questions. However, the time was still the high-living, free-spending Twenties, and pleasure-oriented New Yorkers identified with and admired the dapper mayor; La Guardia did not carry a single one of the city's sixty-two election districts, and lost even in his own ward.

Shortly after Walker's re-election the stock market crash came, and then the Depression. The people of New York, jobless or on short rations, no longer looked quite so indulgently on Walker's relentless pursuit of pleasure. Then in the spring of 1932 Judge Samuel Seabury's investigation of the messy affairs of the city touched James J. Walker himself. The mayor tried to quip and wisecrack on the witness stand, but he was evasive about where all his money had come from, and he showed that he had been an absolute do-nothing as a mayor. When it was over, he resigned and went on another of his many trips to Europe.

In 1933 Fiorello La Guardia ran again, this time on a fusion ticket, campaigning on a promise to replace Tammany with an honest administration. The opposition vote was split between a Tammany hack and an independent Democrat, who got more than half the vote between them, but La Guardia was elected. He was sworn in at midnight on December 31, 1933, in a quiet ceremony in a private home; a few minutes later he picked up the phone and ordered the arrest of "Lucky" Luciano, the city's most notorious crook.

La Guardia was rotund as well as short. His clothes were always rumpled, and he

wore a big Western hat, which made him appear to be playing the part of a comic. Instead of the deep voice one would expect to come from such a stocky body, his tones were high-pitched and rose to a shrill when he became excited. Though often insensitive to the feelings of others, he was easily offended. For one thing, he was very conscious of his short stature. Once, when an associate made a joke about a short man who was applying for a city job, La Guardia took it personally and screamed, "What's the matter with a little guy? What's the matter with a little guy? What's the matter with a little guy?" Yet he was seen to walk over to a bystander even shorter than he, pat him on the shoulder, and call him "Shorty."

He worked long and hard at being mayor, but he put so much energy into it that he made it look like fun. He was an inveterate chaser of fire engines, showing up at every big blaze with a red fireman's hat perched on his head. During a newspaper strike he went on the radio to read the comics to the city's children, not so much to keep the kiddies up to date with what was happening in the funny papers as to dramatize the strike. He had pushcarts banned from the streets because most of the peddlers were Italian and they perpetuated a stereotype that the mayor, with his Italian background, resented. The same was true of organ-grinders, against whom he waged a bitter campaign.

When he was to lead the combined bands of the Police and Sanitation Departments, the stage manager asked him whether he wanted a spotlight played on him. "Hell, no!" the mayor said. "Just treat me like Toscanini!" Along with this great ego went a true love of political battle and an ability to be ruthless. "I invented the low blow," he once said, and on another occasion, "I can outdemagogue the best of demagogues."

He served three terms, retiring in 1945. His administration was one of the most honest New York has ever known, and he left the city with new schools, bridges, parks, and low-cost housing. He died in 1947.

The Brown Bomber

I t's *Louis* shuffling forward. . . . It's *Louis* stalking his man. . . . It's *Louis* with a left and another left to the midsection, and *Louis* with a right to the jaw. . . ." The voice always had the urgency and timbre of gravel pouring down a chute, and on many a hot summer's night it reverberated up and down every Elm and Locust and Walnut Street in America, every tenement-lined block in Harlem, and across the barracks-dotted grounds of Army posts from coast to coast. These were the late Thirties, the years before air conditioning was common, when windows were thrown open to catch the errant breezes of a summer night, when radio held America in thrall, and when a tawny, saturnine, quick-fisted young man, an Alabama sharecropper's son, held ab-

solute sway over the heavyweight division.

It was in the summer of 1934, when John Dillinger dominated the nation's headlines and St. Louis' fabled Gashouse Gang was clawing its way to the National League pennant, that Joe Louis (born Joseph Louis Barrow) turned to professional pugilism after winning fifty of fifty-four amateur bouts. Public attention was turned elsewhere—Max Baer had just dethroned the heavyweight champion, a huge, shambling imported pacifist named Primo Carnera—when Louis made his debut as a paid killer against one Jack Kracken. Kracken was, in a line penned by sports scribe Red Smith for another occasion, "a blameless youth in the prime of his mediocrity," but his vitreous mandible collided with our hero's left hand

about midway through the first round and the career of Joe Louis was launched.

Louis' freshman year was a busy one. He destroyed no fewer than twelve opponents, the most notable of whom was the now justifiably forgotten Lee Ramage. Ramage assumed a horizontal posture in the eighth round and maintained it until he had the referee's assurances that hostilities had been terminated.

By late spring of 1935 Louis had added ten more victims to his string, including the hapless Ramage, who fell into his swoon with considerably more alacrity on the second go-around. At this juncture Louis' manager, John Roxborough, and trainer, Jack Blackburn, decided their tiger was ready for more dangerous prey and matched Louis with Primo Carnera. Louis spent some fifteen minutes assiduously belting his man in the tripes. In the sixth round the belly-weary Italian dropped his hands in an attempt to protect the devastated area from further abuse. Louis thereupon decked him with a left and two rights to the jaw. The former champion righted himself with some reluctance—only to be wronged again by his tormentor. The referee put a merciful end to the carnage.

By this time Louis was a hot property. After disposing of Kingfish Levinsky in one round at Chicago, he was matched with Max Baer, who possessed a formidable array of skills but who somehow had contrived to lose his championship to James J. Braddock, a man with little going for him but the desire born of desperation.

Baer was the first holder of bona fide credentials that Louis encountered (his brief reign as champion notwithstanding, Carnera was, in the elegant parlance of the trade, a bum). They met at Yankee Stadium on September 24, where a game but dead-beat Baer—he had punched himself into a state of exhaustion in the first furious minutes of the bout—was disposed of in four rounds.

Louis' next opponent was Paulino Uzcudun, "the broad-shouldered bull of the Basque." (The sports writers of the Thirties, incipient Homers all, were much given to fixed, and preferably alliterative, epithets; Louis himself became known as the Brown Bomber after such sobriquets as the Dark Destroyer and the Tan Panther failed to stick.) Paulino's flaw was curiosity; after frustrating Louis for three and a half rounds by hiding his head in his hands, he decided to risk a brief glimpse of what the paying customers had come to see. Whether he saw anything at all is debatable. He certainly missed seeing a pistonlike right, and the debate ended in a shower of bicuspids, molars, and incisors.

Louis then flattened a worthy named Charley Retzlaff in the first round and was matched with Max Schmeling, who was known to the prosodists of the time as the Black Uhlan. Schmeling had studied Louis' oeuvre and thought he detected a weakness in the young master's style: Louis was "a sucker for a right." Schmeling's insight proved to be correct. The Brown Bomber was floored by a right in round four and iced by another in the twelfth. A wiser young man climbed into the ring with Jack Sharkey, a former champion, two months later.

Sharkey by then was an elder statesman as athletes go, and boasted of the "case-hardening" that would prove to be Louis' undoing. True to his word, he landed a terrific face to Louis' fist in the third round, and sat out the rest of the evening.

Louis disposed of his next six opponents in a total of twenty-five rounds and then, on June 22, 1937, met James Braddock in Chicago for the heavyweight championship. Braddock, who had come off relief to divest Max Baer of his title, was the sentimental favorite and had the crowd roaring when he dropped Louis with a sneaky right in the first round. In the second round, however, the tide turned; soon Braddock was flailing his arms like a man besieged by hornets. Blood was shed by both parties in the next two rounds, and again by Braddock in the sixth. Braddock tired fast in the seventh, dropped his guard in the eighth, and paid for his indiscretion by absorbing a lethal right to the jaw. Three years after his professional debut, Joe Louis was heavyweight champion of the world.

After three successful defenses of his title, Louis was rematched with Schmeling, who, according to his compatriots, would once again demonstrate the validity of Hitler's theory of the Master Race. Much has been made of the second Louis-Schmeling bout by those who would impute to Louis more social and political awareness than he may in fact have possessed. Unarguably it was a grudge match, but whether Louis was really bent on disproving Hitler's racial theories or was merely concerned with eradicating the single blot on his professional escutcheon is a moot point. In any event, Schmeling was demolished in the first round in the only indisputable display of gratuitous viciousness that Louis ever staged.

After laying the ghost of the first Schmeling fight, Louis embarked in earnest on his "Bum of the Month Club" campaign. In 1939 John Henry Lewis and Jack Roper lasted less than a round apiece, Tony "Two Ton" Galento succumbed in four, and Bob Pastor got his comeuppance in the eleventh, after running like a thief for ten rounds.

So it went through '40, '41, and early '42, until Louis' induction into the Army, where he served mostly as a fund raiser, morale booster, and coiner of epigrams ("We are on God's side"). In 1946, with the war over, he signed for a bout with Billy Conn, who five years earlier had outmaneuvered him for twelve and a half rounds before throwing caution to the winds. During his preparations for the second Conn fight Louis got off the second of the mots that established his reputation as the Bernard Shaw of the prize ring; told by a reporter that Conn might be too fleet for him, Louis riposted: "He can run but he can't hide." Conn ran neither fast nor far enough; the fight ended in the eighth round.

After the second Conn fight, Louis knocked out Tami Mauriello in a single round, barely beat Jersey Joe Walcott in two separate outings, and retired after fourteen years of professional mayhem. An ill-advised comeback attempt in 1950 started badly with a loss to Ezzard Charles. Louis then won eight consecutive bouts, but with nothing like the old authority. In October, 1951, Rocky Marciano wrote finis to a legend by destroying in the eighth round a fat, balding, short-winded travesty of one of the few bright baubles that the Thirties had produced.

Droughts, dust storms, mechanization, and the Depression combined to drive thousands of farmers from their lands. Abandoned farms like this Montana homestead were common throughout the Plains and the South as family after family pulled up stakes and headed west, many to join the hordes of migratory workers in California. It was a grim prospect, but there was little choice. "I didn't sell out back there," as one migrant put it. "I give out." Dorothea Lange's photograph, opposite, bears testimony to the broken dreams and spirits of those uprooted from their homes.

Time of Troubles

The President moved left, and for the majority of the nation the shift revived hope. But it was a hope born of desperation, for Depression life remained grim and was better than before only in small ways. Employment was up slightly. Income was up slightly. But for more than six painful years now, longer than any recession in American history, the economy had stagnated, resisting nearly as much the improvisations of the New Deal as the action of the once-revered laws of the market to move the country off dead center.

And somehow even the universe itself seemed malign. To add to the economic and spiritual woes of the Depression there were physical disasters: droughts, great dust storms, floods. The result was an immense restlessness, a slow kindling of hate. Yet if America in those years seemed, unaccountably, to have run out of luck, it was not really an accident, not an entirely impersonal affliction. For the droughts, dust storms, and floods were the predictable vengeance of the land.

Americans, always a profligate people, had disregarded the warnings of conservationists and ecologists. Contemptuous of the jeremiads of the "crackpots," heedlessly expending the natural riches that lay so easily at hand, Americans polluted the streams of the industrial East, cut down the evergreen forests of the North Central States, and wore out the soils of the cotton and tobacco South with generations of destructive single-crop farming.

Now the very soil of the Great Plains blew away. The result was a new migrant horde fleeing the disaster.

The origins of the disaster lay, to be sure, well in the past. Displacing the Indians on the great belt of semiarid land that lay far west of the Mississippi between the fertile prairies and the Rockies, the cattle barons had long ago overgrazed a region of minimal rainfall and precarious soils. Then in their wake came the sodbusters, farmers with their moldboard plows, to tear up the topsoil, turn under the buffalo grass, and plant their wheat.

The farmers who came to the Great Plains were a mixed lot. There were new immigrants, like the Scandinavians and Ukrainians, who, as late-comers to the feast, too often had to content themselves with the semiarid marginal lands of the West. There were as well farmers of old American stock, responding to the call of the frontier, or urged onward by overpopulation and worked-out soils behind them, or, most irresistible of all, lured by the big money promised by World War I prices for wheat. For whatever reasons, they farmed land that ought never to have come under the plow—and farmed it badly as well, disregarding the admonitions of agriculturists, who pleaded for contour plowing to check erosion and for stands of trees planted as windbreaks to hold the soil.

Elsewhere in the nation Americans could practice careless farming methods without catastrophic consequences. In the Northeast and the Middle Atlantic States forty or fifty inches of rain fell each year; the Olympic Peninsula in the Pacific Northwest was drenched by seventy-five inches. But in the great arc stretching from North Dakota through Oklahoma and Texas the average rainfall was a skimpy fifteen to twenty inches, just enough to bring crops through to harvest. In a dry year plants withered and died.

The spring and summer of 1933 were dry, the autumn days were hot. On November 11, 1933—fifteen years after the armistice stillness along the Western Front in France—the dust began to blow, a great black cloud that twenty-four hours later darkened the sky over Chicago, the next day over Albany, and the day after that swept out to sea.

The dust blew all that autumn and winter. It drifted in the lee of fences; it seeped through the cracks in windows and doors, defying the frantic defenses of farm wives and powdering kitchens and bedrooms and front parlors with a nasty, omnipresent black grit; it killed livestock, buried farm machinery, and made it necessary to turn on car headlights and street lights at noon.

Author Sherwood Anderson, reporting on the ravaged countryside and the ruined lives, told that the people spoke incessantly of "dust storms that came out of South Dakota, out of the plains beyond the Missouri, making the skies black at midday." Anderson quoted a small-town newspaperman: "I have an uncle who took up a farm out there. It was a farm until he plowed it. Then it blew away." By the newspaperman's story, his uncle went about over his fields picking up Indian arrowheads that had been buried a foot underground. "The dry soil that had been plowed had drifted like drifting

snow. He had planted trees and they were all killed. The fences were buried under the dust drifts."

By the summer of 1935, according to a W.P.A. survey of the time, the proportion of farmers on relief in the twelve states of the drought area far exceeded the national average, which was 1 out of 9. In New Mexico, the hardest hit of all, the number was 4 out of every 9; in South Dakota, 1 out of 3; in North Dakota and Oklahoma, better than 1 out of 4.

Anderson had found, early in the disaster, a certain truculent pride among the stricken farmers, an unwillingness to admit to hopelessness or to acknowledge any poor farming practices. "I guess if God wants to send rain he doesn't have to ask us," one farmer, too proud to pray, told him. There was anger against the "foreigners" who came to gape at their miseries. "On the whole," one retorted angrily, "I think we'd rather you writers let us alone." But as the months of tragedy mounted, the defiant spirit began to crack.

Farmers abandoned their lands. For a few brief months early in the Depression, there had been a migration to the land as jobs dried up. Now the disaster in the Great Plains reversed the trend. There was a new exodus from the drought areas, terrifying in its volume. In jalopies that often ran on faith alone, the farmers took to the roads in a great horde, moving ever westward to a new and fancied El Dorado. John Steinbeck described the migration in his monumental *The Grapes of Wrath*:

[Highway] 66 is the path of a people in flight, refugees from dust and shrinking land, from the thunder of tractors and shrinking ownership, from the desert's slow northward invasion, from the twisting winds that howl up out of Texas, from the floods that bring no richness to the land and steal what little richness is there. From all of these the people are in flight.... Carloads, caravans, homeless and hungry; twenty thousand and fifty thousand and a hundred thousand and two hundred thousand. They streamed over the mountains, hungry and restless— restless as ants, scurrying to find work to do—to lift, to push, to pull, to pick, to cut—anything, any burden to bear, for food.... They were hungry and they were fierce. And they had hoped to find a home, and they found only hatred.

Hatred they certainly found. Originally lured westward by rumors of work in the great industrialized farming enterprises of California and the Pacific Northwest —the ranchers had even distributed misleading leaflets in Oklahoma, the Dakotas, Nebraska, Arkansas—the Okies, as they were quickly dubbed, came in droves too numerous even for the heartless contractors, who had hoped to beat wages down to near-subsistence level. Townspeople and farmers found themselves threatened by the drifting horde. Local food stocks were too strained, jobs too few, charitable resources too meager, to support the influx. Vigilante bands, backed by county and state police, barred the highways, turning the migrants away. There were pitched battles, beatings, killings. In the fruit camps, when they were lucky enough to find work, the migrants lived in leaky shacks or in tents, next to noisome outhouses or open trenches, which were the only toilet facilities.

 ections of the backlands were greatly depopulated by the migration—the number of migrants was officially estimated at better than 200,000 by 1939. A government survey in 1936 of seven counties in southeastern Colorado, a region typical of the disaster, found that of 5,689 homesteads reported, 2,811 had been abandoned. Of those that remained in use, half or more were in such circumstances that they were sooner or later forfeited to banks and Eastern insurance companies, which found themselves reluctant landlords in a profitless wasteland.

Drought and dust storms did one thing for the farmer that all the farm programs had not been able to accomplish: they raised prices. Cutting crops in 1933 by one-third, and the following year by one-fifth, the natural disaster pushed prices upward, a rise that did not falter when on January 6, 1936, the Supreme Court invalidated the A.A.A.'s controversial crop-restriction features. The price rise, of course, did nothing for the farmer whose crops had been completely burned by drought or blown away; it was a complete mockery for the man who had already lost his farm.

The exodus from the farm lands, many of which had been marginal at best, promoted agricultural efficiency as well. A new breed of businessmen farmers—many of them "suitcase farmers," who held steady jobs in town and only farmed during the few crucial months in spring and autumn—shouldered aside the family farmer who loved the land but worked it badly. Banks and entrepreneurs invested in mechanical equipment and consolidated the patchwork of small and inefficient traditional farmsteads, thereby laying the foundation of the large-scale agriculture that was, in effect, to feed the world in World War II.

Even the floods—that vengeance of the rivers whose watersheds had been denuded by rapacious lumbering and eroded by single-crop farming—were not utterly without social benefit. Stuart Chase described the floods in *Rich Land, Poor Land*:

In 1936 the Merrimac, Connecticut, Hudson, Delaware, Susquehanna, Potomac, Allegheny, and Ohio all went wild. The Potomac was up twenty-six feet at Washington and long barriers of sandbags protected government buildings.... Pittsburgh was under ten to twenty feet of water and was without lights, transport, or power. The life of 700,000 people was paralyzed. The food supply was ruined, the steel industry at a standstill.

In such circumstances the old complacent indifference to the urgings of the conservationists could not endure. The great dam building program of the New Deal received a new impetus; the A.A.A., struck down by the Court early in 1936, arose again in the guise of a soil conservation program called the Soil Conservation and Domestic Allotment Act. Under the new act part of an annual appropriation of half a billion dollars was regularly earmarked to encourage farmers to divert production from soil-depleting crops like cotton and tobacco to soil-enriching crops like vetch and clover, as well as to encourage them to learn soil-building techniques like contour plowing, strip cropping, and the use of artificial fertilizers. During the three years it operated, the scheme enrolled close to four million farmers. The soil conservation plan provided thereby a desperately needed relief from bankruptcy as well as it restricted production by removing some lands from cultivation, helping to ensure their future fertility.

Any farmer could demand the minimum payment of ten dollars yearly—a meager payment but in the depressed lands of the cotton South any money was important. The over-all volume of payments was huge: $370,000,000 in 1936, $460,000,000 in 1937, $494,000,000 in 1938.

Though the program was meant to salvage the farm sector, its effects, and those of many other New Deal agricultural aid programs, were often curiously inconsistent. Like as not, the poverty-stricken tenant farmer was as much hurt as helped by programs that were designed to save agriculture as a whole but that funneled a disproportionate share of the aid to landlords and entrepreneurs, whose need was less pressing.

When the landlord received a stipend from the government in return for restricting production, he was, naïvely enough, "expected" by the framers of the act to divert a fair share of these funds to his tenants. But the simplest expedient for the landlord was to accept the government stipend and restrict production by turning the luckless tenants, white and black, off the land to fend for themselves. By making cash available, the program also motivated the landlord to dispense with human and animal labor altogether and employ tractors, mechanical harvesters, and all the other machines that replace living muscle. Small farms were thus consolidated into huge tracts, eliminating the small-family tenant tract of the past, so that "tractored off" soon became a familiar phrase in the Depression years.

The problem of farm tenancy was, in any case, growing acute by the Thirties for causes that cut deeper than the Depression itself. According to the President's Committee on Farm Tenancy, a group convened to study this evil in 1937, tenancy had risen from a mere quarter of all American farmers in the year 1880 to a whopping 42 per cent by 1935. Almost one-half of the farmers in the South, nearly one-third in the North, and one-quarter in the West were tenants; and in the single-crop areas, where cotton, tobacco, or wheat was grown, there was scarcely any diversification of effort to supplement the tenants' meager cash income.

Worst off of all the tenant farmers were the sharecroppers, those with no capital at all, nothing to sell but their inefficient labor, families operating in a savage buyer's market that gave the owner all the advantages. Equally divided between whites and blacks, the sharecroppers of the Deep South were an exploited, helpless mass, existing on a near-starvation diet of fatback and meal, which left them afflicted with pellagra and, in late winter, scurvy.

The whites had the advantage of skin but little else; an "uppity" black tenant who sought to challenge accounts at the farm store that lent him seed and sold him supplies might easily find himself dragged off and lynched. Even for the whites, a too active curiosity, a too daring show of self-respect, could mean a flogging or worse.

According to a W.P.A. survey of seven cotton states in 1934, sharecropper income in the Mississippi delta was a shocking ten cents a day. The average for all such farmers in those seven states was a scarcely lordly seventy-one dollars per person per year.

Nor were bad diet and low income the only grievances. To these had to be added foul living conditions (in North Carolina, the most progressive of the states studied, sharecropper housing averaged a value of $417 as against $194 for Negro tenants in Alabama) along with absence of schooling for the young, loss of pride, the constant uprooting of homes and ties as the exploited croppers sought new and better masters year after year.

Statistics in any case can scarcely tell the story. More vivid by far is the account of the degradation of the Southern sharecropper compiled by James Agee and photographer Walker Evans. Commissioned by *Fortune* to study the evil, they produced a report far too grim and it was rejected. Published as a book in the late Thirties, it sold very poorly, but did circulate in a kind of underground world of East Coast intellectuals and Hollywood script-writers as an unofficial classic, to re-emerge to public view only in our time.

More acceptable to the general public by far was Erskine Caldwell's *Tobacco Road*—which reduced the subanimal plight of the sharecropper to a bawdy joke—a book that later became one of Broadway's biggest hits. But the reality of peonage in the Deep South was anything but a joke, for as Agee recorded it:

From March through June, while the cotton is being cultivated, they live on the rations money.

From July through to late August, while the cotton is making, they live however they can.

From late August through October or into November, during the picking and ginning season, they live on the money from their share of the cottonseed.

From then on until March, they live on whatever they have earned in the year; or however they can. . . .

During five to six months of the year, of which three are the hardest months of any year, with the worst of weather, the least adequacy of shelter, the worst and least of food, the worst of health, quite normal and inevitable, they can count on nothing except that they may hope least of all for any help from their landlords.

Negroes, like the Okies, were set adrift in the Depression. Actually there had been a black migration for some time, and the first effect of hard times was to slow down this movement. For however brutalizing the life of black peonage on the land might have been, it was life still. On the land the black could hope to scratch a meager livelihood from the depleted soil, but in the ghettos of the North, despite the old myth of freedom, the black man fared badly. He was the first to feel the effects of market contraction, barely eking out a living at all as whites struggled for traditionally "nigger" jobs.

The effect was to slow the migration, but not to halt it. Fleeing a brutal racial oppression—there were 285 lynchings in Mississippi between 1900 and 1931, 132 in Alabama, 302 in Georgia, and 68 in the comparatively relaxed border state of Kentucky—six hundred thousand blacks had made the trek north in the Twenties, while in the Thirties the number fell by half. But though the migration diminished, in many regions its effect was still great: during the Thirties the state of Pennsylvania, with its shut-down mines and stagnant industry, lost three hundred thousand in population overall, but gained twenty thousand Negroes, who had followed the road of illusion north.

What they did once they got there was something else again. By the middle of 1934 more than half the black population of the Northern cities was on relief, while only 13.3 per cent of the whites needed financial help. Nor did the original social legislation of the New Deal accomplish much for the Negro: he was seldom employed in jobs covered by social security, seldom allowed into the white unions that Section 7a of the N.I.R.A., and later the Wagner Act, did so much in the Thirties to encourage.

Inevitably racial tensions in the North sharpened. For the white majority the Thirties was an era of only slowly awakening social conscience. For the most part white America was content to chuckle at the buffoonery of blackface Amos 'n' Andy and Madame Queen on the radio or to be amused by Octavus Roy Cohen's caricature of Negro life embodied in the antics of one Florian Slappey, who appeared regularly in the pages of *The Saturday Evening Post*. If the Negro was accorded any dignity at all, it was only in the role of faithful family retainer. It was somehow construed a triumph for American good feeling that a Negro, Hattie McDaniel, won an Oscar in 1939 as best supporting actress for her portrayal of a good slave to Vivien Leigh's Scarlett O'Hara in *Gone With the Wind*. Bill "Bojangles" Robinson no doubt stirred similar kindly feelings as perennial film mentor to little Shirley Temple.

There were the athletes, too, like Jesse Owens, who had his larger utility, it seems, in puncturing Adolf Hitler's boasts of Nordic superiority at the 1936 Olympics. And even more tellingly, there was the taciturn and self-effacing but deadly heavyweight Joe Louis. Unlike his predecessor Jack Johnson, the new black champion offended nobody and called forth no hysterical quest for a "white hope," but a clue to the mood of the ghetto might have been the scenes of wild joy on the nights when Louis destroyed his white opposition.

Hardly an accident, amidst the sharpening racial competition for jobs, was the founding in Detroit in 1930 of the Black Muslim Movement by an unstable visionary, W. D. Fard, to proclaim the evil of the "white devils" (who were to be destroyed at a future Armageddon). In 1934 the movement fell under the leadership of Elijah Muhammad, an out-and-out racial separatist and a brilliant organizer determined to establish a new dignity for the black man by enforcing a regimen of Spartan self-denial on his flock, while maintaining unremitting hostility toward the world of the whites.

Still, the active solicitude of the President's wife for the Negro, for which she was to reap a harvest of hatred, together with the slow opening of federal jobs to the black, did something in those years to lay the groundwork for possible racial cooperation. Important, too, was the new literary emphasis on the suppressed American Negro, who now, for the first time, emerged as more than a passing figure in an American letters grown socially conscious. If nothing in the Thirties had quite the same impact as Harriet Beecher Stowe's *Uncle Tom's Cabin* had had in the nineteenth century, or if no single writer of the Thirties could quite evoke the tragedy of the American Negro and the lie at the heart of American assertions that all men are created equal as had Mark Twain with his Nigger Jim in *Huckleberry Finn*, still a vast volume of work was being produced that focused on the problem.

Among white authors, Erskine Caldwell at least once approached literary distinction with *Trouble in July* before retreating to comic prurience in his later work. William Falkner's blacks—in novels like *Light in August* and novellas like *The Bear*—could not fail to arouse white sensibilities.

Not many of the literary reputations of the preceding decade were to survive the Depression years intact. It is very tempting to state that a new note of high seriousness now dominated the best-seller lists, but that was not the case. If romantic escapists like Joseph Hergesheimer and James Branch Cabell had sunk into oblivion, still there was Hervey Allen with his interminable *Anthony Adverse* and Margaret Mitchell with the equally lengthy *Gone With the Wind*, a hazy re-creation of the ante-bellum South and Reconstruction, to replace them.

The real shift came in the work of serious men, because having deep sensibilities, they could not write in the old way. H. L. Mencken, perennial deflator of the self-complacency of American values, could hardly function freely in a world in which afflictions stronger than Mencken's tongue chastised the old money-obsessed middle classes. The outrageous invective that had been Mencken's stock in trade was endurable only in a world of certainty; when the middle-class ethos collapsed in 1929, the essentially smart-alecky Mencken found himself without a calling. He was never to make the transition successfully to the new age. He retired to his study, there to produce a monumental history of the American language, which is likely to endure as his best single work.

More poignant was the case of F. Scott Fitzgerald. The spokesman for the "lost generation" of the postwar years continued to write after the crash, but he found little readership in a world suddenly conscious of the viciousness of money and class. Fitzgerald chronicled his own decline in his novel *Tender Is the Night*, the story of a doomed expatriate wedded, like himself, to a schizoid wife, and then retreated to Hollywood to spend his remaining years.

"Songs of social significance," as the Broadway hit *Pins and Needles*, produced by the International Ladies' Garment Workers' Union, had it, were now the rage. Curiously, some radical social critics, like John Dos Passos, who had once assaulted war and capitalism in *Three Soldiers* and in his massive trilogy *U.S.A.*, began a drift to the right. Other writers spoke steadfastly for the Left. Typical of the socialist-tinged realism that became the vogue was James T. Farrell's chronicle of the decline and fall of a lower-middle-class Irish youth, *Studs Lonigan*, which details the tragedy of a life completely without purpose and with no values but those of the street-corner gang.

Ernest Hemingway, prodigiously gifted still, gave up his explorations of the lost generation for a retreat to an apolitical world of big-game hunting in *Green Hills of Africa* and of brave bulls in *Death in the Afternoon*, but he seemed to be simultaneously developing a political consciousness, which emerged in *To Have and Have Not*, a rejection of individualism in which the isolated hero while dying grasps his mistake. After his experience in the Spanish Civil War, Hemingway assessed

the threat of fascism in *For Whom the Bell Tolls*. Sinclair Lewis, too, turned his pen against fascism in his novel *It Can't Happen Here*, published in 1935, the story of an American demagogue who makes himself dictator. The novel, which was inspired in large part by the activities of Huey Long, was not Lewis at his best, but the provocativeness of its theme, at a time when dictatorships were fastening themselves on nations elsewhere in the world, made the book widely read.

Nathanael West's surrealist and mordant fantasies *Miss Lonely Hearts* and *The Day of the Locust*, two social commentaries revealing the spiritual desolation at the heart of contemporary life, were not the kind of novels that book club readers could be expected to accept. Less competent, but far more popular, was the leftist sentimentality of playwright Clifford Odets, who burst on Broadway with his one-act *Waiting for Lefty*, now a less-than-convincing call to union action. Odets could seemingly do no wrong in the Depression years and went on to write *Golden Boy*, an implausible tearjerker in which the hero breaks his hands by fighting in the prize ring and ruins them for his true calling, the violin.

The general intellectual drift was clearly to the left, a drift greatly encouraged by the rise of fascism in Europe—though a good many intellectuals found themselves unable to accept communism after witnessing the Stalinist tyranny at work in the Soviet Union. Intellectuals were hard-hit by the Depression and not surprisingly proved vulnerable to communist arguments that capitalism was collapsing, for in those years it was seemingly unable to feed its own or to assure economic and social justice.

A college education guaranteed little in the Thirties. A 1934 survey of graduates of fifty-four colleges and universities revealed 12,420 unemployed teachers, 2,845 unemployed engineers, 2,436 unemployed business executives. Of the colleges listing unemployed alumni, Ohio State led with 2,097. The University of Chicago reported 1,798 and even lordly Princeton 450. Disenchantment with the "system" was not hard to explain.

Typifying the plight of men driven to wander by economic necessity was a W.P.A. case study published in 1937, which recorded the odyssey, in no sense unusual, of a white migratory worker in the early and middle Depression years:

June–August, 1932: jackhammer operator on railroad

construction at Liberty, Missouri; wages $4.80 a day.

September, 1932: railroad extra-gang laborer at Hays, Kansas; wages $3.20 a day.

October, 1932: railroad extra-gang laborer at Cheyenne, Wyoming; wages $4.50 a day.

February–March, 1933: pipeline construction laborer at Topeka, Kansas; wages $3 a day.

April–October, 1933: building construction watchman at Kansas City, Missouri; wages $1.25 a day.

February–May, 1934: railroad extra-gang laborer at Wamsutter, Wyoming; wages $2 a day.

June–September, 1934: railroad extra-gang laborer at Topeka, Kansas; wages $2.80 a day.

Abstract analysis of the plight of such men suggests, on the evidence of European politics, that they were tinder for revolution, the very proletarian material that a totalitarianism of the Left or the Right might well have ignited. The Revolution—of the Left, especially—was widely heralded by the disillusioned intellectuals of the time. But the long-awaited "radicalization of the masses" did not, in fact, occur. What happened? Except for a brief period at the turn of the century, when the essentially Populist Industrial Workers of the World came close to capturing the true spirit of the American worker, the revolutionary parties of the Left looked to sterile European models and thereby doomed themselves to defeat.

The real aspirations of the American wage earner were merely to be that, a wage earner, not the wielder of sole political power. The opportunities before the American unions were immense, but they were slow to sense the opening that depression gave them. In 1930 there were fewer than three and a half million union members in the United States—the number had remained static throughout the previous decade—and the initial effect of depression was to force the number down to 2,689,000 in 1933. For one thing many workers, employed only part time if at all, could not afford to pay union dues. For another, frightened men succumbed to the antiunion pressures of employers operating in a buyer's market for labor and holding the whip hand.

Under the conservative policies of the American Federation of Labor, founded years before by Samuel Gompers, a man who envisioned union labor as limited to skilled workmen tightly organized into craft guilds, membership had risen only slowly. Then, in three years in the 1930's there was a gain of better than a million, but chiefly as a result of the more favorable climate provided by the New Deal, particularly Section 7a of the N.I.R.A. But if unions were to make the great breakthrough to industrial power, a new model of organization was needed and a new technique of combat as well.

eapons, organization, and charismatic leadership were all provided at this point by shaggy-maned John L. Lewis—descendant of generations of exploited Welsh coal men—who organized the first great industrial union in America, the United Mine Workers. The U.M.W. responded truly to the needs of the time, not merely by its aggressiveness, but by its vertical unionization, that is, the organization of all workers in the entire industry into a single union. In the American Federation of Labor, each craft—carpenters, masons, iron puddlers, plumbers—formed a separate union. It was a mode of organization that tended to fragment labor and limit its ability to pressure capital.

Rebellious labor leaders broke with the A.F. of L. at the 1935 convention and established the Committee (later Congress) of Industrial Organizations. The results of the new dynamism were dramatic: between 1936 and 1937 union membership nearly doubled, rising from a little less than 4,000,000 to 7,000,000. By 1940 there were to be nearly 9,000,000 union laborers in the United States, most of whom, despite Lewis' own antipathy to President Roosevelt, firmly supported the Democratic party and the New Deal.

Militant the C.I.O. was. According to *Fortune* magazine's survey in November, 1937: "From May 1933 to July 1937, a period of little more than four years, there were some 10,000 strikes drawing out no less than 5,600,000 workers. This was aside from all the thousands of quickies, sitdowns, and other protests that tied up industry during that period. . . ." And as *Fortune* went on to note, fully half the strikes fought in 1936 and the first six months of 1937 were fought for a principle: union recognition, usually of the C.I.O., as sole bargaining agent for labor.

But the employers struck back in a bitter industrial war, fought without real quarter on both sides. The traditional weapons of the bosses had always been the yellow-dog contract, by which a would-be worker agreed not to join a union; the company union, a captive organization that enabled an employer to turn away any outside union; the black list; and the lockout. Now these devices had been outlawed by the New Deal's labor legislation. What were the employers to do? Illegal always, but normally invoked as a last resort, was the use of strikebreakers.

The most highly developed form of employer counterattack was the Mohawk Valley Formula of Remington Rand, so-named from the location of the firm's plant in upper New York. As *Fortune* put it:

If you were a union man in Remington Rand's Ilion plant in 1936 you were one atom in the working out of a new force, which, amid charges and countercharges, accusations of prejudice, partisanship plotting, and worse, was to be analyzed and defined by the National Labor Relations Board as the Mohawk Valley Formula. The nine steps of the Mohawk Valley Formula it found to include: (1) conducting a forced balloting under the direction of foremen to misrepresent the strength of the union, calling strike leaders "agitators," forming a Citizens' Committee under threat to move the plant; (2) arousing the community by calling for "law and order" because of "wholly imagined violence"; (3) calling mass meetings of citizens; (4) calling for armed deputies; (5) starting a back-to-work movement; (6) setting a date for opening the plant; (7) staging the opening theatrically; (8) turning the "locality into a warlike camp"; (9) keeping up a campaign of publicity to convince the remaining strikers that the plant is in full operation.

To accomplish its purposes, Remington Rand, according to National Labor Relations Board findings, paid one Pearl L. Berghoff the sum of $25,800 for supplying two hundred guards and "missionaries." There was another $30,000 paid to Foster's Industrial and Detective Bureau, and a further $25,000 to the William J. Burns International Detective Agency.

Such payments were scarcely unusual, as the Senate hearings conducted in the mid- and late-Thirties by Wisconsin Senator Robert La Follette's investigating committee were to reveal. And often enough there were murders and beatings by the company sluggers as well as the more usual fomenting of trouble by *agents provocateurs* and spying on union members by paid informers.

As always, violence engendered counterviolence, and that in turn induced a new round of escalation. In February, 1936, workers at Akron, Ohio, rubber plants adopted the system known as the sit-down strike, the occupation of the employers' premises in order to prevent the lockout and the maintenance of production by imported scabs and goons.

Quickly spreading, the technique was adopted by the striking employees of the General Motors plants in Detroit, Michigan, in 1936, leading to widespread public demands that Governor Frank Murphy (later to join the Supreme Court) call out the National Guard to evict the strikers bodily. Murphy refused, thereby making himself something of a left-wing hero. General Motors finally capitulated in February, 1937. The huge United States Steel Corporation surrendered on the issue of exclusive bargaining with a single union without offering up a fight in 1937, but the group of smaller steelmakers known as Little Steel adamantly refused to bargain with the steelworkers' union. Violence erupted outside the gates of the Republic Steel plant in South Chicago on Memorial Day, 1937. Four strikers were killed and almost one hundred injured. Not until 1941 did the C.I.O. have agreements with all the members of Little Steel.

THE EYES AND EARS OF THE WORLD
4.

Steadily, almost imperceptibly, the world powers moved toward war. Bullying, threatening, cajoling, the expansionist regimes of Germany, Italy, and Japan pressed their demands, and the democracies, led by England and France, yielded, a little at a time, always in the hope of achieving peace. This charade of aggression and appeasement reached its culmination in the Munich Agreement of 1938. Early that year Hitler, emboldened by his unopposed annexation of Austria, had begun a campaign against Czechoslovakia, threatening to "liberate"—by force if necessary—the German-speaking peoples of Czechoslovakia's Sudetenland. Backed by Italy, Germany became more belligerent; to stave off war, England and France intervened. An agreement signed by England, France, Germany, and Italy in Munich in September, 1938, gave Germany the Sudetenland in return for a promise of peace. It was the free world's last concession. Six months later Hitler took the rest of Czechoslovakia. Appeasement was clearly not the way to peace.

Ambitious for control of China, Japan became increasingly belligerent, and the force of her aggression began to alarm democracies of the Western world. The bombing of Chinese civilians after the fall of Shanghai in 1937 set world opinion strongly against Japan. The United States formally condemned her actions, but it was the Japanese bombing and machine-gunning of the U. S. gunboat *Panay*, near the city of Nanking in December, 1937, that outraged the American press and public. Japan officially apologized and the United States accepted, but the incident produced severe tensions between the two countries. Above, the sinking of the *Panay* on the Yangtze River; at right, Chinese refugees flee their burning homes after a Japanese bombing attack on the city of Chungking in late May of 1939.

The Munich pact of 1938 gave Hitler a free hand to absorb the Sudetenland and paved the way for German partition and annexation of the rest of Czechoslovakia. At left, Mussolini, Hitler, interpreter Schmidt, and Britain's Prime Minister, Neville Chamberlain, at Munich conference in September; below; Hitler parades through the streets of Asch on a tour of his newly acquired Sudetenland; and at bottom, Vienna's Dollfuss Square (named for Austria's ex-chancellor, who was assassinated by Nazis) is renamed Adolf Hitler Square after annexation in March, 1939.

UNDERWOOD & UNDERWOOD

ADOLF HITLER PLATZ

PHOTOWORLD

UPI

Controversial printed matter was banned during Hitler's regime, and book burning became a favorite Nazi occupation. Below, Nazi students feed the flames of censorship in 1933. Right, Hitler addresses new Austrian subjects in Vienna's Heldenplatz, 1938.

The Spanish Civil War became a bloody battleground for rival foreign factions: German Nazis and Italian Fascists on the side of General Franco's Nationalists, and Russian Communists aiding the Loyalists. Above, Spanish civilians outside Madrid in 1939.

In August, 1939, Russia and Germany signed a nonaggression pact (at right, Soviet Minister Molotov signs treaty, with Stalin and Nazi Minister von Ribbentrop at rear), opening the way for Hitler to invade Poland. Russia, for her part, was given a free hand in Finland, the Baltic States, eastern Poland, and eastern Rumania. Below, a Finnish ski battalion during the Soviet-Finnish winter war.

Louis D. Brandeis

Willis Van Devanter

Pierce Butler

Benjamin N. Cardozo

Charles Evans Hughes

James C. McReynolds

Harlan Fiske Stone

Owen J. Roberts

George Sutherland

The King in Check

Roosevelt's first Court appointment, Hugo Black, right, and Vice President John N. Garner; opposite: the "nine old men" of the Supreme Court.

It was January this time—the date of Inauguration Day had been moved forward to shorten the period of marking time between old and new administrations. But in January, 1937, no disconsolate and defeated incumbent rode with the President-elect to the Capitol rotunda to hand over his constitutional authority. Franklin Roosevelt had won again, by the greatest landslide in American history, and the day, for him at least, was one of total rejoicing. If his defeated enemies, right and left, detested him, the nation as a whole had vindicated his four years in office.

Only the dripping winter skies and the solemnity of the Chief Justice of the United States, stately old Charles Evans Hughes, stood in contrast to the cheer of the victor as he took his oath again, hand on the Dutch family Bible, cellophane-wrapped to protect it from the dampness. Would he support the Constitution of the United States? He swore that he would—and in after years admitted that he had meant, of course, the Constitution as a flexible, living document, not a barrier to progress.

The President moved to the lectern and in the pattering rain unfolded his typescript. "We of the Republic pledged ourselves to drive from the temple of our ancient faith those who had profaned it," the President intoned, in clear allusion to the money-changers he had castigated in his first inaugural address four years before. We did this, the President said, "to end by action, tireless and unafraid, the stagnation and despair of that day."

Yet instinctively as a nation "we recognized a deeper need—the need to find through government the instrument of our united purpose to solve for the individual the ever-rising problems of a complex civilization. Repeated attempts at their solution without the aid of government had left us baffled and bewildered. . . ."

The nation, he asserted, had at last opted for government intervention in order to find "practical controls over blind economic forces and blindly selfish men." Much had been done. Now timidity and greed had begun to appear again. Yet, and here his voice rose to a passionate intensity, at this very moment tens of millions were still "denied the greater part of what the very lowest standards of today call the necessities of life."

For, said the President, "I see millions of families trying to live on incomes so meager that the pall of family disaster hangs over them day by day.

"I see millions whose daily lives in city and on farm continue under conditions labeled indecent by a so-called polite society half a century ago.

"I see millions denied education, recreation, and the opportunity to better their lot and the lot of their children. . . ."

In words that were to be repeated throughout the country again and again, he spoke of "one-third of a nation ill-housed, ill-clad, ill-nourished."

He would, he promised, continue to lead the American people "along the road over which they have chosen to advance."

The rain dripped from the sky, the wind tugged at the sodden flags, the crowd filed away.

What loomed ahead, unseen by the public, was no mere clash of policies such as the campaign just ended had fought out: fiscal responsibility versus reckless spending, individual freedom versus an alleged Rooseveltian propensity for dictatorial control. The new issue was to cut to the very heart of the constitutional order: the responsibility of one arm of government, the executive, to act and of another, the courts, to review.

In theory, the Founding Fathers had long ago settled the issue. There was, as every school child knew, to be a three-way division of government into congress, executive, and judiciary. The business of the Congress, which represented in effect the will of the people, was to make laws. The business of the executive, who in effect acted for the people, was to carry them out. And the business of the Supreme Court, in effect the conscience of the people, was to see that the executive's acts jibed with written law.

But this was mere theory. In practice, the powers of all three divisions of the government had always overlapped. When special committees of Congress investigated an "evil" — Teapot Dome, say, or the scandalous behavior of Wall Street speculators prior to 1929 — ostensibly this was done to obtain background information on which to base future legislation. But, in fact, a Senate banking investigation or a House un-American activities investigation judged "witnesses" and "defendants," men not formally accused under law and not protected from caprice and from the somewhat savage

prejudices of the investigators by the elaborate system of court justice.

And when the executive or Congress set up administrative bodies like the Federal Trade Commission, the Securities and Exchange Commission, or the National Labor Relations Board to regulate economic behavior, those bodies also functioned as courts, finding on issues, assessing penalties, enjoining acts.

Indeed, on just this constitutional issue were the host of New Deal agencies — S.E.C., N.L.R.B., N.R.A., T.V.A., A.A.A. — to be challenged again and again, and nearly as often as not to be struck down by the courts.

But less noticed was the fact that the courts, ostensibly the least self-aggrandizing of the three branches of the government, nevertheless repeatedly invaded the legislative prerogatives of Congress. For under the American system of law, judges searched for guidance in historical "precedents," some of which had only marginal relation to the matter under consideration and were consequently subject to broad interpretation. Thus, whatever theory said, American judges did not merely interpret law, they made it.

ll this was legitimate enough, and the great John Marshall, fourth Chief Justice of the United States, opined that of all the branches of government the courts were the least likely to usurp, since their powers of enforcement largely depended on others. The ability of the federal courts to make law was therefore limited in scope. The problem was that in an era of stormy change, of New Deal innovation, the mere power to deny ceased to be purely negative and became a positive ability to negate the entire New Deal program. For amply endowed as the Supreme Court was with judicial majesty and wisdom, it was preeminently a political court, broken into a Left, a Right, and an uneasy Center.

On the left were three men who were the heroes of a reform movement reaching back into the last century. There was the drawn, pale Louis D. Brandeis, well over eighty, a labor lawyer, dubbed long ago the People's Advocate, the first Jew appointed to the Supreme Court. He had been chosen by Woodrow Wilson over the bitter opposition of conservative legal leaders, including William Howard Taft and Elihu Root. There was Harlan Fiske Stone of New York, former dean of the

Columbia Law School, a distinguished legal scholar and later to be Chief Justice, chosen by Calvin Coolidge as a reward for his services in Cal's administration as Attorney General. There was Benjamin N. Cardozo, again of New York, quite possibly the finest legal mind of all, and this on a Court supremely well endowed. Cardozo was also a Jew and a man who had made a brilliant reputation as chief justice of the New York State Court of Appeals before Herbert Hoover, urged by progressive Republican Senator George Norris of Nebraska, called him to Washington. These three men were, significantly, products of the Northeast of the United States, the center of urban, industrial, and banking life, and were sensitive to the problems of ethnic minorities.

But the right wing did not lack for good minds either. It had elderly Willis Van Devanter of Wyoming, a Taft appointee dating from 1910 and, predictably enough, a staunch defender of the frontier ideology of small government, free enterprise, and the devil take the hindmost. There was James Clark McReynolds of Tennessee, a man who displayed all the virtues, and all the vices, of the Bourbon South, though as one of Woodrow Wilson's Attorneys General he had been an active trust buster. There was another Westerner, George Sutherland of Utah, a Harding appointee and a sound jurist. And there was, finally, the least of these intellectually, Pierce Butler of Minnesota, a former railroad man, the business conscience incarnate, hated by the conservationist bloc. As a university trustee, Butler had a way of hounding professors whose politics he did not like, but, then, Butler himself had failed in constitutional law at college.

Between the two wings stood Owen Roberts of Pennsylvania, at age sixty-four a young man for this Court. He was a former corporation lawyer, conservative but unprejudiced, a man who had hounded the oil peculators of Teapot Dome and Elk Hills for Calvin Coolidge and had been named to the bench by Herbert Hoover. And, finally, there was the Chief Justice himself, dignified, solid, bearded Charles Evans Hughes, no stranger to political battles, the almost-President who had nearly beaten Woodrow Wilson—only to wake in the morning and find that California had done him in.

Hughes had once before sat on the Court. Appointed by Taft, he resigned to run for the Presidency in 1916. Later, having served Harding and Coolidge as Secretary of State and fathered the Washington Naval Treaty

of 1922, he was raised to the position of Chief Justice by Herbert Hoover in 1930.

There had been warnings of trouble ahead. Had not the President on the occasion of his inaugural address with careful emphasis declared: "The essential democracy of our Nation and the safety of our people depend not upon the *absence* of power, but upon lodging it with those whom the people can *change* or *continue at stated intervals* through an honest and free system of elections."

To whom had the President addressed the threat, if threat it was, other than to the Court? Congress, and the President himself, were subject to "change" or "continuation," as the people chose. Only the Court stood lofty and unassailable, above the immediate wishes of the masses.

Time and again, often by narrow margins, it had negated the innovations of the New Deal. It had done so conscientiously, but in the interests of a business ethic that the nation at large had discarded, or, at the very least, had come to distrust.

In the spring of 1935, in *Schechter v. United States*, the Court had found for the defendants against the whole structure of industrial-commercial planning embodied in the N.R.A. "Extraordinary conditions do not create or enlarge constitutional power," the Chief Justice declared, dismissing the plight of eight million unemployed in favor of principle. Then in January of 1936, by a vote of 6 to 3, the Court, in *United States v. Butler*, struck down the concept of agricultural planning and the control of farm surpluses as embodied in the A.A.A.

In both the Schechter and Butler cases there was genuine ambiguity; "honest" men could differ about the meaning of the law. But even conservative legal opinion held that the Court had gone an extra mile to invalidate the Guffey-Snyder Coal Conservation Act, an innocuous bit of legislation that seemed to suffer only from guilt by association with its grander New Deal siblings.

In the summer of 1936 the Court, voting 5 to 4, revealed that it was concerned with more than the federal government's invasion of the constitutional "reserved rights of the states." No more favorable to local New Deals than to the national New Deal, the conservative four—Van Devanter, McReynolds, Sutherland, and Butler—joined this time by Roberts, found against a New York State minimum wage law in the Morehead case. Even Chief Justice Charles Evans Hughes was disturbed: in the midst of a wild gale blowing at sea the old men of the Court seemed more concerned with proprieties at the captain's table than with keeping the ship afloat.

The President declared to the public a few days after the Morehead case that the Court had in effect created a "'no-man's-land' where no Government—State or Federal" was empowered to act. Clearly the Wagner Act, establishing the National Labor Relations Board with the power to protect unions, was in jeopardy—and along with the Wagner Act the whole right of the government to legislate in humane ways for the mass of the nation.

Ways to circumvent the hostile federal courts had been debated within the inner circle of the New Deal for more than two years; there was no lack of proposals, including the straightforward one of constitutional amendment. The President rejected that one out of hand: "Give me ten million dollars," he said, "and I can prevent any amendment to the Constitution from being ratified by the necessary number of states."

Besides, the President was in a punitive frame of mind. The Court had struck at him; now he would strike back, humiliating his foes.

He bided his time, and when he moved, it was without consulting his Cabinet, the Democratic leaders of Congress, or the liberal threesome on the Supreme Court itself. Clearly the victim of overconfidence, certain on the basis of his massive electoral sweep that the nation would follow where he led, he discussed his plans with no one except his Attorney General, Homer Cummings.

Having searched the files of the Justice Department, Cummings had dredged up a plan for federal court reform dating back to 1913—and it was the work of none other than frosty old Justice McReynolds himself, Attorney General when he had proposed it. The McReynolds proposal called for retirement of a federal judge at an age stipulated by law and appointment of a new colleague if he did not retire. The President was jubilant. He would extend the McReynolds proposal to the Supreme Court itself.

For the President, ever playful, even at the serious business of statecraft, the irony of the situation seems to have tipped the balance against mere prudence. The results were to be disastrous. Setting out to destroy his enemies, the President, on the morrow of his great election victory, came within an ace of destroying himself.

On the afternoon of February 4, 1937, a summons went out to the Cabinet, the Speaker of the House, the chairmen of the Senate and House Judiciary Committees, and the Democratic party whips. The next morning the bombshell burst in a Cabinet room in which were assembled a dozen or so of the most powerful men in the land. Of all who gathered there, only two or three had any inkling of what was to come.

The President presented his arguments for infusing the Supreme Court with new blood. The federal courts were swamped, he said; the Supreme Court itself had denied 87 per cent of the petitions before it without citing any reason for its failure to act. He pointed out that from its number of six, as established in the original Judiciary Act of 1789, the Court had fluctuated several times in the past: it had decreased to five in 1801, was restored to six the next year, was up to nine in 1837, and then, after going to ten in 1863, it settled in 1869 at nine. The President now proposed that when a judge reached the age of seventy, a younger judge be appointed to help him, up to a maximum of fifteen justices on the Supreme Court. This, the President asserted, would relieve the personnel of the federal judiciary, who were too few in number to handle all the business loaded on them and often forced to work long past their years of physical and mental vigor.

All this was contained in the message he sent that day to Congress, in which he stated that "a constant and systematic addition of younger blood will vitalize the courts and better equip them to recognize and apply essential concepts of justice in the light of the needs and the facts of an ever-changing world."

All the old Roosevelt charm, it appears, was present that morning, but the ruse was transparent and the meeting was glum. Only Harold Ickes seemed joyful. Vice President Jack Garner, who was a powerful conservative force within the Democratic party, said not a word. Nor did most of the other grandees assembled, among them Speaker of the House William B. Bankhead and Chairman of the House Judiciary Committee Hatton Sumners.

Outside the Cabinet room Sumners broke his silence to announce he was parting ways with Roosevelt. That afternoon, when the message reached Congress, he joined the vigorous opposition to the bill. Garner expressed his feelings as he stood in the Senate lobby by holding his nose as if he detected a bad smell. The Republicans, by a masterly tactical stroke, kept opposition to the bill from forming along party lines. It was the Democratic conservatives in Congress, joined by many New Dealing liberals like Burton Wheeler of Montana and Tom Connally of Texas, who led the attack.

Among the causes of opposition was Roosevelt's popularity itself. The very strength of his personality, the very depth of the worship of the multitudes for him, made uneasy those thoughtful men who understood that they lived in an age of political leaders able to manipulate the masses—witness Mussolini in Italy and Hitler, then consolidating the power of Nazi Germany. This suspicion was easy to trigger, and the American Congress was, in any case, by tradition the foe of a strong President.

The Supreme Court was, moreover, despite the Depression, an institution much revered by a people who revealed themselves throughout the Depression decade to be not radical, not revolutionary, but fundamentally conservative by temperament.

 or was Congress, itself an institution with more than its share of windy septuagenarians, likely to accept the argument that a man automatically becomes senile on reaching the age of seventy. Senator Carter Glass of Virginia was seventy-nine and was deeply offended that the President did not seem to know. He pointed out that the great English jurist Sir Thomas Littleton had written his classic treatise on property when well past seventy. Even Rooseveltian partisans were forced to admit that one of the consistently forward-looking and truly "young" minds on the Court was that of octogenarian Louis Brandeis.

Roosevelt had laid his prestige on the line because, as one of his admirers put it, his "Dutch was up." Part of the reason for the radical reform of the courts seemed to vanish when, in the spring of 1937, Justice Roberts revealed that his negative decision in the Morehead case, outlawing the New York minimum wage, had been based on technical grounds alone, and in *West Coast Hotel Company v. Parrish* he voted with the liberals, 5 to 4, in favor of a Washington State minimum wage. Evidently social security and all the actual and prospective federal wage and hour legislation were not in such deadly jeopardy after all. And if this possibility was mere suspicion in March, in the following month the Court upheld the Wagner Act, Roberts again joining with his liberal colleagues.

In May the Court announced the decision of Justice Van Devanter to retire, opening the way for a 6 to 3 liberal majority among the justices. And moving to counterattack, now that Roosevelt's arguments on the need for change were revealed as absurd, Chief Justice Hughes "replied" to a letter of inquiry from Senator Burton Wheeler and conclusively proved that the administrative operations of the Court had been efficient indeed.

It was Roosevelt, not the Supreme Court, who, in Ickes' phrase, found himself far out on a limb. And now Chief Justice Hughes—who had tactfully brought Roberts on the liberal team, had exploded the President's charges of senile inefficiency, and had no doubt helped prod Van Devanter into retirement—was busily sawing off that limb.

Yet even so the President would not desist from his plan. Senator James F. Byrnes asked ruefully: "Why run for a train after you've caught it?" Texas Jack Garner sulked in Texas, thereby denying the administration its most effective legislative lobbyist in the Senate. The once solid New Deal ranks were breaking. The President would not hear.

But it was death that finally struck down the plan. Roosevelt's manager of the fight in the Senate, Joe Robinson, charged with the hopeless task in exchange for the promise of a seat on the Court, was physically unequal to it. Exhausted by the struggle, desperately attempting to patch a meager majority together, one morning he dropped dead in his apartment across from the Capitol. With that the New Deal push for Court reform —or chastisement—died too.

Five days after Robinson's death, even Roosevelt's close political ally and heir, Governor Herbert Lehman of New York, declared against the bill. The bill was recommitted on July 22, 1937, without mention of the Supreme Court at all. "Glory be to God!" Senator Hiram Johnson yelled. The battle was over, and it was the first Roosevelt defeat.

In the history of men and empires, when the tide of fortune turns, it often runs out with astonishing speed. For more than eight years—first as governor of New York, then as President of the United States—it had seemed that Franklin Roosevelt could do nothing wrong. Now, scarcely six months into his second administration, it seemed he could do nothing right.

The first miscalculation, the abortive Supreme Court fight, had grown directly out of vanity and overconfidence. Now stung by defeat, punitive and bitter, but suddenly grown indecisive, one of the canniest political infighters of all time seemed to lose judgment. For one thing—and this was the most humiliating turn of all—the economy began to play him false. Though Depression life had remained grim after the brief New Deal honeymoon of 1933, after about 1935 there was improvement. The emergency relief measures of the New Deal had softened the edge of suffering for millions and had put some money into circulation. Gradually the economy inched upward, rising, according to the Federal Reserve Board, from an industrial production index of 69 in 1932 to 121 in the summer of 1936. That was only a few points off the 1929 high (though, to be sure, the population too had grown, so that things were far from rosy and millions were still unemployed).

For these improvements the New Deal had not been slow to take credit. The President in 1935, speaking in Charleston, South Carolina, fairly trumpeted out the news: "Yes, we are on our way back—not just by pure chance, my friends, not just by a turn of the wheel, of the cycle. We are coming back more soundly than ever before because we are planning it that way."

And now, suddenly, in 1937 the bottom dropped out of the economy. The Dow-Jones average, which had reached 190 in August plummeted to 115 by October. On October 19 a wave of selling hit the market as 7,290,000 shares were traded. And it was not only the market. Steel production dropped from 80 per cent of capacity to a sickening 19 per cent as manufacturers with overstocked inventories canceled orders for steel and began laying off workers, only in turn to reduce the purchasing power of the nation still further. By the beginning of 1938 there were some ten million men and women unemployed, and things did not improve much in the spring.

The old Depression had been the Hoover Depression. This was the Roosevelt Recession with a vengeance, for it was the federal government's mistaken policies that had triggered the fall.

The truth is that the business community, which hated the President with a frequently obscene passion, had never really understood him. For all his talk of money-changers in the temple, and despite their abuse of him for "mortgaging" the country's future by crazy spending policies, Franklin Roosevelt was essentially an economic conservative. He believed in balanced budgets, and in the spring of 1937, in order to "reassure" business, he had even cut back federal spending. The great public works programs, the relief programs, were trimmed way down. And having just collected nearly two billion dollars in social security taxes, for the first time in years the government took in more money than it spent.

The result of taking so much money out of circulation was ruinous. Now what was Roosevelt to do?

Not even Roosevelt himself knew the answer, for he had never been a theoretician, or even a scholar, of economics or anything else. His way was to learn from men, letting the contending forces play about him almost as if, in a curiously detached way, he himself wondered which voice would win.

The recession sparked a combat within the inner circles of the New Deal. There were the conservative forces, essentially budget balancers and probusiness men, pre-eminent among them Secretary of the Treasury Henry Morgenthau, who as early as 1936 had argued, with a peculiar indelicacy under a crippled President, that it was time to "throw away the crutches" and see if the economy "could stand on its own feet." Arrayed against the Treasury Department crowd was a phalanx of New Dealing minds—Harry Hopkins, Harold Ickes, Marriner Eccles and Lauchlin Currie of the Federal Reserve, the President's sometime speech writer and confidant Tommy Corcoran, William Douglas, then rising to notice on the S.E.C., and Solicitor General Robert Jackson. These men argued that the business community would not take up the slack in the economy if government spending ended, for businessmen were essentially irreconcilable as far as a New Deal administration was concerned, perversely determined to damn the men that sought to save the country no matter what they did, even to balancing the budget.

According to Governor of the Federal Reserve Eccles, the monetary role of the government was to act as "compensatory agent in this economy; it must unbalance its budget during deflation and create surpluses in periods of great business activity." That is to say, the government should spend itself into debt in hard times and put money aside in good.

All very Keynesian by the sound of it, except that Eccles claimed in after years that he had then never heard of the eminent British economist John Maynard Keynes, whose precedent-setting work *The General*

Theory of Employment, Interest and Money had appeared in 1936. The President, though, did know Keynes, but since he was hardly an intellectual, he could not really understand him. The Roosevelt strong suit was pragmatism, practicality. Did it make sense? was the characteristic question. Keynes, of course, did not make sense. He was merely, as the weight of learned opinion has it today, right.

According to Keynes, classical economics was simply dead wrong. It held that in bad times the market would contract, prices would fall, weak producers would be shaken out until, restored to "health," the market would again begin to function as demand came into balance with supply. But Keynes set all this classical theory on its head. In bad times the government was to spend and spend, levying low taxes, with the seemingly paradoxical result that recovery would be achieved by creating a deficit.

For presidential advisers like Harold Ickes and Harry Hopkins, Keynesianism did make sense, since it justified what they, in a less theoretical way, wanted to do anyway, namely spend money on relief or build enduring works. In fact, there were few genuine Keynesians among the New Deal inner circle—and the tragedy is that an innovative and bold administration thereby irrevocably missed its chance to go down in history as having accomplished the cure of depression by organized, deliberate, and above all peaceful means. Instead it would be war that would cure America and build its later prosperity.

The economic battle raged in the White House through the cheerless autumn and winter and spring of 1937–38. And growing more and more short-tempered, angered as he was by his foes in Congress, both within and without his own Democratic party, who were preparing a massive counterattack on the New Deal, the President tended to ignore the pressing economic crisis in favor of the political wars, for which he still had some zest.

The New Deal enthusiasts nurtured his resentment, urging a punitive campaign against those who had failed the President in the unfortunate Supreme Court battle. The President, in any case, hungered for fun, for the exhilarating experience of the cheering crowds, the "people," who, he was convinced, still idolized him. He was right in a way. The people still adored their President. But that did not mean that they really liked his policies, for the nation, even though battered by a near decade of depression, remained fundamentally conservative. It had not opted for revolution, nor even for political radicalism.

In September, 1937, when the Presidential Special had chugged its way across the Midwest and the West, the wildly cheering crowds still came out to see the man who was the incarnation of their hopes. But the American people who cheered him on his circuit were partly pragmatists too. If he could not deliver prosperity, they were not going to translate their liking for him as a man into real power by chastising rebellious members of his party at the polls.

The President called a special session of Congress, which convened on November 15, 1937, and asked it to pass, among other things, a new farm program and legislation setting up wage and hour standards. But Congress was not listening to the President; after five weeks it adjourned without giving him any of the things he wanted.

he regular session of Congress, which met just after the beginning of 1938, was a little more fruitful. It produced a refurbished A.A.A., which empowered the Secretary of Agriculture to fix marketing quotas whenever there was enough of a surplus of an export farm commodity to endanger the price level. Acreage allotments to each grower were also authorized, and prices were to be further supported by loans to farmers on their surplus crops, allowing growers to store crops and sell them in years of scarcity. Congress also passed a law setting minimum wages for many enterprises in interstate commerce and —indicative of the darkening shadows over the world— authorized a billion-dollar expansion of the Navy.

For all the A.A.A. planning, there were crop gluts again and sharply falling prices. In 1938 Secretary of Agriculture Henry A. Wallace warned his colleagues that the country could not stand another good harvest, that it "would be sunk." As the decade ended, the cotton carry-over in any single year was nearly three million bales greater than it had been in 1932.

When the spring of 1938 came at last, the President, dispirited and exhausted, slipped away to Warm Springs, Georgia, for a rest. His associates were worried: they had never seen him, as one put it, so "beat." But the economic ills of the nation would not wait, and on

April 2 Harry Hopkins and National Youth Adminis-trator Aubrey Williams went to Warm Springs to talk to the President. Wearily Roosevelt leafed through their memoranda, wearily he heard their arguments. Finally, abandoning his dream of balanced budgets, the President gave in. It was to be more spending. A little less than two weeks later, the President sent a package to Congress asking for a rejuvenated public-spending program. In June a Congress still hostile to him but un-willing, with an election year coming, to void a pork-barrel bill, authorized three and three-quarter billion dollars, a vast sum for the time. Included in this was nearly one and one-half billion dollars for Harry Hopkins to distribute through the W.P.A. and lesser sums for the N.Y.A., low-cost housing, and other classic measures that had marked the New Deal of Roosevelt's first term.

Morgenthau, bitterly reflecting on his failure, toyed with the idea of resigning his post as Secretary of the Treasury. ". . . the cards are all stacked against us," he told his angry aides. "They have just stampeded him like cattle."

But the President had not been stampeded. He had, if anything, held out too long. His foray into the back-lands the following summer to chastise the Democratic dissidents, during which he lashed out at the "Copper-heads" in his party who had refused to support him in his Court fight, netted him precisely nothing. Though he successfully backed Senator Alben Barkley over Happy Chandler in Kentucky and lukewarm New Dealer Senator Elmer Thomas over his opponent in Oklahoma, both would have won anyway. For the rest, his "purge," as the campaign became known, was an unmitigated disaster. He would not even tackle a local grandee like Pat McCarran in Nevada. He failed ut-terly in his effort to unseat old Senator "Cotton Ed" Smith in South Carolina and Senator Millard Tydings in Maryland.

Nor did the Democratic party as a whole fare well in the November elections. The Republicans added eighty seats in the House of Representatives, seven in the Senate. They came back from a 39.6 per cent showing in 1936 to 47 per cent two years later.

"The old Roosevelt magic has lost its kick," General Hugh S. Johnson, now a sullen anti-New Deal Washing-ton columnist, had cried on the occasion of the Supreme Court defeat. "The diverse elements in the Falstaffian army can no longer be kept together and led by a melo-dious whinny and a winning smile." He seemed right.

Economic breakdown, Democratic party discipline a shambles, near defeat at the polls, bankruptcy of imagination; the New Deal seemed played out.

But by a supreme irony regeneration lay just over the horizon—the "salvation" of a new war.

The Turbulent Years

By the middle of the Thirties Americans had weathered the first shock of the Depression and were developing a new awareness of the nation's social ills. Labor pickets, such as those in Joe Jones's *We Demand* (above), were taking up the cudgel against management with renewed vigor (and new effectiveness). Intellectuals whose faith in capitalism had been destroyed by the Depression were joining the crusade for socialism (as early as 1932 author Edmund Wilson and fifty-two cosigners issued a manifesto rejecting "the lunacy spawned by . . . the much-adulated immensely stupid and irresponsible 'business men'"); and artists, novelists, and playwrights were espousing the causes of society's oppressed minorities. But toward the end of the decade, as war clouds darkened Europe, the nation turned from domestic problems to a social disease of far graver concern: ". . . the epidemic of world lawlessness," as President Roosevelt put it, was threatening America herself.

Nine Old Men

On February 5, 1937, after the Supreme Court had invalidated many New Deal programs, including the N.R.A. and the A.A.A., the President sent to Congress a bill for the reorganization of the judicial branch of the government. It was to become known as Roosevelt's court-packing plan and was, in fact, an attempt to change the predominantly conservative structure of the Supreme Court by appointing one additional judge for each justice over the age of seventy who declined to retire (up to a total of six). (Above, the "nine old men" of the Supreme Court as they were caricatured in *New Masses* magazine, left to right: Justices Roberts, Butler, Brandeis, Van Devanter, Chief Justice Hughes, Justices McReynolds, Sutherland, Stone, and Cardozo.) Even the Court's critics were shocked, and the Democratic-dominated Congress (caricatured opposite) balked at such tactics. Roosevelt went on the air to assure the public that his proposal would "provide a reinvigorated, liberal-minded Judiciary necessary to furnish quicker and cheaper justice," but to many it still smacked of court packing. On July 22 the bill was returned to the Senate Judiciary Committee, and there it died. It was a victory for the independence of the Court and a crushing defeat for Roosevelt.

YOUR CHILDREN LIKE THESE LOW RENT HOMES

OHIO
WPA ART PROGRAM

**CEDAR-CENTRAL APTS.
2202 EAST 30TH STREET**
CLEVELAND METROPOLITAN HOUSING AUTHORITY

The Government and Art

"Art in America is being given its chance and there has been nothing like it since before the Reformation," proclaimed author Ford Madox Ford of the Works Progress Administration (W.P.A.) arts program. As part of that program the Federal Art Project (launched in 1935 along with similar projects for writers, actors, and musicians) put thousands of painters, sculptors, and designers to work adorning America. Posters like those at right gave support to a variety of causes, and the poster above announced an exhibition of one of the project's most ambitious undertakings, the Index of American Design, a massive compilation of renderings of American crafts and folk arts. And across the country W.P.A. murals—such as Edward Laning's immigrants on Ellis Island (the artist is shown at work), opposite, and Reginald Marsh's harbor scenes on the dome of the New York Customs House, opposite top—left an indelible stamp of the period on the nation's buildings.

KEEP YOUR FIRE ESCAPES CLEAR

F. H. LaGUARDIA
MAYOR

LANGDON W. POST
COMMISSIONER
TENEMENT HOUSE DEPT. OF THE CITY OF NEW YORK

A panel from William Gropper's Construction of a Dam *(above) in the Department of the Interior building shows a dynamism typical of W.P.A. murals. Below, Civil War scenes by Jared French.*

Above: panel of James M. Newell's heroic The Evolution of Western Civilization in Evander Childs High School library in New York. Below: right, study for Arshile Gorky's Newark Airport abstract mural, destroyed during use of the airport by the military; left, Karl Knaths's Composition.

Nature dealt the country two severe blows in 1937 and 1938. In January, 1937, one of the worst floods in American history rolled through the Ohio valley, leaving hundreds dead and hundreds of thousands homeless. In places the river was almost eight feet higher than it had ever been before, and it inundated Cincinnati's Coney Island (top), washed out roads and railways, and carried trees, debris, and wreckage of homes (including, top left, the submerged houseboat of one Sam Simpson) along with it. The following year, on September 21, a tropical hurricane struck the New England States, sending a tidal wave over Providence, Rhode Island, uprooting huge trees (opposite, a street in New London, Connecticut), and flattening buildings (above) throughout the area. The death toll was over six hundred.

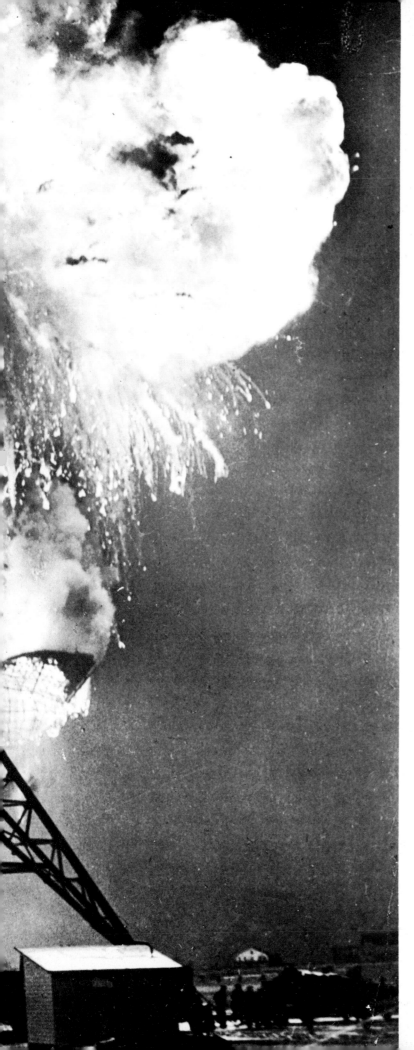

Death of the *Hindenburg*

On May 6, 1937, after a successful crossing of the Atlantic, the giant hydrogen-filled zeppelin *Hindenburg* dipped gracefully toward its mooring mast in Lakehurst, New Jersey, and burst into flames (left). Within minutes, it was reduced to a heap of smoldering wreckage (above top) as rescue workers gathered helplessly about. Thirty-six people were killed (above, caskets of the dead await shipment to Germany), sixty-one miraculously survived. The cause of the explosion was never determined, but the tragedy put an end to dirigible passenger flight.

Labor Comes of Age

Strikes and violence continued on the labor front, but by the late 30's the workingman was bargaining from a stronger position. Early in 1937 in Flint, Michigan, the United Auto Workers staged the first successful sit-down strike, below, forcing General Motors to come to terms. It was a major victory, and the sit-down spread to other areas. (Opposite below, the tactic is carried a step further by F. W. Woolworth employees in Detroit.) But unionism still met strong resistance. At right, U.A.W. organizers Walter Reuther (later to become U.A.W. chief) and Richard Frankensteen show the effects of Ford's strong men during an unsuccessful attempt to organize the Dearborn plant in May, 1937. Ford held out until 1941.

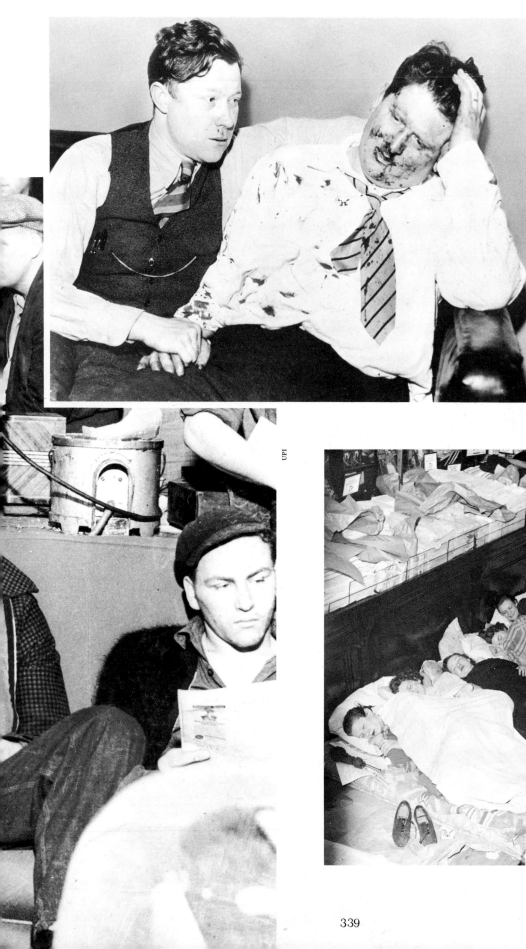

UPI

PHOTOWORLD

339

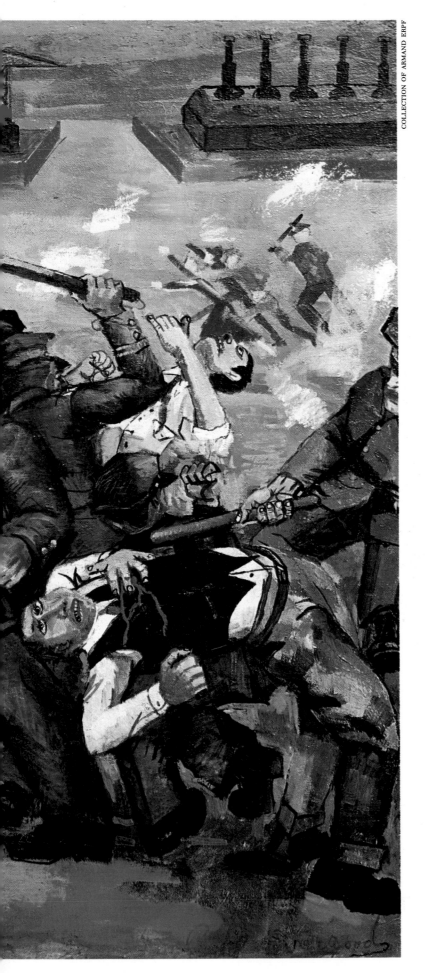

Labor's first gain in the steel industry was deceptively peaceful. In March, 1937, John L. Lewis, vociferous leader of the Committee for Industrial Organization, won acceptance of his union by the giant United States Steel without raising his voice, but the victory struck terror in the hearts of smaller steel companies. Their adamant refusal to recognize the union touched off a number of outbreaks, the most violent occurring at Republic Steel on Memorial Day. Philip Evergood's *American Tragedy*, at left, painted in part from news photographs like the one above, portrays the brutality of the police in driving off unarmed picketers at Republic's South Chicago plant.

In the Public Eye

The three figures here had only one thing in common: they made news in the 30's. Pretty Amelia Earhart (right), as the first woman to fly the Atlantic solo, stole the hearts of Americans in 1932 and was mourned in 1937 when she was lost over the Pacific. Evangelist Father Divine (below with his "angels") had a wide following, many of whom worshiped him as God and attended his "heavens," or religious communes. Though denigrated by some as a cultist, he helped many through his job placement service and soup kitchens during the Depression. Albert Einstein (opposite), formulator of the theory of relativity, made news in 1939 when he wrote to President Roosevelt warning of Nazi gains in nuclear fission. The message spurred United States development of the atomic bomb.

"the endless moving changed them"

John Steinbeck was well acquainted with the hardships and poverty of California's migratory workers. During the Depression he lived with these dispossessed farmers and sharecroppers of the South and Middle West in his native Salinas valley in California, and in 1939 he published a searing and compassionate account of their plight in his masterly The Grapes of Wrath. *The novel, excerpted here, stirred the American conscience and won a Pulitzer Prize in 1940. Steinbeck, whose works include* Cannery Row, Tortilla Flat, *and the more recent book* Travels with Charley, *was awarded the Nobel Prize for Literature in 1962.*

The moving, questing people were migrants now. Those families which had lived on a little piece of land, who had lived and died on forty acres, had eaten or starved on the produce of forty acres, had now the whole West to rove in. And they scampered about, looking for work; and the highways were streams of people, and the ditch banks were lines of people. Behind them more were coming. The great highways streamed with moving people. There in the Middle- and Southwest had lived a simple agrarian folk who had not changed with industry, who had not farmed with machines or known the power and danger of machines in private hands. They had not grown up in the paradoxes of industry. Their senses were still sharp to the ridiculousness of the industrial life.

And then suddenly the machines pushed them out and they swarmed on the highways. The movement changed them; the highways, the camps along the road, the fear of hunger and the hunger itself, changed them. The children without dinner changed them, the endless moving changed them. They were migrants. And the hostility changed them, welded them, united them—hostility that made the little towns group and arm as though to repel an invader, squads with pick handles, clerks and storekeepers with shotguns, guarding the world against their own people.

In the West there was panic when the migrants multiplied on the highways. Men of property were terrified for their property. Men who had never been hungry saw the eyes of the hungry. Men who had never wanted anything very much saw the flare of want in the eyes of the migrants. And the men of the towns and of the soft suburban country gathered to defend themselves; and they reassured themselves that they were good and the invaders bad, as a man must do before he fights. They said, These goddamned Okies are dirty and ignorant. They're degenerate, sexual maniacs. These goddamned Okies are thieves. They'll steal anything. They've got no sense of property rights.

And the latter was true, for how can a man without property know the ache of ownership? And the defending people said, They bring disease, they're filthy. We can't have them in the schools. They're strangers. How'd you like to have your sister go out with one of 'em?

The local people whipped themselves into a mold of cruelty. Then they formed units, squads, and armed them—armed them with clubs, with gas, with guns. We own the country. We can't let these Okies get out of hand. And the men who were armed did not

Philip Reisman's ink drawing of migrants is one in a series inspired by The Grapes of Wrath.

own the land, but they thought they did. And the clerks who drilled at night owned nothing, and the little storekeepers possessed only a drawerful of debts. But even a debt is something, even a job is something. The clerk thought, I get fifteen dollars a week. S'pose a goddamn Okie would work for twelve? And the little storekeeper thought, How could I compete with a debtless man?

And the migrants streamed in on the highways and their hunger was in their eyes, and their need was in their eyes. They had no argument, no system, nothing but their numbers and their needs. When there was work for a man, ten men fought for it—fought with a low wage. If that fella'll work for thirty cents, I'll work for twenty-five.

If he'll take twenty-five, I'll do it for twenty.

No, me, I'm hungry. I'll work for fifteen. I'll work for food. The kids.

You ought to see them. Little boils, like, comin' out, an' they can't run aroun'. Give 'em some windfall fruit, an' they bloated up. Me. I'll work for a little piece of meat.

And this was good, for wages went down and prices stayed up. The great owners were glad and they sent out more handbills to bring more people in. And wages went down and prices stayed up. . . .

And now the great owners and the companies invented a new method. A great owner bought a cannery. And when the peaches and the pears were ripe he cut the price of fruit below the cost of raising it. And as cannery owner he paid himself a low price for the fruit and kept the price of canned goods up and took his profit. And the little farmers who owned no canneries lost their farms, and they were taken by the great owners, the banks, and the companies who also owned the can-

neries. As time went on, there were fewer farms. The little farmers moved into town for a while and exhausted their credit, exhausted their friends, their relatives. And then they too went on the highways. And the roads were crowded with men ravenous for work, murderous for work.

And the companies, the banks worked at their own doom and they did not know it. The fields were fruitful, and starving men moved on the roads. The granaries were full and the children of the poor grew up rachitic, and the pustules of pellagra swelled on their sides. The great companies did not know that the line between hunger and anger is a thin line. And money that might have gone to wages went for gas, for guns, for agents and spies, for blacklists, for drilling. On the highways the people moved like ants and searched for work, for food. And the anger began to ferment.

345

Hollywood Goes Moral

Mae West poses seductively for the 1933 Paramount production I'm No Angel. *She certainly was not, though she managed to sneak by the Code regulations despite a swaggering gait and certain suggestive overtures to her leading man, Cary Grant. She even received a word of congratulations from the Central Association of Obstetricians and Gynecologists for popularizing the natural plumpness of the female figure. Miss West, whose well-rounded figure then measured a natural 36–26–36, was, the group concluded at its annual conference, "a boon to motherhood."*

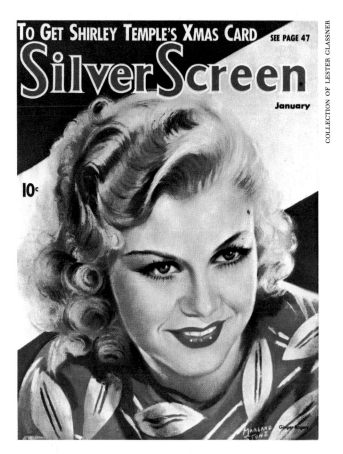

TO GET SHIRLEY TEMPLE'S XMAS CARD SEE PAGE 47

Silver Screen

January

10c

WHAT HOLLYWOOD LOVERS GIVE

Silver Screen

NOVEMBER

10c IN CANADA 15 CENTS

CLAUDETTE COLBERT as Poppaea in "The Sign of the Cross"

By the middle of the decade Hollywood had solved most of its technical problems (sound had evolved from a cacophonous garble to more or less intelligible communication, and color bore at least some resemblance to the hues one might encounter in nature), but a new problem—censorship—arose to plague the film makers. In 1933 the National Legion of Decency was formed, and by 1934 it had pressured the movie industry into enforcing the Production Code, a self-censorship plan until then largely ignored. Sex and sin were banned, and Hollywood suddenly went moral. But while it

definitely took some of the spice from life, there were other subjects, and the industry proved itself adaptable. Comedy was big, with such stars as Will Rogers, the Marx Brothers, and W. C. Fields (below, assisting Charles Sellon in *It's a Gift*, 1934). Ginger Rogers (above left) waltzed with Fred Astaire in light romances, and Claude Rains (below left, terrorizing Una O'Connor) provided thrills as *The Invisible Man*, 1933. Gone were such spectacles as Cecil B. De Mille's 1932 sex-and-the-Bible production, *The Sign of the Cross*, with Claudette Colbert (above) as the vamp.

Bedimpled Shirley Temple was the darling of the 30's. Below, Shirley shares the spotlight with Jack Haley and Alice Faye in a military tap routine from Poor Little Rich Girl, 1936. At right, tough-talking Humphrey Bogart holds hostages (who include Leslie Howard and Bette Davis, in foreground) in The Petrified Forest, 1936.

Clockwise from below: Katharine Hepburn and Fred MacMurray in 1935 film version of Booth Tarkington's 1921 Pulitzer Prize winner, Alice Adams; *John Garfield and Priscilla Lane in* Dust Be My Destiny, 1939; *Oliver Hardy, Mae Busch, Stan Laurel in* Sons of the Desert, 1934; *Walt Disney's* Pinocchio, 1940; *Victor Jory and Anita Louise in* A Midsummer Night's Dream, 1935; *Isabel Jewell and Ronald Colman in* A Tale of Two Cities, *released during 1935.*

349

At left, Jean Harlow stretches sensually for a publicity shot—to the query posed below, the obvious answer is "plenty."

JOAN CRAWFORD IN "NO MORE LADIES"

"MOVIES"

SEPTEMBER
10¢

NRA
CODE

COMPLETE
MOVIE
STORIES
"LES MISERABLES"
"CALL OF THE WILD"

NORMA SHEARER

WHAT DOES HARLOW HAVE?

Norma Shearer, above, played society ladies; Barbara Stanwyck, below, was starred in Ladies They Talk About, *1933.*

COLLECTION OF LESTER GLASSNER

Above, the Marx Brothers—Groucho, Chico, and Harpo (displaying wounded leg)—in the 1935 comedy A Night at the Opera. Below, Ginger Rogers and Fred Astaire flank a 1936 still from Tarzan Escapes, with Johnny Weismuller and Maureen O'Sullivan fending off the lions. Weismuller made the transition from Olympic swimming champion to Tarzan jungle hero in the early 30's. He was one of several Tarzans.

COLLECTION OF DION MC GREGOR; LEFT AND RIGHT: CULVER PICTURES

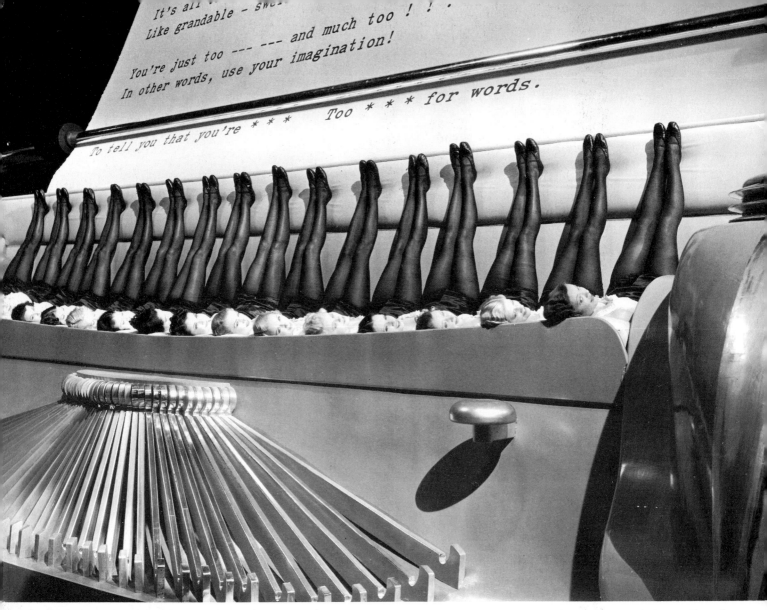

It's all ...
Like grandable – swe...

You're just too --- --- and much too ! ! .
In other words, use your imagination!

Too * * * for words.

To tell you that you're * * * Too * * * for words.

Above, a 1937 Busby Berkeley musical Ready, Willing, and Able, *all just too marvelous for words*. Below: left, Gail Patrick, Robert Light, William Powell, *and* Carole Lombard *in* My Man Godfrey, 1936; *right*, James Stewart *as a young senator in* Mr. Smith Goes to Washington, 1939.

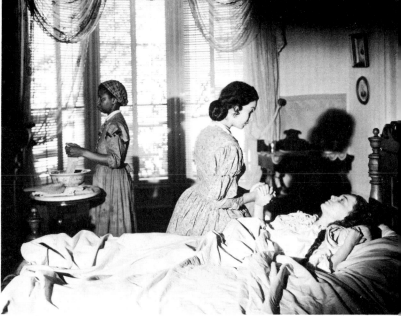

Swashbuckling Errol Flynn in the lusty The Sea Hawk, *1940.*

Butterfly McQueen, Vivien Leigh, and Olivia De Havilland in David O. Selznick's Gone With the Wind *(above), 1939. Below, Bert Lahr, Jack Haley, Ray Bolger, and Judy Garland in musical* The Wizard of Oz, *1939.*

John Carradine, Spencer Tracy, and Freddie Bartholomew in Captains Courageous, *1937, with Tracy playing a fisherman.*

Gary Cooper and Jean Arthur in Mr. Deeds Goes to Town, *1936.*

Below, Irene Dunne (foreground) sashays through a little number in Show Boat, *1936, as Paul Robeson, Hattie McDaniel, and Helen Morgan look on.*

On Stage

Despite setbacks caused by the Depression, some of America's best theater was produced in the middle and late 30's. The W.P.A.'s Federal Theater Project provided a creative outlet for thousands of unemployed stage people, there was the experimental New York Group Theater, with such impressive young talents as Harold Clurman, Lee Strasberg, and Elia Kazan, and of course there was Broadway. Clockwise from above are scenes from memorable performances of the 30's: Dorothy Stickney and Howard Lindsay with brood in *Life with Father*; Monty Woolley as the incapacitated and truculent house guest in *The Man Who Came to Dinner*; arguing angels in the satirical hit of the International Ladies' Garment Workers' Union, *Pins and Needles*; Martha Scott (center) and Evelyn Varden in Thornton Wilder's Pulitzer Prize-winning *Our Town*; Claire Luce and Broderick Crawford in *Of Mice and Men*; and chorus girls in George White's *Scandals*.

Cole Porter, Richard Rodgers and Lorenz Hart, and George Gershwin were masters of the Broadway musical, with tunes like those above. Opposite, Ethel Waters belts out "Heat Wave," from Irving Berlin's As Thousands Cheer. Left, the famous Lynn Fontanne and Alfred Lunt, husband and wife team, as they appeared in the mildly licentious Amphitryon 38.

A Blow at Bigotry

In 1935, after a performance by Marian Anderson in Salzburg, Austria, Arturo Toscanini was moved to observe, "What I have heard today, one is privileged to listen to once in a hundred years." Few could deny the American contralto's great art, but there were those who would deny her a place to practice it. In 1939 the Daughters of the American Revolution, one of whose stated purposes is "to cherish, maintain, and extend the institutions of American freedom," refused Miss Anderson, a Negro, the use of their hall for a concert in Washington, D. C. Despite the vocalist's world renown and protests against racial bias, the Daughters (who inspired Grant Wood's 1932 painting below) were not dissuaded. With the support of Eleanor Roosevelt (who resigned from the D.A.R.), Harold Ickes, and many other public figures, Miss Anderson gave her concert on the steps of the Lincoln Memorial (opposite), where she sang to a crowd of some seventy-five thousand on Easter Sunday. Mitchell Jamieson's W.P.A. mural (above) commemorates the occasion.

A Royal Visit

In the summer of 1939 America received a royal visitation. Arriving in Washington on a sweltering day in June, King George VI and Queen Elizabeth of England were greeted by a twenty-one-gun salute, a formation of bomber planes, and crowds of wildly cheering people. After a state dinner the royal couple were entertained at a White House concert, which included performances by Marian Anderson, Kate Smith, and a cowboy balladeer named Alan Lomax. The visit included a tour of Mount Vernon (above, the King and Queen alight from their car at the Washington Navy Yard for the trip down the Potomac), a trip to the New York World's Fair (opposite top, Her Majesty—with orchid bouquet—seated with King in open tractor train), and a traditional American beer-and-hot-dogs picnic at the President's Hyde Park estate (opposite, in a prepicnic pose, the Roosevelts flank the King and Queen, with the President's mother center). Then the British monarchs prepared to leave for Canada enroute to their war-threatened country across the Atlantic. As they boarded the train, the President called out, "Good luck to you! All the luck in the world!"

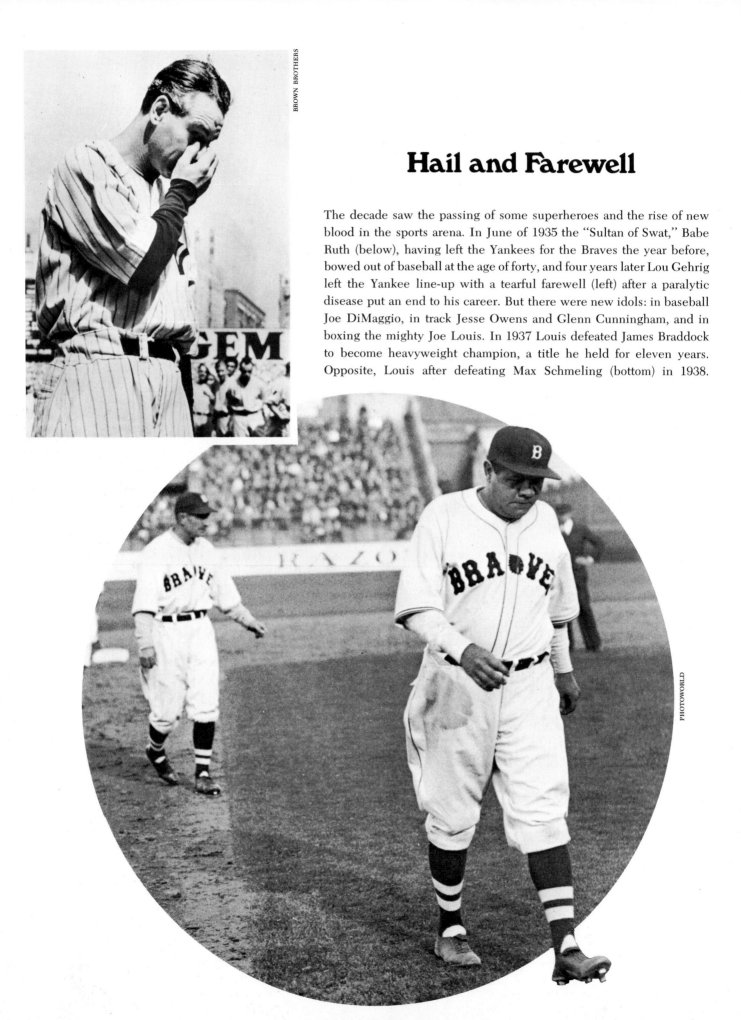

Hail and Farewell

The decade saw the passing of some superheroes and the rise of new blood in the sports arena. In June of 1935 the "Sultan of Swat," Babe Ruth (below), having left the Yankees for the Braves the year before, bowed out of baseball at the age of forty, and four years later Lou Gehrig left the Yankee line-up with a tearful farewell (left) after a paralytic disease put an end to his career. But there were new idols: in baseball Joe DiMaggio, in track Jesse Owens and Glenn Cunningham, and in boxing the mighty Joe Louis. In 1937 Louis defeated James Braddock to become heavyweight champion, a title he held for eleven years. Opposite, Louis after defeating Max Schmeling (bottom) in 1938.

BROWN BROTHERS

PHOTOWORLD

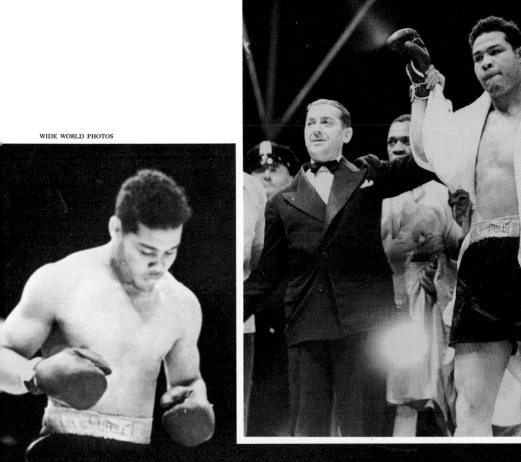

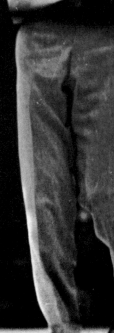

FEDERAL BUILDING

NEW-YORK WO

World of

On April 30, 1939, the New York World's Fair opened, and visitors (sketched at right by Perry Barlow for *The New Yorker*) poured into the grounds at Flushing Meadows. Symbolized by the Trylon and Perisphere (centered above on a desk-scarf souvenir), the fair was dedicated to the World of Tomorrow. And what a world it was to be. General Motors conducted awed visitors in moving chairs over a serpentine highway of the future, General Electric exhibited the first TV studio, and Dr. Albert Einstein explained the mysteries of science in a superspectacular *son et lumière*, in which cosmic rays

364

Tomorrow

were utilized to suffuse the fairground with multicolored light and pulsing sound. For those who sought thrills, there was a parachute jump (left), and for those who sought more than a hot dog, the French Pavilion and the Belgian Brussels (later to become Manhattan restaurants) provided welcome gastronomic relief. Most of the foreign nations (with the notable exception of Germany) had exhibitions, and the only shadow over an otherwise splendid opening was the nagging question, Would the nations all be as friendly in tomorrow's world as they seemed on that opening day?

The Great Debate

As Hitler's army overran the Low Countries and France and stood at the very door of England, the debate over America's foreign policy intensified. Should we be aloof or aid our friends? One of the strongest advocates of isolationism was a group called the America First Committee. Dedicated to avoiding American involvement in the war at any cost, it numbered among its members and sympathizers such influential figures as Senators Gerald P. Nye and Burton K. Wheeler, author

Kathleen Norris, industrialist Henry Ford, and aviator Charles Lindbergh. On the other side was the powerful Committee To Defend America by Aiding the Allies, founded by writer and journalist William Allen White. Its purpose was to gain aid for Britain without directly entering the war. The argument raged into 1940 and 1941, but from the very intensity of the debate it was clear that America could not sit quietly on the side lines while Europe was engulfed in war.

APPEASING A POLECAT

"Above all, let us stop this hysterical chatter of calamity and invasion," admonished Charles A. Lindbergh even as Germany was smashing through Belgium and Holland. Lindbergh was not the only "good citizen" who believed the war was strictly a European affair. Opposite, Senator Burton K. Wheeler of Montana, Charles Lindbergh, and Kathleen Norris attend a rally of the isolationist America First Committee, and above, the senator and the flier draw fire from the Philadelphia Record in August, 1941, for their "appeasement" tactics. Others, such as William Allen White (left), urged intervention in the form of arms for Britain.

Home-Grown Nazis

imieden ▲ die Zukunft

Among those of decidedly isolationist persuasion were numbers of American Nazis, notably a group called the German-American Bund, founded in 1936 by Fritz J. Kuhn (opposite top). Its members established camps (above, Camp Nordland in New Jersey and the slogan "We forge the future"), aped Nazi dress, and goose-stepped through the streets (left, a Bund parade in Yorkville, New York). Violently anti-Communist and anti-Semitic, Kuhn advocated dismissal of all Jews from influential positions "if the United States is to be saved from Communism." There were other fascist groups: William Pelley's Silver Shirts ("the cream, the head and flower of our Protestant Christian manhood," according to Pelley), the German Legion, the Hindenburg Youth Association, to name a few. Their aims were the same: to promote the fascist cause and to keep America from joining the Allies.

The Nation Prepares

Notwithstanding fascists and isolationists, America was preparing for war. Despite lobbying mothers who staged a Death Watch (opposite below) in the Senate reception room, Congress authorized the nation's first peacetime conscription, and on October 29, 1940, Secretary of War Henry L. Stimson (blindfolded, opposite) drew the first draft number as Roosevelt (far left) looked on. Within weeks young draftees (like those below, headed for Fort Dix, New Jersey) were being shipped off to training camps. In addition, the President stepped up national defense production and the shipment of arms to Britain, including fifty World War I destroyers (one of which is shown at left) to fight Nazi U-boats.

Willkie Tries

The decade ended, appropriately enough, with a challenge to the new order. In June of 1940 the Republicans met in Philadelphia and nominated Wendell Willkie (taking ovations, opposite) as their presidential candidate. Opposing third-term candidate Roosevelt, Willkie barnstormed the country (above, in Ohio), charging the President with perpetuating "one-man rule" and warning of the danger of "an American totalitarian government." The voters, however, seemed little concerned with the possibility of domestic dictatorship, and Roosevelt was re-elected. He had assured Americans their boys would not "be sent into any foreign wars"; he did not dwell on how close to home the war was coming.

NO MAN IS GOOD THREE TIMES

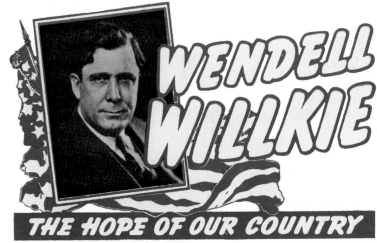

WENDELL WILLKIE

THE HOPE OF OUR COUNTRY

America's role in the war abroad was a matter of endless discussion during the late 30's and early 40's. Legislators (like William Gropper's bombastic senator above) debated the pros and cons of intervention while students (like the University of Chicago group opposite) staged antiwar rallies across the country.

Isolation or Intervention?

Grim as it seemed at the time, the recession of 1937–38 proved in the end to be only a small eddy in the mainstream of American history, but that end could not then be seen. Domestic developments in that short period provided critics of the administration with ample opportunity to point out that the economic expedients the New Deal had resorted to with such feverish activity over the past five or six years were of dubious permanent value. For those who viewed with alarm the very thought of a planned society, here was proof enough that their fear was well-founded.

In 1935, at the high tide of the New Deal's success, Roosevelt had told a responsive audience in Charleston, South Carolina, that so much progress had been made because "we planned it that way." By early 1938 those brash words were recalled as a mocking echo of an empty boast. What sort of planning had led to the terrible need of Chicago children who early in 1938 looked for food in garbage cans, of desperate Cleveland families turned scavengers among the spoiled produce dumped in the streets by markets at the close of day, and of some few, at least, who took their lives in despair or who died of malnutrition? Once again fear was loosed, fear, among other things, that American democracy, for all its past accomplishments and its glowing promises for the future, had lost its way and had stumbled into a slough from which there was no means of escape.

But as the months passed a path did open, a way that led the nation at an accelerating pace toward the greatest productivity it had ever known, toward a new, commanding sense of common purpose, and, inexorably and by supreme irony, into the frightful blood bath of World War II. While America had preoccupied itself throughout the unprecedented trials and threats of the Depression years with desperate efforts to preserve and reinforce the safeguards of democracy, in Europe other governments had been abandoning such cumbersome ways in favor of direct, forceful, and ruthless action to further their destinies. Italy and then Germany under Mussolini and Hitler emerged as totalitarian states where concepts of law and order were ghoulish parodies of any civilized norm. Russia had, of course, long since demonstrated how methodically and mercilessly civil and individual rights could be suppressed by the state when suppression served the purposes of those in power.

There were more than a few Americans for whom such quick and absolute "solutions" to social and political problems had a strong appeal. After all, as even the truest American citizens repeatedly, if half humorously, observed, Mussolini had quite miraculously made the Italian railroad trains operate on time. And while the Roosevelt administration had enrolled homeless and destitute American youths to reforest cutover land and clear firebreaks in woodlands, Hitler had been putting German youths into uniforms and encouraging them to strut through the streets in search of dissidents with Nazi aims and methods. The dramatization of Sinclair Lewis' antifascist novel *It Can't Happen Here* was a great popular success. But there were those who thought or feared that a fascist revolt just might happen here—and others who hoped it would. The German-American Bund and the Silver Shirts, both strongly profascist and anti-Semitic organizations, spawned their own little Hitlers. On the other hand, men like Theodore Dreiser and Upton Sinclair lent their names and influence to Communist-supported organizations in the sincere hope that by doing so they could help to defeat the evils of fascism before they seriously infected American attitudes and America's interest in maintaining peace in the world. For many liberals, young and old alike, the professed ideals of communism seemed to offer an antidote to the ills that had so recently and so miserably afflicted the capitalist societies of the Western world.

Under the circumstances, at a time when old, established certainties were being challenged from many sides, such aberrations were probably in the nature of things. An even more serious menace to the public weal, it seemed to thoughtful, concerned people, came from within the government itself with the creation of the congressional committee under the chairmanship of Representative Martin Dies of Texas to investigate evidences of un-American activity in the country. The zealous chairman conducted his hearings with such a flagrant disregard for judicial conduct and for the rules of evidence that Eleanor Roosevelt likened them to the work of the Gestapo—the Nazi secret police—in Germany. According to one report, the House Un-American Activities Committee had discovered that Shirley Temple, the child movie star, had Red affilia-

tions, and Harold Ickes amused an audience in Tacoma, Washington, by referring to "a burly congressman leading a *posse comitatus* in a raid upon [her] nursery to collect her dolls as evidence." Nevertheless, as war clouds gathered over Europe, and America felt increasing concern for its own security, Congress, backed by public opinion, renewed the committee's mandate and its funds. A special Senate committee headed by Senator Gerald P. Nye of North Dakota, also more resembling the Inquisition than a fair-minded body, was able, during a series of hearings that lasted from May of 1934 into 1936, to convince a host of Americans that manufacturers of munitions and other materials of war—"merchants of death"—had tricked the country into the First World War in order to sell their products. Because it provided a simple explanation for American entry into the war and a ready scapegoat, the merchants of death theory appealed to millions of Americans determined never to become involved in another war.

Though disturbed and confused by the deplorable state of domestic affairs during those years, Roosevelt was obliged to turn his attention more and more to the nation's foreign relations. By a curious coincidence, on March 5, 1933, *The New York Times* had carried in adjacent columns on its front page an account of Roosevelt's first inauguration the preceding day and a confident prediction that Adolf Hitler would be elevated to power that very day—as he indeed was. It could not then be foretold, of course, how fatefully the separate missions of these two leaders would come into conflict in the dozen years that followed. The second half of Roosevelt's long administration, until his death in 1945, was above everything else concerned with the containment and defeat of Hitler and his allies. Both men died in the same month of the same year, April, 1945, before the last battles were fought, Roosevelt within clear sight of victory, Hitler in suicidal despair over the certainty of defeat.

In the course of the social and economic reforms Roosevelt undertook as part of the New Deal, he experienced more bitter vituperation than had virtually any other President in American history. This was something different from the malice directed at him by Jew-baiting fascists because of his tolerance of their enemies. Nice old men and women of good fortune and respectable pedigree referred to the President as That Man, rarely by his name—an abominable man, a high-born Hudson valley patrician, properly schooled at Groton and Harvard, who had turned traitor to his class. He had questioned the probity and social responsibility of big business and finance, and he had lent his support to the long-deferred claims of union labor. And in circles whose interests conflicted with such developments this was reprehensible.

In those circles and elsewhere there were many who were sure they detected in the President's utterances and in his programs a lust for power. His efforts to pack the Supreme Court seemed to be evidence enough of that. Such apprehensions, coming at a time when the bogy of dictatorship loomed large and frightful, found exceedingly fertile soil to root in. Actually the matter of the conservative bias of the Supreme Court settled itself shortly after Roosevelt's plan to add new and younger members had been rejected as a needless abandonment of constitutional principle. Through resignations and retirements of a number of the "nine old men," the President was able to reconstitute this eminent body with men of his own choosing, worthy men like Hugo Black, Felix Frankfurter, William O. Douglas, and others, who found the Constitution a more flexible instrument than had their immediate predecessors. The integrity of the Court had been preserved, and the President was relieved of a problem he was much better off without.

Other Americans feared that he was willfully leading the country toward war, and even today some earnest people apparently continue to believe that this was true, although it is altogether unlikely. The roots of the policy that brought this country to its ultimate decision in 1941 are deep and tangled, but the main strands of their growth can be traced through the brief years that separated the two world wars. When the first of those wars started in 1914, there was general agreement that this was no business of ours. Even after our decisive participation in that frightful strife, there was a strong tendency in America to write it off as an imperative, perhaps, but momentary "foreign entanglement." As the popular song went, it was soon "over over there," and after that brief foray into the nettlesome disputes of the Old World, America could return to the tranquil isolation of the New World, and in that distant retreat set a shining example of peaceful enterprise for others to follow—as George Washington had long before observed that the nation must do to fulfill its highest destiny. Convinced of its own strength, long turned inward by geographical circumstance, and skeptical of the advantages of international involvements, America hastily washed its hands of Europe's perplexities and beat a retreat to "normalcy." Doughboys returning from that "great crusade" hoped never again to see the Statue of Liberty except from the back side.

Woodrow Wilson pleaded that the nation must not retire from the responsibilities it had incurred, that "at whatever cost of independent action" governments must act together to do away with the old war-breeding order of international politics. "The League of Nations," he argued, was "the only hope for mankind. . . . Shall we or any other free people hesitate to accept this great duty? Dare we reject it and break the heart of the world?" But his plea was in vain. And while the average American ignored the world congress that with American participation might have contributed substantially to world peace, forces leading toward war were set in motion.

In 1921 and 1922 the United States Senate did ratify complicated international treaties, in which the reduction of naval armaments and certain other measures aimed at reducing the threat of war were agreed upon. However, significantly, among these agreements a four-power treaty between this country, Britain, France, and Japan carried the specific proviso that "there is no commitment to armed force, no alliance, no obligation to join in any defense." All the treaties were, in fact, toothless. Subsequent efforts to encourage disarmament were hardly more effectual. In 1928 the United States, along with sixty-one other nations, signed the Kellogg-Briand Pact, which solemnly outlawed war as a solution to international differences. The force of world opinion, it was ingenuously held, would be the principal deterrent in case of trouble.

Shortly after Roosevelt's first inauguration in 1933, almost three-quarters of the twenty thousand college youths who responded to a nationwide poll declared they would not willingly serve in the armed forces in time of war; almost half of them further stated they would not fight even if this country were invaded. This sort of pacifism was, to be sure, not a purely American phenomenon. There were similar demonstrations in the British universities, where the famous Oxford Pledge—"Resolved, we shall not serve King and Country"—gained wide support. That spirit did not altogether diminish in the years immediately following. In 1935, the nadir of the Depression, large numbers of

American students staged a country-wide show of solidarity against war. (Their slogan, "Build schools—not battleships," has a strangely topical ring some thirty years later, during America's agony in Vietnam.) The youths were not alone in their protest. Ladies' clubs protested against toy soldiers, and some even proposed the abolition of Memorial Day, with its custom of decorating military graves. Men of the cloth felt their churches should register disapproval of the crime of war.

A long debate over the question of America's entry into the World Court dragged on from 1926 to 1935, when it came to an inglorious conclusion. "We are being rushed pell mell to get into this World Court," Senator Huey Long objected, with characteristic spleen, "so that Señor Ab Jap or some other something from Japan can pass upon our controversies." Somewhat more succinctly and more profanely, Senator Thomas Schall of Minnesota shouted from the Senate floor, "To hell with Europe and the rest of those nations!" A more summary expression of isolationist attitudes would be difficult to find.

On a considerably higher level Roosevelt had, in his first inaugural address, told his countrymen: "In the field of world policy I would dedicate this nation to the policy of the good neighbor—the neighbor who resolutely respects himself and, because he does so, respects the rights of others. . . ." This was isolationism of a different order. In much this spirit President Hoover had already started to pull American troops out of Nicaragua, as Roosevelt would withdraw them from Haiti, to the satisfaction of Latin Americans generally, whose "Yankeephobia" was all but chronic. Thus, also, in 1934 Roosevelt renounced the right of America to intervene in the affairs of Cuba. In 1936, during the course of the Mexican revolution, America's ambassador to that country, Josephus Daniels, resolutely refused to take action when oil interests in this country demanded forceful protection of their investments below the border. Members of the Liberty League in New York and Chicago thundered at such "mollycoddling" of the foreign plunderers, but saner heads prevailed and relations between the two nations gradually improved. Such gestures by no means transformed the image of a rich and acquisitive Uncle Sam into a popular figure south of the Rio Grande, but at least they gave fair evidence that this country had no aggressive military aspirations in that area, and when the President visited South America in 1936, he

was hailed everywhere as "el gran democrato."

The United States obviously had little to fear from its neighbors to the south, except as these in their relative impotence might fall victim to Nazi stratagems and serve as advance posts for some future aggression. (Both Argentina and Chile, for example, had large populations of German descent, and in both countries vigorous Nazi organizations had been formed.) To the north, Canada, with its historic Anglo-French orientation, was, of course, stoutly antifascist and under the imperial wing of Britain to boot. But since the first signs of Japan's overriding militancy in the Orient and since Hitler's first cynical maneuvers in Europe, the news from east and west had become increasingly foreboding.

By 1937 the shadows of a world-wide debacle had already fallen and were lengthening. Six years earlier, in September, 1931, halfway around the globe, Japan had invaded Manchuria, the first step in an expansionist policy that within a decade would lead to the devastation of Pearl Harbor and its long, sanguinary aftermath. The moral force of the Kellogg-Briand Pact signatories had proved ineffective.

I n 1935 Hitler all but tore up the Versailles Treaty and openly prepared for a war of conquest. That same year Mussolini, heartened by Hitler's audacity, overran Ethiopia as one ridiculously easy step toward re-establishing the ancient Roman Empire; humanitarians around the world cringed when Vittorio, Mussolini's son, described the bombing of earth-bound natives as "exceptionally good fun." The next spring, in March, 1936, Hitler ordered his army into the demilitarized Rhineland, in violation of the Treaty of Versailles.

Meanwhile, by lending their support to the reactionary nationalist faction in the Spanish Civil War, Nazi Germany and Fascist Spain assured the long, despotic rule of General Francisco Franco in that troubled land. Two or three thousand young American idealists and liberals enlisted with the Spanish Loyalist forces, serving in the Abraham Lincoln Brigade and other units; most of them died, in vain. The sad futility of their efforts and of the cause they supported was recalled in Ernest Hemingway's poignant novel *For Whom the Bell Tolls.*

Three times in three successive years beginning in 1935, Congress passed Neutrality Acts designed to minimize the possibility of this country's being swept into the maelstroms that threatened to engulf Europe and Asia alike. The third act, passed in 1937 and expanding on the earlier two, prohibited the export of munitions to belligerents, gave to the President full authority to ban shipments of certain other "articles and materials" (presumably oil, scrap iron, and such strategic commodities) unless they were paid for before leaving the United States and then carried in foreign ships, and forbade Americans to travel on ships of belligerent nations. The cash-and-carry provision was clearly devised to protect Americans from loss if exported goods were captured or destroyed. The traditional American principle of freedom of the seas had been thrown overboard for a narrow self-interest.

Even as the bill was being passed there were predictions that it might well prove futile. One fatal defect was that it did not discriminate between belligerents. Germany, Italy, and Japan were already relatively well armed. To apply the Neutrality Act would only penalize the more pacific and unprepared nations— England, France, and China—with whom Americans at large sympathized, who were later to be our allies, and who sorely needed our support as hostilities abroad approached and actually began. As the New York *Herald-Tribune* caustically observed, the act seemed designed to preserve the United States from intervention in World War I, twenty years late, rather than in the one then brewing. Nevertheless, noninvolvement appeared to be the mood of the nation, for several weeks before the third Neutrality Act was passed, a Gallup poll concluded that 94 per cent of the American public felt that the nation's main policy should be staying out of foreign wars instead of trying to prevent them from breaking out.

"My own impression," wrote Claude Bowers, United States ambassador to Spain, two months later, "is . . . that with every surrender the prospects of a European war grow darker."

As though in answer to his foreboding, in that same month, July, 1937, Japan again attacked China. Power in Japan had been largely consolidated in the hands of military leaders who believed their nation's manifest destiny led toward territorial expansion and economic hegemony in Asia. The populous Chinese cities of Nanking and Canton were unmercifully bombed and a

few months later the United States gunboat *Panay* was sunk in the Yangtze River. That particular incident was quickly apologized away and compensation paid. However, the underlying intent to drive Americans out of China was transparently clear from the subsequent destruction by the Japanese of American hospitals, missions, and other properties in that country.

 s a reprimand to the Japanese war lords many American college girls eschewed silk stockings and American chain stores boycotted Japanese manufactures, with no measurable influence on the course of events—especially since both American and British firms were selling large amounts of scrap iron and oil to Japan for use in the Japanese war machine. Application by this country of the Neutrality Act would have deprived China of materials necessary to her cause. So, incongruously, exports flowed from America to both belligerents. And the slaughter of innocents at Nanking and Canton was, as American correspondents wrote, largely accomplished "with materials furnished by American companies for a price."

The pace of such ominous developments around the world was quickening. On October 5, 1937, the President delivered a memorable speech in Chicago, in which he spoke of the breakdown of international order and law, which had begun a few years earlier and was spreading so rapidly; he pleaded the cause of peace in the world and proposed a "quarantine" of the contagious disease of war. America, he concluded, hated war, hoped for peace, and was actively searching for peace. Those last two sentiments were roundly applauded, but the use of the word "quarantine" aroused a fear in certain quarters that he had in mind some plan for collective security among peace-loving nations, an idea that was anathema to isolationist congressmen, who therewith spoke loudly of impeaching the President. Ridiculous as such a reaction seems, it reflected the almost superstitious dread that had for so long been attached to the expression "entangling alliances." As first used by Thomas Jefferson (and subsequently attributed to George Washington) the phrase had none of the implications that had been read into it for convenient purposes over the years. The President intended in his speech to reassure isolationist Americans that they could preserve their sanctuary even if the rest of the world went up in flames.

There were those who, from a sense of moral obligation, and others who, indeed, from a sense of self-interest or of strictly military caution, felt that the nation should immediately exert its influence, at whatever cost, to turn the tide of aggression. Reflecting the opinion of the latter faction, in December, 1937, Ickes wrote in his diary, "Certainly war with Japan is inevitable sooner or later, and if we have to fight her, isn't this the best possible time?" To realistic military minds that attitude made good, hard sense, but such saber rattling grated on the ears of the majority of Americans. Japan and China still seemed infinitely remote from Main Street. Would it not be best to get out of the Orient and stay out?

But the nation's mood was starting to change. Early in 1938 Congress authorized the expenditure of more than a billion dollars on new naval vessels of various sorts; the country was starting the development of a two-ocean navy to police both the Pacific and the Atlantic. The President also asked for a substantially larger army. Both coasts of the nation, he suggested, might be attacked at once, and even inland cities bombed. That very year, it was subsequently revealed, Hermann Göring, the chief of Hitler's *Luftwaffe*, was asking German aircraft designers for planes that could reach New York with their bombs. The American sanctuary might have become a prime target for the *Luftwaffe* if things had continued to go Hitler's way.

And things did continue to go Hitler's way for a while. In March, 1938, after softening up the country with a Nazi fifth column, his highly mechanized armies swarmed over Austria and "liberated" seven million people without firing a shot. Following up his "strategy of terror," within six months the *Führer* demanded that the German-speaking Sudetenland of Czechoslovakia be ceded to the Reich. It was almost the limit, but not quite. British Prime Minister Neville Chamberlain went three times to Germany to talk to and try to placate Hitler. On the third visit, at Munich in September, 1938, in company with French Premier Edouard Daladier, Chamberlain, in spite of the treaty obligations of both Britain and France, persuaded the Czechs to yield—in fact abandoned them to the growing forces of evil. Returning to London, Chamberlain assured his countrymen that he brought them "peace with honor. I believe it is peace in our time." Winston Churchill

believed otherwise. "Britain and France had to choose between war and dishonor," he said. "They chose dishonor. They will have war."

The news reached America as it was cleaning up and counting the dead after an unprecedentedly devastating hurricane that swept over Long Island and New England earlier in the month. Over six hundred people had been killed; countless venerable trees—the pride of that countryside—had been blown to the ground; many millions of dollars' worth of property had been destroyed. It was a tragedy more immediate and unexpected than the one enacted at Munich so shortly afterward, and it tended to blunt the news from abroad.

Anxieties about the world situation were nevertheless mounting. Hardly a month after the Munich meeting, on Sunday evening, October 30, 1938, fear surged across the nation when ninety-two radio stations carried the dramatic broadcast of H. G. Wells's *War of the Worlds* by Orson Welles and the Mercury Theater, describing an imaginary assault on the Atlantic seaboard by Martians armed with "death rays." Although the performance was explicitly announced as entertainment, it was mistaken for a special news broadcast and it resulted in nationwide hysteria. Nothing had ever demonstrated so conclusively the power of network radio; nothing more clearly revealed the apprehensive mood of the nation's people.

There was reason enough to worry, as the President warned Congress in January, 1939. "Events abroad have made it increasingly clear to the American people," he remarked, "that dangers within are less to be feared than dangers from without. . . . Once I prophesied that this generation of Americans had a rendezvous with destiny. That prophecy comes true. To us much is given; more is expected." And, quoting Washington, he concluded, "This generation will 'nobly save or meanly lose the last best hopes of earth'. . . ." Two months later Hitler quickly took over the rest of Czechoslovakia, that "dagger pointed at the heart of Germany," as it was ingeniously described. Czechoslovakia had been the creation of Wilsonian diplomacy; the main boulevard in the city of Prague had been named for the American President—the man who had so earnestly espoused the cause of self-determination for peoples everywhere. The following month, monkey-style, Mussolini copied the *Führer*'s antics by seizing Albania. England and France were at last preparing for war, for if, as seemed likely, Poland was the next victim on the Nazi agenda, they would simply have to fight. And America was feverishly stepping up the pace of its own preparations for whatever might come. Meanwhile, Franco was winning out in Spain.

Long before such dire developments, New York City had started plans for a huge world's fair that would celebrate the "World of Tomorrow" and expound "the theme of social reconstruction." It opened almost immediately after the rape of Czechoslovakia, which benighted country nevertheless staged an exhibit along with several scores of other foreign nations. Nazi Germany was prominently absent, although Italy and Japan had elaborate displays, as did Soviet Russia. The demonstrations of man's technological triumphs, everywhere featured, were underlaid by a most bitter irony, which could hardly be masked. However, the fair provided diversion for more than twenty-five million visitors during its first year, including, for most of them, a first glimpse of television.

mong the most notable of those visitors were the King and Queen of England, who had come to the United States on an unprecedented good-will tour. (Somewhat earlier a Chicago mayor, seated in the capital of the isolationist American Midwest, threatened to "punch King George in the snoot" if he dared to visit that city.) The royal couple were given a cordial reception, including a picnic at the Roosevelt home in Hyde Park, New York, where they were treated to an all-American menu: hot dogs, baked beans, beer, and strawberry shortcake among other items.

The year before, the Swedish crown prince and princess, the crown prince and princess of Denmark, and the crown prince and princess of Norway had also visited this country and been entertained by the Roosevelts at their home. "It was evident," wrote Mrs. Roosevelt, "that the people of Europe were deeply troubled by the general feeling of unrest and uncertainty on the continent, and were looking for friends in other parts of the world—hence their sudden interest in the United States."

Over the years since 1933 a large number of other foreigners had crossed the Atlantic and been received with cordiality. If Americans were loath to involve themselves directly in the troubles overseas, they did open wide their doors to those who found Europe insufferable, those who were fortunate enough to escape the pogroms and persecutions so methodically undertaken in Germany particularly, and in Italy and Spain. To Americans, watching their newsreels, *il Duce* resembled some pompous, strutting clown, and the *Führer*, with his little mustache and absurd poses, a Chaplinesque sort of buffoon. Both were all too easy to laugh at, from a distance. But to the refugees who had more intimate associations with these figures, they were satanic, literally bloodthirsty, men with unlimited power.

America had never before played host to such a concentration of distinguished immigrants. The roster of those who found haven here during the decade following Hitler's rise to power reads like a *Who's Who* of German intellectuals—Jews, many of them, including scholars, artists, musicians, architects, scientists, and philosophers among others. Various committees were formed in this country to expedite their escape, often by cloak-and-dagger tactics, and to help them find suitable employment in the New World. Many of these eminent men and women came not merely to seek shelter for the duration of the war but to stay and enlarge their interrupted lives through the new opportunities that were opened to them.

This infusion of extraordinary talents had an immeasurable, beneficent, and lasting influence on the cultural climate of this country. With their presence the provincial strain that had long characterized so many aspects of life in America dissolved into a new cosmopolitanism. It is now hard to imagine how this country could have developed as it did over the past generation without the contributions of such architects as Ludwig Mies van der Rohe and Walter Gropius, such musicians as Bruno Walter and George Szell, such artists as Willem de Kooning and Vasili Kandinski, such scholars and writers as Erwin J. Panofsky and Bertholt Brecht, and so on down a long, impressive list.

The most dramatic chapter in the saga of the European refugees was written by a group of physicists—Danish, Hungarian, Italian, and Russian as well as German—who revealed and unleashed the almost incredible potential of nuclear energy, which was under study in Germany at the time. Over the prestigious signature of Albert Einstein they warned the President that action must be taken if the titanic force of an atomic bomb was not to be first released by the hands of a madman like Hitler. However, it was only after Pearl Harbor that the decision was taken to proceed with the bomb. From there the road led straight to Hiroshima four years later.

The number and the prominence of the Jews who arrived during those trying years added volume to a wave of anti-Semitism, whose virulence was unprecedented in the history of this country. Fanatical groups that aped the insane methods of Hitler spread the virus of this hatred with a diligence that was almost worthy of their model, although they were too few and powerless in the face of the law to bring about more serious consequences. Even so, they caused a blight that infected people of less vicious intentions. A poll taken in 1939 revealed that a surprising proportion of the population, especially in the cities of the Northeast, harbored anti-Semitic attitudes, even though they often were expressed as no more than flippant disparagement. The absurd and irresponsible nature of the bias was unmasked when domestic fascists, by some tortured genealogical searching, traced Franklin Roosevelt's ancestry to remote Jewish origins and, on that basis, proceeded to execrate his "Jew Deal." One group went so far, preparing for the day of Hitler's take over, as to use a likeness of the President's head for target practice, a degree of hysterical extremism that could only backfire, scorching the marksmen and attracting sympathy for Roosevelt.

Such demonstrations were, in part, ugly symptoms of the anxiety that beset the nation as it hovered between the miseries of the Depression and the horrible prospect of war. It was hardly a less serious symptom of malaise when, in April, 1939, the Daughters of the American Revolution denied the distinguished and highly accomplished contralto Marian Anderson the use of Constitution Hall for a concert because she was black. Harold Ickes arranged for her performance to be held on the steps of the Lincoln Memorial instead. More than seventy-five thousand persons attended that concert. Miss Anderson was almost overcome by the tribute, following the rebuff. ". . . I could not help but feel thankful," wrote Ickes, "that the D.A.R. and the school board had refused her the use of the auditorium." Two months later the Roosevelts persuaded Miss Anderson to sing Negro spirituals in their home before the King and Queen of England, because, as Eleanor Roosevelt wrote, that couple "would want to hear the music that above all else we could call our own."

Two months after that agreeable social gathering, on August 21, 1939, the entire world was rocked by the news that the Nazis had signed a pact with the Soviet Union, separating the latter from the West, protecting Germany from military confrontation with Russia, and leaving Poland exposed to Hitler's next thrust. Americans listened with disbelief to the news bulletins. Communist sympathizers had to make an abrupt and totally unexpected about-face, an awkward maneuver from which the party in this country never recovered. On September 1 Hitler unleashed the massive German forces against Poland. The *Luftwaffe* quickly annihilated the outnumbered and obsolete Polish air squadrons and bombed and strafed Polish ground forces, cities, and civilians at will, while the German ground forces rolled ahead almost unchecked despite valiant resistance. Two days later Neville Chamberlain addressed the British people on the radio. "I have to tell you now," he said, "that this country is at war with Germany." Both England and France had agreed to yield no further. And that evening in America Roosevelt told his radio listeners: "When peace has been broken anywhere, the peace of all countries everywhere is in danger. . . . This Nation will remain a neutral Nation, but I cannot ask that every American remain neutral in thought as well." Still another poll revealed that 84 per cent of Americans wanted an Allied victory.

THE EYES AND EARS OF THE WORLD
5.

In September, 1939, Germany attacked Poland. England and France, honoring an alliance concluded five months earlier with the Poles, declared war on Germany, and Europe was plunged into the Second World War. Thrusting simultaneously from north, south, and west, the Germans swooped down on Poland and crushed all resistance in little more than a month. The blitzkrieg, or "lightning war," that hit Poland was to characterize Hitler's tactics throughout the war. In April he struck again, with the same devastating swiftness, taking Denmark and Norway. In May his armies overran the Netherlands, Belgium, and Luxembourg, leaving some two hundred and fifty thousand isolated British troops to be evacuated from Dunkirk and opening the way to France. In less than six weeks the French army was defeated. After an abortive air offensive against Britain, Hitler invaded the Balkans and Greece, and then, in June of 1941, turned against his former ally, Russia. There, after initial successes, he was finally checked, and as the war continued, Hitler's fortunes slowly turned.

Hitler's savage invasion of Poland caught the nation off guard, soldiers and civilians alike. Above left, a ten-year-old girl kneels horror-stricken over the body of her sister, killed in a strafing attack on a group of Polish women in a potato field. Some two weeks after the German invasion, Russia, on September 17, 1939, attacked from the east. Above right, a Red army unit enters the border village of Rakov after the defeat of Poland in October. The following spring Hitler took Denmark and Norway. Below, Germans enter a burning Norwegian village.

Germany's next target was France, and on May 10, 1940, Hitler took aim —through Holland, Belgium, and Luxembourg. At top, Belgian sharpshooters fire on approaching Germans after blowing up a rail line south of Antwerp to delay their advance, and left, Nazi shock troops cross the Maas River between Holland and Belgium. Above, British soldiers leave the beaches at Dunkirk during the heroic rescue operation.

In June, 1940, France fell to Germany (above, the victors parade past the Arc de Triomphe in Paris), and in August Hitler launched a bloody assault on England in the Battle of Britain. Below, Londoners dig out after a Nazi air raid; at right, a building near St. Paul's Cathedral (background) collapses under a direct bomb hit.

Along with her assault on land and in the air, Germany waged a relentless battle at sea. Merchant ships carrying desperately needed food, arms, and supplies from the United States to the Allies were attacked again and again by German U-boats patrolling the Atlantic. (Opposite: top, a U. S. tanker aflame after an Axis submarine attack; middle, a Canadian destroyer picks up survivors of a torpedoed merchantman.) In mid-spring of 1941 Hitler overran the Balkans, and in June attacked Russia. But by December, 1941, he was stopped short of Moscow, bogged down by mud (opposite bottom), cold and snow, and Russian resistance.

Arsenal of Democracy

On September 17, sixteen days after the Nazis assaulted Poland from the west, Russia attacked from the east. Within only four weeks after the first German attack, and in spite of heroic resistance, the last Polish opposition was violently suppressed. Even while the murder and destruction were still going on, Roosevelt called Congress into special session, on September 21, to consider repealing the arms embargo provision of the 1935 Neutrality Act and applying a cash-and-carry formula to munitions — in short, giving England and France immediate access to materials of war they desperately needed. It was too late to rescue Poland, but there might yet be time to save the remaining Allies — and America, perhaps, in the bargain — from some similar fate.

Only twice in its long history, the President pointed out, had this country deviated from a policy of insisting on the right of neutrals to freedom of the seas in times of war. Each time our surrender of that right had proved bootless. The Nonintercourse and Embargo acts of Thomas Jefferson's administration, during the Napoleonic Wars, so long ago and so early in our national experience, had completely failed to serve their purpose. And now the neutrality legislation of 1935–37 was not only working against the vital interests of the nation but was helping to deepen the shadows that were falling over the world at large.

Roosevelt's plea loosed a storm of isolationist sentiment and propaganda, much of it Anglophobic. John Bull was pictured as a far worse ogre than Hitler. Father Charles Coughlin exhorted his followers to dissent. Form letters by the hundreds of thousands flooded the Senate, appealing to that body to "Keep America out of the blood business." And, according to *The New York Times*, Henry Ford insisted that the sole purpose of repeal was "to enable munitions makers to profit financially through what is nothing less than mass murder." However, the press, many public bodies, and the majority of the public stood solidly behind the President. After almost two months of heated and bitter debate in Congress, the embargo was repealed on November 4, 1939, putting sales of munitions to belligerents on a cash-and-carry basis.

Only a few weeks after the arms embargo was lifted, American opinion was further

The run across the Atlantic with U. S. supplies for the Allies was fraught with peril. At left, British-bound maté-
riel travels in convoy for protection against U-boats; above, a British convoy shelled by Nazis in English Channel.

outraged when Soviet troops invaded Finland. That tiny country was the only one that had met every installment on its old World War I debts to the United States, a display of probity and conscientiousness that especially endeared it to Americans and made the rape by Russia even more odious. But the isolated nation could draw little practical support from the large well of American sympathy, and Russia completed her conquest almost unhindered, meeting no obstacles other than those provided by the brave but terribly outnumbered Finns.

However outrageous the aggressions overseas were, and however deep was the concern for the Allied cause, the majority of Americans still had no heart for intervention in the war. Roosevelt, keenly sensitive to public opinion, felt it was necessary to reassure his countrymen on this point during the debate over the arms embargo. "The simple truth is," he remarked, "that no person in any responsible place . . . has ever suggested . . . the remotest possibility of sending the boys of American mothers to fight on the battlefields of Europe." He reiterated this same assurance somewhat disingenuously almost a year later. By then it was later than he cared or dared to admit.

For a few brief months after the Finnish debacle, as the 1930's passed into history, all was quiet on the Western Front. The French had taken their position along the "impregnable" Maginot Line, the Germans behind their Siegfried Line. "Not a gun was fired, not a disturbing sound broke the stillness," an observer recorded. It almost seemed that things would deteriorate into a stalemate, a dreary nonwar of attrition. People referred to the situation as the phony war. The hush that had fallen over the battle front extended to the White House. In March, 1940, Roosevelt wrote that "things here are amazingly quiet." In that seemingly stagnant period the President's popularity reached a new low even for this second term, already marred by grave discontents for which he was held accountable. There were still more than eight million unemployed in the country.

Barely three months later the Nazis had exploded from their entrenched positions and—it still seems incredible—had overrun Denmark, Norway, Holland, Belgium, Luxembourg, and a large part of France, including Paris. The British Expeditionary Force had been pushed back "into the sea." On June 22 France formally capitulated. Hitler was astride virtually all Western Europe and could dance with glee high up on the Eiffel Tower while below Parisians wept—and England now stood alone. Nothing like the blitzkrieg had been known in the history of warfare. It seemed that the world of tomorrow might not be quite like the one still being projected at the World's Fair in New York, which was running into a lackluster second year—minus a few exhibitors.

Like a jackal impatient to feed at a still-twitching carcass, Italy had attacked stricken France from the south in the last days of the Nazi onslaught, fulfilling, as Mussolini told his generals, a previous commitment to the *Führer*. Roosevelt had sent urgent pleas to *il Duce* to stay out of the war and was outspokenly bitter about this stab in the back of Hitler's almost helpless victim. The White House shook off its springtime lethargy. It was time for action, for a call to arms.

Preparing America for the uncertain future was a matter that required time. Roosevelt called on the nation to "harness" all of its material reserves "in order that we ourselves in the Americas may have equipment and training equal to the task of every emergency." In slightly over a year following the President's call, Congress appropriated thirty-seven billion dollars for rearmament and for aid to the Allied countries. The President urged rapid development of a two-ocean navy and production of equipment for a vast—but still nonexistent—army. He also asked the aviation industry to tool up for an annual production of at least fifty thousand planes—a staggering increase over the then-current output of six thousand a year. (In 1944 planes of all types manufactured in the United States totaled almost one hundred thousand.) In the meantime the United States could only hope that the Allies would be able to hold out until they received American help in meaningful amounts.

As the nation began to gird itself for whatever might come, laments over the stagnation of the economy were drowned out by the hum and the roar of busy factories across the land. Whether the New Deal could ever have restored the country to prosperity by further planning and legislation will never be known. It had not done so, in any case, before war industries moved into high gear and manpower was needed as never before.

Matters were complicated by the fact that 1940 was a presidential election year. Roosevelt's second term was drawing to a close and no American President had ever served a third term. Whether Roosevelt himself was contemplating being the first to break the precedent set by George Washington no one could guess. As the summer passed, he kept a sphinxlike silence on the point. Just before the Republican convention in Philadelphia, he threw a bombshell into the ranks of that party by appointing two prominent Republicans to his Cabinet: Henry L. Stimson, a firm internationalist, as Secretary of War and Chicago newspaper publisher Frank Knox as Secretary of the Navy. The move was something other than "dirty politics," as the Republicans bitterly complained. It was an effort to strengthen national unity by developing a bipartisan Cabinet, and it also strengthened the advocates of a militant foreign policy within Roosevelt's administration, offsetting the isolationist bloc in Congress.

Regardless of Roosevelt's own political plans for the future, there were matters of desperate urgency to act upon. Time did not wait either on the American elections or on the gigantic task of converting American industry to a wartime basis. In the closing days of French resistance to the crushing Nazi onslaught, Premier Paul Reynaud had called upon Roosevelt for "clouds of planes," which this country could not possibly provide. When France fell a few days later, Joseph Göbbels, the German minister of propaganda, told his cheering, exultant countrymen that they had "just one more battle to win."

It appeared that that last battle might not cause Hitler too much trouble. The British army, after the fall of France, was left almost barehanded. The British Expeditionary Force, though saved from Dunkirk in a heroic evacuation, had left most of its equipment behind, and there was considerable difficulty resupplying the men even with rifles. With the nation in this precarious position, Winston Churchill sounded his rallying cry to his people and his defiance to the Nazis: ". . . we shall defend our island, whatever the cost may be, we shall fight on the beaches, we shall fight on the landing grounds, we shall fight in the fields and in the streets, we shall fight in the hills; we shall never surrender. . . ."

But in spite of the brave words, all that protected the island kingdom was the surrounding sea, which the Royal Navy controlled, and the Royal Air Force, which was greatly outnumbered by the *Luftwaffe*. Hitler prepared for invasion, for which his generals had no real heart, and while he hesitated, Britain braced herself. Elderly men trained with fowling pieces, rescue squads

were formed and drilled, trenches were dug across fields where enemy troop-carrying gliders might land. And from the United States came stocks of rifles and artillery pieces to re-equip the army.

Then, in mid-July of 1940, Hermann Göring began throwing his bomber squadrons and their fighter escorts at Britain in an attempt to soften the island for invasion. The Royal Air Force was outnumbered by about three planes to one, but the pilots of its Spitfire and Hurricane fighter planes showed such superior spirit and resolve that they destroyed two German aircraft for every one they lost. "Never in the field of human conflict was so much owed by so many to so few," said Churchill of the outnumbered, bone-weary R.A.F. pilots. British cities, especially London, suffered frightfully, but though Göring turned to night bombing in an attempt to escape punishment, he was in the end forced to admit total defeat and give up his aerial assault on Britain.

During that summer of heroic battles in the air, however, Britain was suffering seriously at sea, where lay the island's lifelines. Nazi submarines were sinking British ships at an alarming rate, cargo vessels and their convoying warships alike. American foreign policy had always assumed the presence of a powerful Royal Navy policing the high seas. But since the start of hostilities, almost half the destroyers of the British navy had been damaged or sunk. And because invasion still threatened, the need for replacements was crucial. Churchill pleaded for help—and quickly, if Britain was to be saved.

On September 3, 1940, after several months of agonizingly difficult negotiations, through which Roosevelt had to thread his way with constant regard for public opinion and strong congressional opposition, the President announced an arrangement whereby fifty aging American destroyers from World War I would be transferred to Britain in exchange for leases on a series of British bases in the Western Hemisphere, from Newfoundland to Trinidad. It was a masterly stroke of strictly personal diplomacy, in which by a legalistic maneuver he bypassed Congress altogether. The President referred to it as "the most important action in the reinforcement of our national defense that has been taken since the Louisiana Purchase." That historical parallel was hardly accurate, but his audience got the point.

And Churchill remarked that the British Empire and the United States "would now have to be somewhat mixed up together."

To a relatively small but highly opinionated segment of the population this sort of involvement with a belligerent power was anathema. An advertisement placed in leading newspapers by the St. Louis *Post-Dispatch* declared: "Mr. Roosevelt today committed an act of war. He also became America's first dictator. . . ." Just a few days after the President's announcement, a group called America First also raised its voice in protest. Fearful that any degree of participation in wartime activity would undermine the democratic process, they spoke of the possibility of a negotiated peace, especially since they foresaw no physical danger to this country in Hitler's actions. Some earnest men of indisputable patriotism, true public servants like Senator Robert A. Taft and Chester Bowles, held to such a point of view. At the same time, however, support for the group came from the Coughlinites, Nazi sympathizers, and other extremists, who placed upon it the kiss of death. Isolationism lingered but waned. Although the President dismayed his critics, he had acted in accord with the prevailing sentiment of the nation. With all its implications the destroyer deal was widely accepted.

It was a fateful month. In mid-September, two weeks after the transfer of the destroyers, and in spite of vehement protests from its isolationist members, Congress called more than a million civilians to serve in the army and put hundreds of thousands of reservists on active duty. It was the first peacetime draft in the history of the nation and reflected a grimly realistic mood, which was born of recent events. That same month, also, Japan started a new advance in the East by invading Indochina, and almost immediately thereafter, with high ceremony, signed a treaty of alliance with Germany and Italy, a pact directed primarily at the United States.

During the turbulent summer months the candidates for the Presidency had been nominated. The Republicans settled on Wendell L. Willkie, "the darkest of dark horses," a likable country-born big-city lawyer of German descent, a utility magnate who had stoutly challenged the T.V.A., and an internationalist. Roosevelt, maintaining his noncommittal pose till the first ballot was cast at the Democratic convention, confiding in no one, and making no overt moves to win renomination, was "drafted" by an overwhelming majority on the first ballot. As usual, he was roundly castigated from some quarters for being devious and power-hungry. "Caesar thrice refused the kingly crown," wrote a former senator, "—but this Caesar, never!"

Roosevelt pointed out that as President during these months of national crisis, he had neither the time nor the inclination to engage in "purely political debate." He hardly needed to. As Commander in Chief of the Army and the Navy he was constantly in the public eye, and he had its ear as he went on the air, guiding the nation in its feverish haste to rearm and to strengthen its defenses. The great majority of newspapers was against his candidacy; Henry Luce of *Time-Life-Fortune*, Joseph Patterson of the New York *Daily News*, and finally the editors of *The New York Times*, among other important opinion makers, all declared for Willkie. But the President's persuasive charm on the radio was never more effective. In November the people, by a popular vote of 27,000,000 to 22,000,000, chose to reject Willkie and keep Roosevelt in office.

Shortly after the American election, in December, 1940, Hitler proclaimed in a stormy address that there could be no reconciliation between Germany on the one hand and Britain and America on the other, only war to the finish. "There are two worlds that stand opposed to each other," he ranted. And, he added, "I can beat any other power in the world. . . ." (In Tokyo it had already been announced that war between Japan and America seemed inevitable.) Within a few weeks Roosevelt responded to Hitler's harangue in a fireside chat. Quoting the *Führer*'s own words, he emphasized for his fellow Americans the evil intentions of the Nazis and the threat they held for the United States. It was already apparent that England could not conquer the Axis singlehandedly and that she was rapidly running out of the resources necessary to protect herself. America must provide greater help quickly.

With full confidence that he had a mandate from the people to support the Allies, the President addressed Congress early in January, 1941, proposing a plan to get more war aid to the beleaguered democracies overseas at almost any cost and risk. "In the future days, which we seek to make more serene," he remarked, "we look forward to a world founded upon four essential human freedoms." He went on to name the four freedoms: freedom of speech and expression, freedom of every person to worship God in his own way, freedom from want, and freedom from fear. The United States, he advised, must give unlimited support to people everywhere who were defending those freedoms at such great sacrifice. In pursuance of his recommendations, Congress on March 11 passed the Lend-Lease Act, which enabled the President to provide arms and other supplies by sale, transfer, exchange, or lease to any country whose defense he considered vital to American interests. That arrangement had the great advantage of preventing a postwar controversy over debts such as had followed World War I, causing much bitterness. Countries that received lend-lease aid might also refit their ships in American ports and receive what defense information this country could supply. Now, as Roosevelt observed, the United States had truly become the "arsenal of democracy." In the course of the years that followed, lend-lease aid totaled more than fifty billion dollars.

eanwhile, the situation of the Allies became more serious. In April the British forces in Africa were pushed back to the border of Egypt by a German-Italian counteroffensive. German troops in Europe swarmed over Yugoslavia and Greece and then used paratroopers to conquer the island of Crete, while Russia and Japan signed a mutual nonaggression pact in Moscow. Around the globe, in Singapore, British, Dutch, and American military planners framed a strategy to combat further Japanese aggression. In May a German submarine sank an American ship off the coast of Brazil. That same month, in the North Atlantic, the British battle cruiser *Hood* was sunk by the German battleship *Bismarck* (which in turn was sent to the bottom by the Royal Navy three days later). On May 27 Roosevelt proclaimed an unlimited national emergency.

With the Lend-Lease Act the United States had dropped all pretense of neutrality. Almost immediately after passing it, this country seized all ships belonging to the Axis powers that were then in American ports and followed this action by freezing all the American assets of those nations. By agreement with Denmark the United States assumed responsibility for defending Greenland as essential to the security of the Western Hemisphere. A few weeks later the President announced that armed American ships would patrol the Atlantic, establishing an American defense zone far out into the ocean. And with the proclamation of a

national emergency he warned the world that this country would "actively resist" any and all attempts of the Nazis to gain control of the high seas.

Nothing in the sequence of violent and ominous events had prepared the world for the shattering surprise of June 22, 1941, when Germany, with Finnish and Rumanian support, suddenly turned on Russia with a furious assault along a two-thousand-mile front from the Arctic to the Ukraine. The alliance between the two powers had been from the start an unnatural one and one that Hitler, on his part, had fully planned to betray when he considered the time ripe. For several months during the summer and autumn his armies surged forward until by mid-November they reached the outskirts of Moscow.

The turn of events made strange bedfellows. In the estimate of Allied governments, Hitler was a much more serious danger than Stalin, and America and Britain both moved at once to help Russia. Lend-lease was immediately extended to our improbable new ally to enable the Red army to tie up a large part of the German army on the Eastern Front. And soon the German army would be bogged down in Russia, for Hitler had made a disastrous blunder.

The German assault on Russia hardly affected developments elsewhere in the world during the summer. Early in August, Winston Churchill and Franklin Roosevelt held secret meetings on American and British warships in Argentia Bay off the coast of Newfoundland and afterward issued a joint statement of principles known as the Atlantic Charter. With this document—a resounding declaration of "certain common principles" concerning the liberation of the oppressed, the destruction of tyranny, the freedom of the seas, and mutual security in the postwar world—the two leaders in effect raised the war to the level of a crusade for righteousness and truth. The charter did not outline a particular program of action, but its positive tone of resolution and courage and fortitude buoyed the spirits of men everywhere outside the camp of the enemy.

For the President, leading a nation not yet at war, it was an audacious gesture. At home he still faced some serious opposition to the course he was following. Such distinguished figures as former President Hoover and labor leader John L. Lewis believed and stated publicly that America had no stake in the war that was raging and should stay out of it. The month of Roosevelt's dramatic meeting with Churchill, an extension of the draft law passed the House of Representatives by the margin of a single vote. When that law had first been under debate, it was decried both by some military experts and by apprehensive congressmen. "A conscript army made up of youths trained for a year or two," protested one senator, "compared to Hitler's army, is like a high school football team going up against the professional teams they have in Chicago and New York." Hanson Baldwin, *The New York Times* authority on military matters, agreed in principle. For a while—indeed, until industry tooled up to provide sufficient weapons—the preparatory maneuvers of the newly created large conscript army resembled an amateur play. Army units, totally without heavy equipment, went through their exercises with broomsticks labeled machine guns and trucks doing duty as tanks, stovepipes substituting for antitank guns and beer cans taking the place of ammunition.

But the circumstances that had made necessary such makeshifts were rapidly changing, and congressmen were lagging behind public opinion. Almost a year before the question of continuing the draft was considered, one of the many Gallup polls indicated that more than half the population was already willing to risk even war in supplying the aid that would help Britain survive. Since America had begun to rearm, her arsenal had grown phenomenally. The Lend-Lease Act, and the progressively more adamant position this country had taken since, were a challenge Hitler could not ignore. But he was wary enough to caution his admirals against action that might galvanize American opinion and draw the United States into war. However, with American vessels watching over the Allies' shipping lanes, and German U-boats determined to stop enemy traffic, an incident was bound to occur that would carry this country to a fuller commitment. In September, 1941, the American destroyer *Greer* was attacked (though not hit) and Roosevelt immediately declared that German or Italian vessels of war would enter waters necessary for American defense at their own risk. ". . . when you see a rattlesnake poised to strike," he said, "you do not wait until he has struck before you crush him." The nation applauded. On October 17 the American destroyer *Kearny* was torpedoed and eleven sailors were killed, although the stricken vessel was able to steam to safety in the harbor of Reykjavik, Iceland.

On Navy Day, October 27, the President made a speech that was virtually a call for action. "The shooting has started," he declared. "And history has recorded who fired the first shot. In the long run, however, all that will matter is who fired the last shot. . . ." The President was grim. "I say that we do not propose to take this lying down. . . ." But he had little choice. Congress was not ready to take the final step, and neither were most of the people. Only three days after the President spoke, the destroyer *Reuben James* was torpedoed and sunk by a German submarine in the North Atlantic with the loss of one hundred and fifteen members of her crew. Playwright Robert E. Sherwood, who had become a Roosevelt speech writer and idea man, later recorded that the general public seemed more interested in the Army–Notre Dame football game than in the sinking of the *Reuben James*.

That same month the President insisted that American goods must be delivered under the American flag wherever the United States chose to send them. "I say to you solemnly," he told Congress, "that if Hitler's military plans are brought to successful fulfillment, we Americans shall be forced to fight in defense of our own homes and our own freedom in a war as costly and as devastating as that which now rages on the Russian front. Hitler has offered a challenge which we as Americans cannot and will not tolerate." No "peacetime" President had ever used such bellicose language.

On the other side of the world, as Japan watched America and Britain consolidating their defenses, the war lords of that Far Eastern country became increasingly restive. According to one observer, they had already decided, in January, 1940, that "they must be prepared to fight the United States and the British Empire jointly" to further their interest. They had watched the fall of Holland and France and the peril of Britain before the Nazi onslaught and decided that the Asian empires of those countries were ripe for plucking, provided they used overpowering force and provided the United States fleet at Pearl Harbor did not intervene. As early as 1940 United States Ambassador Joseph C. Grew in Tokyo warned his government that unless the United States cleared out of the Orient altogether, a "head-on clash with the Japanese" was inevitable. Some American military advisers actually wished to withdraw the fleet to the Pacific coast. General George Marshall himself argued against taking any strong action in the East lest that distract our attention from the European crisis.

With the German invasion of Russia, Japan's Siberian flank was almost automatically made secure. In the meantime American embargoes were putting serious pressure on the Japanese economy, geared to war as it had become. Almost all Japan's petroleum products, so vital to a military machine, were imported from the United States. If that small nation was to proceed with its plans for a Greater East Asia Co-Prosperity Sphere (to include China, Indochina, Thailand, British Malaya, the Netherlands East Indies, and the Philippines), it needed the precious oil; if the United States totally stopped such exports, Japan would have to take over oil fields elsewhere, by immediate conquest. Or, and this was unthinkable, it would have to renounce all schemes for further aggrandizement. Plans for conquest, leading ever to Pearl Harbor, had long been made, a "secret" well-known to the State Department. American appeasement came to an end on July 26, 1941, when, by executive order, the President froze all Japanese assets in this country and all trade with Japan was abruptly stopped.

On December 6, 1941, in a personal appeal, Roosevelt called upon Emperor Hirohito to restrain his war lords for the sake of humanity. By then, however, those schemers had perfected their master plan and by then the Japanese assault fleet was already drawing within striking distance of Pearl Harbor. The next day the United States suffered the greatest naval defeat in its entire history when Japanese airplanes made their raid on the Hawaiian base. A day later we were at war with Japan. Three days after that Germany and Italy formally declared war on the United States. It was the end of American isolationism. A new era was born of the bloody conflicts that now raged around the world. The President reported to the people on December 9:

On the road ahead there lies hard work—grueling work—day and night, every hour and every minute. I was about to add that ahead there lies sacrifice for all of us. But it is not correct to use that word. The United States does not consider it a sacrifice to do all one can, to give one's best to our Nation, when the Nation is fighting for its existence and its future life.... We are going to win the war and we are going to win the peace that follows.

From the end of the First World War to Pearl Harbor,

America had gone through a revolutionary cycle that affected virtually every aspect of life. Looking back from the beginning of the 1940's to the beginning of the 1920's seemed like scanning a much longer period than a mere score of years. The Twenties had been introduced by the passage of the Volstead Act, which outlawed the sale of alcoholic beverages, and by Harding's summons for a return to "normalcy" after the unnatural stimulation of the war years. Long before the Thirties had run their course, prohibition was remembered as a hopelessly quaint miscarriage of national good sense, the return to normalcy as a vain attempt to recapture a nostalgic past. Those who voted for Harding in 1920, it was later observed, did so "in the spirit of a certain mythical bird which flies through the air backward because it does not want to see where it's going, but likes to look where it's been."

Looking backward at the Twenties from the next decade, however, gave a different prospect. The shameful ineptness of Harding's Presidency and the extreme inactivity of Coolidge's administration, in view of what followed, seemed almost too improbable to accept as true and recent history. "Mr. Coolidge's genius for inactivity," Walter Lippmann had written, "is developed to a very high point. It is a grim, determined, alert inactivity, which keeps Mr. Coolidge occupied constantly." At the time, to be sure, everything was going so well—or so it seemed to those who ruled the nation's economy—that no one wanted anybody to tamper with anything. Both Harding and Coolidge were elected by large majorities. But the thought of either of them leading the country during the difficult years of the Thirties is enough to arouse disquieting reflections on the perils and paradoxes of the democratic process. Herbert Hoover was a man of a different stamp, but it was his extremely bad fortune to be President in 1929, when the "permanent" plateau of prosperity turned into a nightmare of depression. Almost a century before, Walt Whitman reminded his countrymen that they had traveled roads "all even and peaceful" and learned "from joy and prosperity only." Suddenly there were unexpected troughs in the road, deeper than any others that had yet been discovered in past American experience, and joy and prosperity were in very short supply. But there were also new peaks of social awareness. The self-indulgent hedonism of the Twenties was quickly dismissed as a passing aberration of the American spirit. Concern for the public weal, so insistently urged by the New Deal, left a deep and lasting imprint on the national conscience. The large problems of social security, housing, the rights of labor, and the role of government in matters of general welfare replaced what were in retrospect the fleeting and relatively trivial questions that had been raised by prohibition, war debts, and the escapades of "flaming youth."

With his Presidency Roosevelt recaptured for that office authority that had all but vanished in the past dozen years, such authority, indeed, as had not been matched at any time before, unless it was in the term of George Washington and, perhaps, those of Andrew Jackson and Abraham Lincoln. By reorganizing and enlarging its functions and using the power vested in him to the full, he converted the Presidency into a modern instrument of government suited to the needs of the times. Subsequent Presidents have been heirs of this enhanced responsibility.

The New Deal by no means succeeded in everything it had undertaken to do. Indeed, as earlier suggested, it may have been on the verge of a general failure, in economic areas at least, when stepped-up production for national defense and for war finally got the factory wheels turning again. And this left open the disturbing question of whether the capitalist system, as it was generally accepted in practice and principle in this country, could flourish without the stimulating injections of large expenditures for military machinery. Nevertheless, before war intervened, the Roosevelt revolution had already altered the whole concept of our federal government in many ways. The laissez-faire state of old, respected tradition had been irreversibly transformed into the social service state. At last that issue, which had burned fitfully in past years, was now, it seemed clear, permanently settled. Constructive collective action, war or no war, was now to be as respectable as individualism had been before. As the Thirties faded into history the frolics of the Twenties seemed irresponsible and remote from the realities that had to be faced, from the problems that had to be met if not mastered. Reviewing the developments of that later decade, in 1939 Eleanor Roosevelt expressed her belief in the programs of the New Deal. "They helped but they did not solve the fundamental problems . . ." she told an audience of youths, at least some of whom would soon risk their lives defending the values Americans continued to hold dear. "I never believed the Federal government could solve the whole problem," she said. "It bought us time to think." And she asked in conclusion, "Is it going to be worthwhile?"

On the Brink

On December 29, 1940, President Roosevelt told the nation, "We must be the great arsenal of democracy," and he pledged every effort "to help the defenders who are in the front lines." Less than three months later Congress passed the Lend-Lease Act, authorizing the President to supply arms and aid to Britain and her allies to fight the Axis powers. United States ships escorted Allied convoys in the Atlantic, and shipyard welders like the one above were at work expanding a two-ocean Navy. In July, 1941, American troops relieved British soldiers defending Iceland, and the following month President Roosevelt and Prime Minister Churchill drew up a statement of common aims and principles in the Atlantic Charter. The two nations divided the Atlantic into defense zones, and in September, after several Nazi submarine attacks on United States ships, Roosevelt issued a shoot-on-sight order against German and Italian ships entering the west Atlantic. Meanwhile across the Pacific another Axis power was threatening. On December 6 Roosevelt sent a personal plea to Japanese Emperor Hirohito "to restore traditional amity and prevent further death and destruction in the world." The next day Japan bombed Pearl Harbor.

American industry was being converted from peacetime uses to production of guns, tanks, and other matériel. At left, giant M-26 tanks roll off a converted auto assembly line in Grand Blanc, Michigan; opposite, the U.S.S. Atlanta is launched from a Navy shipyard in New Jersey. In March, 1941, Congress approved lend-lease, enabling hard-pressed Allied countries to obtain U. S. arms without direct payment. Not everyone was in favor. Massachusetts women below saw it as a step toward war.

In August, 1941, President Roosevelt and British Prime Minister Churchill (seated above) exchanged visits aboard their respective ships, the Augusta *and the* Prince of Wales, *off Newfoundland and drew up a set of common postwar aims known as the Atlantic Charter. While not a binding alliance, it cemented friendship and respect between the two nations. Already the previous month, U. S. forces had been sent to replace British troops in Iceland. Opposite: top, American infantrymen arrive in Reykjavik, Iceland; at bottom, United States Marines build Icelandic barracks.*

In September, 1940, some sixteen and a half million men between the ages of twenty-one and thirty-six became eligible for the draft as America's first peacetime conscription was authorized. The following year the draft was extended, but some of the boys were still training with broomstick guns and other ersatz equipment. Above, recruits practice tank warfare with rifles and wooden antitank guns during a drill in upstate New York. Opposite top, soldiers train with a genuine 105 millimeter howitzer, and right, infantrymen attack under simulated battle conditions.

On September 11, 1941, a week after a Nazi U-boat attacked the U.S.S. Greer in the Atlantic, President Roosevelt (above) announced an order to shoot on sight any German or Italian warships in American defensive waters. Such ships, he warned, would enter the west Atlantic "at their own risk." Nonetheless, on October 17 the U. S. destroyer Kearny (opposite top) was torpedoed west of Iceland, killing eleven (opposite, crew members survey damage), and two weeks later the Reuben James was sunk, with the loss of over 100 men.

405

At right, Japanese Ambassador Kichisaburo Nomura (left) and special envoy Saburo Kurusu with Secretary of State Cordell Hull (center) prior to final Japanese-American negotiations in November, 1941. U. S. demands included withdrawal of Japanese forces from China and Indochina and a multilateral pact of nonaggression. Japan's rejection did not reach Hull until December 7, as bombs were falling on Pearl Harbor. Above, a Japanese carrier flight-deck crew salutes pilots taking off for Hawaii.

Acknowledgments

The Editors appreciate the generous assistance provided by many individuals and institutions during the preparation of this book. They especially wish to thank the following:

Addison Gallery of American Art, Phillips Academy, Andover, Massachusetts: Mrs. Anne Blake Smith
Thomas Hart Benton
Brown Brothers, New York City
Butler Institute of American Art, Youngstown, Ohio: Mrs. Alice B. Goldcamp, Clyde Singer
Rick Carrier, New York City
Chicago Historical Society: Mrs. Mary F. Rhymer, John S. Tris
Cincinnati Art Museum: Betty L. Zimmerman
Geoffrey Clements, New York City
The Conde Nast Publications Inc., New York City: Paul H. Bonner, Jr.
Mrs. William Cotton
Culver Pictures, New York City: Robert Jackson
Mrs. John Steuart Curry
Dallas Museum of Fine Arts: Carol Robbins
Detroit Institute of Arts
J. Doyle DeWitt, Hartford, Connecticut
Downtown Gallery, New Orleans
Evander Childs High School, Bronx, New York
Everson Museum of Art, Syracuse, New York: Virginia Ruppe
George Eastman House, Rochester, New York: Mrs. Ann McCabe, Thomas Barrow
Ben Goldstein, New York City
Greenwich House, New York City
Michael Harwood
Mrs. John Held, Jr.
David Hoffman, Whitestone, New York
Imperial War Museum, London, England
Jay Jacobs
Paulus Leeser, New York City
Lester S. Levy, Pikesville, Maryland
Library of Congress, Washington, D. C.: Mrs. Renata Shaw, Virginia Daiker, Milton Kaplan, Leroy Bellamy
Life magazine, Time Inc., New York City: Mrs. Vassilia Moore
Mrs. Jean Lipman
Mrs. John McCrady
Mrs. Reginald Marsh
Metropolitan Museum of Art, New York City: Mrs. Margaret Nolan, Harriet Cooper
Museum of the City of New York: A. K. Baragwanath, Charlotte LaRue, Sam Pearce, Melvin Parks
National Archives, Washington, D. C.
National Gallery of Ireland, Dublin, Ireland
New Britain Museum of American Art, New Britain, Connecticut: Mrs. Lois Blomstrann
New School for Social Research, New York City
New-York Historical Society, New York City: Martin Leifer
New York Public Library, New York City: Elizabeth Roth
The New Yorker magazine, New York City: Mrs. Ruth C. Rogin
Paramount Pictures Corporation, New York City: Stuart Kahan
Pennsylvania Academy of Fine Arts, Philadelphia, Pennsylvania: Mrs. Diana M. Gray
Philadelphia Museum of Art
Photoworld, New York City: Lenora Weber

Mr. and Mrs. Alfred Easton Poor
Rehn Gallery, New York City: John Clancy
Henry T. Rockwell, Bronxville, New York
Franklin D. Roosevelt Library, Hyde Park, New York: Paul McLaughlin
Sy Seidman, New York City
Time Inc., Index Department, New York City: Barbara Sachner
Underwood & Underwood, New York City: Milton Davidson
United Press International, New York City: Stan Freidman
Whitney Museum of American Art, New York City: Mrs. Denny Judson
Wide World Photos, New York City: Fred Cantey
Wisconsin Historical Society, Madison, Wisconsin: Paul Vanderbilt

The Editors also make grateful acknowledgment for permission to use material from the following works:

The American Mercury, August, 1925, "Salesmanship" by Clarence Darrow. Copyright 1925 by The American Mercury, Inc. The excerpt on salesmanship on pages 96–97 reprinted by permission of *American Mercury,* Torrance, California.
The Grapes of Wrath by John Steinbeck. Copyright 1939, copyright © renewed 1967 by John Steinbeck. The excerpt on pages 344–45 reprinted by permission of The Viking Press, Inc.
Hard Times by Studs Terkel. Copyright © 1970 by Studs Terkel. The excerpts on pages 198–99 reprinted by permission of Pantheon Books, Inc., a division of Random House, Inc.
The New York *Herald* and New York *Tribune,* October 19, 1924, a report of the Notre Dame-Army football game by Grantland Rice. Copyright 1924 by New York Tribune, Inc.; renewal copyright 1952 by New York Herald Tribune, Inc. The excerpt from this account on page 120 reprinted by permission of W.C.C. Publishing Company, Inc., New York, New York.
How To Win Friends and Influence People by Dale Carnegie. Copyright © 1936 by Dale Carnegie; renewed © 1964 by Dorothy Carnegie. The excerpts from this book on pages 280–81 reprinted by permission of Simon and Schuster, Inc.
Life Begins at Forty by Walter B. Pitkin. Copyright 1932 by McGraw-Hill Book Company, Inc. The excerpt from this book on pages 280–81 used with permission of McGraw-Hill Book Company.
Main Street by Sinclair Lewis, copyright 1920 by Harcourt, Brace & World, Inc.; renewed 1948 by Sinclair Lewis. The excerpts on pages 42–43 reprinted by permission of Harcourt, Brace & World, Inc.
The Man Nobody Knows by Bruce Barton. Copyright 1925 by The Bobbs-Merrill Company; renewal copyright 1952 by Bruce Barton. The excerpt on advertising on pages 96–97 reprinted by permission of The Bobbs-Merrill Company, Inc., Indianapolis, Indiana.
Of Time and the River. The excerpt on pages 266–67 reprinted with the permission of Charles Scribner's Sons from *Of Time and the River,* pages 329–32, by Thomas Wolfe. Copyright 1935 Charles Scribner's Sons; renewal copyright © 1963 Paul Gitlin, Administrator C.T.A.
The Prince of Wales and Other Famous Americans by Miguel Covarrubias. Copyright 1925 by Alfred A. Knopf, Inc. and renewed 1953 by Miguel Covarrubias. The Valentino caricature on page 165 reprinted by permission of Alfred A. Knopf, Inc.
This Side of Paradise by F. Scott Fitzgerald. Copyright 1920 by Charles Scribner's Sons; renewal copyright 1948 by Zelda Fitzgerald. The excerpt from this book on pages 58–59 reprinted by permission of Charles Scribner's Sons, New York, New York.

Index

C

CABELL, JAMES BRANCH, 80, 309

CAGNEY, JAMES, 208 (pictured)

CALDWELL, ERSKINE, 308

CALLOWAY, CAB, 136 (pictured)

CAMPBELL, ALAN, 299

CANNON, REP. JOSEPH, 64 (pictured)

CANTOR, EDDIE, 155

CAPONE, ALPHONSE, 85, 110 (pictured), 111, 166–67 (biography)

CARDOZO, JUSTICE BENJAMIN N.: 227, 321; caricatured, 318, 328–29

CAREY, HARRY, 207 (pictured)

CAREY, JOYCE, 211 (pictured)

CARNEGIE, DALE: *How to Win Friends and Influence People*, excerpt from, 280–81

CARNERA, PRIMO, 302

CARRADINE, JOHN, 353 (pictured)

CÉLINE, FERNAND-LOUIS, 13 (quoted)

CENTRAL ASSOCIATION OF OBSTETRICIANS AND GYNECOLOGISTS, 346

CENTURY OF PROGRESS EXPOSITION (1933). *See* Chicago World's Fair

CERMAK, ANTON, 225

CHAMBERLAIN, NEVILLE, 315 (pictured), 380 (quoted), 382

CHAPLIN, CHARLIE, 122, 126 (pictured)

CHARLES, EZZARD, 303

CHASE, STUART, 307 (quoted)

CHAVEZ, CESAR, 198–99 (quoted)

CHICAGO WORLD'S FAIR (1933), 264–65 (illus.)

CHILDS, MARQUIS W., 221 (quoted)

CHRISTIAN, GEORGE, 89 (quoted)

CHUNGKING, 314–15 (pictured)

CHURCHILL, ALLEN, 140 (quoted)

CHURCHILL, WINSTON: and Atlantic Charter, 393, 400 (pictured); on British air force, 391; on defense of England, 391; on exchange of American destroyers for British bases, 391–92; on Hitler's aggression, 235; on Munich Pact, 380; on unemployment insurance, 156

CIVIL WORKS ADMINISTRATION, 253

CIVILIAN CONSERVATION CORPS, 232, 252 (illus.)

CLARK, RUSSELL, 297

CLARKE, EDWARD Y., 31

CLEMENCEAU, GEORGES: 13–14, 15, 16; quoted, 14, 17

CLEMENTS, ROBERT L., 244

CLIQUOT CLUB ESKIMOS, 128 (pictured)

COHEN, OCTAVUS ROY, 309

COLBERT, CLAUDETTE, 347 (pictured)

COLLINS, FLOYD, 146–47

COLMAN, RONALD, 349 (pictured)

COLOSIMO, "BIG JIM," 85, 166

COMMITTEE OF INDUSTRIAL ORGANIZATIONS, 293, 311

COMMITTEE TO DEFEND AMERICA BY AIDING THE ALLIES, 366

COMMUNISM: in America, 242–43, 310–11, 376; in Europe after World War I, 19, 22–23

CONN, BILLY, 303

CONNALLY, SEN. TOM, 323

CONNELLY, MARC, 298

CONSERVATION, SOIL, 305, 307

CONSERVATIVES: opposition to New Deal, 242, 247, 248, 320–22, 376–77

CONSTRUCTION: during Depression, 202–3

COOK, ROY, 293 (quoted)

COOLIDGE, CALVIN: 67, 90–91 (pictured), 182 (quoted), 291, 298, 395; administration, 79–86 *passim*

COOPER, GARY, 353 (pictured)

CORCORAN, THOMAS, 324

CORNELL, KATHARINE, 211 (pictured)

CORRELL, CHARLES J. *See Amos 'n' Andy*

COUGHLIN, FATHER CHARLES E., 241, 244–45 (quoted), 286, 287 (pictured), 389

COURT PACKING PLAN, 321–23, 329

COUZENS, SEN. JAMES, 155

COWLEY, MALCOLM: quoted, 37, 80

CRAFTS, DR. AND MRS. WILBUR, 28 (quoted)

CRAMER, CHARLES F., 68, 71, 72

CRAWFORD, BRODERICK, 354 (pictured)

CRAWFORD, JOAN: pictured, 103, 209

CREEL, GEORGE, 12

CRÈVECOEUR, MICHEL GUILLAUME JEAN DE, 14 (quoted)

CRIME: in the 20's, 84–86, 110–13, 166–67; in the 30's, 270–71, 296–97

CULBERTSON, ELY, 213

(pictured)

CUMMINGS, HOMER, 322

CUNNINGHAM, GLENN, 362

CURRIE, LAUCHLIN, 324

CURRY, JOHN STEUART: lithograph by, *Line Storm*, 277; painting by, *Baptism in Kansas*, 139

D

DANIELS, JOSEPHUS, 378

DARROW, CLARENCE: 33–34; pictured, 145, 148; "Salesmanship," excerpt from, 96–97

DAUGHERTY, HARRY M., 66–72 *passim*

DAUGHTERS OF THE AMERICAN REVOLUTION, 358, 382

DAVIS, BETTE, 348 (pictured)

DAVIS, ELMER, 229 (quoted)

DEARBORN, MICH., 217

DEBS, EUGENE V., 70

DE HAVILLAND, OLIVIA, 353 (pictured)

DE KOONING, WILLEM, 276

DELANEY, JACK, 116 (pictured)

DE MILLE, CECIL B., 124

DE MILLE, WILLIAM C., 122 (quoted)

DEMPSEY, JACK, 83, 116, 117 (pictured)

DENBY, EDWIN N., 72

DEPRESSION OF 1920–21, 158

DEPRESSION OF 1929–39, 158–60, 177–84, 192–201, 214–23, 305–12

DEWEY, JOHN, 243 (quoted)

DIAMOND, JACK "LEGS," 112 (pictured)

DIES, REP. MARTIN, 376

DIETRICH, MARLENE, 206 (pictured)

DILLINGER, JOHN, 270 (pictured), 296–97 (biography)

DIMAGGIO, JOE, 362

DIONNE QUINTUPLETS, 238–39 (pictured)

DOHENY, EDWARD L., 72

DOLLFUSS, ENGELBERT, 239 (pictured)

DOS PASSOS, JOHN, 310

DOUGLAS, JUSTICE WILLIAM O., 324, 377

DRAFT, 370–71 (illus.), 392, 393–94

DRAGONETTE, JESSICA, 274 (pictured)

DRESSLER, MARIE, 208 (pictured)

DROUGHT, 256–59 (illus.), 305–7

DUNKIRK, 383, 385 (illus.)

DUNNE, FINLEY PETER,

410